THE UNSETTLED PLAIN

THE UNSETTLED PLAIN

An Environmental History of the Late Ottoman Frontier

CHRIS GRATIEN

Stanford University Press
Stanford, California

STANFORD UNIVERSITY PRESS
Stanford, California

© 2022 by Chris Gratien. All rights reserved.

No part of this book may be reproduced or transmitted in any form or by any means, electronic or mechanical, including photocopying and recording, or in any information storage or retrieval system without the prior written permission of Stanford University Press.

Printed in the United States of America on acid-free, archival-quality paper

Library of Congress Cataloging-in-Publication Data

Names: Gratien, Chris, author.
Title: The unsettled plain : an environmental history of the late Ottoman frontier / Chris Gratien.
Description: Stanford, California : Stanford University Press, 2022. | Includes bibliographical references and index.
Identifiers: LCCN 2021032901 (print) | LCCN 2021032902 (ebook) | ISBN 9781503630895 (cloth) | ISBN 9781503631267 (paperback) | ISBN 9781503631274 (ebook)
Subjects: LCSH: Human ecology—Turkey—Cilicia—History. | Rural population—Turkey—Cilicia—History. | Land use, Rural—Turkey—Cilicia—History. | Cilicia—Environmental conditions. | Turkey—History—19th century. | Turkey—History—20th century.
Classification: LCC GF679.C55 G83 2022 (print) | LCC GF679.C55 (ebook) | DDC 956.4/6015—dc23
LC record available at https://lccn.loc.gov/2021032901
LC ebook record available at https://lccn.loc.gov/2021032902

Cover art: Julie M. Gratien
Cover design: Rob Ehle

CONTENTS

Notes for the Reader vii

INTRODUCTION 1

1   Upland Empire   23

2   The Stench of Progress   56

3   Second Nature in the Second Egypt   94

4   Fallowed Years   139

5   A Modern Life of Transhumance   180

Acknowledgments 231

List of Archives and Libraries 235

List of Abbreviations and Acronyms 237

Notes 241

Index 311

NOTES FOR THE READER

This work refers to sources in several languages other than English, especially Ottoman Turkish and Armenian. All translations of primary sources are my own, with the exception of sources from Greek, translated by Polina Ivanova, and any secondary translations cited in the endnotes.

I have transliterated Ottoman Turkish words according to the spellings and conventions of modern Turkish. When quoting transliterated sources, I have preserved the spellings of the editor.

In Turkish words, the following letters diverge from what an anglophone reader may expect:

c is "j" as in "jam" (*muhacir* meaning "immigrants" is pronounced mu-ha-jir, the name Cevdet is jev-det, *mucuk* meaning "mosquito" is mu-juk, name of Ceyhan River is jey-han, and so forth)

ç is "ch" as in "cheese" (the toponym Çukurova is pronounced chu-kur-o-va, the honorific *çelebi* is che-le-bi, the toponym Çokmerzimen is chok-mer-zi-men)

ğ is silent and elongates the vowel in modern standard Turkish (the ğ is silent in the name Kozanoğlu, the name Dadaloğlu, *huğ* meaning "hut" and so forth) ş is "sh" as in "fish" (the ethnonym Avşar is pronounced av-shar, the name Yaşar is ya-shar, *aşiret* meaning "tribe" is a-shi-ret, and so forth)

Some Armenian words along with titles of sources in the notes are conveyed in the original Armenian. Names in most cases are transliterated phonetically according to the pronunciation of Western Armenian within the text and consistent with WorldCat.org entries in citations.

The spellings of proper names and toponyms adhere to the conventions of transliteration, unless there is already a commonly used spelling in English (Marash, Hadjin, Khaldun, Pasha, and so forth).

All sources, including suggestions for further reading, are cited in the endnotes.

Materials with Islamic lunar (*hicri*) calendar and Ottoman solar (*rumi*) calendar dates have been converted to the Gregorian (*miladi*) calendar using the date conversion tool of the Türk Tarih Kurumu at ttk.gov.tr/tarih-cevirme-kilavuzu/.

THE UNSETTLED PLAIN

Cilicia in the late Ottoman period. Key to place names, Ottoman name with modern name in parentheses: Ayas (Yumurtalık); Çokmerzimen (Dörtyol); Hadjin (Saimbeyli); Kars-ı Zülkadriye (Kadirli); Namrun (Çamlıyayla); Sis (Kozan); Zeytun (Süleymanlı). Map by author.

INTRODUCTION

Ömer was born in a Central Anatolian village called Taf during the early decades of the Republic of Turkey. His family was well off for the area. Ömer was educated. And though it was no place for a young man with big aspirations, the little place where he grew up had its charms. The winters were cold and bleak, but with the return of spring, the bracing mountain air gave way to refreshing breezes. It was a wonderful place to spend the summer. The village was set in a region of expansive plateaus, or *yaylas*.[1] Ömer's ancestors, the Avşars, once visited those highlands each year with their flocks to pass the warm months in comfort, surrounded by bountiful, green grass and wildflowers. They would travel hundreds of kilometers between the Central Anatolian plateau and the lowlands of Çukurova on the Mediterranean coast, following pasture, water, and fair weather. But a few generations before Ömer was born, the Ottoman government settled them in villages. By the early twentieth century, the world of a people that had once traversed an empire had become very small.

Ömer was young at the time of his engagement to a girl named Hacca. He really loved her, and he was eager to get married. But marriage was often a family affair. Something happened that caused Ömer to abruptly leave the village behind and head for the fertile lowlands in the south that had become the center of Turkey's cotton industry. According to those who knew the story, his sudden departure that summer was the result of a falling out with his family (*küskün gitmiş*). Perhaps they quarreled over his engagement to Haçça. Perhaps Ömer planned to make some money and come back for her. There were certainly other young men who had gone to Çukurova and returned with money and gifts, wearing brand-new suits purchased from tailors in the bustling markets of Adana. There, they found work in the cotton fields and factories that employed tens of thousands of migrant laborers. Çukurova was a place where a kid like Ömer could build a new life or return to his old one as a new man, provided it did not chew him up and spit him out like so many bales of cotton.

Ömer's mother had begged him not to leave their village. She feared for his safety in the big city. "Don't stay in Adana, my son," she implored. "A *mucuk* will get in your eye." *Mucuk* was the word for a type of mosquito in her Turkish dialect.[2] The mosquito here was metaphorical. She simply meant that misfortune might strike him out of nowhere. There were many hazards awaiting a naïve country boy in a place notorious for exploitation and vice, and there were certainly other men who had gone to Çukurova and never come back. Missing her son and consumed by worry, she made the same long journey to Adana to retrieve him, only to be met with her greatest fear upon arrival. Ömer had died. Some said that he was stricken by the evil eye of envy. But the culprit was no metaphorical *mucuk*; it was an actual mosquito that got him. Ömer had contracted malaria. It was a common ailment during Adana's notorious summers, and though it was not always lethal, Ömer probably had not been exposed to the disease before in his highland village. Many a strapping young man like him had traveled to Adana for work during those years and met the same fate. Yet his mother seemed to blame herself. "While he was dying, he turned to the wall for help," she recalled in horror, realizing that he had had neither family nor doctor to care for him in his last moments. The trauma inspired her to write a poem, "The Lament of Ömer, Son of Durmuş Ağa." One verse reads as if she imagined his final, feverish thoughts: "I'm getting on a truck. I'm going to Kayseri. I don't want to die. I'm going to see Haçça."

Ömer meant the world to someone, but he was not the kind of person whose life would normally enter the annals of world history, nor was the place he lived. His village has changed names multiple times, making its history harder to trace. Today, they call it Dadaloğlu, in recognition of the local belief that the famous bard by the same name is buried there. Dadaloğlu's poetry had championed the resistance to a government decree that the nomadic populations of the region settle in fixed villages during the 1860s. His most memorable line—"the decree is the Sultan's, but the mountains are ours [*dağlar bizimdir*]"—was a claim to sovereignty in a moment when the future of these communities became a central question of the Ottoman Empire, which deployed more than 10,000 men armed with modern weaponry to enforce the settlement orders. Dadaloğlu had distilled the defiant sentiments of these communities concerning a pivotal moment in their history. Without his songs, they might have been lost to time, so it made sense to rename a village born out of that history in his honor. In the Avşar villages, the practice of preserving songs that commemorate important moments as Dadaloğlu once did continued into the twentieth century. They have been transmitted orally across generations. Like the refrain "the mountains are ours," Ömer's story was known to people his age, who preserved it alongside hundreds of other tales of tragedy and heroism. Thanks to Ömer's mother and those who learned her song, his eight-verse tale of love and loss lives on today.[3]

When compared with the archival record, sources for history like these songs follow a more complicated path to survival. An archival source is preserved by an institution for a given purpose, but its survival does not require that anyone else deem it to be valuable. For a folk song such as the "Lament of Ömer" to survive, others must learn it and repeat it. Members of a community must accept it as valuable in some way, internalizing its words, melodies, and rhythms, and making it their own. Only the greatest hits could survive generations.

Why then did Ömer's community preserve this song, which described something far more personal than the collective struggle of Dadaloğlu and his contemporaries? Maybe it survived as some form of cautionary tale. Maybe the story resonated with the experiences of other families. For some, Ömer was family. Yet from afar, it may seem that there have been so many Ömers and Haçças over the years and so many laments composed about them, such timeless stories are ostensibly outside history altogether. But in fact, their story is of great value for writing the little-known history of their community, and its significance extends far beyond their remote villages. It was part of a much larger historical epic, the same one documented by

Dadaloğlu. The place where Ömer was born, the economic forces that drew people like him to Adana, and even the malaria that killed him embodied the experience of a recent process that transformed rural societies. They were facets of the late Ottoman frontier, a space that defined a century of political, socioeconomic, and ecological change and reshaped life in the Middle East.

This book is about the remaking of Ömer's world—Çukurova and its mountainous hinterland—between the Ottoman Tanzimat reforms of the mid-nineteenth century and Turkey's development programs of the mid-twentieth century. In some respects, what follows is a familiar history of the late Ottoman Empire, only it has seldom been told with rural people and places at its center. They made up the vast majority of the Ottoman population. The administrative and commercial decisions made in Istanbul and the provincial capitals were ultimately about them. They were also the pioneers of the "late Ottoman frontier," an internal zone of settlement and environmental transformation in the provinces of the empire. The history of these small but numerous spaces collectively shows how Turkey and other post-Ottoman states were the product of agrarian transformation. The remaking of society and politics in the Ottoman world entailed a remaking of rural environments, and in the process, how people understood and ordered the environment also changed. Though the frontier experience in the Ottoman Empire was not the same in all places, Çukurova was in many ways a microcosm of the empire's transformation. In this study, it begins as a swampy, sparse winter pasture for nomads on horseback in which direct Ottoman authority over the countryside was limited. By the end, it will be overtaken by fields of cotton tended by farmers who sing the laments of once-powerful provincial lords and humble shepherds atop their tractors "like the song of a former, foreign world."[4]

The fertile lowland of Çukurova became a late Ottoman frontier because merchants and Ottoman officials alike deemed it to be an unsettled plain. Few permanent villages existed there. Its main economic function was as seasonal pasture. The long process by which Çukurova came to be mostly grazing land for pastoralists like Ömer's ancestors was cast as a historical aberration from a civilizational ideal. Through policies of forced sedentarization, village construction, and agrarian commercialization, Çukurova did become a densely settled region, encompassing not only the large cities of Mersin and Adana but a total of at least seven cities with a population of more than 100,000 today. In this regard, the dynamics of the Ottoman frontier survived long after the Ottoman state itself, revealing a line of historical continuity amid the breakup of a centuries-old empire.

But in serving as a point of continuity, the frontier experience left Çukurova unsettled in another sense. For rural people, the theme of this century of history was disruption, displacement, and dispossession. In the pages that follow, each group that lived in the late Ottoman countryside will have its turn at exile: pastoral nomads of the Taurus Mountains; Muslim villagers violently expelled from the Balkans, Crimea, and the Caucasus; seasonal laborers from Anatolia and Northern Syria; Armenians deported by the Ottoman government; prisoners of war; Kurdish refugees; "exchanged peoples" on both sides of the Aegean; and eventually, every villager who moved to the city because the nature of village life had forever changed. Their experiences reveal how societies in the modern Middle East were forged through intersecting displacements and movements of people.

The narrative of this work is diachronic, but the subjects of analysis that recur throughout the five chapters that follow are rhythmic. Despite the significant changes that occurred over the period examined in this book, each chapter returns to dimensions of continuity that manifest not through static states but rather through percussive repetition of familiar modes and melodies that can be conceptualized as "refrains."[5] These refrains arise not only from "natural rhythms" that have long fascinated historians of the Mediterranean but also from the new rhythms of increasingly complex systems of economic production and the modern institutions that order nature and time itself.[6] The refrains in this study contain interacting rhythms of seasonal migration, agricultural labor, capitalist production, bureaucratic function, and mosquito reproduction. The continuities and the gradual evolution of these refrains drive this story of movement, ecological upheaval, and social transformation.

A major contention of this book is that the disease that killed Ömer—malaria—was fundamental to the unsettled ecology of the late Ottoman frontier and its rhythms, more a product of recent developments than the primordial scourge it is often assumed to be. Caused by a blood-borne parasite transmitted between humans by mosquitos, malaria was present in the Mediterranean for millennia. Only in recent decades have public health measures and mosquito eradication programs nearly eliminated malaria in Turkey. Yet prior to the advent of modern biomedicine, people possessed means of mitigating malaria's impact rooted in an intimate knowledge of local geography and a seasonal conception of space. Long before Ömer's encounter with the disease in the city of Adana, people in the region avoided malaria's impacts through seasonal migration between the mountains and the lowlands. That was one thing groups like the Avşars shared with even their most sedentary and urban neighbors. However, the major forces that shaped the late Ottoman frontier—the modern state, capitalism, war, and science—each changed the region's ecology and rhythms. In the process, malaria became widespread in new ways as the practices that enabled local people to mitigate the risk of disease and maintain their livelihoods were eroded. Though it was an old ailment, malaria in its modern form was an artifact of rural dispossession.

This history of malaria reveals a new political history of the late Ottoman world, but it was not removed from the more well-charted political violence associated with imperial fragmentation, communal conflict, war, and state-building. On the socioeconomic level, the Ottoman frontier produced a new landed elite enriched by the labors of a new class of agricultural workers. On the communal level, the creation of a new rural ecology placed new groups of settlers and migrants in conflict with local people, while commercial competition created an additional arena of conflict between ethnoreligious groups. Though contention was a persistent feature of the new spaces created by the frontier, large-scale war and political strife during the Ottoman Empire's final decades accelerated processes of displacement and dispossession. The environmental history of the late Ottoman frontier does not explain the political conflicts that shaped the region. Yet it demonstrates that those conflicts did not emerge from ancient enmities. They unfolded in novel spaces produced by migration, displacement, political reform, and commercialization.

For many, the experience of the late Ottoman frontier was one of violence and loss, but its history is also full of examples of resistance and resilience. People subjected to settlement policies that threatened their livelihoods, like the communities that rallied around Dadaloğlu's cry of "the mountains are ours," fought and won battles to preserve aspects of their ways of life within a new Ottoman order. People who faced ethnic cleansing and genocide found ways to survive in the direst of conditions, and refugees from distant lands built new lives in the Ottoman countryside against formidable odds. Cultivators and workers defied the demands of the market and maintained local practices while still participating profitably in an increasingly uneven world economy. And even though the entire project of the modern state appeared at times antagonistic to their culture, rural people preserved a sense of place and forms of local knowledge and memory long after the world they came from was irrevocably changed. The past acts of resistance and strategies of survival studied in this work reveal how the creation of the modern world entailed concerted destruction wrought far from centers of political power and capital. Those who endured and resisted this destruction have not received the attention they deserve. Their lives provide a window onto other ways of knowing and being in a present where the narrative of progress is increasingly replaced by a prophecy of impending environmental catastrophe. There is no going back to the world they came from. But the legions of people who resisted developments once simplistically cast as progress "show us how to look around rather than ahead."[7]

In the pages that follow, many actors will emerge in this multivocal history of environmental transformation in Çukurova and its mountainous hinterland. Bandits, bureaucrats, immigrants, landlords, workers, doctors, tourists, shepherds, goats, and mosquitos will each have their moments at center stage. Their experiences have been preserved in archival documents, memoirs, newspapers, local histories, and folklore in Turkish, Armenian, and a host of other languages that constitute the fragmentary and international source base for the history of a region that was never the center of a unified modern state. In bridging linguistic and temporal gaps in the historiography of the Ottoman Empire and exploring environmental themes largely ignored by extant work, I hope to have achieved a narrative that not only enriches the study of the modern Middle East but also underscores its relevance for scholars of other times and places. I also hope to have done justice to the historical experience of the actors foregrounded in this study and the place they made or called home. But this is not just the history of that little world over the course of a century of change. It is the history of the unmaking of their worlds and the making of ours. Let's call it a history of "the world and a very small place" in the Ottoman Empire.[8]

Environment, Empire, and Indigenous Ecology

Though there are relatively few English-language publications about it, there is a precedent for using a place like Çukurova to write about something bigger. This work is influenced by the greatest chronicler of rural life in Southern Anatolia: the novelist Yaşar Kemal. In an interview from 1960, he addressed the notion that he would eventually run out of material writing about his native Çukurova. "What would that even mean?" he asked. "Could Çukurova ever run out? [*Çukurova biter mi*]."[9] The next year, his award-winning novel *İnce Memed* was published in an English translation, permanently adding this small region of modern Turkey to the annals of world literature.[10] Born to Kurdish refugees from Eastern Anatolia who settled there during the World War I period, Yaşar Kemal found Çukurova to be an inexhaustible source of inspiration. And over a career that continued up to his death in 2015, he never really ran out of Çukurova to write about. He published dozens of books, most of them dealing with the lives of rural people in the region, how they have transformed, and how they remained the same. When asked to reflect on his work and his choice to focus almost solely on Çukurova, Kemal frequently appealed to universalism. For Kemal, to write about Çukurova was to write about the human experience through his subjective lens. He was not *just* writing about Çukurova. And in this regard, Kemal was not alone in writing about it. As he once put it, "Tolstoy was writing about it, Dostoyevski was . . . no writer can be a great novelist if they don't have a Çukurova. Stendhal also wrote about his own Çukurova. I've written about Çukurova as much as anyone else."[11]

Kemal followed the dictum of "write what you know," but his work was also guided by political commitments that always drew him back to rural people. His early work employed ethnographic methods born out of an affinity for songs and stories that began in childhood. He would go on to use the fragments of human experience contained in those songs and stories to author novels of epic proportions. Kemal's first publication, however, was a collection of laments from the Çukurova region, songs by rural people like the one that commemorated the aforementioned Ömer's untimely demise. For him, the lament genre, or *ağıt*, which typically involved a song composed for a person who died a tragic or heroic death, was not just an expression of the relationship between an individual and an author. He wrote about laments as cultural palimpsests, songs that could be modified and added to by other interpreters to bring their own experience into the living composition. The familiar laments that circulated in Çukurova were not songs about individuals; they were frames for narrating the experience of a community rooted in a multilayered past.[12] Kemal regarded the people (*halk*) of Çukurova as a cultural repository not just of that region but of human history and genius itself. "I've always wondered: why is a woven carpet as beautiful as a Picasso painting," he mused in one interview. "It's because its design is 10,000 years in the making."[13]

Many social historians of the late Ottoman Empire and modern Turkey find inspiration in Yaşar Kemal's approach, which brings to life the stories of ordinary people in ways that the archive cannot.[14] Yet if recent scholarship is any indication, the longstanding strain of Ottomanist scholarship concerned with peasants, pastoralists, and "provincial" people so dear to the late Yaşar Kemal once held a place of higher prominence in the field. Suraiya Faroqhi, who has been writing about the provincial history of the Ottoman Empire for over half a century, has critiqued this trend in terms of a methodological shift, noting that since the cultural turn of the 1980s, Ottoman studies had turned its back on the rural people who made up the vast majority of the empire's population but have "left very few traces of their cultural orientations."[15] If the cultural turn did leave them behind, it is because the operative definition of culture privileged elite written and material culture. By treating human ecology—the relationships between human beings and their environments—as a dimension of culture, however, we can access a whole world of cultural orientations that is yet to be properly explored.

Recently, scholars have returned to the role of rural people in Ottoman life, thanks in part to the emergence of environmental history, defined here as the study of humans and their past relationships with "the rest of nature."[16] Environmental history has reinvigorated the study of agrarian spaces in the former Ottoman Empire, drawing greater attention to factors like soil, water, plants, and animals that were fundamental to that polity but treated as marginal in political narratives of its history. The first works of Ottoman environmental history focused mainly on the empire itself as an "ecosystem," in the words of Alan Mikhail.[17] This framework allows for the study of cyclical and repeated flows of people, biota, and material, and their role in constituting political and economic life over a broad region. Similarly, large-scale events like epidemics, epizootics, and climatic change may be studied on an imperial level to demonstrate the role of environmental factors in political histories. Newer scholarship explores relations and phenomena that are only legible on a smaller scale, moving away from framing Ottoman environmental history in a manner that reifies the field's state-centered bias, which erases the texture of local ecologies.[18]

Writing good environmental history requires much more than thinking of nonhuman factors as agents and forces in history; it means understanding that the environment and human culture mutually constitute one another. It also requires accounting for how people understood their environments and acted upon those understandings. It means not only looking to new sources about the history of the environment but rereading familiar sources with an "ecocritical" lens, which is to say, in Robert Kern's words, "to recover the environmental character or orientation of works whose conscious or foregrounded interests lie elsewhere."[19] An ecocritical reading of sources in turn means taking seriously past actors with radically different worldviews, interrogating conceptions of "nature" itself, and uncovering anthropogenic dimensions of environments one might otherwise regard as natural. This work also adopts the perspective of political ecology, defined here as a "postpositivist understanding of nature and the production of knowledge about it, which views these as inseparable from social relations of power."[20] Environmental historians draw on the natural sciences, but scientific expertise cannot be taken at face value. The very practices by which nature has been constructed as an object of inquiry have also served political projects that usurped rural people in both cultural and material terms for the purpose of reordering the environment to suit the needs of the modern state and capital.

If people like Ömer are still marginal in the field of Ottoman studies, they are increasingly important within the environmental humanities turn toward indigenous ecology. As an analytical category, the term *indigenous* can be juxtaposed with a host of entities associated with colonialism, capitalism, and globalization over the past centuries: the settler, the plantation owner, the corporation, the technocratic state, and so forth.[21] If the environmental history of human societies over the past few centuries could be summarized in a word, it would be *usurpation*—of local people, of their communal and political formations, and of their ways of knowing and ordering nature. Plants, animals, microbes, and a range of ecological practices pertaining to agriculture, water management, resource extraction, and manufacture that were initially confined to specific regions have spread—albeit unevenly—throughout the world.[22] Local ecologies have also been reoriented by production for the demands of a global market as opposed to more local networks. In the process, indigenous understandings of nature were maligned as economically inefficient and environmentally irresponsible, especially in areas subject to European colonialism, as scholars such as Diana Davis have convincingly demonstrated.[23] This process of dispossession involved what Jason Moore describes as a reordering of the environment to produce "cheap nature" that served the extractive systems associated with the capitalist world economy.[24]

As a result of these developments, the world saw the greatest-ever rise in human population, but it was accompanied by escalating economic disparity. Pollution and environmental destruction have likewise occurred unevenly. Climate change is the greatest expression of this process.[25] Environmental activities that have produced wealth in primarily temperate regions of the world disproportionately threaten environments nearest to the equator and the poles, and pose the greatest immediate threat to communities whose relationships with their lived environments are often least mediated by technology. Megacities have emerged in places most likely to be devastated by climate change, ranging from the arid southwestern United States to the historically shifting Bengal Delta. Amitav Ghosh has called this revolution "the great derangement," inverting Polanyi's notion of "the great transformation" to fashion a more dystopian understanding of what modernity is and what it holds for our future.[26]

This monograph belongs to a growing number of studies examining the erosion and destruction of indigenous ecologies over the past two centuries throughout the making of the world ecology. Though it was part of the Ottoman Empire, Çukurova is kin to a variety of places. Like Beringia in Bathsheba Demuth's *The Floating Coast*, they are places far from sight that endured dramatic changes once spotted by the rapacious gaze of capital.[27] Like La Huasteca in Myrna Santiago's *The Ecology of Oil*, they are unique environments stripped down to produce commodities and extract resources for the market, only to become sites of conflict between workers and owners.[28] Like Bengal in Debjani Bhattacharyya's *Empire and Ecology*, they are liminal environments entirely reordered to support a population of millions for the profit of a few.[29] And like so many important corners of the globe, Çukurova has long awaited an environmental history of internal colonization "buried under the national space" of modern historiography.[30]

The Late Ottoman Frontier

Like so many such places, Çukurova was a settlement frontier, a space where modern societies were produced through what James Belich terms the "settler revolution."[31] These frontiers saw foreign people, ecologies, and state forms imposed upon local communities in some fashion, and they were ubiquitous in nineteenth-century empires. What follows will certainly harken to the history of the American West, the Russian East, French Algeria, South Africa, and a host of other examples of the "unending frontiers" inherited from early modern empires.[32] The Ottoman frontier is special among this club, not just because it has barely been included within its historiography, but also because the Ottoman Empire was contracting as a territorial entity. Over the course of its last century, the tricontinental empire lost provinces in Europe and North Africa to incursions by European empires and uprisings by national independence movements. By its end, all that was left was Anatolia, Thrace, and the lands of the Arab Mashriq.

The historiography of the late Ottoman frontier is currently most robust at the empire's edges in North Africa, the Arabian Peninsula, and the borderlands of Eastern Anatolia and Iraq. It shows that even while losing territory, Ottoman officials harbored expansionist visions.[33] Thomas Kuehn's work on late Ottoman expansion in Yemen and its "Tanzimat imperialism" has explored how in seeking to secure its frontiers, officials adopted an approach to local communities that resembled the practices of modern European colonialism in the production of both knowledge and political difference.[34] However, less distant from its major centers, the Ottoman Empire produced a different and, in some ways, more intense frontier experience in the Balkans, Anatolia, and

Syria. The wars and territory it lost in the Black Sea region, the Balkans, and the Aegean produced millions of refugees who settled in the remaining Ottoman domains. Designated as *muhacir* (pl. *muhacirin*), the vast majority of these refugees were Muslims, and they received Ottoman nationality.[35] A new immigrant class became the vanguard of an empire-wide program of *iskân*, or settlement, projected not out into the wild expanses of a territory in the process of being conquered but rather into pockets of sparse population and contested hegemony that had been part of the empire for centuries. Meanwhile, as Isa Blumı notes, "finance capitalism created a particular kind of refugee exposed to a form of exploitation that increasingly scoured the earth for cheap labor."[36] Migrants of various sorts became central to the commercialization of the Ottoman countryside and the emergence of local forms of capitalism, which further expanded the environmental frontier.

The fate of the Ottoman Empire's new class of settlers became intertwined with the reform of the Ottoman government known as the Tanzimat, aimed at reasserting central imperial control to increase tax revenues and meet the needs of a growing, modern conscript army. The provinces became the site of a bold program of rural reorganization which Milen Petrov has aptly described as "Tanzimat for the countryside."[37] The project of Tanzimat for the countryside began in full force after the Crimean War (1853–56), when provincial reform became central to government policy. New land tenure policies, infrastructural projects, water and forest management, and the promotion of novel crops and commercial agriculture were accompanied by efforts to settle millions of migrants throughout the empire. The Tanzimat government also employed its own nomadic population in this settlement program, sometimes by constructing new villages and compelling pastoralists, such as Ömer's Avşar ancestors, to change their modes of habitation. Though its policies took different forms and brought different impacts from region to region, in total Tanzimat in the provinces amounted to an "Ottoman civilizing mission." The policies initiated under the Tanzimat reforms continued to shape the Ottoman countryside under Sultan Abdülhamid II, as well as under the Committee of Union and Progress (CUP) that usurped him in the constitutional revolution of 1908. The Republic of Turkey—largely built by former CUP figures and other former Ottoman officials—expanded the vision of the Tanzimat even further.

Although frontier settings varied widely from place to place within the Ottoman Empire, the imaginaries of the frontier were portable. Similar rhetoric was applied to settlement in regions with environments very different from Çukurova's. The most striking example perhaps is the Ottoman project to settle Cretan Muslim refugees in Cyrenaica (eastern Libya) at the turn of the twentieth century, recently examined by Frederick Walter Lorenz. These migrants were envisioned as a vanguard of Ottoman civilization and cultivation in an area dominated by nomadic communities that were cast as "savage" in official discourse. Moreover, just as in Çukurova, Ottoman officials promoted the idea of developing Cyrenaica as a "second Egypt," gesturing to how the project of the late Ottoman settlement frontier was tied to the idea of recovering the wealth lost through territorial contraction in the Balkans and Egypt's de facto independence.[38]

The late Ottoman frontier was a frontier in three senses. It was a "frontier of the state," a space in which new forms of state presence were asserted or reasserted in rural settings.[39] It was also a settlement frontier involving millions of people on the move. Finally, it was an ecological frontier, one in which novel plants, animals, microbes, methods of land use, modes of agrarian production, forms of resource extraction, and environmental understandings emerged in tandem with the processes of state-building, settlement, and commercialization. Key to the concept of frontier as defined above is that the most important spaces of the Ottoman frontier were not necessarily regions of political borderlands. They were pockets of transformation within the Ottoman provinces, and there is a growing body of work dealing with these spaces, though not always under the precise heading of frontier and more frequently under the heading of provincial reform.[40] The concept of the frontier not only sharpens our understanding of what was taking place in such spaces but also draws attention to what they shared. When treated as a collective, these disparate provinces reveal a common story that was central to the remaking of Ottoman society. Çukurova's historical experience contained many of the dynamics typical of the frontier moment.

One such dynamic, which has received the most attention, is conflict between Muslims and Christians. The expulsion of Muslims from formerly Ottoman lands and the localized rebellions and massacres in many provinces during the late Ottoman period served as the backdrop for confessionalized conflict on the imperial scale. In Çukurova, escalating antagonisms culminated in the massacres of 1909, which claimed the lives of thousands of Armenians throughout the Adana region. Along with the anti-Armenian pogroms of the 1890s, the 1915 Armenian genocide, and other violence against Christians in the empire during World War I, the Adana massacres have defined how the history of this region has been discussed. The Muslim-Christian divide that widened during the war years in turn shaped the postwar conflicts that birthed the Republic of Turkey. New scholarship is revealing just how important the political economy of provincial society is for understanding the political transformation of the Ottoman Empire and events like the Armenian genocide as well as their centrality in the making of the Republic of Turkey and the former Ottoman territories.[41]

The violence that accompanied the end of empire has loomed large for justifiable reasons. It has been the main interest for anglophone scholars who have studied the history of the Çukurova region. There is of course much more to the region's history. Both the teleologies of ethnic cleansing and genocide as well as the contrivances involved in avoiding their discussion have skewed the historiography of the Ottoman Empire. However, I do argue that the frontier experience was central to how communal relations changed. Attending to the spatial dimensions of the frontier sharpens the impression of simultaneous "convergence" and "divergence" that defines the current scholarly consensus on communal relations in the late Ottoman Empire.[42] The same process that birthed the cosmopolitan cities of the late Ottoman Mediterranean like Izmir, Salonika, Beirut, and Mersin fostered conflict in the countryside. The transformation of what Nicholas Doumanis studies as "intercommunality"—a quotidian, lived experience of social bonds across confessional divides—must be understood within the context of significant population movements and socioeconomic changes.[43] They produced a shared Ottoman culture among an emergent urban class but also created new social rifts. These rifts were distinctly modern, though they cannot be reduced to a single cause associated with modernity as such. Rather, the frontier was a key spatial component in a complex process that produced drastic results in its rawest manifestations.

For many, the notion of "frontier" in English gestures to the specificities of the American context, where the word transformed from merely being synonymous with borders or geographical limits to take on a "special civilizational or emotional meaning… as a liminal zone associated with a distinct culture."[44] In using the term "frontier" for the Ottoman context, I highlight what was common about the conceptualization of space across different empires of the period, where the practices of empire shared a great deal despite the sometimes distinct genealogies of their discourses. Indeed, this study warns against the reductive, deterministic role that the frontier played in early American historiography under the influence of Frederick Jackson Turner's frontier thesis. In bringing rural spaces to the center of questions about late Ottoman transformation, the frontier does not offer simple answers. Rather, it challenges us to grapple with the diversity of local contexts, the multiplicity of their historical experiences, and the extent to which the historiography of the late Ottoman Empire unduly reflects an urban bias. That bias has flattened the narratives of how the empire changed, as well as conventional understandings of the modern societies that emerged from the post-Ottoman world.

From Cilicia to Çukurova

The name Çukurova refers to an interconnected region centered on the city of Adana and the port of Mersin, each of which boasts more than a million inhabitants today. The region lay roughly at the geographical center of the late Ottoman Empire on the Eastern Mediterranean littoral at the historical junction of Anatolia and Syria (and Turkey's present-day border with Syria). In the mid-nineteenth century, Adana's population was just around 30,000, still making it the region's most populous city. Many of the other significant urban settlements of today had not yet been founded. The dramatic metamorphosis of Çukurova was the consequence of commercialization of agriculture and the export of cotton, wheat, sesame, and rice beginning in the nineteenth century. This process has been studied by Meltem Toksöz in one of the few academic monographs about the Adana region to be published in English.[45]

The name Çukurova gestures to that region's recent environmental transformation. The label *çukur* connotes a depression. Coupled with the geographical feature of a plain, or *ova*, the name Çukurova signifies "lowland."[46] During the Ottoman period, this was not a name for an entire region but rather for the large plain between the Taurus and Amanus mountain ranges and the Mediterranean coast. In other words, Çukurova was once the swampy outback of the much larger region that the name describes today. Making modern Çukurova entailed filling the plain with people, houses, and farms as it became Adana's late Ottoman frontier. Though these lowlands were on the margins of settlement for rural people throughout most of the Ottoman period, they now contain all the region's major cities and most of its economic activity. The modern name of Çukurova thus attests to the centrality of this process in redefining a region with a much longer history.

Previously, a historical name for this space was Cilicia, a toponym that stretches back millennia in some form. It was used as a provincial designation under many centuries of Roman rule.[47] For most of the past millennium, Cilicia's true center of gravity was not the fertile lowlands but rather the mountainous hinterland. During the medieval period, Cilicia was united as an independent kingdom under Armenian dynasties. After that, principalities, or *beyliks*, descended from Turkic groups that migrated to Anatolia under the Seljuks claimed most of historical Cilicia, governing as largely independent rulers in alliance with states like the Mamluk Sultanate. Both groups ruled over the cities of the lowlands, but their power was rooted in control over the mountains. When the Ottoman Empire incorporated the region during the conquests of the early sixteenth century, these communities continued to hold considerable political sway and carved out spheres of autonomy. The history of Çukurova as a late Ottoman frontier begins with the story of how the centralizing Ottoman government reasserted its presence in Cilicia during the mid-nineteenth century, catalyzing many of the changes that occurred in the following century.

Chapter 1 of this book explores how the frontier of Çukurova was the product of developments that unfolded over several centuries and the entanglement of local political power and autonomy with local ecology shaped by seasonal migration between the mountains and the lowlands. It places particular emphasis on the temporal space of the *yayla*, summer quarters located in the Taurus and Amanus Mountains, as the defining feature of this ecology. The *yaylas* were frequented by the nomadic pastoralists who made up much of the population in the Cilicia region by the outset of the nineteenth century. They capitalized on the availability of vegetation at different elevations over different parts of the year. However, the *yayla* was no less important to urban populations as a site of refuge from the summer discomforts of intense heat and malaria, which spread in the lowlands during the warm months of the year. Muslims and Christians alike from every walk of life participated in the rhythm of migration between the mountains and the lowlands, and their ecological understandings, though divergent from modern biomedical knowledge, were well founded in the epidemiological realities of the lowlands. However, their movements also endowed the *yaylas* with political significance. Despite attempts by the Ottoman Empire to reorient the region over the course of the early modern period, the position of the mountains in Cilicia endured, and those who controlled them became key to the Ottoman project of provincial reform that was coming with the Tanzimat.

Chapter 2 explores the making of the modern state and the role of settlement policy in the lowlands of Çukurova within the broader goals of the Tanzimat during the 1860s and 1870s. It identifies the environmental impacts of settlement on migrants and forcibly sedentarized pastoralists, pointing to mass mortality from malaria and starvation as an experience shared across many groups. It explains how Ottoman settlement policy was part of a civilizing mission articulated by statesmen like Ahmed Cevdet Pasha, who saw settlement and cultivation as fundamental to the reform of the empire. It also shows how the populations subjected to settlement resisted Ottoman policy due to the spread of malaria it catalyzed. Their resistance prompted the Ottoman government to adjust policies to make them more consistent with the ecological realities of the region.

Chapter 3 is about capitalism and its role in the remaking of the Cilicia region during the last decades of Ottoman rule. Some imagined Cilicia was "the Second Egypt" due to its perceived agricultural promise, especially for growing cotton. In addition to studying the unique local form of capitalism that emerged in Cilicia, this chapter considers how this commercial economy engendered unevenness as well as rifts in agrarian society that contributed to the dynamics of the 1909 Adana massacres. It also charts the emergence of seasonal labor rhythms that brought workers to Cilicia from all over the empire, and how with the spread of malaria and other health issues as systemic problems within these groups, the Ottoman government established new medical institutions and targeted a more thorough environmental overhaul of the countryside. Cotton did not remake Cilicia in an instant, but by 1914, the "second nature"[48] born out of plantations and new lowland settlements increasingly defined local experience of the environment.

Chapter 4 demonstrates how war and displacement impacted Cilicia in social and environmental terms. It studies the long World War I period from 1914 to 1923. Mobilization for war destabilized the economic production of the Adana region, and with the deportations of the entire Armenian population and Muslim refugees fleeing into the region, Cilicia—like other parts of the empire—became a zone of mass displacement. The war also fueled ecological transformation. On one hand, the Ottoman state and its agents took on a greater role in the agrarian domain. On the other, malaria took on a novel form due to the conditions of war, resulting in an unusually virulent malaria epidemic with an improbable epicenter at a *yayla* in the Taurus Mountains. After the war, France invaded Cilicia to establish a colonial mandate, but France's short years there were merely an encore of wartime displacement and turmoil. As a result of these conflicts, Cilicia as a space shared by Muslims and Christians was destroyed, and the name "Cilicia" itself fell out of use in Turkey. However, many of the environmental trajectories in the region that were set during the Ottoman period endured.

Chapter 5 studies how science and technology were harnessed by the nation-state in the Republic of Turkey to further remake the late Ottoman frontier it had inherited. It explores the early republican period through World War II to the transition to democratic rule in Turkey during the 1950s. Science became an integral component of the relationship between the government, provincial society, and the environment in the realms of agriculture and medicine. The Adana region became a laboratory for testing technologies of governance, particularly through a comprehensive malaria control campaign. Out of the technocratic consensus that emerged within the republican state, a militant discourse about nature and the economy itself emerged. At the same time, a romantic understanding of nature fixated on the mountains and the *yayla* as a space of bourgeois leisure. Yet the fetishization of the mountains and the pastoralist communities that once controlled them only occurred once such communities were pushed to the margins. The process of settling the late Ottoman frontier culminated with the gentrification of mountain spaces by the new urban elite and middle class, as science, technology, and medicine facilitated a radically new experience of rural landscapes.

Malaria and Modernity

In addition to exploring how the state, capitalism, war, and science reshaped the Ottoman frontier, this book develops an argument about the changing relationship between human societies and diseases such as malaria that arise from a complex set of ecological factors. Malaria was the paramount disease of the settlement frontier, because when people changed their modes of habitation and malaria was part of the local ecology, new infections were likely to ensue.[49] According to current biomedical understandings, malaria is an illness caused by two main variants of blood-borne parasites: *Plasmodium vivax* and *Plasmodium falciparum*. The more deadly *falciparum* requires warmer temperatures to thrive and was therefore more likely to spread in the warmer climates.[50] *Vivax* produces milder symptoms but results in recurring infections that could also prove deadly, especially to children. The parasite that causes malaria reproduces within various species of the *Anopheles* mosquito and is transmitted from one person to another by the mosquito's bite. Because of this complex chain of transmission, malaria existed to varying extents in many parts of Europe, Asia, and Africa that were warm enough to support the parasite and various anopheline vectors. It spread to the Americas with the Columbian Exchange.[51] During the summer months, most of the inhabited world is warm enough to support at least certain forms of malaria under the right conditions. Because the same environments associated with human habitation are amenable to mosquitos, James Webb has rightly called malaria "humanity's burden," a "primordial companion" of human societies and the "oldest and cumulatively the deadliest of the human infectious diseases."[52]

Malaria was not uniformly present in all times and places, however. Its impact was contingent on many factors. And one must not apply "mosquito determinism" to the course of political events.[53] Twentieth-century biomedicine's burning fixation on the mosquito as the vector of illness can blind us to the ways in which culture and politics also shaped disease as something entangled with all other facets of life.[54] Premodern people in Cilicia had sophisticated malaria avoidance strategies that shaped their patterns of movement and settlement in a variety of ways. Settlement, commercial agriculture, war, and technology each interacted with those patterns as well as with the reproductive capacities of mosquitos and the malaria parasite. In many cases, these interactions fueled malaria's spread. The disease became deeply entrenched within the local ecology even as science and medicine developed new ways of treating malaria and modifying mosquito habitats. However, the burden of malaria was not felt equally by all of humanity. In Çukurova, subjects of Ottoman settlement policies, seasonal workers in the burgeoning plantations, people displaced by war, and villagers far from the center of medical infrastructure disproportionately contracted malaria and died from it. Thus, malaria was a form of "silent violence"[55] in the making of the modern world that was masked as a natural and inherent feature of "tropical" environments.

In other words, the history of malaria is political. It speaks to hidden forms of inequality and dispossession not easily quantified in economic terms. Despite its historical importance in many parts of the Ottoman world, it has not received much attention from Ottoman historians. Yet its history is also not uniquely Ottoman. As the work of Katerina Gardikas has recently shown, modern Greece's independence from the Ottoman Empire during the early nineteenth century did not liberate it from a remarkably similar experience with malaria to what will be described in this work.[56] So while not outside of politics, malaria is a historical question that forges thematic and material connections across political boundaries. Its history is still in the making, as malaria at present kills hundreds of thousands of people each year, and mosquito-borne illnesses require continued monitoring for new strains, as well as new areas of spread and resurgence. In fact, malaria is far from the only major public health issue of today that is rooted in the conditions of a highly commercialized and interconnected world. The deadliest such diseases may await us in the decades to come.

In part, this history of how the making of the modern world changed the nature of epidemic disease explains why colonial settings became sites of malaria research and discovery, and why national public health projects became so preoccupied with malaria eradication during the twentieth century. Diseases like malaria were not only impediments to economic activity; to a large extent, they were manifestations of the ecologies created by colonialism and capitalism.⁵⁷ Yet the primary goal of this book is not to expose the ravages of colonialism, capitalism, and war, nor is it to question the outsized role of biomedicine in shaping modern society, though these are critiques certainly served by the arguments and material presented in each chapter. The function of malaria in this work is to recenter the lived and embodied experience of ordinary people in the past like Ömer, whose story graced the first pages of this introduction. They were the people whose labor and loss built the modern world. It is worth reflecting on what it cost them.

{ CHAPTER 1 }

UPLAND EMPIRE

The Indigenous Ecology of Ottoman Cilicia

Unbearable summer heat is a constant refrain in descriptions of the Cilicia region. A familiar folk song set in its geography revolves around escape to higher ground: "Come summer, it's a fire, the heat of July / a ferocious wolf, becomes every fly / it would pain my heart to see you die / rise, my flamingo, let's go to the *yayla*." This song appears in the collection of Ahmet Şükrü Esen, who spent the early decades of the twentieth century gathering the tales and laments of formerly nomadic Turkish communities in Southern Anatolia.[1] For such communities, the highland summer pasture of the *yayla* was the most important feature of the landscape. In this song and others he collected, the *yayla* was often synonymous with *sıla*, or home.[2] It is a testament to how would-be nomads still maintained a sense of belonging to place.[3]

The summer retreat to the mountains was a special time of the year for many communities in Ottoman Anatolia, so it is no wonder that Turkish folklore is replete with fond descriptions of it. One song, entitled "Yaylalar," conjures the familiar feelings of longing for the mountains: "If only the summer months would come / Wouldn't that breeze blow oh so gently / All the birds longing for home / Can you see the partridges of the *yayla*?" With references to gently blowing breeze, migrating birds, and longing for the *yayla*, this song bears all the linguistic markers of the poetic tradition associated with Turkic pastoralists in the work of folklorists. Yet this latter song was the composition of an Armenian bard from the town of Marash, preserved in Armeno-Turkish within a diasporic memorial volume as a testament to the region's natural beauty.[4]

Divergent Turkish and Armenian memories of the late Ottoman period have usually been written about in juxtaposition, but when read side by side on the level of daily life, convergences like this shared appreciation for the *yayla* emerge between what were normally held as two very distinct communities. They attest to the deeper ordering of everyday life that once transcended communal divisions. This chapter studies how the *yayla* as a shared temporal and spatial dimension of culture in Cilicia was integral to the local ecology, and in turn how that ecology shaped society, politics, and the historical evolution of the region up until the Tanzimat reforms.

The figure of the *yayla* has most often appeared within the historiography of the Ottoman Empire as summer pasture for pastoralists within a static binary of seasonal migration between winter and summer quarters. While the *yayla* was indeed central to the lives and livelihoods of herding communities in Anatolia, seasonal migration to the *yayla* was about more than finding pasture. Seasonal migration was also a conscious malaria avoidance strategy, which is why it was shared between people with entirely different communal formations and ways of life, including urbanites who had no economic incentive to engage in such movements. The *yayla* was a refuge from what local people understood as the insalubrious summer heat of the lowlands. Retreating to the mountains during the summer was central to notions of wellbeing for most people in Ottoman Cilicia. Participation in these rhythms served as a good index of an intimate and longstanding relationship with the environment that can be characterized as an indigenous ecology. Outsiders were often unaware that the *yayla* existed, and the rhythms associated with it were at odds with the increasingly commercialized ecology of the nineteenth century.

Cilicia's ecology was not unchanging. Rather, the centrality of seasonal migration to the *yayla* was reaffirmed and strengthened over several centuries of change in the region. The pages that follow consider how the environment and politics of Cilicia had developed up until the eve of mid-nineteenth-century provincial reform. I examine both Ottoman and Western European views of the region, demonstrating that the frequent accounts of Cilicia as a malarial backwater reflected the prejudices of "epidemiological orientalism" but also represented a failure to account for local ways of being in the region's environment. Then, I explain how Cilicia's diverse communities shared in a rhythm of transhumance and why seasonal movement between the mountains and the lowlands as a conscious malaria avoidance strategy was integral to life there. Next, I briefly outline Cilicia's long history as a borderland and discuss how during the high medieval period both Armenian "lords of the mountains" and the heads of Turkic pastoralist communities established political power in Cilicia through control of mountain spaces that were beyond the reach of imperial states. Finally, I explore how the early modern Ottoman government displayed flexibility in engaging with such forces of local autonomy as a feature of what Karen Barkey calls "segmented rule," often attempting to settle mobile populations but never carrying out a systematic and sustained effort to sedentarize the population of Cilicia.[5]

A Country with Two Climates

Cilicia is the historical name for an interconnected geography similar in size to Switzerland. It encompasses the Central Taurus Mountains, the Amanus Mountains, and the adjacent lowlands, especially the Cilician plain of the Mediterranean coast, which at the beginning of the nineteenth century contained the cities of Adana and Tarsus in the west and the lowlands of Çukurova and the Ceyhan River basin in the east. Ottoman Cilicia itself was not a bounded territory but rather a web of social and material connection and movement between urban and rural communities. However, with the provincial reforms of the Ottoman Empire, most of what I describe as late Ottoman Cilicia became part of the Ottoman province, or *vilayet*, of Adana in 1869 under four districts, or *sancaks*: the provincial center of Adana, the mountainous and coastal western Sancak of İçil (which included Mersin), the inland Sancak of Kozan encompassing the town of Sis and the mountainous subdistricts in the north, and the Sancak of Cebel-i Bereket, centered on the Amanus Mountains and surrounding lowlands. The Sancak of Marash was also part of historical Cilicia and had strong links to the provincial capital of Adana in the late Ottoman period, but it was governed either as a piece of the Vilayet of Aleppo or as an independent district. The coastal area surrounding the port of İskenderun, although it lay on the western side of the Amanus Mountains and closer to Adana, was also under the Vilayet of Aleppo due to its being the primary maritime outlet for the city of Aleppo.

Contrasts in elevation define the environment of the Cilicia region. Because the mountains trap the moisture of the coast, Cilicia's environment differs from neighboring regions of Central Anatolia and Northern Syria, which are considerably more arid. Moisture from the sea and plains, which becomes fog, rain, and snow as it meets with mountains, waters the mountain slopes, nurturing large swaths of pine and cedar that during the Ottoman period comprised some of the most impressive Anatolian forests. The Taurus and Amanus ranges surround the wide and fertile Çukurova plain, which is crosscut by rivers, most notably the Seyhan and Ceyhan and their tributaries. Runoff from the mountains feeds those rivers, endowing the delta plain with rich and well-watered soil.[6] Some areas around the Seyhan and Ceyhan Rivers were historically quite marshy as a result of frequent flooding. Much of the Mediterranean shore, especially near the river deltas, is still made up of wetlands. Before the twentieth century, the extent of wetlands in Cilicia was much greater. For example, the Karabucak, or "Black District," swamp in the south of Tarsus was once so vast that on an Ottoman map of Çukurova from the 1870s it was shown as an enormous green lagoon dwarfing the small city.[7]

During the warmer half of the year, the Cilician lowlands are notoriously hot and muggy. The period from June until the end of September is the heart of Adana's warm season, which is hotter and longer than in neighboring regions. Average high temperatures stay above 31°C/87.8°F.[8] Adana was often mentioned among the tropical regions, or "warm countries (*bilad-ı harre*)," of the Ottoman Empire alongside Greater Syria, the Hijaz, Iraq, Yemen, and North Africa.[9] An Ottoman agronomist remarked in an 1888 publication that summers in the Adana region were "warmer than the summers of the coasts of the Alexandria and Egypt (İskenderiye ve Mısır) climes."[10] As more standardized descriptions were generated throughout the late Ottoman period, the infamy of Cilician summers grew, whether in a Russian Armenian survey of Cilicia that characterized the summer heat as "unbearable"[11] or in the letter of a British consul who griped that summer in Adana was "tropical and far more trying than in India."[12]

Just a few days' walk from the urban centers of the lowlands, another climate prevails. Ottoman writers put that region in the same climatic zone as parts of inner Anatolia, such as Sivas and Ankara, and sometimes referred to it as the "*yayla*" clime.[13] The highlands of the Taurus Mountains in the north and the Amanus Mountains of the eastern part of the plain were known for their cool summer temperatures and fresh breezes. The average high temperature in the mountains during the summer typically hovers around 22°C/71.6°F. The average annual temperature in mountain towns of the Cilicia region is comparable to that of Budapest, meaning that to enjoy the climatic difference between the mountains and the plains of Cilicia in strictly latitudinal terms, one would have to traverse the northern half of the Ottoman Empire at its territorial peak. A memory volume compiled by former Armenian inhabitants of Cilicia put it simply: "Cilicia has two types of climate."[14] Historical sources frequently described the mountains and the lowlands as two separate geographies with distinctive environments and cultures.[15] As far back as antiquity, Cilicia was conceptually divided into a "flat" or "smooth" Cilicia of the plains and a "rough" Cilicia of the mountains.[16]

Although different parts of the Cilicia region were home to very different environments and ways of life, they were connected by the movement of people between those environments. At the beginning of the nineteenth century, a few hundred thousand people lived in Cilicia. The largest city was Adana, which contained about 30,000 people during the mid-nineteenth century. Marash and Tarsus were similar in size. İskenderun was the largest port, but its population was only in the thousands, and its commercial links to the cities of Cilicia were fairly limited. Mountain settlements in the region were comparatively dense. The predominantly Armenian towns of Hadjin and Zeytun in the Taurus Mountains boasted populations in the many thousands and were surrounded by clusters of villages.

Most of Cilicia's inhabitants were rural, usually residing in highland villages or engaged in various patterns of seasonal migration. There were many groups identified as seasonally nomadic tribes, or *aşirets*, by the Ottoman government. They formed the majority of the region's population, but they were far from being a monolithic segment. Some spoke dialects of Turkish and others Kurdish, and the boundary between these ethnic categories was not always well defined. In the center of Cilicia, the Avşars were the largest such group. They migrated between the lowlands of Çukurova and a large plateau called Uzunyayla beyond the Taurus Mountains in what became the Vilayet of Sivas with the administrative reforms of the 1860s, while others moved upland toward Marash and Elbistan in the summer. Among the large tribes cited as wintering in Çukurova were the Cerid and Bozdoğan. In the eastern portion of Cilicia, similar groups moved on an east-west axis between the Amanus Mountains and the lowlands on their eastern and western flanks.[17] Groups wintering on the eastern side of the Amanus Mountains were the Delikanlı and Çelikanlı, consistently described as Kurdish in the sources of the period. Most pastoralists of the eastern portion of Cilicia were recorded as tent-dwelling nomads as of the mid-nineteenth century. In the western part, the population was also primarily pastoralist and identified as belonging to *aşirets*, but these communities tended to move between fixed villages and the summer *yaylas* in the mountains. The foremost among them were the Menemencizâdes based in Karaisalı, not far from the city of Tarsus.[18]

Cilicia's pastoralists mainly herded sheep and goats, with the more nomadic groups tending toward a greater proportion of goats. Their economies were based on dairy production, wool, weaving, commerce, and varying degrees of agriculture. Some of the people who moved between the Taurus Mountains and the coastline between Silifke and modern-day Mersin were identified as *Tahtacı* in reference to their reliance on lumber from the mountain forests as part of their livelihoods. Other groups in Cilicia, such as the *Devecis*, or cameleers, made their living off long-distance transport and the breeding of pack animals, moving in a semi-nomadic fashion but not engaging primarily in the herding of livestock.

Most of the rest of the population of Cilicia was made up of villagers who also engaged in some form of pastoralism but devoted more energy to agriculture. Wheat and barley were the main staples. The mountains were also conducive to terraced agriculture and the maintenance of orchards. The cities of Adana and Tarsus were also surrounded by such orchards, which doubled as spaces of leisure during the summer. In the lowlands, sesame and small quantities of cotton were harvested. In the Central Taurus, especially around the towns of Feke and Hadjin, a large part of the Muslim population was identified by the label *Varsak,* signifying their descent from Turkic communities that had settled in the region over prior centuries. The label of *Ulaşlı* was applied to a similar group in and around the Amanus Mountains.[19] The Armenian population of the mountains was concentrated in the areas of Hadjin and Zeytun in the north and Bahçe in the Amanus Mountains. The ecclesiastical center of the Cilician Armenian community was based in the Catholicosate of Sis, a town at the edge of the plain near the ascent into the mountains in the Sancak of Kozan. At the beginning of the nineteenth century, the lowland town of Çokmerzimen (modern-day Dörtyol), located along the coast between the Gulf of Iskenderun and the Amanus Mountains, was an emergent site of Armenian settlement in rural Cilicia that would grow throughout the late Ottoman period.[20] In the west, the Mediterranean coast and adjacent Taurus Mountains also contained a large concentration of Greek Orthodox population near Silifke. One other enclave was the district of Rum (signifying its Greek Orthodox character) in the Central Taurus, a key commercial stop on inland trade routes.[21] While the Greek Orthodox community of Cilicia had particular links to the inland towns of Bor and Kayseri, the Cilician Armenian community also had links to Marash and Aintab in the east.[22]

Both of these groups were among the many communities found in the principal lowland cities of Adana and Tarsus.[23] In these cities, as in the other major towns of the Cilicia region, Turkish was the dominant language, although a sizable population of Arabic speakers attested to the enduring connections between lowland Cilicia and the Levant. Outside these cities, most of the lowland village population was Muslim, hailing from the same communities found throughout Cilicia. During the nineteenth century, a growing number of Nusayri cultivators from the area of Antakya and the coast of Northern Syria began to settle permanently in the Cilicia region.[24] The Nusayris, who spoke a dialect of Arabic and belonged to the same religious community as modern-day Alawites of Syria, were regarded as outsiders by the majority of Cilicia's urban population, but they would become a substantial component of the rural population by the early twentieth century.[25]

Epidemiological Orientalism

Cilicia has occupied a relatively minor place in the historiography of the pre-nineteenth century Ottoman Empire. It was sometimes characterized by outsiders as an insignificant backwater. Well into the twentieth century, the lowlands of Çukurova were known for the rampant spread of malaria during the summer months. Looking back, Turkish social scientist Mübeccel Kıray stated that Çukurova had been "no more than a badly drained, fever-ridden, thinly populated country" prior to modernization. This description has found its way into much of the subsequent anglophone scholarship on the region's recent history.[26] However, Ottoman Cilicia's inhabitants probably would not have described their region in this way. In fact, some of the features that made Cilicia seem wild or unproductive from one perspective were the very facets of daily life most cherished by its diverse communities.

The idea that the Cilician lowlands were fever-ridden became deeply entrenched during the early modern period. Western authors almost universally depicted this area as insalubrious. Such descriptions go back at least a far as the thirteenth-century travels of Marco Polo, who began his journey east from the Cilician port of Ayas. The account describes Cilicia as "by no means a healthy region, but grievously the reverse."[27] Unpleasant encounters with the region's malarial swamps appear everywhere in early modern accounts of the coastal region of İskenderun (also Scanderoon or Alexandretta). İskenderun was the main maritime outlet for the city of Aleppo, which was one of the largest cities in the empire at its height, and thus, European merchants frequently visited the port.[28] Surrounded as it was by extensive marshes, İskenderun was infamous among early modern travelers, who were wary of disembarking or spending the night.[29] Unflattering reviews by seventeenth-century visitors included these characterizations: a "bad village" with "awful air";[30] "for the most part swampy [*paludoso*] and therefore very unhealthy";[31] a "contagious and pestiferous place";[32] and an "especially sickly place" during the summer because of "an innumerable company of frogs, of a greate bignes, which cry almost like ducks" that would find their way to the town and "for want of water dye there, and infect the ayre very much."[33] Notable in these accounts of İskenderun's insalubrious environment is that its reputation usually preceded it as word spread to new visitors via more seasoned merchants. By the nineteenth century, European authors were primed to write about the region in this way by the accounts of travelers in whose footsteps they followed.

Though the early modern authors quoted here did not understand the mechanisms of malaria's transmission, they knew that people often fell violently ill and died in such "unhealthy" places, intuitively linking disease to the climate and the bad air of swamps that harbored mosquitos or (in one case) the frogs that might eat them. "The climate paralyzes every thing," a mid-nineteenth-century British traveler wrote. "Our consul had about fifty attacks of fever before he became acclimated." Likening İskenderun to the more familiar Southern Europe, he added that "the rest of the population has the sepulchral complexion of the specters that glide about the roadside inns in the Pontine marshes between Velletri and Terracinn."[34] As İskenderun was a place of much greater importance to European merchants than to the general population of the region, their perspectives also found their way into the Ottoman archival record; the aforementioned consul repeatedly urged the Ottoman government to drain İskenderun's marshes, resulting in a large but ultimately unsuccessful desiccation scheme during the 1840s.[35]

These depictions of İskenderun bear the mark of what Nükhet Varlık calls "epidemiological orientalism."[36] During the early modern period, Europeans saw the Ottoman Empire and many European colonies in Asia, Africa, and the Americas as inherently insalubrious. Thus, when a European traveler referred to İskenderun as "the Sierra Leone of the Eastern Mediterranean," we must bear in mind that this perception was based in part on the image of the tropics as the "white man's grave."[37] This point should not call into question whether Europeans did in fact drop like flies in İskenderun, for they certainly did. However, epidemiological orientalism, like other forms of orientalism, calls into question whether Western portrayals, especially negative ones, were accurate or faithful to the lived experiences of people in the Ottoman Empire. As Aaron Shakow notes, the longstanding trope of "Oriental plague" among European commentators might have primed early modern writers and by extension present-day environmental historians to find sickness scattered across the Ottoman geography.[38]

Even though most of the available early modern depictions of Cilicia in Ottoman Turkish and Arabic were also by travelers, they were not nearly so dominated by the disdain that pervades Western European sources. For example, Badr al-Din al-Ghazzi, a Sufi scholar from newly conquered Damascus, visited sixteenth-century Cilicia during the dead of summer, traveling through Syria into Anatolia and toward the Ottoman capital. Offering selections of Arabic poetry all the way, his descriptions of an idyllic countryside rendered in effortlessly rhyming prose were at times puzzling. In the heart of Çukurova near the Misis bridge, he described the air as "humid" and yet also likened it to "the fragrance of ambergris," dedicating a poem to the banks of the mighty Ceyhan River.[39] He described Adana as a wondrous city, likening its fine courtyards, trees, gardens, and waterwheels to those of the city of Hama on the Orontes River in Syria.[40] Al-Ghazzi's account was written for the Ottoman sultan with the goal of currying favor, which may explain the embellished grandeur and beauty of the empire's new provinces in his narrative.[41] Yet there were a few points in his Cilicia travels that wavered into trepidation. Near the Gülek Pass, which serves as Syria's gateway to Anatolia through the Taurus Mountains, the darkness and desolation provoked terror, as did the narrow, winding mountain paths, which al-Ghazzi found so sheer that "monkeys would not climb them and mice would not travel them except in a state of bewilderment and utmost fear and trembling."[42] This uncharacteristically uncharitable description makes more sense if we consider that al-Ghazzi was a consummate scholarly gentleman, whose natural environment was in the lavish salons of exquisite Damascene homes.[43] More generally, we might conclude that al-Ghazzi was simply most comfortable in areas of Cilicia that resembled his native Syria, and his subjective impression of Cilicia's environment differed from those of Western Europeans because of how he read the landscape.

Lack of local knowledge may have been another key factor in why Europeans depicted this corner of the Mediterranean in such miserable terms. The account of a Scottish clergyman and physician named Vere Monro offers a vivid illustration. Monro undertook virtually the same journey as al-Ghazzi, also in a newly conquered Cilicia—this time by Ibrahim Pasha's armies from Egypt—some three centuries later. He described his travels in a two-volume work entitled *A Summer Ramble in Syria*. Apparently unaware of how ill conceived a "summer ramble" through the Cilician lowlands would be, he predictably depicted the area as a backwater. "The marsh, which entirely surrounds [İskenderun], renders it one of the most unhealthy spots in Syria," he recalled. "And the scantiness of the population, together with their sallow complexions and swoln bodies, testify the vindictive influence of malaria."[44] Moving toward Adana through the Çukurova plain, he found that traveling conditions became almost unbearable near the crossing of the Ceyhan River at Misis. "The heat, untempered by a breath of air, was very oppressive; and the flies, which swarmed about us like bees, made it more insupportable," he wrote. "Their bite was so severe that the necks and chests of the horses were dripping with blood . . . Wherever they bit through my clothes, a swelling immediately followed."[45]

After an unanticipated complication sent him back to Beirut, Monro returned to Adana, which he described as largely deserted, to obtain horses and set out for the Anatolian interior. As he neared the Taurus Mountains, his griping halted for one of the first moments in the entire account. "Liberated from thralldom, advancing rapidly to new scenes by the most agreeable of all conveyances, freshened by the dews, and fanned by the breezes from the snowy tops of Taurus, I could imagine no greater delight than I felt." His group ascended "amid scenery of Alpine grandeur" until reaching a village "much like some of those upon the highest ranges of the Swiss Alps."[46] They eventually came to the town of Pozantı, where Monro felt that he had been transported to another world. He found men huddled around a warm fire, "proof that it was not merely imagination which whispered that we had changed the climate within the last thirty-six hours." He learned there that the population had retreated even farther into the mountains. He speculated that the reason for this practice was to take advantage of the salubrious air that prevailed in the highlands.[47]

Monro's depiction might have reflected the growing trend of appreciation for mountain spaces like the Alps in nineteenth-century Europe, but he had "discovered" something that would have been obvious to any local in the region. Since Ottoman travelers who passed through Cilicia had more immediate access to local knowledge, they moved through the landscape in a different manner. Bulus ibn al-Zaim al-Halabi (often referred to as Paul of Aleppo) traveled from Aleppo to Wallachia during the seventeenth century with his father, then patriarch of the Melkite Church. They passed through Cilicia during the months of July and August. He recorded nothing in terms of malaria and discomfort in the Cilician lowlands, and their journey reflected a savvier approach to the landscape than was commonly found among European travel narratives. Their party journeyed only after dark, sometimes leaving cities in the dead of night despite the potential danger of traveling after dark. Bulus and his father also had a Türkmen agha in their company, which might explain why they lodged in Türkmen encampments and villages during parts of their journey, which included a visit to Tekir in the Taurus Mountains. There, the account mentions a stay at the renowned Ramazanoğlu *yayla*, apparently referring to the Turkish word *yayla* within his Arabic text.[48]

The *yayla* was a temporal space, a highland plateau used as a summer home by communities that spent the winter in the lowlands. Though they were rarely mentioned in early modern European accounts, the *yaylas* of Cilicia were legendary. The seventeenth-century account of Evliya Çelebi also mentioned the Ramazanoğlu *yayla*, stating that there were seventy great *yaylas* in the Ottoman Empire, and the Ramazanoğlu *yayla* was rivaled only by the Bingöl *yayla* in Eastern Anatolia.[49] The eighteenth-century hajj narrative of Mehmed Edib also made note of the Ramazanoğlu *yayla*, described as the summer home of residents of Adana.[50] While the favorable descriptions of Cilicia's *yaylas* in Ottoman accounts contrasted with the negative descriptions of the lowlands in European accounts, these Ottoman narratives did contain similar descriptions of insalubrious lowlands that pointed to a shared conception of climate's impact on the body. Concerning Adana, Mehmed Edib indicated in a matter-of-fact manner that "since its air is heavy [*sakil*], most of the inhabitants go to the *yayla* during the summer."[51] He likewise described the air of Payas—a port just 20 km up the coast from İskenderun—as "very heavy." But at Payas, he also remarked upon the boon of the "incomparable" *yayla* in the nearby Amanus Mountains that it possessed.[52]

The *yaylas* of the Amanus Mountains near Payas also appeared in Evliya's account as spaces where the pastoralists of the region (*Türkmân ve Urbânlar*) would spend six months of the year to "get air and refreshment." According to Evliya, each of the seven *yaylas* was imbued with the power to ward off specific early modern calamities; one was impervious to malaria, and its residents were "very healthy." Another, the Sincan *yayla*, the water of which could cure lepers, was even a site of pilgrimage since, according to Evliya's account, Jesus of Nazareth and his mother had once stayed there. As for Sürmeli *yayla*, which was regularly frequented by the martyr Habib the Carpenter of Antioch, a contemporary of Jesus in Islamic traditions, it was absolutely free of plague.[53] In Evliya's rendering, local beliefs about these incredible *yaylas* were somewhat fantastical. But they referred to the very common conception of the mountain *yayla* as a salubrious space with good air and restorative waters. While the more voluminous and well-known European accounts of Cilicia have resulted in a consistently negative description of the region's climate and environment, local understandings suggest that during the summer, Cilicia was best described as a mountain paradise.

An Indigenous Ecology of Transhumance

The accounts of Bulus al-Halabi, Evliya Çelebi, and Mehmed Edib quoted here attest to the most important dimension of Ottoman Cilicia's ecology: seasonal migration. Local life was structured by an annual retreat to the mountain *yaylas* during the warm months. Such migrations have often been described as transhumance, which is typically understood as a system of herding. The term is of French origin and was first applied to the phenomenon of Alpine transhumance and other cases within Europe. However, in its broadest definition, transhumance is a practice that has emerged in numerous locations throughout the world. While there was no term encompassing the idea of transhumance as a system in Ottoman Turkish, there were many ways of describing communities that engaged in semi-nomadic patterns. The language of administration contained terms that refer to animal husbandry and nomadism or, alternatively, "tribal" designations, such as *aşiret*, *kabile*, *oymak*, and *cemaat*, that were implicitly understood to refer to nomadic or mobile populations.[54] The Ottoman vocabulary also contained notions of temporal spaces associated with transhumance, summer and winter quarters (*yayla/yaylak* and *kışlak*), which came from the pastoralist vocabularies not only in the Ottoman Empire but also in regions such as Iran where Turkic herders have had a long historical presence.[55]

By migrating between different elevations on a seasonal basis, pastoralists could take advantage of differentiated seasons of vegetative growth. For the "tent-dwelling [*haymenişin*]" pastoralist communities in Cilicia, such as the Avşars, the mountain *yayla* referred to a summer pasture. But if later studies were any indication of practices decades prior, the *yaylak/kışlak* binary was an oversimplification of practices. For herders in Cilicia who lived in tents and migrated hundreds of kilometers throughout the year, *yayla* was the name of just one of many different high elevations frequented during the summer.[56] With regard to their practices, *yayla* was shorthand for a summer place that probably comprised multiple stages of pasturing in the mountains.

A *yaylak/kışlak* framework for understanding transhumance is thus a simplified binary that was more legible to nonpastoralist communities, in part because it was more in line with their own movements. For example, during the early twentieth century, scholars began to connect the modes of pastoralism found in Anatolia to broader practices in the Mediterranean. Turkish geographer Cemal Arif Alagöz (more in chapter 5) translated transhumance as *yaylacılık*, which signified the practice of frequenting the *yayla* or the state of being a *yaylacı*, a person who goes to the *yayla*. This choice of words was significant in that a *yaylacı* was not necessarily a nomad in any sense, and the term usually described an urban person who vacationed at a mountain *yayla* during the summer. In fact, Alagöz singled out the Cilicia region as one in which "urban transhumance [*şehir yaylacılık*]" was commonly practiced.[57]

Why would nonpastoralist communities adhere to a seasonal rhythm of migration that served no clear economic benefit? The answer is that summering at the *yayla* was a matter of life and death. This ecology of transhumance, while typically associated with the demands of nomadic pastoralism, was arguably a malaria avoidance strategy first and foremost, as attested by the fact that nonpastoralists engaged in the same summer migrations to the mountain *yaylas* for health purposes.[58] Local communities in Cilicia saw the *yayla* as the antidote to what nineteenth-century Ottoman sources describe as "*vahâmet-i hava*." This term referred to the heaviness, severity, or general bad quality of the climate. It was more or less equivalent to the Latinate word "malaria," signifying bad or foul air.[59] In a miasmatic understanding of disease, bad air produced illness, and specifically, an ailment known in Turkish as *sıtma*, signifying fever and shivering—the chief symptoms of malaria. Long before scientific research demonstrated the *Anopheles* mosquito's role as a vector in malaria transmission, people associated mosquito-friendly environments such as swamps (and their foul airs) with malaria. The perception of bad air and the fevers it gave rise to reflects an understanding of malaria as a "biophysical pathology of the environment."[60] Seasonal migration worked well as a malaria avoidance strategy due to the nature of the mountain environment. In contrast to the lowlands, the mountains had few aquatic spaces for mosquitos to breed in. But the crucial fact was that most of the mosquitos that transmit malaria hibernate at around 10° Celsius, meaning that mountain elevations were much too cold for them during most of the year.[61]

Lived knowledge of the Cilician landscape dictated that the mountains were the more salubrious place to spend the summer and to escape the lowlands for "change of air," or *tebdil-i hava,* when one was ill.[62] Almost every community in Cilicia shared in this practice within the same mountain spaces. In the summer of 1857, for example, the deputy governor of Adana sent a request to the Ottoman government for permission to spend the summer in the *yayla* of Namrun, stating that "most of the population both rich and poor needs to spend three or four months at the *yayla,* as Adana's well-known *vahâmet-i hava* is unbearable during the warm seasons."[63] William Burckhardt Barker, who lived around that time in Cilicia where his father served as British consul, declared in his extensive work on the region that "the poor man will sell any thing he may possess rather than fail to take his family to the mountain during the summer months."[64]

As such, transhumant rhythms were integral to the communal life of urban communities such as the Cilician Armenians. A memory volume belonging to the Armenian community of Sis cited "change of air" as the common approach to dealing with malaria.[65] That volume also displayed a hand-drawn depiction of the Namrun *yayla* northwest of Tarsus (see figure 1.1). The diagram marked several locations at Namrun, including a "Turkish" quarter and an Armenian quarter separated by a stream, as well as a place called "cattle *yayla*" in Turkish, a few monasteries, and the old fortress of Lampron that guarded the Cilician Gates during the medieval period.[66] The small space of Namrun contained the summer quarters of both Christians and Muslims from Adana and Tarsus, a summer pasture for animals, and numerous sites of religious and historical importance. Armenian mountain settlements also played an important role in the seasonal rhythms. In another memory book about the mountain town of Hadjin, an Armenian doctor in California and former resident described his native village as "a marvelous summer place," using the word *amranots,* which is a close synonym of the Turkish words *yayla* and *sayfiye* (coming from Arabic and also meaning "summer place").⁶⁷ It was common for Armenians of Adana to summer in Hadjin with residents of Hadjin in turn descending to the city during the winter, thereby integrating the different Armenian settlements in Cilicia.⁶⁸

The Greek Orthodox, or Rum, community of Cilicia was smaller than that of the Armenians. They were concentrated in the city of Tarsus (and later Mersin) and the villages and towns of the western coast. According to testimonies recorded in Greece following the post–World War I exchange of populations, the summer retreat to the *yayla* had played a critical role in their seasonal rhythms. One former resident of Tarsus stated that "during the summer, only few people remain in the city; the majority of the inhabitants move to the mountains, to avoid excessive heat and the fevers, which plague those who remain in the city."⁶⁹ Another concurred: "The summer is very hot. Everybody goes out someplace, to the vineyards, the countryside, and spends the summer there."⁷⁰ A former resident of a nearby village similarly recalled that "in the summer it was hot, and many people caught malaria. Whoever could leave left to avoid fevers."⁷¹ Former inhabitants of both the villages of the mountains and the coast to the west attested to the apparent centrality of summer fevers in transhumant temporalities. Of the small port of Taşucu, one said that "the brook nearby marshes up in the summers and creates a lot of stagnant water. And then there is the heat. For this reason, we move up to Gökbelen. Gökbelen is 23 km away from Taşucu, and it is higher up. One travels the whole day, from morning till night, by horse to get there. On the way there is Alakilise and [Silifke], and from there too, everyone who can afford to leave leaves."⁷² As for the mountain dwellers, they recalled the salubrious environments of their villages and their benefit to the inhabitants of the coast. One said, "The climate here was excellent. It was up in the mountains, with vineyards, plane trees, and below the plane trees there were springs. Those who didn't have work in [Silifke] in the summers would come up here to spend the summer here."⁷³ A former inhabitant of another village noted, "The summer was cool. The village was above sea level, surrounded by mountains and woods. They kept it cool. People from [Silifke] came here to spend the summer. It was too hot there, and there were lots of mosquitos."⁷⁴

The available sources on local medicine in Ottoman Cilicia demonstrate the centrality of malaria to concerns about health and well-being. It is the most commonly mentioned ailment. Beyond change of air, solutions to

FIGURE 1.1. An Armenian sketch of Namrun and the surrounding area from a memory book published in Beirut in the 1940s. It is oriented northwest to southeast from top to bottom. No. 5 is Bolkar Mountain of the Taurus Mountain range. Old fortress of Lampron is no. 2. Turkish quarter of Namrun at left (no. 4) and Armenian quarter at right (no. 3). "Cattle yayla" farther right at no. 10. Nos. 6 and 9 are monasteries. The paths that come down the mountains and join near Tarsus are not roads but rather the streams that feed into the Berdan (Cydnus) River, which becomes a series of cascades north of the city of Tarsus, situated at extreme bottom left. Source: Prepared for Keleshean, *Sis-matean* (1949), 81, by Dr. H. Der Ghazarian and drawn by Krikor Ulubegyan; reproduced in H. Ter Ghazarean, *Հայկական Կիլիկիա* (1966/2006).

malarial fevers ranged from the practical to the supernatural. Anatolian peasants and townsfolk were accustomed to alleviating the feverish symptoms of malaria with a trip to the bathhouse or consumption of alcohol.[75] An account from the Avşars of the Taurus Mountains cites a remedy for fever that involved wrapping the patient in a sheepskin to let them sweat it out.[76] A former Greek resident of a village near Tarsus noted that "Arabs who suffered from malaria" would tie strings around the branches of the wild pear tree at the Church of St. Paul in search of healing.[77] In Hadjin, locals engaged in a similar practice at the Saint Sarkis Sanctuary on the southeastern side of the town.[78] A Greek activist who worked on the population exchange oral history project noted the use of an incantation (in Turkish), and the Armenian memory volume of Sis referred to the same Turkish incantation that could be incorporated into a charm or amulet.[79] The same incantation of "*Sıtma! Bu iti tutma*" is also attested among Turkish communities of the region today.[80] Malaria did not respect confessional boundaries, and neither did its solutions, even when in the form of a prayer.

Though it appealed more to a modern scientific explanation of malaria avoidance, retreat to the *yayla* was in some way just as magical as a prayer or incantation. Movement to the *yayla* in late April and early May was a time of communal and spiritual significance. The celebration of Hıdırellez, which falls at the beginning of May, was one of the most important feasts in the agrarian calendar. For pastoralists, Hıdırellez was celebrated once the community had reached the *yayla*, meaning that the beginning of the *yayla* season was marked with ritual festivities.[81] Yet Hıdırellez was not a celebration exclusive to those communities; it coincided with the feast of St. George, one of the most important celebrations of the local Christian calendar. Both Muslims and Christians in the Cilicia region celebrated Hıdırellez as a sacred dimension of a shared temporality.[82] An aforementioned Greek man from a village near Tarsus noted that his village had a church of St. George where "Arabs and Turks" would come to participate in the festivities, bringing animal sacrifices and votive offerings.[83] For some inhabitants of Cilicia, the coming of summer, which was followed by retreat to the mountains for pasture and respite, was accompanied by rituals and celebrations that transcended religious boundaries.[84]

Cilicia as a Historical Borderland

Nineteenth-century diplomats, officials, merchants, and travelers wrongly cast Cilicia as inherently insalubrious, but they also often fixated on the themes of decline and ruin. There were indeed ruins of ancient and medieval settlements scattered throughout the region. While there had been seventeen cities in Roman Cilicia as of the fifth century, only seven of these were still significant settlements at all as of the early nineteenth century.[85] The ruins of Anazarbus (or Anavarza), located deep in Çukurova near the Ceyhan River, seemed the most poignant symbol of Cilicia's fall. The site of a once impressive city was virtually uncultivated, though it was endowed with good soil, abundant water sources, and evidence of prior hydraulic sophistication.[86] In a mid-nineteenth century drawing featured in the journal *Le Tour du Monde*, which introduced readers to little-known corners of the world, horsemen with spears stand in the shadow of Anazarbus's decaying fortifications, aqueducts, and columns (see figure 1.2). Such was the state of affairs in Cilicia when it first appeared before the Western gaze.

Impressive though they were, the once mighty settlements of the ancient world had been built upon a very different set of power relations. The nature of slavery in the Roman Empire is the subject of considerable scholarly debate, but it is clear that enslaved laborers were a critical component of Roman society. In fact, Rome's expansion into Cilicia seems to have been a direct consequence of its reliance on the Mediterranean slave trade to sustain plantations in areas such as Sicily, where during the second century BCE, enslaved Cilicians participated in a revolt that lasted about seven years. Rome's invasion of Cilicia to oust the so-called Cilician pirates allowed it to take control of the slave trade in the Eastern Mediterranean.[87] Settlements of the Roman era were inextricable from the practice of slavery in virtually every field, including building and agriculture. In fact, in a fifth- or sixth-century tariff from Anazarbus, slaves were listed as one of the major "items" taxed in the city, right above livestock.[88] That this fact was lost on observers from nineteenth-century empires, which were often no less built on the practice of slavery, is just one example of how Western views of the Ottoman Empire were informed by a rose-tinted view of the classical past.

Recent scholarship challenges the civilizational hierarchies and declensionist narratives that undergirded these perspectives and have implicitly

FIGURE 1.2. This drawing was based on an image from Victor Langlois's *Voyage dans la Cilicie*, one of the first detailed studies of the Cilicia region during the nineteenth century. The artist Pierre-Eugène Grandsire used the sketch of Anazarbus from Langlois's study, adding nomads of his own imagination to enhance the impression. Source: *Le Tour du Monde*, 3:412.

informed much of modern historiography, going so far as to write "against the grain" of the normative assumption that intensive agriculture was simply a natural fact of human civilization.[89] If we assume that the agricultural settlements and cities of Roman Cilicia were predicated on the coercive power of the state to perpetuate a set of economic relations that ultimately rested on slavery, the image of nomads frolicking in the ruins of civilization looks very different, and the question of malaria becomes all the more relevant. As Robert Sallares concludes in his study of malaria in the ancient Italian Peninsula, "Rome was a society with the potential for massive chattel slavery as the basis of the labour force and the slaves had no choice over where to live and die." Roman agricultural expansion fueled the spread of malaria; enslavement was a means of keeping people on land they did not wish to work. This, Sallares notes, resembled the very dynamic that played out in the plantation societies of the Americas.[90]

Cilicia at the outset of the nineteenth century was almost the opposite of the civilizational ideal embodied by the romanticized understanding of Roman civilization. Most of the population did not derive its livelihood from agriculture, and there were few large plantations. The coercive power of the state was limited. This was not a static or timeless status, but the process by which Cilicia became a borderland dominated by pastoralist communities takes us back at least as far as the Islamic conquests of the seventh century, which were preceded by wars between the Sassanian and the Byzantine Empires in frontier spaces like Cilicia. The Byzantine retreat after defeat by the Muslim armies at Yarmuk left the lowlands south of the Taurus Mountains abandoned in military terms. From the Islamic perspective, the Taurus Mountains constituted the farthest extent of the Syro-Anatolian frontier or western *thughur*. Early Arabic accounts described many of the towns in former Byzantine Cilicia as depopulated at that time.[91] As Muslim rulers slowly reoccupied Cilicia's settlements, the landscape was changing due to erosion in the mountains. During the transition between the Byzantine and Islamic periods, marshes appear to have expanded in the Cilicia region around Lake Amik, the plain of Marash, Çukurova, and south of Tarsus with the expansion of the Rhegma (Karabucak) lagoon that, with silting of the Cydnus River, ended the city's status as a port.

The early period of Islamic rule in Cilicia saw increased settlement and economic activity around cities like Tarsus, Anazarbus, and Adana from the eighth century onward. The Abbasids invested in building lowland settlements, and in light of similarities between the Mesopotamian marshes and the marshy lowlands of the Cilicia region, they brought settlers from modern-day Iraq, which is perhaps how Cilicia's distinctive species of water buffalo was first introduced.[92] On the Byzantine frontier, Christian pastoralists continued to move seasonally in a form of transhumance between the mountains and lowland regions, a practice that long pre-dated their being Christian and went back at least as far as the Hittite period roughly two millennia prior.[93]

With Abbasid fragmentation, Cilicia once again became a contested space, and over successive centuries, it was settled by people of two main groups from the east: Turkic pastoralists from the Seljuk heartlands in Greater Persia, and Armenian villagers from the highlands in Eastern

Anatolia and the Caucasus. The Byzantine Empire encouraged Armenian settlement for the purpose of maintaining hegemony following Cilicia's reconquest from the Abbasids in the tenth century. The short-lived annexation of Ani (near the modern-day border between Turkey and Armenia) and other sites in Eastern Anatolia enabled the Byzantines to forcibly resettle Armenians throughout Central Anatolia. Aurora Camaño argues that Cilicia became the ideal location for Armenian migrants in part because the Taurus Mountains provided familiar landscapes for new Armenian settlements. Armenian communities brought the same types of fortifications, monasteries, and agricultural settlements that already predominated farther east.[94] Cilicia felt like home to these migrants, and in the mountains, they enjoyed more autonomy. Their settlement was so impactful that successive heads of Armenian dynasties claiming the title "Lord of the Mountains" came to control the region in their own right with the decline of Byzantine power. At its height, Armenian Cilicia was a bit larger than Roman Cilicia, first as an independent principality and later as a protectorate under the Mongols that played an active role as a buffer state in regional politics, especially during the period of the Crusades.[95]

The Armenian dynasties established their political capital where the mountains and the plains converged: the city of Sis, which would eventually become an ecclesiastical center as well. The mountain towns of Hadjin and Zeytun (then Ulnia) grew during the Armenian period, and the future summer resort town of Lampron (Namrun) was one of many mountain settlements that became the site of enormous fortifications. The feudal economy of Armenian Cilicia featured a low degree of coercion; the fields were tended by tax-paying, small-time cultivators who could take refuge within the many fortifications in times of crisis.[96] The Armenian nobility tended to take up residence in the forested mountains away from the major mercantile cities they controlled.[97] The people of Sis engaged in a pattern of seasonal migration, summering in the mountains as successive generations of Cilicians would do for centuries.[98] Malaria was a disease familiar to the region's inhabitants, as evidenced by medical writings indicating sophisticated understanding of types of fevers and symptoms associated with different kinds of malaria infection.[99]

The Armenian kingdoms of Cilicia were neighbored by the Turkic principalities, or *beyliks*, that emerged out of Seljuk fragmentation. Turkic migration to Anatolia occurred over centuries; the extent to which preexisting populations adopted new identities with the successive arrival of new nomadic groups is a complicated one, but the groups that came to predominate in Cilicia during the medieval period are associated with the Oghuz Türkmen migrations.[100] These groups had become predominantly Muslim, and their spread into Anatolia accompanied the rise of the Seljuks. Turkic pastoralists established seasonal pastures in the Cilicia region while it was still under Armenian rule.[101] Just as the Anatolian highlands had provided a smooth transition for Armenian settlers, the mountains welcomed pastoralists expanding from the east at the expense of former Byzantine subjects. Their preestablished seasonal patterns of migration between winter pastures and the summer pastures of the *yaylak* readily mapped onto the Anatolian geography. They traveled with large flocks and could scarcely afford to stray from sources of pasture for long. Turkic pastoralists thrived in Cilicia in part because the landscape was legible to them. They knew a *yaylak* when they found one, and they knew how precious it could be.

During the mid-fourteenth century, Cilicia witnessed the devastation of the Black Death, which may well have hit the cities and towns hardest. Türkmen *beys* emerged as the new power players in the region, particularly after the Mamluk Sultanate of Cairo captured Adana, Tarsus, and Sis. Much of the Armenian elite fled to Cyprus or points farther west, leaving behind a sizeable Armenian peasantry ruled in the name of the Mamluks by largely autonomous principalities under the leadership of the Ramazanoğlus, based in Adana, and the Dulkadiroğlus, who controlled the Marash region and were based in the town of Elbistan. The Armenian church maintained its position of authority at the Catholicosate of Sis. Under these new dynasties, a large pastoralist population thrived. As the Armenian nobility had done, the new rulers based much of their power in the mountains. In the case of the Ramazanoğlus, the eponymous Ramazan Bey and his brothers had inherited both summer pastures (*yaylak*) and winter homes (in towns like Tarsus and Adana) from their father Yüreğir, so transhumance was built into the polity's organization.[102] This did not mean that the entire region became a pasture of nomads, and in fact some important institutions of urban life were constructed in Adana, Tarsus, and the Ramazanoğlu *yayla*: mosques, *medreses*, *hamams*, inns, markets, *türbes*, and charitable institutions called *imârethanes*. When the Ottomans assumed control of the Cilicia region, the Ramazanoğlus and their charitable endowments (*vakıf*) dominated the landscape.[103] Yet even as the city of Adana would remain the political capital of the region for centuries to come, the mountains remained the true locus of power.

Ottoman expansion into Cilicia was built on the foundations of the Anatolian *beyliks*. While Cilicia came under Ottoman rule during Selim I's conquests of the early sixteenth century, some of the local autonomy of the medieval period remained in place. The Ramazanoğlus continued as hereditary governors of Adana until the early seventeenth century. As for the Dulkadiroğlus, their reign in Marash ended with Dulkadiroğlu Ali Bey, appointed as governor by Selim I, being executed under suspicion of treason during the bloody suppression of the Kizilbash movement that allied with the Safavids of Iran. But this was only after he had fought under the Ottomans and women of the Dulkadiroğlu dynasty had married into the Ottoman royal lineage. Sultan Selim I himself was supposedly born to Ayşe Hatun, the daughter of former Dulkadiroğlu ruler Alaüddevle.[104]

Aided by the acquisition of Egypt, a major center of agricultural production, the Ottoman Empire enjoyed a period of great military and economic strength during the sixteenth century. The Cilician lowlands shared in the agricultural expansion under the *timar* system of land grants to the military elite. Lowland settlements resurged to the extent that mountain fortifications like Namrun, which overlooked the Cilician plains, became redundant.[105] İslamoğlu and Faroqhi argue that Adana briefly switched from being a center of wheat production to a predominantly cotton-producing region by the late sixteenth century. Demand for cotton came from Istanbul, namely, the Ottoman palace. However, unlike in other parts of the empire, the population of the lowlands did not rise very significantly at the time, so it seems, because a commercial crop became dominant and therefore did not offer the same opportunities for the creation of small farms. Rice may also have been an ascendant commercial crop around Sis and Marash, as evidenced by an early seventeenth-century tax farm register.[106] İslamoğlu and Faroqhi hypothesized that labor took the form of "coerced cash-crop labor" mediated through the internal power relationships of the *cemaats,* or tribal communities.[107]

Meanwhile, the mountain ecologies resembled a familiar Mediterranean blend of subsistence crops and pastoralism. The district of Zeytun reflected a crop distribution common to the highland settlements: most land was devoted to wheat and the rest to fruit trees and garden vegetables.[108]

The sudden economic rise of the lowlands was short-lived. The ascendant cotton industry of Cilicia may have simply declined for market-driven reasons.[109] But the seventeenth and eighteenth centuries were a period of generalized agrarian crisis in the empire. Recent scholarship demonstrates that the Little Ice Age, a period of extended global cooling, brought significant changes to the Anatolian environment. Average global temperatures only diverged by a degree or two during this period, but these slight variations resulted in unfavorable weather conditions that spurred agrarian crisis in Europe, the Middle East, and China.[110] Sam White has argued that climatic changes, which made Ottoman peasants more vulnerable to drought, led to the abandonment of villages and favored the more resilient and flexible modes of pastoralism among tribal populations, who were often armed and capable of expanding their pasture at the expense of adjacent settlements. The lack of state hegemony in the countryside during the period of Celali rebellions, themselves fueled by agrarian collapse, compounded the abandonment of settlements.[111] The Armenian traveler Simeon of Poland noted that around Zeytun, once-populous Armenian villages had been largely vacated as a result of Celali raids.[112]

Some have argued that the issue of malaria attested in early modern sources was a byproduct of the changes described here. In *The Waning of the Mediterranean*, Faruk Tabak hypothesized that changes in the hydrography of the Mediterranean lowlands brought on by the Little Ice Age led to a rise in malaria rates during the early modern period.[113] Shakow also notes that the rapid rise in cotton planting in formerly uncultivated lands around the Ceyhan River that occurred during the sixteenth century may have brought with it *P. falciparum* strains of malaria that flourished in the Cilician lowlands and spread to other regions.[114] McNeill meanwhile asserts that the malaria of the Cilician lowlands, which was a function of the hydrological "disorders" occurring there in the form of swamps, had been the consequence of erosion in the highlands of the Taurus Mountains over centuries, which resulted in increased deposit of silt and runoff into the plains.[115] These factors and the crisis of the seventeenth century encouraged another population shift back toward the highlands, the places where some of the most quintessentially Mediterranean economic activities—viticulture, olioculture, and pastoralism—thrived.[116]

The Resilience of Transhumance

Since Albert Hourani's important intervention that reframed the eighteenth century through the rise of local notables, or what is often referred to as "the age of ayans," the early modern period has come to be seen less as one of Ottoman decline and more as one of restructuring and imperial rule through local clients and intermediaries.[117] In this view, provincial elites were no longer feudal holdouts within an imperial system but rather representatives of local communities within a segmented or tiered form of rule in which the Ottomans did not strive to attain uniform political relations throughout the various provinces of the empire.[118] As Ali Yaycioglu has recently argued, these notables from various backgrounds even became "partners of the empire" during the Ottoman attempt to reestablish an imperial order during the Age of Revolutions at the turn of the nineteenth century.[119] In Cilicia, these prospective partners of empire were the *derebeys*—"lords of the valley"—who were critical to securing the obedience of largely pastoralist communities.

The work of Andrew Gordon Gould has demystified these elite figures sometimes cast as noble savages or lawless brigands. As the name suggests, the *derebeys* derived their power from control of mountain spaces, but in doing so, they extended their influence into the lowlands that the communities they ruled frequented on a seasonal basis. The *derebeys* were tribal notables who entered the local elite by controlling regions to legitimate their positions as de facto governors of their respective realms. Some of these leaders even earned important titles during the nineteenth century. The leading *derebeys* in the Cilicia region ultimately maintained their positions by holding in check the heads of other groups with even more localized power bases.[120]

The era of the *derebeys* attests to the ways in which the facets of pastoralist economic life and seasonal mobility were central to the political order in Cilicia during the eighteenth and early nineteenth centuries. Transhumance and power were intimately intertwined. By the 1850s, there were different spheres of local autonomy in Cilicia centered on the mountains. As of the first half of the nineteenth century, the most politically important dynasty in Cilicia was arguably the Menemencizâdes concentrated in Tarsus and Karaisalı. Langlois estimated their ranks at 3,000 households and stated that they possessed approximately 80,000 sheep, 20,000 goats, and 12,000 cows.[121] The Menemencizâdes presided over a population residing largely in fixed villages—not tents—and their elite were hardly simple shepherds. Their patriarch Ahmed Bey lived in an eight-room brick (*kargir*) mansion in Karaisalı that would come to be used by Ottoman officials as the government building in the district following his exile during the 1860s.[122] Ahmed Bey wrote an account of the Menemencizâde family history and in it, the salience of the *yayla* was marked. *Yayla*, *yaylak*, and derivative words are mentioned more than 50 times in his text. The *yayla* season stands out as a time of great significance, and many important events and political discussions in the text took place while the Menemencizâdes were summering or "*yaylanişin*."[123] The Menemencizâdes were only one of many elite families functioning as de facto governors and residing in handsome summer homes. The *yayla* was imbued with political and cultural significance. Those who commanded the *yaylas* dominated political life in the Cilicia region.

On the other side of the plain, a similar amalgam of pastoralist and agriculturalist communities existed in the Amanus Mountains and along the coast. The town of Payas was controlled by Küçükalioğlu Mustuk Pasha.[124] Mustuk's grandfather Halil had attained an official position by controlling the road along the Mediterranean coast, which was an important land route and key point on the route of *hajj* caravans on the way to Mecca and Medina. When threatened by local officials or the imperial government, Küçükalioğlu Halil exploited his position in the mountain strongholds to great effect. In 1817, the governor of Adana tried to exile the family, but with the governor's departure some years later, Mustuk returned to Payas from Marash. A few years later, when the Egyptian army invaded Cilicia, Mustuk was asked to secure the Amanus Mountains, and he remained in place following their withdrawal, eventually obtaining the title of pasha from the Ottoman government in recognition of the vital role he played in local politics.[125] From the vantage point of the Ottoman government, his authority held a number of other groups, such as the Ulaşlıs, at bay, while their mountain villages in the Amanus Mountains, a region referred to as Gavurdağı, defied direct Ottoman state presence. Unlike his predecessors, Mustuk also ingratiated himself to foreign merchants and European consuls in the region.[126] In Mustuk's region, there were a few towns with significant Armenian populations, such as Bahçe and Haruniye, which were also located on the edge of the mountains, along with the relatively new village of Çokmerzimen on the coast.

To the north in Marash, Elbistan, and beyond was the territory frequented by many different groups in their migration between the *yaylas* of Central Anatolia and the winter pastures of the Çukurova plain. Meanwhile, the rural Armenian communities of the region, centered on the town of Zeytun north of Marash, lived in a state of relative independence. Basic tax collection often required the Ottomans to send officials with military support into "the eagles' nest."[127] While Zeytun was often at odds with the local Ottoman officials in Marash, in the district of Kozan, local power could be characterized as a tight alliance between the Armenian Catholicosate in Sis and the family of hereditary governors known as the Kozanoğlus. The Kozanoğlus derived their legitimacy from their prestigious lineage among the nomadic tribes and the sedentary Muslim populations of that part of the Taurus region known as the Varsaks. The Kozanoğlus were established by the eighteenth century, and they maintained their position by excelling at settling disputes between other groups and retreating into their impregnable mountain strongholds in times of conflict.[128] Through their alliance with the catholicoses of Sis, whose constituency in the Kozan region included the inhabitants of Sis and the many villages surrounding the predominantly Armenian town of Hadjin in the mountains, the Kozanoğlus monopolized power in the region. In 1855, a new catholicos, Kiragos II, took office without election, and the Kozanoğlus even helped eliminate the bishops who refused to recognize him. This move may have made both the catholicos and the Kozanoğlus unpopular among a swath of their constituency, but it reflected the extent to which the church and this ruling family saw their interests as intertwined.[129] The alliance and proximity of the two parties was such that in one Armenian source, the Kozanoğlu name appeared nativized as "Kozanyan"—a rare linguistic artifact of a much different time in the history of Muslim-Christian relations in the Ottoman countryside.[130]

James C. Scott has often remarked that "civilizations can't climb hills." Perhaps then in the Ottoman case, the *derebeys* could be seen as the porters of empire. Their position was inextricable from the long history of negotiation and conflict between pastoralist communities in the Ottoman Empire beginning with its initial expansion eastward into Anatolia. The *derebeys* secured their positions by controlling some of the empire's most ungovernable populations and regions. The dynasties like the Ramazanoğlus, who became incorporated into the Ottoman administrative and military apparatus, exercised legitimacy and skill in dealing with such communities. The allegiance of those communities was in turn contingent on their satisfaction with the local dynasties that emerged throughout centuries of Ottoman rule.

Nonetheless, Ottoman statesmen had recognized from an early period that sedentarization might be one way of curtailing local autonomy, when these communities or their elites failed to render taxes or obey imperial authority. However, as Reşat Kasaba has shown, the compromise between pastoralist societies and the Ottoman state resulted in what at times appeared to be a highly symbiotic relationship.[131] The mobility of pastoralist communities made them naturally valuable to military campaigns, and their animals could be used to supply armies. The Adana region, for example, was a major source of camels for the military during the early nineteenth century.[132] As the Ottoman administrative structure encompassed pastoralism through a tax on livestock or on pasturage, pastoralist economies could contribute to the empire's wealth despite its being an agrarian state in its succession to the Roman and Islamic imperial legacies.[133]

In the earlier periods of Ottoman expansion, encouraging tribal settlement was a facet of emerging geographical imaginaries. Rhoads Murphey argued that Ottoman officials thought of settlement policy as part of "taming the wilderness" of the frontier.[134] However, it is unclear that this approach to the northern frontier in the Balkans and Eastern Europe was applied with the same vigor in Anatolia and the Arab provinces. As Sam White notes, much of the land was marginal for rain-fed agriculture and "only nomadic pastoralists could make adequate use of the thin soil and rugged terrain by grazing sheep, goats, camels, and horses, often crossing hundreds of miles to reach upland pastures in the summer and lowland pastures in the winter."[135] In this view, pastoralism represented a means to expand the productive capacity of the land, and not an extensive, inefficient use of potentially agricultural space.

Still, when pastoralist grazing practices created conflicts with settled agriculturalist populations, or when the autonomous tendencies of mobile communities posed a threat to Ottoman hegemony, the Ottoman government looked to settlement as a means of rendering such populations obedient. Amid waves of internal political crisis associated with the Celali rebellions, the Ottoman government attempted to induce nomads to settle at various points during the seventeenth and eighteenth centuries. One such attempt, in the late seventeenth century, targeted the communities of the Cilicia region. The results highlighted some of the challenges of forcing or even merely encouraging nomads to settle in an early modern context.[136] Enforcing settlement orders without the use of overwhelming military force was impossible, and newly settled communities invariably found their settlement locations unsuitable or desired to continue migratory practices. In fact, the communities of Cilicia targeted by these settlement campaigns suffered demographically as a result, with disease and loss of livestock as the major contributing factors.[137] Pastoralist communities usually resisted settlement, if not initially, then soon after these policies were implemented. As Kasaba notes, early modern Ottoman settlement policy did not produce clear results.[138] Throughout the subsequent rise of the *derebeys* in Cilicia, it was difficult for the Ottoman government to pursue any significant sedentarization policy, and local communities did not have any incentive to settle.

When the Ottoman government resumed control of Cilicia in the 1840s after decades of political crisis, sedentarization was once again on the agenda. The return of Ottoman sovereignty accompanied the beginning of the Tanzimat reforms, which were aimed at the reorganization of the Ottoman Empire and the reassertion of imperial authority. Some of the earliest measures adopted by the Ottoman government involved renewed efforts at sedentarization. The province of Aleppo made some attempts at inducing tribal populations on the edge of the Cilicia region to settle in lowland regions. The most ambitious effort involved the Reyhanlıs who lived in the area of the Amik Plain. The Amik Plain was centered on the Amik Lake and the wetlands that surrounded it. A few thousand Reyhanlı households, led by Mürselzade Ahmed Pasha, agreed to partially settle the region in 1844.

Disputes with neighboring communities became barriers to settlement. Though they remained loyal to the Ottoman state, the Reyhanlıs largely abandoned the goal of pursuing sedentary agriculture.¹³⁹ One report stated that the "intolerable" swamps in the Amik Plain undermined permanent settlement of the Reyhanlıs and their nearby rivals, the Hadidis.¹⁴⁰ On the northern edge of Cilicia, more than 1,000 households of pastoralists settled on a voluntary basis in the Pazarcık plain near Marash in 1846. In this case, the terms of settlement were rather accommodating: the pastoralists chose their settlement locale and continued their seasonal migrations.¹⁴¹

Ottoman attempts at sedentarization notwithstanding, the first half of the nineteenth century reaffirmed and strengthened the political independence and mobility of pastoralists. The *derebeys* maintained their pivotal positions within relations between the imperial center and rural communities. Under the conditions of the nineteenth century, Cilicia's pastoralists proved resilient and dynamic actors in the region's political economy. As Toksöz notes, "the nomadic inhabitants of the Çukurova had developed such complex life-styles that no linear evolution from nomadism to seminomadism and then to sedentarization could be discerned."¹⁴² Pastoralists engaged in more limited forms of agricultural production where possible, and as Hourani has warned, "pastors and cultivators may be the same people, or belong to the same community, or live in some kind of symbiosis with each other."¹⁴³ While sheep and goats were sometimes cited as encroaching on agricultural settlements, allowing pastoralists to graze their herds on agricultural land between growing seasons or during fallow periods was often a way of converting agricultural waste, weeds, and grasses into fertilizer. This is one quotidian example of how lifestyles that would later come to be seen as antiquated or primitive actually involved some rather sophisticated shit!

The centuries leading up to the reform of the Ottoman Empire often appear in historical scholarship as the "prehistory" of late Ottoman modernization. Yet the medieval and early modern changes and continuities in rural society were more than the backdrop to the period of reform; in so many ways, they shaped it. While many features of local life in late Ottoman Cilicia dated to the period even before the Roman conquest, the major communal groups in the region were of more recent provenance.[144] Cilicia's landscape had proven familiar and legible to the Armenian villagers and Turkic pastoralists who moved there from the tenth century onward and had produced many generations of native Cilicians by the arrival of Ottoman rule during the sixteenth century. It was their use of the *yayla*, a temporal space within the culture of transhumance, that chiefly signified integration into the local ecology. Nineteenth-century sources rooted in different cultural understandings of environment characterized the region as a wasteland dominated by nomadic pastoralists, but the realities of settlement patterns and modes of agrarian production in Cilicia were much more complex. The social and political order of Ottoman Cilicia rested on a wide degree of deference to the particularities of local life. In exchange for ceding authority to local notables, the Ottoman government could protect its vital interests in Cilicia at minimal cost. In times of crisis for the empire, those local notables could use their position to expand their autonomy, collecting their own taxes and governing semi-independent fiefdoms.

The ecology of Cilicia was by no means static over the centuries leading up to the mid-nineteenth-century reforms, and political life in Ottoman Cilicia was not always harmonious. Local leaders jockeyed with one another, and local communities competed over land and resources. There is no reason to respond to the idealization of empire by overly romanticizing the societies of people who resisted it. Yet the rural population did enjoy some advantages living under the local lords. With the Tanzimat reforms, those advantages became clearer. The *derebeys* served as an obstacle to direct taxation. A population could not be easily taxed without censuses or land registers. The *derebeys* also resisted mass conscription, a practice gradually introduced over the course of the nineteenth century. And though nobody fully realized it at the time, the rule of the *derebeys* protected local populations from the ever-present threat of malaria epidemics by preventing the Ottoman government from limiting seasonal mobility, which was vital to life itself.

In the next chapter, I will examine a pivotal moment in Cilicia's history, as well as in the history of modern states throughout the world: the post–Crimean War context. The decade following what some historians call the first modern war was one of internal conquest. From the Mezzogiorno and the Caucasus to the Great Plains and the Central Asian Steppe, imperial militaries wielding the new toys and tactics of warfare tested in the arena of the Crimean War launched campaigns to consolidate rule and open new regions for economic penetration and settlement. In the Ottoman Empire, this took the form of pacification campaigns against nomads and mountain communities with hopes of achieving sedentarization and uniform governance. At the same time, the Ottoman Empire enlisted hundreds of thousands of Muslim refugees expelled from areas of Russian expansion in the largest settlement scheme the empire had ever known. Cilicia was at the center of these developments, witnessing the most involved Ottoman sedentarization campaign of the period, as well as a large influx of migrants from Crimea and the Caucasus. The goal of provincial reform and settlement policy—*islâh* and *iskân*—was to make the region better serve the needs of the empire through ecological transformation, represented by the rise of cotton production and the conversion of former pasture into new agricultural settlements. While this period would indeed remake the local ecology in a variety of ways, for the rural people most directly affected by settlement, the results were genuinely catastrophic.

{ CHAPTER 2 }

THE STENCH OF PROGRESS

Ecology and Settlement on the Ottoman Frontier, 1856–78

During an official visit, the Ottoman statesman Ahmed Cevdet Pasha toured Çukurova to examine the outcome of reforms instituted there during his tenure as governor of Aleppo. Cevdet had overseen a scheme in 1865 to not only expand agricultural production but also forcibly sedentarize tens of thousands of pastoralists. His itinerary took him deep into the plain, past the ruins of Anazarbus and other sites where settlement had taken place. "As we left Kars-ı Zülkadriye and reached Sis," he wrote, "we passed through three hours of continuous cotton fields. As far as the Kozan mountains on our right and as far as the Ceyhan River on our left, everything our eye could see was cultivated, and the air smelled sweet [*mis gibi*]." Cevdet marveled at the developments he saw unfolding. "Then for a time a bad smell reached our noses," he recalled. "I wonder if there is a carcass somewhere," he remarked to his companion Hüseyin Bey. "It's nothing," he replied. "It's just that we've left the fields and come to a yet uncultivated area. That's where this bad smell is coming from. Last year when we toured Çukurova we had passed through all these bad smells. However, because everywhere was the same, we didn't notice it." The clean, white cotton of progress made the swamps of Çukurova all the more foul. "Now that one part is reformed and cultivated," Hüseyin Bey explained, "the smell of the ruined and deserted areas is more noticeable. After all, the reason for

Çukurova's bad air is its ruinedness [*harabiyet*]. This shows that if it is developed, its air will become finer." Cevdet noted that this statement was supported by the writings of Ibn Khaldun, the medieval scholar whose theories were now being tested. There was an air of progress in the still pungent Çukurova plain.[1]

Cevdet was a keen observer and compelling writer. But on this point, his account proved less fact than fiction. The sweet-smelling rows of cotton that tantalized the pasha's nostrils differed considerably from the memory of the summer after settlement in Çukurova's villages reflected in Yaşar Kemal's *Binboğalar Efsanesi*. "All summer long the plain reeked of carrion," he wrote. "The mosquitos were merciless. The malaria was disastrous. That summer previously unseen epidemic diseases ravaged the area. Çukurova was full of animal and human skeletons."[2] Though *Binboğalar Efsanesi* was a novel, Yaşar Kemal's narrative was rooted in local memory of forced settlement that was very much alive in his childhood village near the ruins of Hemite, a fortification dating to the Armenian period of the thirteenth century. His early work documented the songs and folk traditions of the very communities forced to settle under Cevdet's governorship. One verse about Hemite perfectly described the swampy environs of the new settlements: "the west wind doesn't blow, the flies descend / the nights are hot, the mosquitos sting / you can't drink the water, it stinks of algae / Oh Lord, if only we could get back to the *yayla*."[3]

These divergent olfactory impressions reflect competing interpretations of what the Tanzimat reforms meant for Ottoman provincial society. What officials cast as a modernization project, local people remembered as a violent rupture. The resettlement scheme in Çukurova, an episode that might earn a few sentences in the conventional narratives of the Tanzimat, was a catastrophic moment in the histories of the communities it targeted. Implementation of the Tanzimat reforms entailed creating new villages in spaces where agricultural settlements were scant. In the span of about a decade, the Ottoman government enlisted more than 100,000 people in its settlement project in the region. The settlements were premised on the notion that the creation of villages would render the people governable and economically productive. If comprehensive reform was the goal, settlement would be the means. But the environmental underpinnings of Ottoman settlement policy were flawed, even according to understandings of the period. Tens of thousands of people died as a result, and by the end of the 1870s, many of the settlements had been abandoned.

This chapter focuses on the making of the modern state in Cilicia. It studies the impact of the Tanzimat reforms for provincial society implemented between the Crimean War (1853–56) and the Russo-Ottoman War (1877–78). Through the figure of Ahmed Cevdet Pasha, I explore why and how Ottoman officials employed the discourse of a civilizing mission and began to see Çukurova as a settlement frontier. Ottoman settlement efforts, though momentous, had agonizing consequences for rural populations in small corners of the provinces like the Çukurova plain. People struggled to survive in the new villages, and malaria was rampant. By reconstructing the ecological imaginaries of both Ottoman officials and local populations, I show that the death and hardship settlement brought were not merely incidental. While settlers complained of malaria, statesmen like Cevdet sought comfort in the belief that settlement and cultivation were the only antidote to the malarial wastelands of the Ottoman countryside. In the end, the discontent caused by settlement forced the Ottoman administration to relent. Provisions accounting for the seasonal impact of malaria became central to the creation of future settlements. As a result, the longstanding transhumant temporality of Ottoman Cilicia was not destroyed but rather rearticulated through a new social contract, in which pastoralism remained stigmatized but the importance of seasonal migration for health purposes was enshrined in state policy.

Cilicia and the Tanzimat

The reform of the Ottoman state during the nineteenth century was incremental and could be characterized as an attempt to recentralize imperial authority to stave off major territorial losses. However, reform was also about introducing new practices and institutions—mass conscription and direct taxation being the two most consequential for ordinary Ottoman subjects. The most ambitious period of reform, the "liberal" years of the empire, began after the Crimean War.[4] While the Tanzimat reforms are conventionally dated to the 1839 Gülhane Edict, the Reform Edict of 1856 (*Islâhat Hatt-ı Hümâyûnu*) was the real beginning of the Tanzimat in the provinces. The Reform Edict established theoretical equality among all Ottoman subjects regardless of religion, reorienting political dynamics within non-Muslim communities but also with regard to intercommunal relations. Then, the 1858 Land Code called for the registration of all property and the distribution of deeds (*tapu*) to landholders. The primary goals of this reform were to increase tax revenue and keep rural people on the books and cultivating the land. However, as will be clear in the coming chapters, the land code and the introduction of transactable private property paved the way for radical socioeconomic change and the consolidation of large landholdings, often at the expense of small-time cultivators and pastoralists.[5] Meanwhile, the 1864 Vilayet Law created a new system of provinces (*vilayet*, pl. *vilayat*) and subdivisions within the empire, instituting a greater administrative presence of centrally appointed officials and creating a provincial council, or *meclis*, in each provincial capital to address local affairs. The new vilayets were promoted by the liberal statesman Midhat Pasha, who first implemented provincial reforms in the Danube province of the northern borderlands and subsequently in Baghdad on the eastern frontier.[6]

Cilicia was a region typical of many of the dynamics that the Tanzimat reforms targeted. The Ottoman Empire's hegemony there was not robust. During the 1830s, Cilicia was occupied by the army of the rogue governor Mehmed Ali Pasha, who sought to build his own empire in Egypt. Led by his son Ibrahim Pasha, the Egyptian army invaded Syria and came close to marching on the capital itself before retreating to Cilicia and establishing a border with the Ottomans at the Taurus Mountains. This region was of strategic importance for Egypt because it contained vast forests, and Egypt was largely reliant on import for timber.[7] In Cilicia, Ibrahim Pasha attempted to institute some of the changes that would later take place during the Tanzimat, in terms of reform of local government. But with the Egyptian withdrawal at the beginning of the Tanzimat period, the local notables who had come to the fore over the course of the prior century remained critical to the Ottoman Empire's control over the mountainous hinterland. The decisions of the local government were still largely guided by the interests of local factions.[8] Implementing provincial reform would require both negotiation and conflict of interest with the local elite, such as the *derebeys*.

The Crimean War was possibly the largest geopolitical conflict that had ever involved the Ottoman Empire up to that point. The Ottomans, supported by Britain and France, fought an expanding Russian Empire in multiple arenas of the Black Sea region. Only during the first decades of the nineteenth century had the Ottoman Empire begun relying on conscription to fill the ranks of the military, and the Crimean War was the biggest test of its conscript army. In Cilicia, however, most local leaders refused to comply with the Ottoman government's call to send troops to fight.[9] This abstention was no doubt popular among their communities, as a large percentage of the Ottoman soldiers who fought in the war perished, mainly of disease.[10] The one prominent local figure who complied came from the Kerimoğlus: Asiye Hatun, known by her nickname of Kara Fatma.[11] She led a unit of cavalry onto the battlefield, where she left two of her own teeth, subsequently earning a medal for her service.[12] The fact that the only prominent tribal figure from Cilicia to cooperate with the war effort was also apparently the only female officer to fight on any side of the Crimean War sums up the extent to which political life in Cilicia was an exception to the Ottoman Tanzimat rule.[13]

Some non-Muslims also recoiled against dimensions of the Tanzimat reforms. The Reform Edict of 1856, which allowed for freedom of religion, theoretically promised greater parity among different religious groups in the empire. But it also opened the door to the first Protestant missionaries in the Cilicia region, who were viewed with hostility by the highly influential Armenian clergy and elite. The American mission in Aintab quickly began to branch into other cities with large Armenian populations, such as Marash and Adana. However, when they expanded their activities into the mountain villages, conflict erupted with local notables. American missionaries were expelled from the town of Hadjin, and the head of the short-lived Hadjin mission was killed under dubious circumstances on the Payas road in 1862.[14] Meanwhile, the village of Zeytun rebelled against the authority of the Sancak of Marash, just as it had done periodically since the eighteenth century. The Ottoman government sent troops to take the town, but the Zeytuntsi rebels inflicted considerable losses and held their ground long enough for the Armenian patriarch in Istanbul and French diplomats to intercede.[15] Mustuk Pasha of Payas was credited with helping to prevent the type of mass communal violence that had occurred in Mount Lebanon and Damascus just a few years earlier under similar circumstances.[16]

As conflicts between the state, its subjects, and the local notables who dominated political life endured in the mountainous hinterland, the Adana-Tarsus region was quickly emerging as a site of commercialization. A local cotton industry grew under Egyptian rule, resulting in the creation of large landed estates and migration of people from Egypt and Syria into the Cilician plain.[17] The 1858 Land Code and demand created by the US Civil War accelerated the creation of cotton plantations during the first half of the 1860s.[18] The cotton craze of the 1860s was buttressed by articles in *Ceride-i Havadis*, an Ottoman newspaper founded by a British journalist that reported continuously on the US Civil War and the potential profitability of cotton cultivation.[19] Over the first half of the 1860s, cotton exports from the Adana region increased rapidly.[20] The tiny port of Mersin quickly became a center of commercial activity. The amount of land under cultivation in the region roughly doubled.[21] The Ottoman government encouraged landowners in Adana and elsewhere to plant cotton by allowing them to import Egyptian seed duty free.[22] Cotton gins were introduced to speed up the process, and workers from Eastern Anatolia were encouraged to migrate to Adana every spring to meet the sudden rise in demand for labor during the planting season.[23]

This cotton boom did not have an immediate impact on the eastern portion of the Cilicia region surrounding the Ceyhan River, but another large-scale conflict promised a different sort of agrarian transformation there. As the Russian military violently expanded its control over Crimea and the Caucasus, Muslim refugees fled into the Ottoman Empire. Russian expansion following the abolition of serfdom in 1861 involved the settlement of large numbers of Christian subjects in predominantly Muslim regions. The local Muslim inhabitants, who in many cases had long resisted Russian authority, were often compelled to either convert to Christianity and relocate to other parts of the Russian Empire or flee under the threat of violence.[24] When they arrived in the Ottoman Empire, these migrants were designated as *muhacirs*, a term that is somewhat ambiguous and can be understood to mean either "immigrant" or "refugee," both of which would suit the experience of these communities.[25] The Ottoman government looked to employ these people toward the settlement of uncultivated land in the countryside through the Muhacirin Commission under the auspices of the Ottoman

Ministry of Interior.²⁶ In the first half of the 1860s alone, hundreds of thousands of Nogays, Circassians, Chechens, and other Muslim communities from the expanding Russian sphere claimed the Ottoman Empire as a new home.²⁷

Çukurova was a prime region for migrant settlement in the post–Crimean War context. While land grabs were rapid around Adana and Tarsus, east of the city of Adana, there was a great deal of land that could be classified as "empty land" (*arazi-yi haliye*) that was uncultivated or exploited for pasture or other purposes by local inhabitants. During the 1860s alone, tens of thousands of Muslim *muhacirs*, mostly identified as Nogays and Circassians, were settled in this area around the Ceyhan River on such lands. According to settlement procedures, these communities were registered, and land was divided up through cooperation with their leaders and those who were literate or "could follow directions [*söz anlar*]."²⁸ These settlers were expected to integrate into the budding cotton economy, and upon the recommendation of the governor of Adana, the settlers received free cotton seed in order to participate in this rapid growth.²⁹

Many of the Circassian *muhacirs* in the Cilicia region disliked these lowland settlements and preferred to settle in the highlands, which more resembled their home regions in the North Caucasus. However, when they were resettled, conflict ensued. One example is the resettlement scheme at Uzunyayla. As the name suggests, it was a large highland plateau, "a vast wilderness (*badiye*) that could settle eight to ten thousand households and a rare location known for the fertility of its land."³⁰ In addition to the *muhacirs* of Cilicia, thousands of Circassian migrants dispersed throughout the provinces of Sivas and Ankara found their final destination in Uzunyayla.³¹ The Circassians were given a village called Aziziye (modern-day Pınarbaşı)—named for the new Ottoman sultan Abdülaziz—to settle and raise their horses. Wide and empty though Uzunyayla was, it was not entirely vacant. The plateau was frequented each summer by the Avşars, who grazed their animals on the mountain pastures. This was probably the first time in the local memory that such an enormous settlement had been created by the state; Aziziye was a community of thousands of people, speaking an unknown language, that had essentially dropped out of the sky. When they found houses being constructed on their *yayla* in the summer of 1861, they attacked and scattered the *muhacirs*, destroying the structures that had been built. Although it was evident that military force would be needed to prevent such incidents from recurring, Ottoman officials were reluctant to send troops because the Avşars were too numerous and "savage" to be dealt with easily.[32]

Around the same time, Circassian *muhacirs* came into conflict with the Armenian community of Zeytun in the midst of its rebellion against the Ottoman government. Small disputes over land escalated into large-scale fighting between the two communities, and after the Armenians killed a reported total of more than 500 Circassians and the latter were unable to successfully retaliate, leaders representing the two parties apparently worked out a truce, agreeing not to attack and rob each other, to conduct commerce freely and move between their adjacent settlements, and for each to punish their own for any transgressions that might occur.[33]

While the Ottoman government continued to deal with each of these issues separately, the period of the 1864 Vilayet Law brought a more comprehensive approach to establishing state presence in the Cilicia region, which became entirely subsumed under the Vilayet of Aleppo. Prior to 1864, Adana had been a provincial capital in its own right, and within five years, it would once again become the capital of a separate Vilayet of Adana. One of the main purposes for the temporary creation of a vast province of Aleppo that stretched from the Taurus Mountains to the Syrian Desert was the political reform of the rural districts where figures like the *derebeys* (see chapter 1) still enjoyed a wide degree of autonomy. In 1865, the Ottoman military dispatched about 9,000 infantry and a few thousand horsemen armed with modern rifles and cannons to the Cilicia region. Derviş Pasha, the commander of this special force, called the Fırka-i İslâhiye or Reform Division, had recently overseen a successful pacification campaign in Montenegro. The newly appointed governor of Aleppo, Ahmed Cevdet Pasha, also traveled with the army, which landed in İskenderun in May 1865.[34] Their initial goal was to pacify the tribes of the Cilicia region, proceed onward into the mountains to establish central authority in the Armenian town of Zeytun, and then possibly continue farther into the mountainous hinterland toward Hısn-ı Mansur and Dersim to carry out further reform and forced settlement.[35]

Over the course of the next year, the Reform Division proceeded to secure the surrender of as many of the region's *derebeys* as possible and to settle the pastoralist populations into fixed villages in Çukurova. They offered amnesty to those who had previously avoided paying taxes or who had evaded conscription. Nonetheless, many initially rebelled against the Reform Division's calls for surrender. In the Amanus Mountains, some of the local leaders, including the relatives of the recently deposed and exiled Mustuk Pasha, launched an extended resistance. In some cases, segments of a particular community resisted.[36] The rebellious lyrics of the bard Dadaloğlu reflected the spirit of resistance to the Ottoman state at the time: "The state made the decree about us. The decree is the Sultan's, but the mountains are ours."[37] Resistance was rooted in a communal claim to the landscape and environment of the Cilicia region that transcended the limits of Ottoman authority to intervene in the lives of subjects.[38]

Those who resisted the Reform Division were met with violence. In some cases, the army burned the houses and tents of communities that refused to resettle.[39] Yet given the scale of its program, the Reform Division achieved its objectives with relative ease. Some local leaders collaborated willingly. Kara Fatma, for example, welcomed the commission and helped appoint an area of settlement for the Cerids, which became a new district of Cerid.[40] Most of the other local *derebeys* accepted lucrative salaries and positions elsewhere in the empire in exchange for their cooperation. The last holdout to the Reform Division was Kozanoğlu Yusuf Agha, who commanded a sizable band of rebels that resisted the army in the Taurus Mountains for months. When he was finally apprehended, he was sentenced to exile in Istanbul. If we believe Ahmed Cevdet's account, he was killed by a guard during a failed escape attempt; other sources indicate that he was deliberately assassinated.[41] Kozanoğlu would eventually be remembered as a martyr by many in the Cilicia region. Yet as Gould notes, the Reform Division by and large dealt with notables who were willing to comply diplomatically, even allowing these notables to enter the imperial elite.[42] In this regard, the Reform Division represented a continuation of the Ottoman Empire's pragmatic approach to the local *derebeys* and the *aşirets* whose allegiance they commanded. This dimension of the Tanzimat was not a great departure. The real novelty of the reforms in Cilicia was in the vision of the region's future and the settlement policies that would be adopted to reshape the environment and society of the rural hinterland.

An Internal Frontier

J. H. Skene, the British consul in Aleppo during the 1860s, penned an evocative description of the environment in Ahmed Cevdet's sprawling province of Aleppo. It typified a physiocratic logic that was becoming conventional wisdom in certain circles by the mid-nineteenth century. "Fertile plains pant for the plough, and copious streams to irrigate them feed only pestilential marshes," he wrote, lamenting that nomads "encroached on arable land," as if a natural law of usufruct were dictated by average rainfall. Where herders saw abundant pasture in marshy lowlands, commercially minded men like Skene saw fertile soils "panting for the plow." Where the local pastoralists might have seen verdant mountain plateaus, Skene saw "stately forests rot[ting] on the mountains, and rich ores crop[ping] out unheeded from the rocks."[43] His view was a common one in an era in which European capital roved the globe in search of untapped potential for profit. But during the nineteenth century, Ottoman officials also began to share this gaze. The new forms of land use and resource extraction that accompanied the Tanzimat period colored how they saw the environment. Whereas two centuries before, Evliya Çelebi had described Çukurova—that is, the lowlands around the Ceyhan River—as *adem geçmez*,[44] in essence, no man's land, once insignificant regions like Çukurova now suddenly appeared as frontiers of expansion filled with opportunities to address a host of problems confronted by the Ottoman state of the Tanzimat era.

In world-historical terms, it may seem odd to describe a small region like Cilicia as containing a frontier. But in its nineteenth-century context, Cilicia was practically a world unto itself, requiring days on end to traverse by foot or by animal. By those standards, the lowlands of Çukurova—and particularly the upper plains along the Ceyhan River—were exceptionally vast, especially given the sparse distribution of settlements across the open and marshy landscape and the relative lack of reliable roads. The name Çukurova, or "the low plain," derived from the region's low elevation and concave quality. Surrounded by mountains and hills, from the perspective of Cilicia's inhabitants, the sea-level terrain appeared as a wet depression beneath the normal plane of settlement. Aside from the dikes on its southern portion and whatever ferries and fords might be found, an Ottoman map from the 1870s revealed just two crossings of the Ceyhan River: the stone bridge at

Misis and two roads near the ruins of Hemite on the northeastern bend of the river.[45] This territory was the true heart of the Çukurova plain, a flat but marshy and muddy expanse that two French travelers, Favre and Mandrot, described as a "large sponge."[46] East of Adana, there was only one town in Çukurova—Sis, on the northern edge of the plain—that could comfortably boast more than 1,000 inhabitants. The distance between Sis and the next largest cluster of settlements, around Payas and İskenderun in the south, was roughly 100 km. In between was the heart of the lowlands in which pastoralists wintered their flocks. During the period between 1856 and 1880, most of the new settlements created in the Cilicia region were located in this largely unsettled plain.

The first great era of settlement in Cilicia occurred in the immediate years after the end of the Crimean War during the late 1850s. Between 1856 and 1865, hundreds of thousands of Nogays, Circassians, Chechens, and other Muslim communities from the expanding Russian sphere came to the Ottoman Empire. The first to arrive in Çukurova were Nogay Tatars from Crimea and the Caucasus. Their settlements were clustered around Yarsuvat (modern-day Ceyhan) on the banks of the Ceyhan River, which would emerge as the main center of population. Soon after, Circassians and Chechens arrived from the North Caucasus and were settled in villages on both sides of the Ceyhan River.[47] Distinguishing between these groups in the archival record is not always easy. Sources from the period sometimes conflate different groups of *muhacirs* who had the same legal status and arrived from a similar region, even though they spoke different languages. Numerical estimates are likewise fragmentary and conflicting. According to Ahmet Cevdet, the initial group of Nogay migrants contained 2,000 to 3,000 families. Using detailed numbers from the Ottoman archives, Hilmi Bayraktar put the Nogays' numbers at more than 20,000 people.[48] As for the Circassians, one Ottoman source refers to 2,000 families from Çukurova being resettled in the Taurus Mountains after the initial migration from the Caucasus, although this may not have been a complete estimate of the Circassian population.[49] A British source referred to the Nogays and Circassians interchangeably and cited their initial immigrant population in Çukurova as 15,000 *families*.[50] Consideration of the available estimates puts the number of *muhacirs* who settled in Çukurova between 1856 and 1865 in the tens of thousands, possibly around 50,000 people.

The next group of settlements created in the Cilicia region was related to the activities of the Reform Division. Toksöz describes these settlement policies in Cilicia as "the most direct involvement of the central state" in the remaking of the regional political economy.[51] Sedentarization was applied throughout the Cilicia region, but Upper Çukurova was the main locus of village construction. At least 3,800 houses and 35 villages were built for these communities under the auspices of the Reform Division, paid for by the Ottoman government and private donations.[52] Whereas the Nogay settlements were centered on the Ceyhan River, the settlements created by the Reform Division were centered on the newly founded district centers of Osmaniye and İslahiye to the east and the rebuilt town of Kars-ı Zülkadriye in the northeast of the plain. One of the larger villages created during this period, and one that remains until this day, is Cevdetiye, named after Ahmed Cevdet Pasha. The general principle applied during these settlement activities was to place communities in proximity to their winter quarters, although there were exceptions. (See the map at the front of this book to understand the approximate layout of these settlements.)

There are no reliable population registers of these communities for the period in question. In Ottoman sources, they were described collectively as *aşirets,* or tribes. As of the 1850s, the study of Langlois put the Türkmen and Kurdish population of Cilicia at around 80,000. Of those, he considered more than one-quarter to be already sedentarized (though they were transhumant), their populations being largely concentrated in the western portion of the province of Adana. As for those considered nomads, who moved between Upper Çukurova and the Taurus Mountains, they included tribes like the Avşar, Karakayalı, Sırkıntı, Kırıntılı, Lek, Cerid, Tecircli, Bozdoğan, and others.[53] Based on the data, 50,000 would be a reasonable estimate of the number of people at least nominally subjected to forced settlement in Çukurova, but the numbers could have been much higher depending on interpretation of extant population data.[54]

After the completion of the Reform Division's activities in 1868, more migrants began to arrive in the Adana province, including 1,500 from the North Caucasus in 1869.[55] A third concentrated period of settlement in Çukurova occurred approximately between 1876 and 1880, around the time of the Russo-Ottoman War (1877–78). The newcomers included Crimean

Tatars, Circassians from the Caucasus, and Muslims from the former Ottoman Balkans. In addition to the district in the immediate vicinity of Yarsuvat, they were settled farther north along the Ceyhan River toward the ruins of Anazarbus, as well as farther east in the district of İslahiye.[56] The years preceding and following the Russo-Ottoman War constitute one of the most chaotic periods of the empire's final century, and precise figures for this group are elusive.[57] One register suggests a figure of around 16,000; others around 6,000.[58]

During this period of settlement between roughly 1856 and 1878, four local administrative centers were established that today are major urban centers: Ceyhan, Osmaniye, Kars-ı Zülkadriye (Kadirli), and İslahiye. If we consider that Mersin (now Çukurova's second largest city and one of the ten largest cities in Turkey) was born out of the cotton boom of the 1860s, the high Tanzimat period between the two wars was unquestionably foundational for the making of modern Çukurova and its population centers. Although there would be many more immigrants in subsequent decades of the Ottoman period and early republican period, no settlement in Çukurova founded after the 1860s has become a large urban center. Thus, the settlement policies of the high Tanzimat period appear as singularly transformative in the long run. However, these policies were quite contentious at the time, and although the official narrative of the Ottoman government would obscure negative facets of settlement, many people died or fled the villages constructed for them, because of disease, famine, and inability to make a living from the land.

Although the Çukurova region absorbed as many as 100,000 settlers as it became the center of the post–Crimean War frontier in Cilicia, by the end of the 1870s, foreign accounts suggested that most of the settlements built during the intervening period had failed to live up to expectations. Favre and Mandrot described the population centers beyond Tarsus, Adana, and Sis as nothing more than "miserable villages dispersed here and there along the edge of the plain and even more dispersed in the mountains."[59] Lt. Ferdinand Bennet, a British consul in Anatolia, described the communities settled near the new town of Osmaniye, remarking that the people "live in reed or rush wigwams rather than homes, roughly thatched and affording as one would suppose hardly any protection in winter. They are the crudest dwelling places imaginable, and it is painful to notice debris of former stone or mud houses in the many villages where they now prefer to use reeds."⁶⁰ The biases of Bennet, who did not consider the structures these communities lived in to be "homes" and conflated them with the "wigwams" of North America, reflected the consistently disdainful tone of European narrative accounts in the Ottoman Empire during this time. However, it is still clear that the results of settlement policies during the high Tanzimat period did not live up to the ambitious designs of their framers. Many of the settlements that had been created during the 1850s and 1860s were largely abandoned by the 1870s. As it seemed, migrants and pastoralists struggled to make a new home in the villages built by the Ottoman government. Extant material provides enough evidence to state that the majority of those settlers must have been severely impacted on the bodily level by malaria, cholera, and other diseases, as well as impoverished by famine and loss of livestock. A large swath of this population, in many cases entire families and communities, died or fled elsewhere during this process.

The fundamental impact of settlement on local communities in Cilicia was high mortality. Nobody kept detailed statistics about this mortality; only during the 1870s did the Ottoman government start taking somewhat reliable censuses of the regions in question. The few quantitative statements about population decline in the Çukurova settlements seem at first glance to be exaggerations. The Nogays who settled around Yarsuvat were the first to arrive in the region. By 1880, Lieutenant Bennet wrote that their numbers had diminished *by 80 percent*, plummeting from an original population of 15,000 families to just 3,000.⁶¹ Favre and Mandrot made similar estimates regarding the Nogays and the Circassians who settled in Çukurova at that time.⁶²

The tribes settled by the Reform Division from 1865 onward might not be expected to have fared as poorly, though the scant available information suggests otherwise. Ottoman documentation referred to "the loss of a great many lives in terms of population and livestock [*nüfusça ve hayvanatça pek çok telefat*]."⁶³ Bennet said the same, estimating that roughly half of the people settled by the Reform Division in Çukurova had died "after three or four summers on the plain" and their flocks had dwindled accordingly.⁶⁴ Quantification using the imperfect Ottoman population records also indicates that a perceptible population decline occurred in the district of Osmaniye when compared with the core districts of the province of Adana.⁶⁵ In subsequent decades, it would be clear that either the people themselves or their identities had been decimated. Estimates of the Türkmen and Kurdish population of Cilicia in the 1890s were only half of what they had been in the mid-century statistics of Langlois.⁶⁶ These figures are particularly striking during a period in which the natural population growth of the empire was rising, and the state was finally developing the capacity to count and account for most of its inhabitants.

Estimates of mortality among the migrants who came after the Russo-Ottoman War of 1877–78 were no less staggering. Bennet said that half of the refugees had died already by 1880.⁶⁷ Another British consul reported in 1879 that, of a new batch of immigrants who came to the İslahiye region—roughly 2,000 families—most fled or died so that only 25 families or so remained.⁶⁸ An Ottoman report stated about these refugees in the Adana province that "most of them [*ekserisi*] are getting sick and dying due to *vahamet-i hava*."⁶⁹

This last document points to the overarching impression that disease, namely, malaria, was the biggest factor in the high mortality in the new frontier settlements. Malaria was the ailment synonymous with settlement in the global context, and though references to disease were not always specific, malaria was the affliction most often mentioned by name. The spread of malaria was in turn a consequence of the environments that the Ottomans targeted for settlement. Natural sources of standing water, such as swamps, marshes, rivers, and lakes, make good environments for mosquitos. For example, E. J. Davis said of İslahiye, a new settlement named after the Reform Division (Fırka-i İslahiye), "it was a very marshy and unhealthy place" at the time of settlement, "and *corvée* laborers, masons, and carpenters, had been sent from Marash to build houses for the forced immigrants. The health of the place had, however, not much improved. The country is so level . . . that very little would be needed to make a good carriage road . . . But the unhealthiness of the country would be a great obstacle to colonization."⁷⁰ He had a similar impression of Osmaniye: "It is a primitive little place, with a cold, bracing air in winter, but in summer it is nearly deserted, owing to malaria. The people live almost entirely by their flocks and herds, and, although the soil is fertile, there is but little cultivation."⁷¹ Favre and Mandrot said of the Circassians that "they have been cruelly decimated by fevers and disease of all kinds."⁷² Malaria, described either through the symptoms of fever or references to the bad air, was the main complaint of refugees and pastoralists alike. An English traveler from the 1870s said of migrants settled in Çukurova that "they spoke most bitterly of being forced to live out on the great plains, with no towns near enough to trade with, and always suffering from fever."⁷³

While malaria was an endemic presence that threatened the lives of settlers, epidemic diseases that tended to travel quickly across the empire were also introduced through movement of settlers and troops. For example, during the autumn of 1865, a cholera epidemic followed the Reform Division charged with settling the region's pastoralists, and introduced the disease in the Taurus Mountain highlands for the first time.⁷⁴ The outbreak was part of the fourth global cholera pandemic, which had begun in Bengal and had spread to the Middle East reportedly with hajj pilgrims, ultimately killing tens of thousands of them.⁷⁵ Cholera broke out in Egypt in late June, and by mid-August had spread to Iskenderun and Aleppo, where the French consul noted that "the panic among the upper class [was] indescribable."⁷⁶ By October, cholera reached the rest of Cilicia.⁷⁷ Cevdet Pasha noted, during the army's ascent towards Feke in the Kozan region of the Taurus Mountains, that they were continually being passed on one side by funeral processions and on the other by sick villagers being carried away on the backs of animals. "I don't know if the Reform Division was struck by the evil eye or what [*nazar mı isâbet eyledi bilmem*]," Cevdet would remark. But he had been somewhat conscious of how cholera began to spread. When some among Cevdet's detachment showed symptoms of cholera, immediate orders of quarantine were issued; yet one of the commanders in the Reform Division, viewing those orders as unnecessarily inhumane, broke the quarantine and allowed the soldiers to mix. Cevdet noted that following this moment, "by the unknowable intentions of God [*bi-hikmetillahi teala*], cholera immediately spread throughout the detachment."⁷⁸ The presence of tens of thousands of soldiers and animals in Çukurova facilitated the spread of cholera in an already malarial countryside.

Exposure to disease exacerbated the economic hardship of adjusting to a new way of life on new land, and farmers suffering from severe fevers were often too weary to properly work their fields. Pastoralists unaccustomed to agriculture struggled to provide for their families, and lack of access to summer pasture starved young sheep and goats. Meanwhile, the end of the US Civil War and the rise in global cotton production stifled the commercial growth of the first part of the 1860s. Then, during the 1870s, the Ottoman Empire entered what Şevket Pamuk dubbed a "great depression."[79] The immediate result was an agrarian collapse. Between 1873 and 1875 a severe famine rocked Anatolia. In the inland provinces of Ankara and Yozgat, famine was especially concentrated in the rural areas, catalyzed by a period of intense drought. In autumn 1873, reports that grain stores in many of the villages had been looted due to food shortages came in from provinces of inner Anatolia, such as Yozgat, which began to receive grain from İzmit and Sivas.[80] What followed was by no means the first famine to visit the Anatolian heartland, though it may well have been the most pronounced. Somewhere between 100,000 and 250,000 people died during these years of crisis.[81]

During this crisis, the province of Adana was geographically fortunate in that it was less vulnerable to drought than more arid inland regions. The Adana region supplied emergency grain to Cyprus, for example, in 1872 as shortages emerged elsewhere.[82] Nonetheless, the 1873 harvest reflected severe effects of drought; wheat production of Adana amounted to just 20 percent of the prior year's total. The following year, the harvest in Adana was strong, and it emerged as one of the principal towns that became a refuge for those fleeing starvation in the countryside, only to become the place of their deaths.[83] The *New York Times* reported in January 1875 that as a result of famine in Anatolia, "50,000 persons have migrated from various parts of the country to the City of Adana, half of whom have since succumbed to disease. The strange climate, distress, and extreme rapaciousness of the tax-gatherers aggravate the mortality."[84] E. J. Davis similarly reported that half of the people who had come to Adana during the winter of 1874 had died of disease.[85] Alongside malaria and an unkind climate, dysentery and typhus were cited as the sicknesses that finished off the famished bodies of those who fled to Çukurova in vain. A correspondent for the *London Times* remarked that "the rich are now poor; the poor are dead or have emigrated," and he described meeting small communities of pastoralists and villagers who had sold their animals and fled elsewhere.[86]

The Ottoman government lacked the means to address a public health crisis the likes of what occurred during the 1860s and 1870s. At the time refugees first came to the Adana region, the only doctor available to treat diseases like "malaria and colds [*sıtma ve nezle*]" was the quarantine doctor in Mersin. The places settled by the newcomers were six to eighteen hours' journey from the city of Adana.[87] When cholera broke out in 1865, Adana's sole country doctor (*memleket tabibi*) was not even present at the time. In the end, three doctors were dispatched to investigate.[88] There is little evidence of doctors being sent to tend to the tribes settled in Çukurova during the 1860s, but in 1878, four doctors were sent to different districts of the province of Adana to look after the thousands of refugees waiting to be settled.[89] Similarly, in times of famine, the Ottoman government often possessed a grain surplus but lacked the means to effectively move and distribute it. Although Adana had grain to spare, transportation during the famine had been inadequate for those supplies to reach the interior.[90] Even when grain was sent, the possibility that merchants and officials would hoard or sell grain at unfair prices loomed large.[91] Faced with their own economic woes, cultivators and merchants actually sought to export grain from Adana to the Mediterranean in the midst of the 1870s famine, despite its being banned by the Ottoman government, and local officials could do little to stop it.[92]

The Ottoman government fell into deep financial troubles during the 1870s. In 1865, the year of the Reform Division, the Ottoman government took on more debt than in any other year of the decade.[93] The government's debts soon mounted to the point of default in 1875. The empire was compelled to establish a debt administration that placed a significant portion of its budget under the control of foreign entities.[94] Thus, while officials understood that engineering the environments of new settlements was a critical component of ensuring their viability, the Ottoman government did not have the means to do so. For example, an 1870 proposal concerning the draining of swamps around Payas to make the region more habitable ended in the conclusion that the admittedly necessary measure was unaffordable.[95]

The failures of settlement policies in Cilicia resulted in a high death toll, but to say that disease and displacement led to a large number of injuries and deaths does not fully encompass the nuances of the impact of settlement on the communal and family level. Disease, hunger, and death destroyed the morale of the communities in question. The loss of loved ones to the calamities that accompanied settlement was often memorialized in the form of laments, some of which were later recorded by folklorists in Turkey. Unlike the fighting involved in resistance to settlement, the impacts of settlement knew no rules of battle. Quite the contrary, children were disproportionately vulnerable to these factors. Disease and hunger were more deadly for them, and the nature of malaria infection made it a grave danger for both infants and their mothers. Children born to women who contract malaria during pregnancy often suffer from low birth weight, making them more vulnerable to various illnesses and leading to high rates of neonatal mortality.[96] The way that malaria interacts with pregnancy also has harsh results. The intermittent fevers typical of *P. vivax* infection that are normally manageable become more severe and even fatal; malaria during pregnancy greatly raises the risk of miscarriage or infant death. Women with malaria are at high risk of dying during or immediately following childbirth.[97] In this regard, a malaria epidemic could be experienced by local communities as more cruel than war.

The notable impact of settlement on children of both refugees and settled pastoralists at the time seemed abnormal to many observers. Bennet remarked that in the villages of Çukurova there were "hardly any children."[98] Another British consul described some refugees settled in Çukurova, saying, "it is really terrible to see these half-starved, fever-stricken wretches and the little skeleton babes tugging at the empty breast."[99] An Ottoman report on the condition of the settled tribes in Çukurova stated that "while they were previously raising many able-bodied men of age suitable for military service, now this is rarely seen."[100] Settlement had led to the loss of an entire generation. Among rural communities of the Adana region—especially those claiming tribal descent—those years were memorialized in songs of longing for the mountains laden with feelings of sickness, displeasure, confinement, and loss on the plains. For many, settlement was as Dadaloğlu's songs had characterized it: "the end of the world [*kıyamet*]."[101] The name Çukurova signified a lowland, but the word *çukur* could also mean "a pit or grave." This connotation was the one most befitting what those subjected to settlement policies experienced.

The Ottoman Civilizing Mission

"Whether this was an experiment or not I know not," the aforementioned Lieutenant Bennet remarked in his account of what appeared to be deeply flawed settlement policies in Çukurova.¹⁰² Decades later, in the midst of World War I, a young Ottoman intellectual and member of the Committee of Union and Progress Ahmed Besim (later Atalay) arrived at a harsher judgment of Tanzimat-era settlement policy in the region. "Raw settlement means annihilation [*kuru iskân imha demektir*]," he wrote. "An age-old life and livelihood cannot be changed suddenly." The Reform Division did not merely "settle" the tribes, "no, it killed and buried them," he exclaimed.¹⁰³ Ottoman officials had not intended for tens of thousands of people to die as a result of the reforms in Cilicia, but had that been the intention, it is doubtful that they could have exacted a more immense toll. Bennet's characterization of a failed "experiment" might have been apt. Thanks to the voluminous writings of Ahmed Cevdet Pasha, there is little need to speculate as to how the intended outcome of settlement was imagined. He explicitly represented the activities of the Reform Division and the broader efforts to settle Çukurova in terms of a civilizing mission that entailed both a cultural and an environmental transformation of the region.

Born in modern-day Bulgaria, Ahmed Cevdet was arguably the most important figure of the reform period in the Ottoman Empire. He received a well-rounded and traditional education, in part from his grandfather, a cleric who came from a long line of Ottoman officials in their region. As a young man, Cevdet moved to Istanbul to continue his studies in the schools of the capital. Soon after completing his education, he developed a relationship with Mustafa Reşid Pasha, one of the main architects of the initial Tanzimat reforms. Cevdet subsequently occupied positions within the Ottoman state, playing an increasingly prominent role in the development of the judiciary and education systems. He influenced numerous legal reforms, including the 1858 Land Code and the completion of the Mecelle, the first codified corpus of Hanafi Islamic law. But his first major task as a civil servant was to write a history of the Ottoman Empire, the first volume of which he completed before assuming the governorship of Aleppo. He would continue to work on this twelve-volume history during his career as a statesman.¹⁰⁴

Cevdet's understanding of history and politics reflected the influence of Ibn Khaldun, who had written seminal works in those fields within the context of political upheaval in Muslim Iberia and North Africa during the fourteenth century, serving as an itinerant statesman in many different courts. Cevdet even produced his own translations of Ibn Khaldun's work, but he was far from the first Ottoman interpreter of the Khaldunian tradition.[105] Among Ottoman statesmen, Ibn Khaldun's ideas on politics and the rise and fall of civilizations had provided a useful framework for thinking about the cyclical degeneration and revival of the Ottoman state. The Khaldunian framework was highly dialectical, juxtaposing cultivated but corrupted urban societies with more vigorous and cohesive nomadic tribal configurations. Ottoman authors deployed Khaldun's concepts in different ways as he became more widely read over the course of the seventeenth and eighteenth centuries. They read his remarks about urban decadence to comment on the crisis or "disorder" they saw in Ottoman society. They did not perceive political crises as symptomatic of an inherent flaw within the Ottoman state; they found in Ibn Khaldun an explanation of why periodic crisis and revival were natural.[106]

Cevdet's understanding of society was rooted in Khaldunian conception of stages of civilization that stretched back at least as far as the turn of the eighteenth century in Ottoman thought. He opened his *History* with the following assertion about the linear progression from nomadic to village to urban life:

> Humans are civilized in nature, meaning that they cannot live separately like beasts, but rather they need to help each other by forming societies [*cemiyet*] from place to place. These human societies are of various orders and the society of tent-dwelling [*hímenişin*] tribes is of the lowest order, which, by procuring the basic human needs, reach the aim of procreation—the fruit of the tree of life. However, they are deprived of knowledge, the productive sciences, and all the complete human attributes that are the result of the shape and form of civilization [*medeniyet*]. Just as village people [*ehl-i kura*] are considered to be forsaken by the proper influences and results of civilization when compared with the inhabitants of large cities, [tent-dwelling tribes] likewise remain farther from civilization than village people.[107]

Cevdet's *History* served as a metanarrative of the Tanzimat informed by

Ibn Khaldun's concepts. But as Christoph Neumann points out, Cevdet inverted the relationships between important concepts such as education and civilization, arguing that the latter is a product of the former, in contrast to Ibn Khaldun. Cevdet's understanding of civilization was founded on the premise that the inevitability of rise and fall—expressed in the life cycle of states described by Ibn Khaldun—could be broken by reform.[108] Through the Khaldunian framework, he created a distinctly Ottoman or Islamic vocabulary with which to narrate a state-centered vision of progress. If we read Ibn Khaldun's work as articulating and analyzing particular historical problems, we can read Cevdet's as the latest in a line of Ottoman thinkers weighing solutions to those problems.

For Cevdet, the primary solution was a reassertion of imperial authority through reform, or *islâh*. The term *islâh* implied setting things right as opposed to overthrowing an established order. "Revolution," or *ihtilal*, as it appeared in his history, was a negative process. He used the term to describe the French Revolution as rebellion and disorder.[109] In one of the early drafts of his report on the Reform Division, Cevdet subconsciously revealed how he saw similar disorder as entangled with Cilicia's mountainous geography. The original title Cevdet gave to the report, "Some Geographical Circumstances of the Places Controlled and Reformed by the Reform Division" (*Fırka-i İslâhiye maarifetiyle zabt ve islah olunan yerlerin bazı ahval-ı coğrafiyesi*), was rather conventional. However, he crossed out the word "geographical [*coğrafiye*]," replacing it with the word *ihtilaliye* signifying rebellion, thereby dramatically changing the title (see figure 2.1). With a single modification the "geographical circumstances" of Cilicia were somehow morphed into seditious events.

Cevdet depicted the uncivilized nature of the region as embedded in the mountains, and he framed the settlement activities and reforms as an attempt to conquer the mountainous spaces inhabited by semi-autonomous communities. "Since the time of conquest, Gavurdağı—that is, Cebel-i Bereket—has been in a state of rebellion," he wrote. The tribes were "Seljuks" that joined with the Ottomans during the conquest, but "because the inhabitants were savage and the terrain difficult [*ahâlisi vahşî ve yerleri sarp olduğundan*]," most of the region was never brought under Ottoman rule.[110] "The Ottoman state has never entered the mountains of Kozan," he declared,

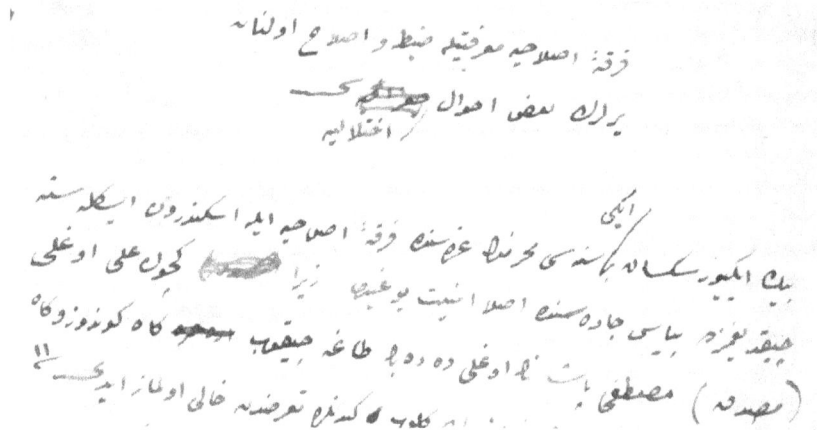

Figure 2.1. Image of title of Ahmed Cevdet's report on Reform Division with *coğrafiye* crossed out and replaced by *ihtilaliye*. Source: Ahmed Cevdet, "Kozan ve Gavur dağı hakkında layiha," AK, Muallim Cevdet (MC)-Yz B0031 956 CEV (1 Harziran 1282 [13 June 1866]).

and in the mountains of Gavurdağı, the people had "remained in a state of ignorance."[111] Thus, they had persisted in a "state of rebellion," rendering the mountains a "den of thieves" and a place where criminals could "escape the clutches of the state," all while rebellious tribes roamed the wilderness.[112] While his narrative mainly focused on tribal populations, Cevdet considered the Armenian town of Zeytun within the purview of the military campaign due to previous rebellions there, affirming the linkage between mountains and resistance to state order. In fact, the grander vision of the Reform Division, not only encompassing Gavurdağı and Kozan, but also marching up through the Anti-Taurus Mountains to Dersim, clearly illustrated his understanding that the mountains themselves were a barrier to the Tanzimat and that to fully implement reform, a complete subjugation of the numerous communities that inhabited them would be necessary.

Though the Reform Division came with the rhetoric of military pacification, Cevdet's civilizational hierarchy enabled him to present settlement policies not as conquest but rather as an invitation to join the civilized fold. The Reform Division's overtures to holdouts to come out of the mountains and submit to the rule of law declared, "The Sultan has sent to you a book and a sword. Those who obey the book have no business with the sword, and otherwise, the sword is ready."¹¹³ The exorbitant expense of building houses for nomads, for which Cevdet was mocked in the capital, was a physical expression of the change he envisioned.¹¹⁴ By building villages for those communities, the Reform Division could theoretically accelerate the civilizing process that the Khaldunian framework presented as natural and gradual. However, the civilizing mission went far beyond instantiating the accoutrements of village life. Cevdet saw the moral component of civilization as equally intertwined with the Reform Division's mission. He ensured that mosques and sharia courts were built in the vicinity of new settlements, as he considered the local Muslim population to be ignorant of proper Islamic practice.¹¹⁵

The mountains represented a barrier to state reform, but the lowlands of Çukurova represented an opportunity. "Çukurova is an unknown world [*bilmediğimiz bir âlem*]," Cevdet marveled in his account of the Reform Division. "The tips of the spears of passing Kurdish horsemen cannot be seen, as if the power of the vegetation displays all of its majesty and splendor here," he remarked, adding that "even if it does not rain, the plains are nourished by the gentle dew that descends upon the earth at night." This image of a perfect state of nature with clear streams running through "emerald-green meadows" attested to Çukurova's bounty. But with a tone of apprehension, he added: "while the francolins taking flight all around and the herds of gazelle bounding to and fro add cheerfulness/prosperity [*şenlik*] to this charming prairie, the wild boars as well as the various snakes that one meets at every turn bring fear/savageness [*vahşet*]."¹¹⁶ He lamented, "What good is it when because of its being the roaming grounds of tribes, there is no sign or indication of agriculture or human labor [*insan emeği*] to be found?"¹¹⁷

Cevdet resembled his Western European contemporaries in his tendency to see the potential for redemption and revitalization among the architectural ruins of the Çukurova plain. It became common during subsequent settlement activities to choose sites of ancient cities and fortresses as places of village construction.¹¹⁸ When settling the Bozdoğans in Hemite, the Reform Division benefited from the rich quality of the stones from old structures that turned up continuously during the digging of foundations.¹¹⁹ Cevdet took these ruins as a sign that the area had once supported a flourishing civilization and was thus poised to again swell with cultivators and inhabitants.

His most boisterous claim to a grander imperial heritage was made during the process of gathering stone to erect new villages near İslahiye, when they came across a slab bearing a Greek inscription. According to Ahmed Cevdet's account, it read, "Here is where Alexander set down his penal code." Veracity notwithstanding, this account conveyed how he understood the activities of the Reform Division in the region. In rebuilding the fortifications of the ancient past, they were rebuilding a fallen civilization, and with that civilization came the rule of law.[120] İslahiye's very name, which commemorated Cevdet's reforms, was a symbol of restored imperial authority.

Settlement was a cornerstone of Cevdet's civilizing mission in Cilicia, and malaria was the greatest barrier. Though there is no evidence of concrete steps taken to mitigate malaria risk in the new settlements, the dangers of malaria were known to both settlers and officials. Cevdet's letters to his wife during the campaign reflect the extent to which Çukurova's bad airs were at the forefront of concern for his own well-being. "Currently we are with the imperial army encamped on the high hills near Iskenderun, and thanks be to God, all of us are in good health. I have no troubles other than being apart from you," he wrote in one letter to Adviye Rabiye soon after his arrival in Cilicia.[121] "There's nothing to worry about," he assured in another. "Thank God that even though the days are a bit hot, we set up camp in high places. They receive air and one can breathe there [*hava alır ve teneffüs olunur*], and so we are in no condition to complain."[122] Concerns about the local climate traveled in both directions between the couple. "It's starting to get hot. Don't stay in Istanbul," Cevdet warned his family back home. "Although it's even hotter here, we are setting up camp in elevated and open places and then leaving."[123]

Cevdet, much like the subjects of settlement policy, believed that the new settlements in Çukurova were being established in insalubrious environs. But he did not believe that the bad climate impacted all people equally. In his reflection upon how the settlement of Circassians in Çukurova and later at Uzunyayla played out, he emphasized how Circassian bodies, which were a product of their temperate, mountain homeland, were ill suited to the hot and humid lowlands of the Cilicia region. According to Cevdet, the Circassians settled in Çukurova had been moved to Uzunyayla "because mountain people cannot live on the plains." This flexible but ultimately deterministic understanding of the relationship between bodies and environments cut the other way as well. For example, Cevdet claimed that Tatars from Kuban settled in Çukurova would be able to handle the climate because they were from a river-valley region of Crimea.[124]

A similar logic regarding acclimation is visible in how the Ottoman government chose to settle different communities of Cilicia under the Reform Division. They were all ostensibly native to the same region, and the principles of settlement dictated that they would construct villages in their lowland winter quarters; however, there were some notable exceptions in practice. The Karakayalıs, who summered in the plateaus of Mount Bolkar near Ereğli and wintered in Çukurova were appointed vacant lands to cultivate in their winter quarters to prevent their future disturbance of people in the Taurus Mountain villages. Yet despite their depredations, the provincial government in 1865 allowed for them to continue migrating and raising animals because, "since they have long been accustomed to the *yayla* [*menülkadim yaylaya alışmış oldukları cihetle*]," they could not be expected to suddenly encamp in "warm locations [*mevaki-i harre*]."[125] Such documentation shows that Ottoman administrators were cognizant of the ways in which local people interpreted their own environments.

Most groups were not afforded such flexibility. Cevdet squared the reality of settling people in regions where they would likely fall ill by citing the idea that malaria, though often part and parcel of frontier settlement, could ultimately be eliminated through the process of settlement and cultivation. He ascribed these ideas once again to Ibn Khaldun, who in his *Muqaddimah* referred to historical precedents in which negative health impacts of the environment were eliminated through continued habitation and persistent expansion of cultivation in a particular area. For example, one passage from the *Muqaddimah* stated that "where there are few inhabitants, the air is not helped to move and circulate, so it remains stagnant. Its putrescence increases and its harmfulness grows . . . We have seen the contrary occur in places founded without regard for the quality of the air. At first, they had few inhabitants, and, consequently, the occurrence of disease was high. Then, when the (number of) inhabitants increased, the situation changed."[126] Cevdet explicitly referred to Ibn Khaldun in his commentary on the relationship between malaria and settlement and remained steadfast in the idea that the expansion of agriculture would clean the air of the Çukurova plain.[127]

This dialectical understanding of the relationship between malaria and settlement was not unique to a Khaldunian understanding of ecology, and it would recur in sources from the Ottoman period. In his own description of Cilicia, E. J. Davis declared that "wherever the virgin soil is opened, virulent marsh fever seems to burst forth and smite down all around, and nothing but generations of patient culture can subdue the soil afresh, and render this plain a safe abode for man."[128] Decades later, when malaria was better understood by medical doctors, the conventional wisdom persisted. Feyzullah İzmidi, who led the late Ottoman battle with malaria, stated in his university lectures that "malaria likes unworked lands and desolate, empty countryside. It cannot hold up in the face of civilization and the efforts of mankind."[129] An Armenian doctor who led a medical mission to Cilicia after World War I similarly attributed the endemic malaria of the region to its lack of cultivation.[130] And Cilicia was not an exception in world history. New settlements of the global frontier were frequently tied to malaria epidemics, and while settlement did bring environmental change, malaria often remained a pervasive dimension of such environments for many generations. In this regard, the Tanzimat-era settlers of Çukurova were part of a much larger social history of malaria, not only in the Ottoman Empire but throughout nineteenth-century empires.

However, it is significant that Cevdet articulated his understanding of civilization and ecology through a Khaldunian framework rooted in a long tradition of Ottoman statecraft. Many have noted a shift in Ottoman governmentality during the nineteenth century toward modes of action and representation that appear "more colonial," particularly with regard to nomadic populations.[131] Andrea Duffy suggests that the shift in attitude toward nomads in the Ottoman Empire and the evolving interpretation of Ibn Khaldun reflected in nineteenth-century Ottoman writings were influenced by new, Western interpretations of Ibn Khaldun read into colonial contexts such as Algeria.[132] This was certainly the case, to some extent, by the founding of the Turkish Republic. Yet a pivotal figure such as Ahmed Cevdet complicates this picture. While certain dimensions of the Tanzimat were clearly influenced by European legal codes, and many strategies of the Ottoman state were plainly part of the zeitgeist of empire at the time, it was European colonial empires more than the Ottomans that were grappling for the first time with the question of how to govern nomadic pastoralists. Although he displayed some of the same prejudices toward nomadic populations as his imperial counterparts in Britain and France, Cevdet was far from the first Ottoman official to support a sedentarization campaign. Moreover, when Ottoman settlement policy faced resistance, the provincial government ultimately relented in ways one might not expect from a colonial power, displaying the flexibility that long governed imperial policy toward the provinces.

Resisting the Tanzimat

Deep in the Taurus Mountains above Mersin is a town called Atlılar: the village of the "Horsemen." It was founded sometime after the Russo-Ottoman War of 1877–78. Originally called Saadiye, Atlılar was settled by migrants from the North Caucasus who had been placed in the lowlands near Mersin. According to the research of Mehtap Ergenoğlu, they had applied for resettlement on the basis of an inability to adapt to the climate, like so many others of their kind. Some of their descendants remain in Atlılar, which has only a few hundred residents. Atlılar today is probably no larger than the initial settlement, while Mersin has grown from a town of fewer than 10,000 people in 1880 to be a city of more than 1 million. The original settlement of these immigrants has been absorbed by the rapid expansion of Mersin to the west, along the Mediterranean coast, and many inhabitants of Atlılar have long since moved to Mersin or elsewhere.[133] For their ancestors to have relinquished prime real estate to take up residence in a remote mountain village may seem nonsensical. In a collection of writings entitled *Çukurova Yana Yana*, Yaşar Kemal referred to a similar paradox in a passage about landless villagers lamenting their foolish ancestors who had sold or abandoned land "forcibly given [to them] by the state" and "spat in the face" of Ottoman settlement policy.[134]

Though in the long run, such a reaction appears short-sighted, the instances in which people refused, sold, or even abandoned what eventually became valuable property were acts of self-preservation and examples of how local people resisted and reshaped Ottoman settlement policy. Localized resistance to Ottoman settlement policy was entangled with the ecology of settlement from the creation of the first villages in Çukurova. The remote settlements of Uzunyayla were the first prominent example of a successful attempt to push back against the state's orders. The Circassian immigrants who settled there were originally placed in the lowlands but complained to the local government that many within their ranks were falling ill and dying, requesting to be resettled elsewhere. The phrasing of the request was a formulation that appears frequently in the documentary record: they "could not get along with the climate [*abühava ile imtizaç edememek*]," indirectly referring to the impact of malaria. The Muhacirin Commission accepted the petition, and suggested different, "airy" locations of the Cilicia region associated with the longstanding practice of transhumance, such as the Ramazanoğlu *yayla* or the hinterland of Marash, as possible sites, before settling on Uzunyayla.[135] The Circassians were given lands around modern-day Pınarbaşı to settle in and raise their horses. This location could be called a "Little Circassia" within the Ottoman Empire, where *muhacirs* were able to maintain a semblance of their life in the old country. In fact, to this day there is a special breed of horse called the Uzunyayla, a legacy of this episode.[136]

Despite the initial conflict with the Avşars at Uzunyayla, the two communities would eventually reach peace, and in the end, the Avşars also became one of the few pastoralist groups to not only appoint their places of settlement during the 1860s but also secure highland villages as opposed to settling in their winter quarters in Çukurova. This arrangement was brokered through negotiations with the Ottoman government by their leaders, especially a figure named Hacı Bey.[137] The bitter irony of Hacı Bey would prove to be that he fell ill and died soon after settlement in the cold mountains, but the ability of the Avşars to maintain their identity and folklore ensured the transmission of a lament memorializing Hacı Bey's heroic negotiations that preserved their identity.[138] Settlement of the Avşars and Circassians at Uzunyayla would even reach elements of symbiosis. For example, when two branches of the Avşars in the Taurus Mountains, comprising about 400 households, became worried that their animals would perish over the winter in the mountains and that they themselves would be blocked in by snow, the local government permitted some of them to leave their houses to newly arrived immigrants and winter their animals in the lowlands.[139] By contrast, some of the groups that settled in the lowlands saw their communal identities eroded by settlement. Writing some decades later, Besim Atalay observed, concerning the Cerids in particular, that their culture and identity had been almost wiped out.[140]

Armed resistance to the Reform Division during the 1860s had failed, bringing a permanent end to the reign of the *derebeys*. Yet by the 1870s, most of the communities impacted by settlement and the subsequent rise in mortality began to flout the restrictions on movement originally imposed through military surveillance.[141] Rather than reacting with military force, the Ottoman government sought to remediate the situation through a detailed investigation of the preferred practices of each community, their patterns of agriculture and pastoralism, and the reason for their attachment to seasonal migration. This investigation revealed the problems created by the "raw settlement" that Besim Atalay would critique. For instance, a group called the Devecis, or "Cameleers," insisted that they were not a nomadic tribe in the typical sense but rather camel herders whose livelihood was completely derived from facilitating commerce in the region. Village life made no sense to them because they could not become settled agriculturalists. It was only movement that allowed them to make their living at all, which in turn made them integral to local commerce.[142] In general, the study affirmed that each community pursued a distinctive way of life that could not be captured by the blanket orders of sedentarization. For virtually all of them, mobility was essential to self-preservation.

One of Ahmed Cevdet's last acts in the Cilicia region was presiding in 1878 over a twelve-article decree that codified the new parameters of seasonal migration among Cilicia's tribes.[143] It read like a formal contract, granting on paper what had already been accomplished in practice. The first article stated that while nomadism (*göçebelik*) was still prohibited in theory, "from the beginning of July until the fifteenth and finally the end of August, those who need a change of air in other places shall be permitted upon true necessity to go to and return from the surrounding elevated and appropriate areas in the manner that is customary." The precise terms of the agreement varied from tribe to tribe. For the Karakayalı, Kürkçü, and Karahacılı *aşirets*, the transhumant communities of the Menemencis were apparently taken as a model for sedentarization. One article said that the practices of the Menemencis should be adopted by these aforementioned tribes as follows: "The Menemenci tribe sends their sheep, cattle, and camels along with their shepherds to their own *yaylas* by May 15 and the end [of May], stay in their villages in order to harvest the wheat and barley and weed the sesame and cotton fields, go to the *yayla* at the end of June with their wives and children for a change of air, return to their villages in the middle of August and return again to their *yaylas* after drawing and burying the sesame to return to their village along with their animals after spending early September [at the *yayla*], and then harvest the sesame and cotton."

Other communities, such as the Sırkıntıs, were also allowed to go to the mountains with their sheep and goats since "the waters in the villages of the Sırkıntı tribe residing in Çukurova retreat during the summer to the extent that they cannot care for their animals." In this case, a *yayla* at a location called İnderesi in the Kozan district was specified as a summer pasture. The Upper Bozdoğan tribe in Kars-ı Zülkadriye received similar terms. Some of the village populations near Sis and Kars were also allowed to go to the *yayla*, but the inhabitants and officials of Sis and Kars were explicitly prohibited, although the rules stated that "those who have orchards on the *yayla* shall be able to go to their orchards for one to two months during the season in order to pick grapes and boil molasses." The document also mentioned agriculturalist communities near Payas who could go to the *yaylas* in the Amanus Mountains, "which are their own homes," after gathering the harvest.

Most of the pastoralist communities in Cilicia, however, were ostensibly prohibited from bringing their animals to the mountains during the summer. One article referred to "the Kurdish tribes called the Lek, Hacılar, and Kırıntı," declaring that "they are always harming the people and occupying the government by engaging in robbery.[144] Henceforth, they are forbidden to go out to the *yayla*." Despite these restrictions, the law stated that, "if during July malaria falls into their ranks, those who need a change of air along with the rest of the inhabitants are allowed to go out to the suitable and elevated places in the *kaza* of Sis such as Çatma and Üçbek. However, in that case they must leave their animals in their villages." Unlike the communities in the western portion of the province of Adana, who were allowed to adopt the transhumance of the Menemencis, for these three tribes, a complete abandonment of pastoralism was the apparent path offered to sedentarization. "They shall not go out to the *yayla* with their animals, and they like the rest of the inhabitants and tribes will be obliged to practice agriculture," the article emphasized. "It is not permissible for them to be found in huts made from reeds and in a scattered state. They will be made to live collectively in the villages formed by the Reform Division, build themselves houses of stone and mud brick, and properly form villages." Similar restrictions were applied to the Cerid, Tecirli, and Lower Bozdoğan tribes near Payas, who were permitted to go to certain *yaylas* in the Amanus Mountains determined by a government commission for change of air but were not allowed to leave the district or bring their animals to the mountains. Nearly identical constraints were applied to the tribes settled around İslahiye.

The new terms of settlement represented an important shift in how the Tanzimat state approached the local communities of Cilicia. They made clear that both the Ottoman government and its subjects understood seasonal migration as a solution to malaria; first and foremost, malaria was a pretext for these historically mobile communities to continue their annual movements. The agreement represented a turning point in the ecological thinking behind Ottoman settlement policy, and a recognition of health and acclimation as key factors in determining the parameters of settlement and mobility. But in forbidding some groups from taking their flocks with them to the *yayla*, the Ottoman government also carried out an intriguing decoupling of the economic function of the *yayla* and its role as a salubrious refuge. While local practices certainly might have differed, in the official discourse, the *yayla* season was no longer part and parcel of the economic activity of those communities. The *yayla* was purely a retreat for those who could not take the heat of the lowlands.

This turning point occurred in part because immigrants and pastoralists had issued their complaints along those terms. But it was also a product of how recent history demonstrated the validity of those complaints: the frontier environment of Cilicia, however inviting it may have appeared to cultivators, did not yield so easily to the changes envisioned by Tanzimat statesmen like Cevdet. The Khaldunian dialectic that made sense on the civilizational time scale had proven to be the recipe for instant disaster. In stipulating new terms of settlement and seasonal migration, the Ottoman government maintained its right to undertake and adjudicate the ordering of time in the Cilicia region. However, in applying highly differentiated policies that closely resembled the preexisting practices of local inhabitants on the ground, the government affirmed the legitimacy of local knowledge and the rights of obedient subjects to control their own mobility when it came to ensuring the health and well-being of their families.

A further illustration of how the Ottoman government became more attuned to the specificities of local environments and ecologies throughout the settlement experiment of the high Tanzimat period can be in found in the subsequent treatment of refugees from the Russo-Ottoman War who arrived at the end of the 1870s. In response to the well-attested malaria or *vahâmet-i hava* of the Cilicia region during the summer, new migrants settled in lowland villages were additionally assigned corresponding *yaylas* in the mountains, in keeping with local practice.[145] While earlier migrants had been expected to adjust to life in the Cilicia region simply through the process of settlement in villages and adoption of cultivation, experience had revealed that acclimation was not an instantaneous process. As a result, ensuring their adaptation meant instead that settlement policy itself would have to be adapted to afford newcomers an opportunity to seek summer refuge in the mountains, like any other inhabitants of the region. The salubriousness of a particular place would become a central concern of Ottoman settlement policy, as evidenced by later manuals and ordinances. For *muhacirs,* inability to adapt to the local climate was one of the few bases upon which they could apply for resettlement by the end of the Ottoman period.[146]

While both the *muhacirs* and the *aşirets* generally resisted settlement in the lowlands and restrictions on their movements, individual cases reflect the plurality of the late Ottoman frontier experience. These individual cases, though not representative of a general trend, demonstrate that environment was a key factor in settlement, but its role was not wholly deterministic. One case involved a man from Dagestan who sought to create a new agricultural settlement at Akdam and Dikilitaş, about 15 km southeast of Sis. Having been settled in the inland province of Sivas, he petitioned in 1873 for permission to buy and to settle the region with his household, which included enslaved people.[147] In his case, permission was denied by the Ottoman government on the basis that "the severe temperament of the *muhacirs* would not be compatible with the morals and manners of the inhabitants there."[148] This curious judgment may have referred to objection on the part of Armenian authorities in Sis about the settlement of Muslims from the Caucasus so close to the town and its adjacent villages, since during the high Tanzimat period, settlement policy was carried out with some genuine concern for communal harmony and with attention to the issue of demographics.[149] The episode also suggested that the highlands were now seen as the natural home for migrants from the Caucasus.

The frontier of Çukurova, harsh though it was to many, occasionally attracted settlers seeking opportunity. A "daring and resolute" entrepreneur whom E. J. Davis met on his tour of Cilicia provides a useful complement to the experiences of migrants and pastoralists settled in Çukurova. Nikola Arslan from Tripoli (modern-day Lebanon) had settled around the ruins of Anazarbus on the north side of the Ceyhan River just south of Sis. He had recently bought up the property around the abandoned city and brought twenty or so households from his native town as laborers. They lived within the remaining walls of the medieval city, forbidding Muslims to settle among them and warding off "the thievish prowling Circassian" bandits that sometimes robbed the villagers of Çukurova. Indeed, a village marked as the "Chechen" village (modern-day Ağaçlı) on an Ottoman map from the period lay directly south of the ruins, which were roughly 30 km from both Sis in the north and Yarsuvat in the south.[150] Though Arslan had bought the previously uncultivated land from the Ottoman government at a bargain price and the soil was fertile, he was struggling to turn a profit in the wake of a terrible flood that had inundated his property.[151] Arslan, himself the native of a malarial region of the Eastern Mediterranean coast, reported that he had at least enjoyed good health thus far. But the frontier spirit of Arslan, who represented a rare breed of voluntary settlers, was not one often encountered in the region at that time, and it is unclear if his venture lasted.

The environmental frontier of Çukurova was not immediately remade by settlement policies, but the political objective of Tanzimat policy in Cilicia was a success. To some extent, both migrant and tribal communities would continue to have a reputation for lawlessness and for challenging state order. An infamous example is that of Tek Taşak, or One-Nut, who took to the Taurus Mountains and made a peculiar name for himself as a ruthless outlaw during the 1870s.[152] But it is striking that when Kozanoğlu Ahmed Pasha capitalized on the period of chaos that accompanied the end of the Russo-Ottoman War in 1878 to launch a rebellion in the mountains, he received relatively little support, perhaps because the Ottoman government had already made peace with the local tribes.[153] Ahmed Pasha's relative Kozanoğlu Yusuf Agha, who led a rebellion against the Reform Division and was killed as a result, was already a legend in the region. The lament his sister Karakız Hatun wrote about him would immortalize his struggle. Yet the prestigious Kozanoğlu name seems to have lost most of its political cachet by the end of the Tanzimat period.

The fate of the 1878 Kozanoğlu rebellion suggests the real reason why the Kozanoğlu name lived on. As Yaşar Kemal noted, Kozanoğlu's lament was transmitted from one person to another and eventually from one community to another. As it moved, each person could change or add material to reflect their own stories.[154] His legend became a living history of people with a shared past of collective trauma. Much like the refrain of "the mountains are ours," commemorating the resistance of ordinary people who sought to maintain access to their cherished *yaylas*, ultimately overturning Ottoman settlement policy in their region, Kozanoğlu's song was an ode to the nomadic way of life itself. It commemorated an entire society's suffering and survival.

At the outset of his influential study *Seeing Like a State*, James C. Scott noted that "efforts to permanently settle . . . mobile peoples . . . seemed to be a perennial state project—perennial, in part, because it so seldom succeeded."[155] The Ottoman case certainly attests to this observation. In many ways, the Reform Division and the broader failures of settlement policy resembled measures attempted throughout Ottoman history. Whereas Kasaba noted that "the sedentarization policies that the Ottomans adopted in the seventeenth and eighteenth centuries did not produce a permanently settled society," the sedentarization policies of the Tanzimat period succeeded—but in many cases only on paper.[156]

The 1877 *salname* of Adana, an annual publication that would serve as a reference for information about the province as well as a basic source for future historians, maintained the fiction that the Tanzimat had succeeded precisely where it had failed. It mentioned neither disease nor rebellion in its discussion of the prior decade of settlement. For the district of Osmaniye, which had become the marshy tomb of both immigrants and pastoralists over the prior decade, the description was hopeful: "Since the inhabitants of this district were settled and sedentarized [*tavtin ve iskân*] by the Reform Division and its land is of the utmost degree of fertility, the aforementioned inhabitants are working to increase the cultivation of wheat, barley, cotton, sesame, millet, and rice and raise various trees, and they are reaping the fruits of their labors."[157] Similarly, the writings of Ahmed Cevdet Pasha, rich and detailed though they were, offered little discussion of the human cost of settlement. Even the Ottoman archival record was mostly silent. Just a handful of documents about the welfare of these communities emerge from a sea of unprecedented documentation produced by the provincial government during that period. In part because its successes were heralded before they were completed, the project of Tanzimat for the countryside would become a permanently unfinished project. Perhaps nothing quite like what took place in the lowlands of Çukurova between the two wars with Russia occurred elsewhere in the Ottoman Empire, but analogies abound.

The history of violence and resistance in the provinces during the Tanzimat period raises familiar questions: what was the nature of the Ottoman state? Was it actually an empire, and if so, of what kind? Was the Tanzimat "Westernization," or rather "modernization," within an Ottoman framework? Was that modernization merely a defensive one, or was an Ottoman form of colonialism at play?

The Ottoman Empire was the only settler state of the nineteenth century with contracting borders, but we see in it echoes of other instances from the colonial world. The Reform Division's tribal pacification campaigns in Cilicia were certainly reminiscent of contemporaneous imperial expansions in the American West, the French Algerian Sahara, the Italian Mezzogiorno, or the Russian Caucasus.[158] Like the immigrants who settled American lowland frontiers, such as the Chicago region, during the mid-nineteenth century, the settlers of late Ottoman Çukurova were plagued by malaria and other troubles of the road. The Anatolian famines resembled other mass starvation events in Egypt, Brazil, Algeria, Iran, and China that Mike Davis has described as "late Victorian holocausts."[159] Even on the level of civilizational discourse, there are important parallels. Placed alongside contemporary accounts like that of George Custer in the Black Hills, sections of Cevdet Pasha's narrative of the Reform Division's activities read as if they arose from the same context.[160] Yet the backgrounds of military figures like Custer and Ottoman statesmen like Cevdet were different, and so too were their aims.

Cevdet's reforms in Cilicia were not the expression of belief in a manifest destiny to conquer a continent in the name of a Christian civilization. He understood them in light of a long tradition of Islamic statesmen reaching back to Ibn Khaldun, who sought to solve the problems of governance that contributed to the rise and fall of empires. While the conquest of the American frontier was predicated on the erasure of indigenous people and their replacement by European settlers, Cevdet saw the subjects of his reforms as irreducibly part of the Ottoman body politic no matter how they resisted or insisted they were outside it. If the label of a "civilizing mission" seems an odd fit for the Tanzimat experiment, it is because people like Cevdet seemed to take the concept so seriously. Whereas the civilizing mission in India or Algeria was the fig leaf of empire, the Ottoman civilizing mission was the work of empire itself. Even though there are parallels between the death and destruction wrought by the Tanzimat on the Ottoman frontier and the colonial genocides of the nineteenth century, the ways in which the Ottoman state responded to failure and resistance during that period reveal something very different.

Ideologues like Cevdet were the authors of the Tanzimat reforms and their history; however, they were not its sole actors. And not unlike the Saint-Simonian socialists who aided and abetted French colonization of Algeria, it was their enthusiasm more than their ideas that ultimately served the material interests of the states that employed them.[161] While education and cultivation were central to the emergent notion of the Ottoman citizen, on a more practical level, pastoralists and their independence were an impediment to potentially lucrative business ventures. As Toksöz notes, "commercialization required some sort of monitoring of nomads."[162] Whether or not settlement resulted in a successful outcome for those subjected to these policies, by freeing up more land for cultivation, it served the long-term interests of capital during a period of liberalization in the Ottoman Empire.

During the 1870s, many of the professional statesmen who shaped the Tanzimat period advocated for further liberalization and a transition to constitutional government. While Cevdet shared their worldview in many respects, he did not share their dissatisfaction with the Ottoman monarchy. When the Ottoman constitution was promulgated in 1876 and Abdülhamid II took the throne, Cevdet supported the new sultan's efforts to suspend the constitution and reinstate absolutist rule, which succeeded amid the Russo-Ottoman War in 1878. By the time of Cevdet's death in 1895, the Ottoman state had completed a new turn in provincial governance, fixating its anxiety not so much on nomads but rather on non-Muslim subjects of the empire, especially Armenians, who made up a sizable component of the population in Cilicia and the "six provinces" of Eastern Anatolia. Yet most of the Hamidian era would prove one of relative calm in the Cilicia region, as a laissez-faire approach to provincial matters propelled a diverse class of landowners and merchants who profited from cotton export to become the new lords of the lowlands, with the *derebeys* and their constituents coopted or exiled. By the end of the Ottoman period, this new commercial class had cemented its place in the Cilicia region, no longer cast as the mountain stronghold of rebels and bandits but rather as an expanse of plantations destined to become "the Second Egypt" of the Eastern Mediterranean. With the Adana massacres of 1909, a less rosy vision of this new region emerged, as the destabilizing consequences of competition and contention on the late Ottoman frontier abruptly became apparent. Only most observers at the time did not see the links between the slow agrarian transformation and the sudden violence.

{ CHAPTER 3 }

SECOND NATURE IN THE SECOND EGYPT

Capital, Ecology, and Intercommunality, 1878–1914

As the story goes, the summer of 1878 brought hot, rainless days to the Cilicia region and parched its fertile fields. In an atmosphere of escalating panic, Adana's notables and *mufti*, the highest ranking cleric in the city, urged the provincial governor to convene a prayer for rain. This ritual is well attested by those who knew the city during the late Ottoman period. People young and old would participate in the familiar *bodi bodi* recitations, appealing to divine mercy to alleviate drought, saying, "into the well of the grain-hoarder, into the farmers' fields, God give us watery rain."[1] They held the public rain prayer above the Seyhan River in the center of the old stone bridge. But Ziya Pasha, the new governor, was a classic man of the Tanzimat—a renowned poet and leading figure in the Young Ottoman movement, who had supported the short-lived constitutional revolution of 1876. As such, he abstained from what he saw as superstition, using a clever turn of phrase. He told the crowd that he was afraid God might ridicule him for begging for rain when the plain surrounding Adana had been endowed by its creator with bountiful water resources in the rivers that crossed it. Rather than a rain prayer, Ziya would give Adana a new water works project, changing the course of the Seyhan River and by extension the course of history.

That was how legend commemorated Ziya Pasha.[2] His actual project entailed regulation of the Seyhan River's flow by digging a channel on the river north of the town to mitigate the impact of floods.[3] The idea of protecting Adana from inundations was not in itself controversial; there had been many severe floods in the recent past.[4] But the dam project would end up at the center of a larger crisis of legitimacy in the province. In repeated telegrams, a group of Muslim and Christian merchants and landowners wrote they could "no longer bear the unfortunate transgressions of Ziya Pasha, known for his tyranny."[5] A complaint signed by more than seventy residents of Adana enumerated his misdeeds, which included the costly river works, a questionable market reconstruction, and his frivolous spending on a theater built on a lot forcibly expropriated from a local resident to host a company from Beirut to perform his own translation of Molière's *Tartuffe*.[6] Some countered the allegations by attesting to Ziya Pasha's enlightened nature.[7] Ziya likewise defended his own actions, saying that all of his projects were undertaken in the interest of the "public benefit [*menfaat-ı umumiye*]."[8] But the episode left him exhausted and ill. He repeatedly applied to the central government to go the *yayla* for change of air. Then, he died suddenly in 1880, and Adana remained without a governor for months.[9]

Ziya Pasha's governorship was a chaotic coda to an era of heavy-handed state intervention into the affairs of the Cilicia region during the high Tanzimat period. He did not accomplish the feat for which he was later credited. But in spirit, his bridling of the Seyhan River for the public good embodied a new vision of Cilicia—that of the "Second Egypt"—which became the dream of many an Ottoman bureaucrat, European consul, and local merchant over subsequent decades.[10] This chapter studies how that imaginary shaped Cilicia under a new ecological regime dominated by commercial agriculture. The idea of the "Second Egypt" meant that Cilicia would replicate the successes of Khedival Egypt in transitioning from a cereals-based agricultural economy to a high-yield, export-oriented economy that revolved around cotton. Though production would never approach the scale of the Nile basin, as Meltem Toksöz has shown, the countryside of the Adana region did become a commercial space "of shared hegemony between large landholders, export merchants, foreign capitalists, and local bureaucrats."[11] Cotton became the vehicle that drove commercialization and empowered a new class of Ottoman officials, local financiers, and ascendant landlords. They presided over a cotton kingdom built on the labor of sharecroppers, seasonal workers, and local households; the productive energy of Çukurova's soil, water, and sun; tens of thousands of animals and a few tractors; and a very particular local species of what would become known in Turkey as the "white gold."[12]

Comparisons to Egypt were rooted in Cilicia's rich soil, abundant natural water resources, and excellent cotton, but the idea of the "Second Egypt" was also predicated on the creation of "second nature."[13] The term "second nature" refers to dimensions of the environment that may be perceived as natural but are in fact anthropogenic. Ziya Pasha's irrigation scheme to convert the plain into a sprawling network of plantations represents one such manifestation. However, in many ways, the reordering of nature in the Cilicia region produced results that were not intended. Malaria had been part of life in Cilicia well before the rise of cotton, but commercial agriculture led to new ecological conditions that, alongside disruption of seasonal rhythms structured around malaria avoidance, facilitated the spread of the disease. Malaria became just one dimension of a growing economic and spatio-temporal unevenness as cotton's rise spun a tale of two very different plains in the Cilician lowlands. As railways and investment accelerated the pace of life in Adana and Mersin, the eastern frontier of the Çukurova plain remained remote and comparatively lacking in state presence. While the cities became the new centers of economic activity in Cilicia, the hinterland equally rose as the locus of contention between different communities and interest groups, and Ottoman capacity to adjudicate was limited. The communal violence of the 1909 Adana massacres catapulted the region's name into infamy not as a Second Egypt but rather as a would-be hotbed of deep-seated sectarian antagonisms. Yet in many ways, the dynamics of the violence in 1909 were inextricable from how settlement policy and commercial agriculture changed the nature of relations among Cilicia's different communities.

The Political Ecology of Cotton

The comparison between Cilicia and Egypt was rooted in a perceived potential for agricultural development. Otherwise, the two regions could have scarcely been more different. Cilicia had been a sparsely populated margin of the empire for most of its history. The fertile Nile Delta meanwhile had been a veritable breadbasket. Collaboration of state and peasants to channel water to fields of grain fed urban populations throughout the Ottoman Empire.[14] During the nineteenth century, Egypt emerged as a center of cotton cultivation in the Eastern Mediterranean thanks in part to new irrigation projects undertaken by the khedival government. The first stirrings of Cilicia as the Second Egypt occurred under the actual Egyptian occupation of Cilicia during the 1830s. The cotton industry in the Adana region grew, and Ibrahim Pasha's short-lived government undertook irrigation and drainage projects around Tarsus.[15] The subsequent cotton boom of the 1860s had cemented Cilicia's destiny in the eyes of many. Though the rapid growth of the 1860s would not be replicated for the rest of the nineteenth century due to a lingering economic depression, the imaginary of Cilicia as another Egypt reshaped its political ecology.

Although the majority of Cilicia's rural inhabitants had been pastoralists raising sheep and goats, cotton and wheat became chief export commodities from the 1860s onward. In 1908, the region produced more than 60,000 bales of cotton annually, and a British consul reported that the area of cultivation was growing by 5 percent every year; by the end of the Ottoman period, the province of Adana produced more cotton than any other province in the Ottoman Empire.[16] Only about 5 percent of all agricultural land in the Asian provinces of the empire was planted with commercial crops like cotton, sesame, tobacco, and opium. In the province of Adana, roughly 30 percent of farmland was occupied by cotton and sesame.[17] Most of the cotton produced there each year was exported, though roughly one-third remained in the empire.

The destinations of Cilicia's cotton varied greatly from year to year, but in most years, the major sites of textile manufacturing in Britain and France were not necessarily the most important trade partners. Instead, European countries with middling levels of textile production imported large amounts of Cilician cotton. Spain, Italy, Austria-Hungary, Greece, and later Germany were all important outlets.[18] In Cilicia, cotton was sovereign, but the regional economy remained peripheral to what Sven Beckert calls the "European-dominated empire of cotton."[19] Production marched to Cilicia's idiosyncratic ecological rhythms, blending local conditions and foreign demand to create a dynamic economy that served as a center not only within the immediate region but for workers and merchants from throughout the surrounding provinces who saw in the rise of cotton a potential for short- and long-term economic gain.[20]

The spread of cotton was accompanied by distinctive land use patterns. The lowland districts of the Cilicia region reflected an unusual concentration of large landholdings. In some districts, such as the immediate vicinity of Adana, all landholdings were recorded as being more than 50 *dönüms* in area, the largest designation possible in the agricultural census of 1909–10.[21] At the time of World War I, around 30 percent of the region's cotton cultivation took place on "estate-like" *çiftliks*.[22] In Ottoman land regimes, the *çiftlik* was a large private landholding akin to the notion of a plantation.[23] The owners of these large estates were a diverse group, and their properties were often in the thousands of *dönüms*.

In 1858, the Ottoman Empire had instituted a new land code that required the registration of all property and the issuance of a deed (*tapu senedi*). In practice, this did not necessarily produce a wholesale shift. Many parts of the empire did not see large-scale registration until decades later, when it was often carried out by government officials who surveyed local communities and registered their land.[24] But close to the cities, the opportunity to register large amounts of unused or at least uncultivated land was especially ripe. In the 1860s, landowners in Adana and Tarsus began to exploit a policy that allowed them to register uncultivated lands for free.[25] The land grabs were very rapid; E. J. Davis remarked in the 1870s that "almost every acre is utilized."[26] In contrast, another British traveler remarked as of the 1870s, moving eastward, that "cultivation may be said to end at Missis," where the Ceyhan River divided the plain.[27] Only after the Adana-Tarsus region was fully commercialized, by the 1890s, did investors begin to look eastward.[28] In 1882, the Ottoman government had updated its land code to further incentivize the registration of land designated as *mevat*, or "dead," uncultivated land.[29] The code said that landowners could obtain a deed for large swamps—a few thousand *dönüms*—so long as they committed to the land's improvement through drainage.[30] This policy fed the creation of massive estates in the Mediterranean littoral.

By the turn of the twentieth century, a new class of landlords was well established in Cilicia. They came from many walks of life. Armenians, Greeks, and Arab Christians figured prominently. Mediterranean mercantile families like the Sursocks of Beirut owned various properties in Cilicia as well as in the lowlands of the Eastern Mediterranean coast and Alexandria.³¹ But as Toksöz notes, this created the false impression among European observers that solely Christians were acquiring land at the expense of an increasingly dispossessed Muslim peasantry.³² Actually, prominent Ottoman officials were becoming major landowners as well. Abidin Pasha, the Ottoman governor who brought the first railway to the region and is credited with redesigning the city of Adana, was perhaps the foremost among them at one point. He possessed enormous landholdings in the east of Çukurova in the districts of Osmaniye, İslahiye, and Ayas (Yumurtalık)—according to one report, more than 50,000 *dönüms*.³³ Large landholders in later areas of expansion were predominantly Muslim; a document listing nine different landowners and the size of the properties that they used as collateral for loans noted three Armenian landholders, Marie Sursock, and five Muslim men, two of whom were business partners.³⁴ The largest property (5,000 *dönüms*) belonged to Alaybeyzade Mahmud, whom Toksöz described as a "former nomad." Many of the other cultivators in the Cilicia region were in fact sharecroppers working under these large landholders, and again, these contracts also cut across confessional lines.³⁵

Cotton was not the only crop intertwined with this specific pattern of landownership. The rice paddy, or *çeltik*, was another agricultural space that tended to give rise to large estates in the late Ottoman context.³⁶ In Cilicia, rice cultivation was concentrated in the northeast sector of Çukurova and in the lowlands around Kars-ı Zülkadriye, Marash, and Pazarcık. Landowners also could easily convert swampland into rice paddies by invoking the *mevat* article in Ottoman land regulations; the marshy lowlands made a natural fit for the high water demands of rice cultivation.³⁷ These rice cultivators were also a mixed group. By way of example, Hagop Khirlakyan, who would become an Ottoman parliamentarian during the constitutional period, operated a large rice plantation along with Muslim business partners.³⁸ Again like the cotton cultivators of Adana, in Marash, rice cultivators dominated local politics. Resembling Khirlakyan was one of Marash's first parliamentarians after 1908, Kadızâde Hacı Hasan Fehmi, who was the head of the one of the region's wealthiest rice-cultivating families.³⁹

Large landowners were the most salient figures, but they were only one part of the financial equation. A network of trade and lending emerged around the production and export of agricultural products. The main market in Adana was a space of collaboration between the state and local merchants. A primary function of Adana's mayor was to govern the market and organize the merchants.[40] Particularly after the completion of the railroad during the 1880s, cotton, wheat, and other agricultural produce bound for export quickly would make its way west to Mersin, where steamship lines made regular stops in the port of Mersin, along with a multitude of smaller sailing vessels that facilitated trade in the Ottoman Mediterranean. As production grew, Mersin emerged as a center of export and commerce. The population of the port was only about 2,000 in the 1860s. By the 1890s, it had risen to 10,000, and by the end of the Ottoman period to 25,000, meaning it rivaled the old city of Tarsus.[41] There was a market that contained almost 400 shops, 15 coffeehouses, and 3 covered alleys.[42]

Out of the cosmopolitan mercantile space of Mersin arose a community of Greek Orthodox merchants who came to Cilicia to trade and invest. At the center were the Cypriot Mavromatis family, whose members linked local and foreign capital in their different business ventures. They traded cotton and other goods, financed the small-scale industrialization of the region, and worked closely with European consulates. By the turn of the twentieth century, the two most important banks in Cilicia were the Ottoman Bank and Banque Mavromatis et Fils, meaning that domestic institutions far outstripped foreign ones in their overall influence over finance.[43] Landowners required loans to expand their commercial endeavors, and they also needed access to credit for seed, equipment, and land purchases. Agriculture in Çukurova to a large extent operated on annual cycles of debt. In Tarsus, the Menafi Sandığı is an example of a credit office, typically headed by an Armenian merchant and moneylender. Access to such credit was highly differential. Small producers were typically not able to do business with the Menafi Sandığı, which meant they had to look to private merchants for credit.[44]

The importance of credit also grew with the sophistication of agricultural equipment and the move toward mechanization. The first steam-powered agricultural machines were introduced during the 1880s. By 1908, there were dozens of steam threshers and plows in Cilicia, and imports of these items continued to grow in the remaining years before World War I.[45] Cultivators generally did not have their own machines; they looked to individuals who specialized in renting out their machines and labor at planting and harvest times. By 1910, there were 60 threshers, 300 steam plows, 1,000 reapers, 200 pumps, and 50 steam and gas engines in the vicinity of Adana.[46]

The peak periods of agricultural labor in late Ottoman Cilicia occurred during the spring and at the end of summer. As an example, a 6,500 *dönüm* farm in Çukurova had an agricultural labor cycle as follows. Land was evenly divided in three parts between wheat/barley, cotton/sesame, and fallow grassland. Fallow land was plowed in the winter and planted with cotton and sesame in March and April. These crops were gathered in August and September. Then, the land could be planted with wheat and barley in October, to be harvested in May and June. After the harvest, the cultivator could wait until October again to plant grains or leave the land fallow in anticipation of the cotton-planting season in the spring. The farm had about 25 regular hands in the winter and 20 in the summer, along with 12 horses, 60 oxen, 20 buffalo, and 100 dairy cows. However, most of the labor on the farm was done by migrant workers who arrived in April and May, and left after the harvest in the fall. On this particular farm, up to 120 such laborers were employed during the harvest—more than five times the number of permanent staff.[47]

Because of its low population density, Cilicia was highly dependent on migrant labor during the planting and harvest of cotton. Every year, an influx of workers that kept pace with the growing city of Adana in terms of size converged on the region. Estimates ranged from roughly 50,000 migrant workers annually in the 1880s to more than 80,000 annually by the end of the Ottoman period.[48] A report from 1912 indicated that while the population of local agricultural laborers in Çukurova was around 2,000, the migrant worker population could be more than 100,000 (see figure 3.1).[49] Many of these workers were Nusayri Arabs from the coasts of Northern Syria, whose range of settlement had been slowly expanding toward Çukurova.[50] Another significant contingent of workers came from Eastern Anatolia. They were described as Armenians, Kurds, Turks, and Assyrians, who descended from near and far in the mountainous interior provinces, as well as the provinces of the Jazira along the border of modern-day Turkey and Syria.[51] Some came from as far east as the Iranian side of the border. There were even a few hundred Afghan laborers living on the outskirts of Tarsus.[52] Late Ottoman Çukurova also had a small population of villagers from Sudan.[53] Though numbers are hard to ascertain, migration to Adana by Afghans, Bukharans, and Sudanese was significant and sustained enough to pose questions of nationality and whether such people should be counted as Ottoman nationals subject to conscription.[54] While many of the workers were single men, both women and men engaged in seasonal labor, sometimes migrating as family units. A governor of Adana linked this fact to the lack of economic opportunities, saying that men and "even women" of the Taurus Mountains were in a constant state of roaming in search of work.[55]

The annual rhythms of labor migration were sustained by a multinodal network of information. The provincial government played a role by providing information about prospective wages and demand for labor during a given year.[56] This information was disseminated throughout local villages in the empire where a contractor, known as the *elçibaşı*, organized a caravan of workers to make the trip by land. The *elçibaşı* was responsible for negotiating wages and was typically paid his own wage, roughly double, based on the agreed rate.[57] As the main go-between who facilitated the work of villages from all over the empire in Cilicia, the *elçibaşı* would then further play a role in supervising labor in the fields, profiting off worker wages further through small-scale lending and facilitation of gambling. He was often a maligned figure among the workers, known for brandishing an umbrella and a whip.[58] However, the *elçibaşıs* were also responsible for choosing the representatives of workers on a commission in Adana that brought together different sectors of the cotton economy, including local officials and law enforcement, cultivators, and merchants, and was headed by the Chamber of Agriculture. Supposedly established during the Egyptian occupation period, this commission served as the site of negotiation of wages and terms of employment, and it lasted well into the post-Ottoman period.[59]

The life of a migrant worker was precarious. The week began on Tuesday, when workers, employers, and middlemen would congregate at the "farmhand market [*ırgat pazarı*]" on the stone bridge over the Seyhan River in Adana. One observer remarked that on Tuesdays, Adana was a "human sea" due to the presence of tens of thousands of workers in search of employment.[60]

The laborers were responsible for their own lodging and had no guarantee of work. Unlike sharecroppers and other local villagers who had special arrangements with cultivators and landowners, these workers generally did not receive a portion of the agricultural produce, which meant that they were not invested in the crop, and in turn, the cultivator was not invested in them. Çukurova gained a reputation for grueling working conditions that, for most of the Ottoman period, were never much regulated beyond the local level.[61] The workday lasted roughly ten or eleven hours.[62] It was organized around virtually sacred breaks (*soluk*). The workday's end was often marked by a ritualistic chant that alluded to many figures in the daily lives of Ottoman workers, and mentioned by name Ibrahim Pasha, who was reportedly responsible for shortening the work week during his time in Cilicia.[63] The breaks were vital to the workers not just because they needed rest but also because they were given meals provided by the farm. The farms had cooks called *odacıs* who supplied sustenance to the workers. One British consul remarked that "if the food is bad, the men strike at once."[64]

The oral history testimony of a former Greek inhabitant of a village near Tarsus further illustrates the complex labor relations of the Cilicia region and their mediation through state institutions. He said that the villagers themselves did not work the fields but rather worked in factories, such as the flour factory of Sadık Pasha in Tarsus or the Mavromatis textile factories in Mersin. For the planting of cotton, sesame, and wheat, local cultivators would go to the municipality of Tarsus and sign a document asking for workers to be sent. The fields of the village were worked by "Kurds from Sivas," who earned a monthly wage. According to this account, worker and employer maintained good relations, and these seasonal workers were eventually allowed to obtain some of the excess land in the village after a few years of repeat work, ostensibly facilitating permanent migration.[65]

These agricultural workers received a relatively high wage paid in cash, much higher than in most provinces, and one that rivaled those of some urban professions in Adana and that could become substantially higher in periods of great demand.[66] Given that most of these workers came from regions with less economic opportunity, these wages were certainly enticing enough to justify coming to Adana. Since the workers kept one foot in the local village economies of the regions they came from, they might have fallen short of constituting a separate social class.⁶⁷ But despite the disparate origins of these workers, a moral economy concerning the terms of relationships of workers, landowners, or intermediaries governed cotton cultivation in Çukurova, which saw the commodification of wage labor on a scale that was unparalleled throughout most regions of the Ottoman Empire.

The relatively high wages shaped the type of cotton the region produced. Unlike the cotton grown in the United States or new cotton-producing regions like Egypt, where a recently developed strain of American cotton took off during the early nineteenth century, Cilicia's predominant cotton was of an indigenous variety commonly referred to as Levant cotton.⁶⁸ The local species, *Gossypium herbaceum*, known simply as *yerli* (meaning "local") in Turkish, had morphological features that made it distinct from American strains of cotton. *Yerli* fibers were shorter and less white, and the plant required an entirely distinct method of production, harvest, and processing. Whereas the fibers of open-boll American cotton strains were picked directly from the plant, *yerli* cotton fibers were encased in a husk—the word for "boll" in Turkish was *koza*, meaning "pod" or "cocoon"—that allowed workers to pick the entire boll. The cotton was then cleaned during a separate process of removing the fibers from the boll. The closed bolls made *yerli* easier to process in local conditions. Because the fibers were protected, the harvest was not as time-sensitive; workers could gather the bolls all at once rather than making repeated outings to the fields. In addition, *yerli* was drought resistant and could be cultivated without irrigation.⁶⁹

The method of producing and processing *yerli* cotton blended well with local conditions. After cotton was harvested, it was distributed to families of the nearby towns and villages. These locals were primarily responsible for carrying out the important task of separating the *yerli* cotton fibers from the rest of the boll. One Armenian writer described this unique process of "husking [*şiflemek*]" the *yerli* cotton bolls as an integral part of the household economy in the region.⁷⁰ The activity of a multigenerational family seated around a pile of cotton for cleaning (*yığılmak*) is an iconic image of life in Cilicia during this time period (see figure 3.2).⁷¹ A British traveler remarked that "there are several factories in Adana, owned by Armenians and Greeks, where the cotton is separated from the husks, but the same operation goes on in a less extensive way in almost every courtyard in the town."⁷² Through this process, the labor of women and children became commodified within the safe confines of the home. Single women and widows could also take advantage of cleaning cotton as a source of supplementary income. For the cleaning of cotton, these families were compensated either in cash or in kind, receiving, for example, roughly one-eighth to one-tenth of the cotton they cleaned. They could then sell that cotton or use it for their own home spinning and weaving activities, as they liked. Rent was paid at the beginning of November, immediately after the end of cotton season.[73]

Yerli cotton was less desirable on the global market. In repeated instances throughout the late Ottoman period, the government attempted to promote another type of seed, called *iane*, or "subsidy" cotton, to replace *yerli*. The *iane* strain was based on Egyptian cotton and was seen as more suitable for export to major textile producers. At various times, the Ottoman government dispensed this seed to cultivators free of charge.[74] In 1893, the Ottoman government established a model farm in Çukurova to further experiment with American strains of cotton. But foreign seed like *iane* did not take hold in Ottoman Çukurova.[75] One major issue was cross-pollination with the local variety. E. J. Davis remarked that Egyptian cotton tended to "degenerate" and "sink back into the type of the district."[76] There were reports that some cultivators would take free seed, feed it to their animals, and plant *yerli* instead. Even where experimentation with different types of cotton, such as American upland, were met with success, cultivators were reluctant to commit. Unlike *yerli*, American cotton fibers had to be picked directly from the plants in the field. American cotton cultivation was much more labor intensive and had been developed in the unfree labor conditions of modern plantation slavery. At any rate, German manufacturers, who emerged as the main importers of Çukurova cotton at the end of the Ottoman period, liked *yerli* because it blended well with wool, so the cost in terms of labor and irrigation for American strains of cotton did make sense within Cilicia's political economy.[77]

Where workshop and factory settings dedicated to ginning and spinning cotton emerged, they also involved family units. It was common for a single family to be responsible for a single machine, with the different members taking turns on the machine throughout the day. Machines significantly increased the speed and scale of the cotton business. These factories generated

Figure 3.1. The cotton harvest on the Adalı farm in the Ceyhan region, one of the sites of experimentation with American cotton. Source: Georges Tsapalos and Pierre Walter, *Rapport sur le domaine impérial de Tchoucour-Ova*, 76.

Figure 3.2. A postcard depicting a family cleaning cotton bolls on the roof of an Adana home, c. 1919. Possibly by Gaston Mizrahi.

their own electric light, which enabled them to operate for longer workdays or even continuously. Here too, the labor of women and children was vital.[78] One visitor reported that she found hundreds of women and children employed in such a factory.[79] Whereas agricultural production fostered a cyclical rhythm of seasonal labor migration, the budding industries of Cilician towns encouraged permanent migration. In the case of a spinning factory built in Tarsus, houses were constructed for Armenian workers who were to be brought from inland towns, such as Hadjin, Zeytun, and Aintab, to live and work in the factory.[80]

By the end of the Ottoman period, the province of Adana and its growing capital had been fundamentally reshaped by the cotton industry. The Armenian pharmacist and writer Hagop Terzian, who was born in Hadjin, described his new home of Adana as being "like a large and incomparable city because of progress but like a big village because of agriculture."[81] The broad-based participation of many segments of society in Cilicia and the intertwining of business and governance reflected the ways in which the commercialization of the local economy was a phenomenon that transcended communal groups and identifications, linking Muslims and Christians as well as town and country. Business, from local finance to the coordination of migrant and household labor, was heavily dependent on regional and family networks within the Ottoman Empire. The communities drawn into this new political economy, from the mercantile families of the Levant and the Nusayri peasants of the Northern Syrian coast to Armenian, Kurdish, and Turkish villagers who came for work, experienced further social effects through the increase in cash and wage labor, contact with urban settings, and connection to hubs of global migration.[82]

The Uneven Plain

The Adana-Mersin railway, which connected Cilicia's capital to its most important Mediterranean outlet, was one of the earliest rail projects in Ottoman Anatolia. "Improved transport will enable our agriculture, our commerce, and our industries to mutually unite towards augmenting the riches of our district," the governor of Adana, Abidin Pasha, declared at its inauguration in 1884. "The large products of the interior, which all gravitate by a natural law to the sea, will be stimulated to increased energy by the facilities afforded by railway communication. This form of social progress is superior to all others, as its effect is immediately visible and palpable; of this the railways of the world are the silent but material and indisputable witness."[83] The natural gravitation that Abidin Pasha described did shift the axis of movement in the region. Until the 1860s, the mountains had served as the stronghold of local power and political legitimacy, but by the beginning of the twentieth century, the city of Adana was unquestionably Cilicia's center. On the whole, this change was accompanied by an increase in agricultural production and expansion of state institutions, but that development was imbalanced. As a result, the disparities between the fast-paced life of Cilicia's mercantile centers like Adana and the hinterland became greater, accentuating the degree of "spatio-temporal unevenness" in the region.[84]

The mountainous hinterland of the Cilicia region was more densely settled than the lowlands during the early nineteenth century, but during the last decades of the Ottoman period, lowland districts and cities grew much more rapidly. The fastest growing subregion was the Adana-Tarsus-Mersin complex united by the railway during the 1880s. Its population more than doubled between 1882 and 1914.[85] Mersin sprang up from a tiny population to become a town of 25,000 inhabitants by the end of the Ottoman period. Tarsus doubled in size.[86] The city of Adana also exploded from roughly 30,000 at the beginning of the nineteenth century to as many as 80,000 registered inhabitants by the end of the Ottoman period (see table 3.1).[87]

The eastern half of Cilicia also witnessed considerable demographic growth during the last decades of the Ottoman period. The Sancak of Cebel-i Bereket reflected growth on par with the rest of the province of Adana between 1882 and 1914. This growth was in Çukurova but not necessarily concentrated in the settlements created during the 1860s. For example, in May 1866, a number of villages had been formed by the members of Cerid and Tecirli communities around the town of Osmaniye. According to a count in 1916, half had either changed name or disappeared. But four main villages still survived. Two named for Cevdet Pasha and Derviş Pasha, who oversaw the settlement activities of the Reform Division, were among them. The four villages had grown by just 7 percent in fifty years, and one was significantly smaller. Cevdetiye, which was closer to a main thoroughfare, grew the most, from 81 households in 1866 to 103 households in 1916.[88]

Table 3.1. Estimates of Urban Populations in Cilicia, 1864–1935

City/Town	1864	1890	1914	1927	1935	Change
Adana	35,000	55,000	80,000	73,000	76,000	
Tarsus	12,000	15,000	25,000	22,000	22,500	
Marash	25,000	35,000	55,000	25,000	27,000	
Mersin	2,000	10,000	25,000	22,000	23,000	
Ceyhan	2,500	3,000	5,000	7,000	10,000	

The districts at the interface with the Taurus Mountains—Sis, Kars, and Karaisalı—witnessed the lowest population growth. When compared with the rest of the Adana region, the census suggested almost no growth for the Kozan region between 1882 and 1914. This trend was the result of migration toward Adana, Tarsus, and Mersin, coupled with the impacts of the disastrous settlement campaigns of the 1860s. With most of the pastoralist populations settled on the plains and mountain villagers flocking to the city, the mountains were losing importance. The few thriving mountain settlements were also overcrowded, and the carrying capacity of areas like Hadjin was certainly stretched. Such factors were consistent with the reversal of trends in settlement between the mountains and the plains throughout the Mediterranean.[89]

The uneven growth of population in the Cilicia region reflected a growing imbalance of economic activity and resources. The expansion of road networks and railways effectively cut the distance between important urban centers, and steamship traffic at the port of Mersin further accelerated movement. The Ottoman telegraph network, which expanded into the countryside beginning in the 1860s, allowed officials and merchants to communicate basic information very quickly. This story is a familiar facet of the earlier phases of industrial acceleration, or what David Harvey calls the "rapid time-space compression" of capitalist modernity.[90]

The railway provided the most visible form of time-space compression. The provincial *salname* of Adana from 1877, published on the eve of the railway's arrival, provided a list of district (*kaza*) centers and their distance from Adana. By these measures, Tarsus was nine hours from Adana, and Mersin was fifteen. These distances were similar to those of the newly established centers associated with frontier settlement. For instance, the Muhacirin district, where many Nogay and Circassians had been settled, was about nine hours from Adana. The towns that dotted the edge of the plain were between eighteen and twenty-one hours from Adana. Mountain districts like Hadjin and Feke, which are twice as far from Adana as the crow flies, were just a little bit more remote at around thirty-six hours of distance. *Yayla* towns frequented by urbanites, such as Gülek and Namrun, which were the same distance from Adana as was Mersin, were in temporal distance only a few hours farther due to slower and more circuitous travel conditions in the highlands.[91] Yet by train, Mersin was just a few hours from Adana. In a request to move the consular residence from Adana to Mersin, a British official assured that "I can reach Adana by train in two hours."[92] Even if this was a rosy estimate, this meant that travel time between Adana, Tarsus, and Mersin could be cut by roughly 80 percent. Suddenly, a provincial district like Osmaniye was no longer just as far from Adana as Mersin, *it was six times farther* from the provincial capital than was the growing port. The unevenness created by the railroad shifted the balance of Çukurova's economy, which was displayed in the way that mechanization played out. By 1908, there were 22 factories associated with cotton and more than 500 cotton gins throughout the region. Of those factories, 14 were in Adana, 6 were in Tarsus, Mersin, and Yenice to the west, and just 2 were located in Ceyhan. The mechanization of late Ottoman Cilicia ended at the Ceyhan River.[93]

An even more vivid illustration of the diffuse geography of Upper Çukurova and the long distances faced by residents of the area might be the fourteen households of sixty-three immigrants founded near the village of Gümürdülü in 1897. Their settlement was three hours from Gümürdülü along a very bad road, leaving them helplessly disconnected from the main village, which itself was about 50 km northeast of the city of Adana. In their case, the situation was extreme enough to merit resettlement to a village that would be newly founded for them, called Yeniköy, approximately one hour from Cevdetiye.[94] But Cevdetiye, a village founded by Ahmed Cevdet and the Reform Division, was twice as far from Adana as was Gümürdülü. Three hours from Gümürdülü was a tough place to be, but one hour from Cevdetiye was only marginally more central.

Nonetheless, by the turn of the twentieth century, the area around the Ceyhan River was also the main area of growth, as cultivation in the western part of Cilicia was more saturated. Yet this development did not lead to the enrichment of most of the immigrants and pastoralists who were settled in the region over prior decades. In fact, the landholding pattern that emerged there was the same stratified structure as in the western districts around Adana and Tarsus.[95] This imbalance is striking in that it was contrary to the intent of Ottoman economic policy. As Gould has shown, the registration of property occurred in the 1880s, some fifteen years after the settlement campaign of the Reform Division. The landholding pattern that emerged on paper was that of relatively small plots of land registered to individuals.[96] Gould, referencing the ethnographic work of Wolfram Eberhard in the region, hypothesized that land may have been registered to individuals but that in practice, local notables kept the deeds and controlled access to the land.[97] However, it is also likely that many people simply abandoned or sold their land. In addition to a desire to avoid taxes or conscription, settlers, whether pastoralists or immigrants, simply did not want to live in the environments where they were settled. Within this climate, it was possible for land to change hands easily and at a low price, and mortality among early settlers was high. New migrants frequently fled their settlement areas rather than waiting to petition for resettlement, much to the consternation of the Ottoman government. One report indicated in 1908 that more than 800 recent immigrant households had sold their allotted farms and seed for cash.[98]

The tribes settled during the 1860s were largely shut out of the new economy. A British intelligence handbook from the World War I era appraised the situation of the Avşar community as follows: "[They] have become poorer as a result of their struggles with the Turks. They live almost entirely on the produce of their diminished flocks and herds and of their scanty tillage. They cultivate a little barley, but vegetables and fruit are unknown to them . . . They build their own huts, and construct their own rough ploughs, yokes, and thrashing-sledges, but little else. Money is practically unknown to them. Produce is exchanged for clothes, which are brought to them by travelling hucksters."[99] While settlement and administrative reform were aimed at curtailing the power of such figures, in practice the image of the oppressive village agha who controlled large amounts of land and forced local residents to obey his will became synonymous with life in the countryside. Yaşar Kemal's most famous novel, *İnce Memed*, revolves around the struggles that arose from this political economy in Çukurova.[100] Given the relatively egalitarian tendencies of nomadic pastoralist societies and the disruptive influence of settlement in this regard, this economic inequality should be seen as a consequence of the postsettlement world of Çukurova.

An additional factor in this process was the reversal of Ottoman policy toward the communities impacted by the Reform Division, from the 1880s onward. Lieutenant Bennet remarked that Governor Abidin Pasha was "well aware of their past history and can . . . be trusted not to repeat the former inhumanity."[101] The local government was content that so long as pastoralists were law-abiding, sedentarization that could not be achieved by force would be achieved through economic incentive. The unintended consequence was that among the unsedentarized communities, the reempowered notables who had official sanction could become nuisances to the general population. In 1892, the Council of State investigated repeated complaints from the inhabitants of villages surrounding İslahiye regarding the alleged abuses of the Delikanlı and Çelikanlı tribes. Their leaders had not only resisted the settlement orders but began to lord over those settled in the area. One of the people who testified against them was the *muhtar* of a village on the eastern flanks of the Amanus Mountains. He complained that the tribes were preventing other locals from cultivating around a warm spring near the village and forcing them to allow sheep and cattle to graze on the spot. However, because the tribal leaders were themselves part of the local government, the villagers' complaints had long fallen on deaf ears.[102] The Delikanlıs and Çelikanlıs were disrupting the activities of settled agriculturalists in the region. However, the Council of State did not move to initiate significant change. The report of the investigation concluded that "although the tribal *ağas* there generally and especially those in question do not possess morals good enough to befit the description of loyalty, obedience, and proper conduct of the country and civilization [*medeniyet*]," their detractors had clearly "exaggerated" in their complaints.[103] In other words, the conduct of the local tribal notables in İslahiye, while not sanctioned, could be tolerated for the sake of stability. Roughly three decades after the Reform Division's triumphant arrival in Çukurova, the frontier town that was founded by and named after that army (the Fırka-i İslahiye) had become a symbol of its shortcomings.

The Taurus Mountains waned in their importance as a site of pasture, but far from the centers of settlement activity and agricultural expansion, their rich timber resources were increasingly exploited for fuel wood, construction, and of course export from the emerging port of Mersin. From the 1860s onward, much of the exported timber was headed to Egypt and beyond.[104] The Mediterranean trade allowed Egypt to obtain what it had sought when it invaded Cilicia a few decades earlier. According to McNeill, the local Tahtacıs who lived in the Taurus Mountains could be blamed for much of the timber harvest that took place, though their ecological footprint had been relatively minimal historically.[105] Archival records suggest a less clear culprit for the amount of forest that was cut in the Cilician highlands during the late Ottoman period but indicate a general inability of the Ottoman government to keep up with the harvest. Of the almost 700 violations recorded in an Ottoman Ministry of Forests case book pertaining to the province of Adana during the last decades of the Ottoman period, people identified as Tahtacı were responsible for only a small portion and usually small-scale illegal cutting that came with a minor penalty. Large companies operating in the Cilicia region were also responsible for large-scale smuggling along the Mediterranean coasts. The records of the Ministry of Forests suggest that forest regulations were difficult to implement; in addition to many cases of corruption and smuggling, the case notebook for Adana reveals that a substantial number of violators were able to appeal and overturn their charges.[106] In addition to the destruction of forest and depletion of timber resources, the cutting in the mountains brought hydrological consequences, since deforested slopes were vulnerable to rapid erosion. Soil stripped from the land by runoff into the major rivers was thus carried into the lowlands as riverine sediment, leading to silting and the further formation of wetlands in the lowlands.[107]

The most fascinating paradox concerning late Ottoman Cilicia's unevenness in terms of state presence and settlement was the emergence of what was apparently an ascendant community of pastoralists. Around the turn of the twentieth century, references to a group called the Aydınlıs begin to appear frequently in the historical record. They represented a few thousand people.[108] Much like the Avşars and other tribes targeted by the Reform Division, their seasonal migration brought them through the Marash region into Çukurova on an annual basis. Their *yaylas* were supposedly located in the regions of İzmit, Konya, and Bursa.[109] By 1901, there were reports of clashes between police and Aydınlı sheep thieves, leading to discussion regarding their prospective settlement.[110] In 1905, a letter indicated that the Aydınlıs were not registered with the Census Bureau and that they hid themselves in the forests of the Taurus Mountains to avoid being counted. It stated that since their winter quarters were in Sis and Kozan, they should be registered there.[111] When in 1907 the local government had as yet failed to register them, a local official in Kozan and Adana governor Bahri Pasha proposed a settlement policy using military force similar to the ones implemented previously in Çukurova. The Aydınlıs would be allowed to migrate seasonally so long as they built houses in the Adana province and registered their population.[112] This was not implemented, however.[113] In fact, discussions of possible tribal settlement projects during the years leading up to World War I indicate that the Aydınlıs were one of many groups of pastoralists who wintered in various parts of Çukurova that remained outside the pale of settlement policy.[114] They would remain so into the 1950s (see chapter 5).

Feeding the Fever

In 1898, an official in Adana, published a rare, romanticized depiction of the city's summertime climate. He described pleasant strolls in the city's parks along with the wonderful sight of the Seyhan River, claiming that thanks to the gardens and orchards extending all around the city, Adana's *vahâmet-i hava*—its infamous malarial climate—was moderating year by year.[115] Such assertions appear sporadically in the historical record. In 1903, the British vice-consul noted that "the tendency of the climate is to improve under increased cultivation and the consequent disappearance of marshy ground," adding that malaria was still very much present.[116] Just as conceptions of environment had long linked foul air and disease, the changing impressions were always based in part on aesthetics. For example, British intelligence from World War I stated that the climate of Mersin had improved to the point that "the town is quite habitable for Europeans all the year round."[117] The same was not true for most of the region, and other sources continued to assert that malaria was rife in Mersin.[118] The perception that Mersin was habitable for Europeans was linked to the recent predominance of eucalyptus trees. One British traveler noted that "in portions of Mersina may be found a curious resemblance to an Australian town, due partly to the presence of Australian trees, but also to the British influence of those who constructed the railway in a new town of wide spaces and cheap land and hot climate. Approach the low-built railway station along its avenue of young eucalyptus trees—red-gums I think they are—and the illusion becomes almost perfect."[119]

The eucalyptus is just one example of how, during a period of new developments in biomedical knowledge, aesthetic considerations rooted in older perceptions of disease reshaped global environments. Native to Australia and Southeast Asia, the eucalyptus was spread throughout the world by nineteenth-century European empires. The late Ottoman state, where eucalyptus became known as the "malaria tree" (*sıtma ağacı*), played a small part in this phenomenon, promoting its cultivation due to its uses for swamp drainage.[120] To a degree, the fetishization of eucalyptus had an empirical basis; eucalyptus grew quickly and required a large amount of water, and so their presence could help desiccate marshy and moist soil. But eucalyptus was not an antidote to malaria, and its promotion across the world from Algeria to California had more to do with a cultural understanding that considered trees inherent features of ideal environmental conditions.[121] As malaria persisted in Çukurova, it gradually became unclear that the name of "malaria tree" referred to the role of the eucalyptus in combating malaria rather than signifying a correlation between the presence of the plant and the disease. It was one example of how malaria became even more deeply entrenched within the second nature produced during the late Ottoman period.

Water management emerged as a fixation for officials and engineers looking to reshape the environment and curtail malaria. Already in 1870, the *meclis* of Adana adopted a number of desiderata concerning water in the region. They included checking the periodic overflow of the Seyhan River using barrages and planting mulberry and willow trees along its course for the sake of the "cleanliness and quality of the air [*nezafet ve ciyadet-i hava*]." The Ceyhan River was to be used to irrigate the Yüreğir plain in the east. In addition, the Çakıt River, which flowed down the Taurus Mountains and into the Seyhan, would be channeled off to irrigate fields and gardens. These were just some of the measures mentioned in the report that involved changing the courses of rivers and streams for the overall improvement of the province.[122] Yet an 1888 report from the Ottoman Ministry of Public Works still expressed many of the same aspirations of over two decades earlier, indicating pessimistically that there simply was not enough money available for the ministry to carry out the work independently, thus leaving the issue to be someday settled by possibly contracting to a reliable company.[123] Where major environmental interventions did occur, they were often rolled into infrastructure projects, such as the creation of the port of Mersin.[124] In 1883, Ispirakis Efendi cleared the swamps along the roads between Misis, Adana, and Mersin in exchange for a steamboat concession on the Seyhan and Ceyhan.[125] The Adana-Mersin railroad project also aided in draining the marshy region between Adana, Tarsus, and Mersin. Drainage canals were often necessary to prepare the land for railroad construction.

Public works projects were usually not undertaken for the sole purpose of eliminating swamps of any considerable size. The Ottoman Ministry of Public Works did actively promote and fund drainage and reclamation projects—billed as cleaning (*tathir*)—during which improving the "quality of the air" was frequently invoked as a motivation.[126] But the port of İskenderun offers an example of a place where successive administrations worked but failed to adequately drain the swamps that surrounded the city. Ibrahim Pasha had first attempted to do so during the 1830s, but the effects did not last.[127] The first major Ottoman attempt on record was initiated in 1847. It stopped at the docks when the budget proved inadequate to extend work into the swamps surrounding the town.[128] Similar reports on the impact of Iskenderun's swamps on the health of the region were written in 1868 and 1872, with evidence of further measures taken to drain the swamps in 1879, 1893, and 1902, suggesting that the issue of drainage in İskenderun was a persistent crisis brought on by the utter infeasibility of sufficiently altering the environment so as to permanently rid the region of "bad air." Added to this were issues like corruption and embezzlement of money intended for use in these efforts by officials or individuals charged with overseeing the work.[129] The last Ottoman plans for drainage in the İskenderun region reflected the unevenness of any infrastructure projects, indicating the intent of draining areas near the town "sooner [*acilen*]" and the rural areas "later [*âcilen*]."¹³⁰

Some reasoned that the swamps in Çukurova resulted from a lack of definition in the course of the rivers and frequent flooding.¹³¹ The Seyhan River, which flowed through Adana, was of primary concern. Ziya Pasha's aforementioned barrage was aimed at mitigating the damage of the river's frequent floods in the city. But the archival record reflects flooding of the Seyhan and resultant damage to bridges, barrages, roads, and adjacent property roughly every three years over subsequent decades.¹³² All questions about the modification of rivers for flood control led to the larger question of irrigation. While rainfall in Cilicia was sufficient to grow both food and cotton, irrigation was seen as a means of greatly expanding output and diversifying the types of crops that could be grown. Most irrigation projects proposed by foreign engineers and developers were not approved, but they reflected the capitalist imaginaries regarding Çukurova's water resources. A blueprint of the Adana irrigation plan survives in the Ottoman archives, though it does not appear that any such plan was implemented. It consisted of a series of irrigation and desiccation canals radiating out from Adana along the Seyhan and Ceyhan Rivers that would channel water away from swamplands in the south and east of the plain in order to increase the capacity of irrigated land.¹³³ Many consuls and travelers remarked that Çukurova's water resources were wasted. One likened the plain to the Cambridgeshire fens, treeless but unlike them only partially cultivated. "If the population had a little more 'go' in them and were better governed, all might be a perfect garden—a second Lombardy." He conceded that it was not merely a lack of "go" but also concern about malaria that deterred locals from irrigation using the Seyhan and Ceyhan Rivers. "This is a lame excuse of the idle, for the fever cannot be worse than it is," he quipped.¹³⁴

Irrigation would increase economic output in the short term, but it was not necessarily a solution to malaria at all. And when the wrong changes were made, the problem could become worse. For example, the course of the Savrun River, a tributary of the Ceyhan flowing near Kars-ı Zülkadriye, was altered in 1900 to facilitate the construction of a large irrigation canal. This brought stagnant water into new areas near the towns of Sis and Kars, resulting in complaints of health issues from the local inhabitants.¹³⁵ Within seven years, the Ministry of the Interior ordered that the course of the Savrun River must be returned to its original state due to these complications.[136]

The idea that agricultural development and swamp drainage would eliminate malaria was rooted in an older, miasmatic understanding of disease as well as an emergent body of knowledge about the *Anopheles* mosquito's role in malaria transmission during the first decade of the twentieth century. Yet the reordering of nature toward commercial agriculture was in many ways supporting the spread of malaria infections. Local understanding of malaria had emphasized the role of "bad air," but it was also seasonal. The new temporality of state-driven progress clashed with the transhumant temporalities of prior centuries in which people moved seasonally between the mountains and the lowlands. As a quotidian example, in 1901 teachers in the Adana region requested that the school year be shortened so that families could leave for the *yayla* and rural orchards by the end of May. They complained not only of annual discomfort but also of the deaths of young children due to the severity of the fevers and the summer heat. Their pleas ended in a compromise.[137] Similarly, in 1890, requests from the local governing councils of Sis and Kars-ı Zülkadriye to move their operations to the *yayla* in order to escape the effects of the hot weather and malaria—something they probably did regularly—were denied.[138]

A more radical disruption of seasonal movements came with the commercial rhythms of cultivation. The period of May through October was the peak malaria season in Cilicia.[139] These were the months when it was warm enough for the parasites and their vectors to reproduce. Heading for higher elevations had long been an easy solution to the perceived insalubrious nature of the lowlands. Such a rhythm was completely compatible with nomadic pastoralism. But the type of agriculture that emerged in Cilicia discouraged such migration. Cotton was planted at the beginning of spring, wheat and barley were harvested in May and June, and the cotton and sesame were harvested in August and September. These were all normally peak times for malaria infection. Therefore, it was impossible for the commercial economy of Cilicia to function without those involved being exposed to disease risk.

Those most vulnerable were naturally agricultural laborers. Many of the farms were founded on land that had recently been cleared of swamps, and frequent flooding and high temperatures in Çukurova made suitable breeding ground for mosquitos. Although the meals the laborers received throughout the week were an important component of their compensation, Dr. Şerafeddin Pasha (later Mağmumi) considered the diet of the workers to be the foundation of a general state of poor health. He found it was common for workers to be served moldy bread or "rock-hard" pilavs cooked in foul-smelling oils.[140] Underfed and overworked, the laborers contracted malaria not only while in the fields but also in the places where they lodged in Adana. The Karşıyaka neighborhood on the flood-prone eastern bank of the Seyhan River was a common place to stay, as was the recently cleared area by the train station. While some slept in local inns, many workers were reported to sleep in the open-air encampments.[141] An Ottoman report from 1909 described the state of agricultural workers in provinces like Adana as "miserable in every aspect [*ez her cihet perişan*]."[142]

"Mortality amongst the labourers is high," E. J. Davis remarked following his travels in Cilicia during the 1870s. "These poor fellows come down from a pure mountain air to the deadly heat of the Cilician plain; they are exposed all day to the burning sun . . . in a climate always more or less malarious." Workers would return from the fields at the end of the week only to die suddenly of malaria or another disease. As Davis wrote: "a man feels a little ill, headache and shivering come on, he is obliged to retire, and in an hour or two he's dead."[143] Şerafeddin Pasha described seasonal labor as a major public health issue. Fever, sunstroke, and dysentery were the most common afflictions facing these workers, and in addition to being vectors for epidemic diseases such as cholera, migrant workers in Adana supposedly contributed to the province having unusually high rates of syphilis.[144] "They depart mostly from cold regions, walk for weeks, and come to a warm and humid climate like Çukurova," he wrote. "And in exchange for 30–40 pennies, they work under that burning sun and spend their nights in the open. Because of such unhealthy foods [that they eat], most of them just up and die."[145] Samuel Jamentz, an Ottoman-Armenian doctor who grew up in the mountain town of Hadjin, believed that the large number of people migrating back and forth between Çukurova contributed to the importation of malaria into Hadjin's population. He said that Hadjin was "a region endowed with such incomparable climate, mountains, and water," but that workers would return with malaria and other diseases that they contracted in the insalubrious swamps of Çukurova.[146]

Neither employer nor worker was blind to the bodily toll; they may have simply taken it for granted that agriculture and malaria went hand in hand. In his university lectures, Ottoman doctor Feyzullah Pasha commented on the unique danger that malaria posed to laborers using a familiar proverb: "He who plays with the soil digs his own grave [*toprakla oynayan mezarını kazar*]."[147] The common outcomes of laboring on the cotton plantations of the Adana region made it even more maligned for its unkind climate. In the folk songs of Anatolia, the space of *gurbet,* or "exile," which often meant going to somewhere like Adana for work, became one not just of longing but also of sickness. A common formulation heaped curses onto a place such as Adana or merely onto *gurbet* itself, followed by the phrase "he who comes healthy leaves sick [*sağ gelen hasta gider*]," sometimes followed by a refrain such as "*yaylalar, yaylalar.*"[148] A popular version of the song is associated with the Erzincan region of northeast Anatolia. A newspaper article from Adana some decades later attested to the legacy of this experience by invoking that familiar lyric: "Down with Çukurova! He who comes healthy leaves sick [*yıkılasın Çukurova sağ gelen hasta gider*]."[149]

The subject of rice cultivation further demonstrates that while encouraging agriculture was in theory to aid in the elimination of malaria, it often had the opposite effect. Rice had been grown in Upper Çukurova near Sis and Marash from perhaps the beginning of the Ottoman period.[150] During the late Ottoman period, this region emerged as an expanding center of rice cultivation. However, Ottoman health officials became aware that due to the amount of standing water it entailed, rice paddies created cozy havens for mosquitos. The regulation of rice cultivation became the subject of debate among Ottoman technocrats and within the Parliament. The debates were so vociferous in part because landlords figured prominently among legislators. The resistance to regulating rice cultivation was led by a representative of Diyarbekir named Feyzi Bey, a wealthy landowner whose family name of Pirinççizâde can be translated as "Rice-Farmer."[151] Another such figure in the Parliament was the aforementioned Kadızâde Hacı Hasan Fehmi of Marash. In 1909, the Ministry of Interior ruled that the rice paddies (*çeltik*) in his district must be maintained at least 3 km from the city in order to protect public health and ward off malaria.¹⁵² Yet these measures provoked a response from cultivators, who complained that the restrictions were unnecessary and unfair.¹⁵³ What further complicated the picture was that *mevat* land was exempted from the regulations, meaning that landowners could use a rule intended to contribute to the improvement of health conditions in the countryside in order to create rice paddies that almost certainly would do the opposite.¹⁵⁴

Malaria and Medicine

Medicine emerged as one possible solution to the plight of agricultural workers and the broader population. During the late Ottoman period, doctors became increasingly able to treat malaria infections using quinine-based medicines. Quinine could be used in two ways: either as prophylactic throughout peak seasons of malaria infection or to reduce the fevers and save the life of someone already suffering from malaria. In other words, quinine had both preventative and curative applications.¹⁵⁵ As early as the 1720s, Ottoman doctors had written about and experimented with quinine, which is derived from a bark native to the Andes region.¹⁵⁶ Yet it was the rise of mass-produced quinine during the mid-nineteenth century and the identification of the blood-borne parasite that causes malaria during the 1880s that further stimulated the application of quinine as a solution to malaria.¹⁵⁷ The Ottoman government first began experimenting with the prophylactic use of quinine within the ranks of the military and the navy, and results were quite impressive. In fact, malaria infections were virtually eliminated among navy personnel at the beginning of the twentieth century. Widespread government distribution of quinine medicines began in 1902, and according to government figures, by 1908 malaria mortality was reduced by more than half, though the government still recorded thousands of malaria deaths each year.¹⁵⁸

The use of quinine, however, did present obstacles. While the emergence of a pharmaceutical industry centered on the production of quinine medicines had greatly reduced prices by the 1890s, all quinine sulfate manufacturers were in Europe or the United States.¹⁵⁹ This made the Ottoman Empire dependent on imports to meet its high quinine demands, and serious issues of regulation arose. The abundance of inferior or fraudulent medicines led to an 1889 decision to inspect and evaluate all quinine imports on the basis of international standards.[160] Following this decision, there were many cases of inferior medicines imported from France and Germany being refused, and in one case, the Ottoman government was compelled by British diplomats to accept what was claimed to be a shipment of bad quinine.[161] Feyzullah Pasha noted that the quinine available in Ottoman markets was often diluted to the point of inefficacy.[162] Moreover, imported quinine sulfate remained expensive for poorer Ottoman subjects, and because supply flowed first through urban centers, Ottoman villagers were at the end of the supply chain though arguably most in need of medicine.[163]

Nonetheless, the permanent medical establishment in Cilicia helped mitigate the impact of diseases like malaria with a multipronged approach to public health. The imperial government established a network of hospitals and clinics that expanded from the late nineteenth century onward alongside charitable private hospitals mainly run by missionaries, and in addition, the government employed different types of doctors to administer treatment in the provinces.[164] The most important medical initiatives established in Cilicia during the late nineteenth century were arguably the charitable institutions called *gureba* hospitals. The category of *gureba* is semantically rich; it can be taken to simply refer to poor people, appearing as a synonym of *fukara* (the poor). But in fact, *gureba* (the plural of *garib*) connoted "estranged" people, related to the concept of *gurbetçi*, that is, people working and residing away from home, in *gurbet*, who would thus become reliant on the state for medical care.[165] In Cilicia, the main purpose of the *gureba* hospitals was to treat the tens of thousands of seasonal workers who came to the region every year. They were not therefore properly hospitals for the poor as such, since they catered to able-bodied wage-earners, but rather institutions meant to offset the public health impacts of agricultural labor in Çukurova among people without families to care for them.

Gureba hospitals were in operation already by the 1870s, although during the empire's financial woes, it appears that the *gureba* hospital in Adana, funded by the municipal taxes, was struggling to function.[166] The documentation regarding the opening of the hospitals indicates that malaria was the main health issue they dealt with. It refers to workers suffering from the bad air or "climatic effects [*tesirât-ı havâiye*]" during the warm season. The scene in the cities around the time of the harvest must have been unpleasant to observe, as documents describe people suffering of sickness and dying, some on the streets, in poverty and destitution. A letter signed in 1880 by over fifty local officials and other residents, including the Armenian and Greek metropolitans, called for the establishment of a new *gureba* hospital in an "appropriate and airy [*havâdâr*]" part of Adana primarily to treat agricultural workers. "Every year fifteen to twenty thousand *gureba* come to Adana for planting," the letter stated. "Since during the summer season some diseases are occurring due to climatic effects in connection with Adana being a tropical region [*mevâki-i hârreden*], the need here for a hospital is greater than anywhere else." The letter explained that even though there was a hospital in Adana, it was not large or organized enough to deal with the seasonal demand: "Some years most of the *gureba* patients cannot be admitted to the hospital and remain without treatment and therefore they are dying in a miserable state." The proposed new *gureba* hospital was to admit both men and women (*zükûr ve inâs*) in keeping with the demographic makeup of the workers, and of course would be nonconfessional. An economic argument was used to justify the call to the government for this charitable act. Since *çiftlik* owners were obliged to bring workers from outside the province, preserving the health of these *gureba* was fundamental to their operations.[167]

The funding of the *gureba* hospitals reflected the types of institutional relationships that typified commercial production in Cilicia as a whole. While the Ottoman imperial government was expected to provide resources and doctors, the budget was in theory drawn from the municipal taxes. The plans for the Tarsus *gureba* hospital, which was built adjacent to the military barracks, also reveal that funds for the hospital came from both the local churches as well as the Islamic charitable endowments (*evkâf*).[168] As such, the *gureba* hospital was the product of collaboration between imperial and local governments and different Muslim and Christian religious institutions. While such institutions had long engaged in charity, the government-brokered partnership represented a fairly novel development.[169]

In addition to the *gureba* hospitals in the cities, the Ottoman government established clinics in regions with high traffic of migrant workers, such as the İslahiye region. One hospital was located in the town of Bahçe. There, the purpose of the hospital was monitoring and treating syphilis.[170] The

Ottoman government employed medical professionals who not only staffed the hospitals but could also expand the reach of the public health apparatus into the countryside. Adana had a few country doctors (*memleket tabibi*) who stayed within the province.[171] These doctors were responsible for a wide range of medical activities, such as delivering emergency relief and medicine, performing medical examinations, monitoring epidemics, and conducting smallpox vaccinations to reduce infant mortality. In addition, the empire employed traveling doctors (*seyyar tabib*) who circulated in an even wider range. Through these doctors, medical services were expanded into the countryside beyond the better serviced towns and cities.[172] During the earliest stages of quinine use, there were orders for emergency treatment of vulnerable communities, such as newly arrived *muhacirs* by dispatching some quinine along with a traveling doctor.[173] But Şerafeddin Pasha noted the desperate health situation of the Adana region and the utter lack of medical services outside of the city.[174] Moreover, the Ottoman government sometimes exhorted doctors not to abandon the villages they were sent to during epidemics. Pharmacists fearing exposure to infected individuals would also sometimes close their shops during major outbreaks.[175] Just like economy and infrastructure, the disease landscape of late Ottoman Cilicia became more uneven due to experiences of disease differentiated by class and uneven coverage of existing medical institutions.

Plain of Contention

In his memoirs, Turkish politician and Adana native Damar Arıkoğlu depicted the late Ottoman Adana of his youth as a harmonious place: "Turks used to call older Armenian males 'uncle,' and they would call the ones who called them uncle 'my nephew.' Turks would also call older Armenian women '*cici* or *cice*,'" a term of endearment for an adoptive mother. He recalled how "in the summer months, Turks would give their house keys to a poor Armenian family when leaving for the summer home in the Taurus Mountains. That family would both spend the summer here and watch over the house. They would also receive an amount of money in exchange. The homeowner returning from the summer home would find all of his belongings in perfect condition in their proper places."[176] Relations between Turks and Armenians had once bordered on kinship in Arıkoğlu's memory. And the Armenian author Hagop Terzian offered a similar portrayal. "The word *gavur* (infidel) had almost no presence in Adana," he asserted. "Often times it would be impossible to tell Armenian and Turkish youth apart when seeing them going around together. They were not differentiated by face, nor garb, nor manner; they were distinguished by name alone."[177] The intercommunal amity of the late Ottoman period appeared to peak with the 1908 Constitutional Revolution, which manifested as an outpouring of enthusiasm for "Ottoman brotherhood."[178] Along the roads between Adana, Tarsus, and Mersin, a procession of vociferous supporters of the revolution raised money to fund the new government. "Long live the Armenians!" shouted the Turkish participants and onlookers, and their Armenian counterparts shouted back "Long live the Turks!" The entire group cheered in unison: "Long live the Ottomans!"[179]

Arıkoğlu and Terzian used these descriptions of intercommunal harmony as preface to irreconcilable narratives of betrayal.[180] During April 1909, in the midst of a counterrevolution by supporters of Abdülhamid II in the imperial center, Cilicia was rocked by violence beginning in the city of Adana and subsequently in most areas of Armenian settlement in the region. Estimates of the death toll ranged as high as 20,000–30,000. Most of those killed were Armenian. In the city of Adana, the violence played out in the neighborhoods and caused havoc in many parts of the city. In the rural hinterland, the violence resembled the anti-Armenian pogroms of Eastern Anatolia during the 1890s. Certain settlements, such as Çokmerzimen, launched successful defenses.[181] In many towns, entire neighborhoods were left uninhabitable. Thousands of widows and orphans were left behind, and roughly one-third of those orphans would suffer from malaria and other ailments in the coming months.[182] The multitude of burned and mutilated bodies of humans and animals throughout the province became a public health concern for the government.[183] After the Ottoman military under the command of Cemal Pasha restored order to the province, loyalists of the deposed Hamidian regime bore the blame.[184] Contemporary and subsequent observers developed various narratives of the violence, and the episode produced a wealth of documentation from a variety of sources that also contained enough bias to muddle the question of culpability and offered little clarity regarding deeper reasons for the violence.

Many studies have attempted to analyze the violence in Adana during the spring of 1909, but rarely in a wider context.[185] It is dangerous to fixate too much on the particularities of the Adana region and its historical experience when attempting to understand these massacres. After all, such episodes occurred throughout nineteenth-century empires, and instances of localized violence usually occurred within the context of larger political changes. However, the Adana massacres are relevant for understanding the broader socioeconomic transformation of the late Ottoman Empire. In so many ways, they reflected the dynamics of contention that defined the late Ottoman frontier in Cilicia.

The juxtaposition of a previously harmonious coexistence with its destruction by some sort of political rupture was common in memories of communal conflicts that occurred during the late Ottoman period. Yet the dynamics of a particular political moment constituted just one facet of a relative state of "intercommunality" between different communities living side by side. As Nicholas Doumanis has shown in his study of memory among the communities of former Anatolian Greeks, the everyday acts of living together, or coexistence as "intercommunality in practice," were fundamental to conceptions of the other in the late Ottoman context.[186] In this view, it was not so much a commitment to a Pan-Ottoman or regional identity nor abstract ideals like tolerance and coexistence that allowed distinct communities of Muslims and Christians to live side by side for generations; rather, it was the sharing of quotidian bonds and semi-intimate spaces that often bound provincial society together.

The emergent urban spaces of Cilicia during the nineteenth century were certainly sites of intercommunality, as people from all walks of life moved to growing cities like Adana and Mersin. But from the 1860s onward, rural communities were being drawn apart in certain ways. Migration that began with the post–Crimean War influx of Nogays, Circassians, and Chechens continued to bring new people to the countryside who lived in their own settlements. From a strictly linguistic perspective, intercommunality among these groups was difficult. The Turkish, Armenian, and Greek inhabitants of Cilicia's cities and most of the villages spoke Turkish. Most immigrants did not speak Turkic languages; they spoke languages of the North Caucasus that were generally unknown in Anatolia or languages of the Balkans like Greek, Albanian, and various Slavic dialects.[187] Many of the thousands of Muslim refugees from Crete who settled in Adana during the early part of the twentieth century spoke only Greek, meaning that their only colingualists might be any Greek merchants who moved to Mersin.[188] While a common identification as Muslim under Ottoman population categories allowed such people to blend in numerically, an American traveler noted that the Chechens settled near Anavarza still spoke a distinct language *in the 1950s*, meaning that for most of the Ottoman period, many *muhacir* groups constituted distinct linguistic communities in their local contexts.[189]

The district of Ayas in the lower Ceyhan region provides a window onto the staggeringly disparate and recent origins of villagers in Çukurova. The following data were gathered in 1921 by the French administration, but it is more or less accurate for the period before World War I.[190] Of forty-two villages, more than one-quarter were inhabited mainly by the Bozdoğan Türkmens, settled from the 1860s onward, and about another quarter were made up of Muslims from the Balkans. Alongside these two groups were a few Nusayri Arab villages, a Tatar village, a village of Cretan Muslims, a Kizilbash (Alevi) village, the lone Armenian village of Nacarlı, and a "Sudanese Arab" village of people who may have arrived as early as the Egyptian occupation in the 1830s.[191] Villages counted as "Turkish" or partly Turkish made up just under 20 percent. Other elements of the population, such as Nogays, Circassians, and Kurds, were also present but their numers were too small in that district to form a majority in any village. This example is not meant to suggest any sort of hostility between these various groups or to reify these categories, as the French administration in Cilicia was eager to emphasize communal divisions. However, it is evidence that the communities in question had not long cohabitated the same region, since most of the villages were founded by groups that had only settled in Çukurova within a half-century or less.

Even during the Tanzimat era, when settlement policy was aimed at preventing local conflicts, new settlements were contentious. For example, the decision to settle *muhacirs* near a small Armenian village called Acemli initially appeared innocuous but ended in violence. The Armenians had left Acemli for the highlands to escape a small-time *derebey* named Kel Kişoğlu. Around the time that *muhacirs* from the Balkans were settled in the supposedly abandoned village in 1878, Kel Kişoğlu was killed. When the Armenians heard the news and returned to the village, only to find it reoccupied, they complained to the local *kaymakam*, who offered monetary compensation if they would relocate. The Armenians of Acemli refused, and Lieutenant Bennet intervened on their behalf, using his standing as representative of the British government to press the local administration. The *muhacirs* resisted on the grounds that in two years of settlement, more than forty of them had already died, and they could not bear to undergo another exile from a place where they had already endured so much hardship. It was a morbid claim to usufruct rights. Ultimately, the original Armenian occupants won out, and the immigrants were forced to relocate. During their departure, they destroyed the church and many of the houses in the village, so that the original Armenian inhabitants returned to rubble.[192]

The Hamidian turn after the Russo-Ottoman War of 1877–78 brought further shifts in communal relations. Under Sultan Abdülhamid II, Armenian revolutionary organizations with links to the Russian Caucasus and global networks of political radicals sought support in the areas of Armenian majority in the Ottoman Empire.[193] Like the Committee of Union and Progress, which initially formed out of graduates of the Ottoman military and medical schools, the Armenian parties were suppressed by the Hamidian government. During the same period, the Ottoman government armed the so-called Hamidiye cavalry, irregular armies drawn from the predominantly Kurdish populations of Eastern Anatolia. They were designed to help the Ottoman government protect its borderlands with the Russian Empire, but the Hamidian government's anxieties turned toward the Armenian population itself.[194] Both the Dashnaks and Hunchaks, groups founded in Tbilisi and Geneva respectively, began recruiting and operating in Anatolia, seeking to arm village populations against the state. Like these parties, the Hamidiye cavalry benefited from the growing ubiquity of cheaply manufactured rifles during the period.[195]

The first major confrontation with Armenian revolutionaries took place in the province of Bitlis with the Sasun resistance in 1894.[196] The extent to which such uprisings were merely aided or instigated by the revolutionary parties is questionable. Likewise, the singular role of the Hamidiye cavalry in the massacres of Armenians that usually accompanied or followed such events is also debated.¹⁹⁷ However, the broad strokes of the Hamidian turn are clear. Anti-Armenian violence broke out during the mid-1890s in most of the provinces of Eastern Anatolia: Bitlis, Diyarbekir, Erzurum, Mamuretülaziz, Sivas, Trabzon, and Van. The episodes varied from small incidents to mass slaughters, and the Hamidiye cavalry played a role in many of the massacres. In addition to many thousands of Armenians killed during those years, families were dispossessed, women were abducted, and mass conversions to Islam took place in the provinces affected.¹⁹⁸ The massacres not only served as a primary motivation for Ottoman Armenians to migrate to the Americas and elsewhere but also discouraged their return.¹⁹⁹

In 1895, this violence touched the Cilicia region. Armenian communities in the Taurus Mountains at Zeytun and the closely linked village of Çokmerzimen by the coast also staged a resistance, which was accompanied by massacres of Armenians in Marash and the countryside. About this period, Toksöz remarked that "all hell broke loose" between the Armenians and tribes settling in the vicinity.²⁰⁰ That communal relations became so contentious in the Taurus Mountains and near Marash, places where many pastoralists had been forcibly settled and gradually sedentarizing since the Reform Division, suggested that, as Astourian notes, unhappy settlement terms made tribal communities possible hotbeds of animosity due to conflict over land.²⁰¹

Adana remained mostly shielded from the violence of the 1890s, despite stirrings in Çukurova.²⁰² In 1896, an encoded telegram from the governor of Adana to the Ministry of Interior claimed that Adana would be at risk of invasion by Armenian rebels from the mountains that summer. The reason given was that much of the region's Muslim population, including a number of "highly loyal" tribes, would be away at the *yayla*, leaving the area mostly vacated.²⁰³ The implication of this warning was a potentially self-fulfilling prophecy of sectarian bloodshed. In October 1896, the Ministry of Interior received a telegram from the *mutasarrıf* of Cebel-i Bereket warning that a man from Adana named Emin Bey was visiting the heads of tribes in the İslahiye region to foment an attack on local Christians.²⁰⁴ İslahiye had remained one of the parts of the countryside where the political mission of undermining the strength of the local tribal notables during the Reform Division never quite succeeded. These episodes illustrate how local actors perceived the communal violence of the 1890s to be related to prior settlement policies and the reversal of the relationship between the Ottoman state and tribal communities in contested regions.

The shift was not just political but also related to how settlement changed the dynamics of intercommunality. Sedentarization removed important elements of symbiosis between pastoralist communities and the settled village populations of the Cilicia region. In Eberhard's study of the impact of settlement, he suggested that in the pre-Tanzimat social order of Cilicia, pastoralists and villagers achieved a high degree of harmony through their mutually reinforcing economic activities. It was beneficial to allow animals of pastoralists to feed on leftover plant matter at the harvest, not only for the purpose of clean-up but also as a free source of fertilizer. Pastoralists who did not farm were in turn reliant on villagers to sell them grain and other agricultural products, as well as material goods.[205] The movement of pastoralists helped conduct trade between regions with relatively difficult conditions of transport, and pastoralists always had extra meat and milk to sell at periods of high demand, such as religious feasts. With their settlement, such communities had a reduced capacity to share in this equation.

Another dimension of the Hamidian turn that increased the potential for conflict in the countryside was the deliberate placement of new settlements in the vicinity of Armenian centers of population. An 1892 order from the Ministry of Interior indicated that because of Adana's large non-Muslim population, Muslim migrants from the Balkans should be settled on vacant lands near Christian villages to "increase the Muslim element there [*unsur-u islamın oralarda teksiri*]."[206] The Hamidian regime enlisted migrants in a project of demographic warfare. For example, in 1901, immigrants were controversially settled near the village of Nacarlı, the lone center of Armenian population in the coastal district near Ayas.[207] Such policy seemed to be explicitly aimed at pitting Muslims and Christians against each other.

During that same period, Abdülhamid II sought to leave a personal imprint on the region of Çukurova, which had been central to the settlement policies of the Tanzimat period. If Osmaniye and İslahiye were towns named to symbolize the reassertion of Ottoman control during the era of reform, Hamidiye, the new name for Yarsuvat (modern-day Ceyhan), conveyed the symbolic importance of the region to the sultan. The creation of the Çukurova Imperial Farm in this area was integral to the symbolism. Occupying some 60,000 hectares of land between the ruins of Anazarbus in the north and the outlet of the Ceyhan River in the south, the farm never became a major agricultural endeavor. Its primary purpose of raising horses for the military fit with the specialization of the Circassian migrants settled around and within its boundaries. But sources reveal that the farms used only a small part of the area within those boundaries, and in some cases came into conflict with local landowners who already had land deeds for properties in the area. In contrast with most of the properties belonging to the sultan, the Çukurova Imperial Farm generated no tangible revenue.[208]

The lands did occupy a strategic position, however, as their northern edge abutted the farthest extent of agricultural settlement in the vicinity of Sis, at a location called Tılan Farm.[209] Sis remained the center of the communal universe for Cilician Armenians, and the catholicos of Sis (from 1902 to the 1930s, Sahak II Khabayan) was arguably the most important Armenian political figure in the region. The town was perched on the side of a sharp hill where there was a medieval fortress. Much of the surrounding area consisted of low-lying and marshy land. During the first decade of the twentieth century, Circassian immigrants were given some of this swamp land for settlement in this area, located very close to the town of Sis at the Tılan Farm. The farm encompassed some 10,000 *dönüms* of agricultural land owned and used by the monastery of Sis, but half of the land was not under cultivation at the time.

As the dispute that followed in 1907 laid bare, this new settlement was an attempt to curtail the demographic ascendance of Armenians in the Kozan district. The Armenians of Sis knew it was a form of encroachment. The settlers became the natural claimants to ownership of this property by virtue of their habitation and cultivation, but the Armenian authorities sought to defend their ownership. In fact, they claimed that the monastery had been given the properties from the pious endowments of the Ramazanoğlus, the dynasty that governed the region before the Ottoman conquest.[210] The dispute over the Tılan Farm escalated into a violent confrontation that resulted in the killing of a few of the recently settled immigrants.[211] The monastery asserted its rightful ownership over the land and demanded that the settlers be removed. The result was a compromise. So long as Armenians were not brought from another province to settle there, the land could remain under the ownership of the Sis monastery and the immigrants would settle elsewhere.[212] Then, when Bishop Mushegh Seropian toured the Adana province in the spring of 1909 with plans to open a new Armenian agricultural school at the Tılan Farm, the new government affirmed that, rather than allowing "Armenians brought from outside to settle" there, the members of Muslim tribes in the region should be given the land.[213] The territorial fight over the Tılan Farm was a simmering proxy conflict between the Ottoman government and Cilicia's Armenians.

Not all conflicts that arose from the settlement in Cilicia broke down along these confessional lines. In fact, most land disputes in the archival record during the years before the 1909 massacres, whether over fields or *yaylas*, were between new migrants and local Muslim communities.[214] Contention over land was a consistent feature of the frontier's economic transformation. However, economic disputes could become confessionalized. The agricultural business of the big city often appeared distant from such conflicts, but it too played a role in the disruption of intercommunal life. Bağdadizâde Abdülkadir Efendi, a former tax-farmer and wealthy landowner who cultivated sugar beets, failing in his efforts to establish his own sugar factory, offers an example of a powerful figure who stoked anti-Armenian sentiment for his own gain and used the violence of 1909 to pursue personal vendettas.[215]

Seasonal movements, too, contributed to the violence in 1909. One central and often ignored aspect of the infamous Adana massacres was the extent to which the violence involved people who were not from Adana. In Krikor Koudoulian's account of the massacres in the Amanus Mountain town of Bahçe, which was itself very far from the provincial center of Adana, armed bands encouraged by the local *mufti* attacked the Armenian inhabitants of the town and surrounding villages, setting fire to buildings and killing those they could capture. Witnesses reported that the large, organized groups of men attacking the towns and villages had come not from Adana in the west, where the massacres started, but rather from Diyarbekir, Mamuretülaziz, Aintab, Marash, and Malatya, more than 10,000 men according to one estimate.[216] Koudoulian referred to these men as the Hamidiye, alluding to the Hamidiye cavalry, which had only been superficially reformed after the 1908 revolution.[217] Whether or not Hamidiye elements played a dominant role in the massacres, many of the participants hailed from other eastern provinces where communal relations had been characterized by repeated outbursts of violence in which the Hamidiye had been active.

In fact, the Adana massacres happened in the spring as workers from all over Anatolia and Northern Syria were flooding in to participate in what promised to be one of the most productive agricultural years in the region's history. The presence of tens of thousands of seasonal workers in the region augmented the scale of the carnage, as a mob assembled to carry out assaults on the inns where Armenian laborers lodged.[218] More than 10,000 Armenian workers were living near the train station in tents.[219] And of the few hundred Muslims who were killed, most were also workers.[220] In a telegram following the massacres, the new governor, Mustafa Zihni Pasha, would explain that "the region is full of outsiders [*yabancı*]. Especially at crop times every year 50–60,000 workers come here. And this year a lot of workers came. Both [Armenians and Muslims] are obsessed with increasing their number of casualties by exploiting the large number of workers and strangers whose names and circumstances are unknown."[221] In one case, more than 1,000 Assyrian workers who had traveled roughly 600 km to Adana from near Midyat were left stranded without work and unable to return to their villages.[222]

During the Hamidian period, unchecked mobility rose as a security concern in the empire. In order to monitor movement between provinces, the Ottoman government mandated that travelers carry a note of transit, or *mürur tezkeresi*, for purposes such as family visits, work, medical treatment, or change of air.[223] Yet the seasonal movements of workers, which were relatively unsupervised, allowed individuals to travel the empire with relative anonymity.[224] Officials became concerned about the security issues caused by migrant workers along their way and in Adana. Reports from 1894 mention numbers of migrants between 70,000 and 100,000 arriving every year in Adana, Kozan, and Cebel-i Bereket. To supervise these movements, the government created a mobile (*seyyar*) gendarmerie of about fifty soldiers to travel with the worker caravans.[225] Mersin and other such ports also became hubs of migration and human smuggling networks for Ottoman subjects headed for the Americas and elsewhere and possibly returning undetected.[226]

Workers cannot be seen as predisposed toward violent acts any more than another segment of society, but when they did become involved in crimes, they were harder to track.[227] It is also worth considering the extent to which contention played a major role in the lives of migrant workers. The nature of labor relations meant that workers were almost constantly fighting—not about religion and ethnicity, but rather about money. Although they arrived in Adana with promises of expected wage ranges, their pay was usually negotiated on a weekly basis. The value of their labor was determined by the open market, the *ırgat pazarı*, where employers and workers convened weekly in the center of Adana to make arrangements. Arguing with employers, middlemen, and other workers was a general feature of life as a migrant worker in Adana. Migrant workers were also relevant for the discussion of intercommunality because of their uniquely fragmentary social formation. They came from a wide variety of towns and villages, from different corners of the empire, and aside from their companions from the same region, many had few connections in Adana. Whatever their familial or communal identities were back home, when they came to Adana, they were Kurds from Bitlis, Armenians from Harput, and Nusayris from Antakya. It is likely that Muslim and Christian workers saw each other's respective groups as economic competitors at times when work opportunities and wages dipped.

The Adana massacres were not, as was seen by some from the outside, the expression of primordial enmities erupting from within the region's social fabric. They occurred in a socioeconomic world that within a few generations had been completely transformed by commercial agriculture.[228] Cotton did not cause violence, but, as in the "oil complex" of Arbella Bet-Shlimon's study of economic change and ethnicity in Kirkuk, cotton was at the center of an array of social, political, and cultural transformations.[229] The massacres represented yet another dimension of the late Ottoman frontier. These dynamics were usually lost on Western observers who left the best known accounts of the massacres. And they may have been lost on figures like Arshaguhi Teotig, who left Istanbul for Adana to help with relief efforts in fall of 1909. It is clear from her account that the countryside of the region was an unfamiliar and frightening place, and like most who left behind accounts of the massacres and their aftermath, the confessional lens provided a framework for understanding the disparate reasons why individuals chose to participate in the mayhem. Teotig did not witness the massacres, but like many writers of the time, what she heard about them found its way into her narrative, reframed by her vantage point.

Teotig did, however, witness carnage of another variety. Heavy rains brought a severe flood while she was in Adana during November 1909. The Seyhan and Ceyhan rivers rose so high that they met in the plain. The entire city was underwater: the train station, the factories, and even the houses that had been recently rebuilt. In Teotig's account, the flood appeared as divine retribution for the violence that had occurred. Grain reserves were ruined. Many families lost all their property. The poor agricultural workers who lived in some of the lowest lying neighborhoods were most severely impacted. Teotig described what she saw with a measure of schadenfreude: a woman lamenting the loss of dozens of sheep and cows; a man mourning the loss of his entire fortune, left with nothing but the hoe in his hand; soldiers pulling bodies from the overflowed waters that looked like a "sewer." The Seyhan River had washed away the blood that had been spilled some months prior, cleaning up what the people could not.[230] In the wake of the violence and floods, Ziya Pasha's Tanzimat vision of a liberal and modern Adana seemed to be very much dead in the water.

Just as the Seyhan flood did not necessarily have anything to do with the massacres that had occurred during the prior spring, some might suppose that the environmental history of the Ottoman frontier is of comparatively little concern for understanding the well-trodden path of politics in the late Ottoman Empire. Enmities like those expressed in the Adana massacres were certainly not rooted in environmental causes. But the same ecological entanglements that shaped issues like malaria, water, or cotton cultivation in the Ottoman countryside also impacted such events in a variety of ways. All were connected to Ottoman land and settlement policy as well as to the emergent commercial economy, and the ways in which they reordered life in Cilicia. Just as malaria was an old disease that took on a new form under the ecological conditions of commercial agriculture, so too were communal boundaries manifestations of old cleavages that attained new relevance and severity in the transformed space of post-Tanzimat Cilicia.

After the massacres of 1909, the vision of Cilicia as a Second Egypt remained a source of optimism for many. The agricultural economy rebounded within a year, and the cotton harvests of the early 1910s were the most robust in the region's history.[231] One British traveler said that the atmosphere in Adana compared favorably with other Ottoman cities, calling it "a throbbing town . . . with an unmistakable air of prosperity and confidence in the future."[232] Foreign interest in Çukurova cotton increased amid this rapid growth. The German Cotton Society of the Levant greatly expanded its enterprises in Cilicia in the years leading up to World War I.[233] Merchants from İskenderun, which had been indelibly linked to Aleppo, even petitioned the Ottoman government in hopes of having the city attached to the province of Adana in light of the agricultural growth occurring right in the port's backyard.[234] The most significant development concerning the future attested to the enduring image of Cilicia as the Second Egypt: a concession of the former Çukurova Imperial Farm of Abdülhamid II to two French aristocrats, Paul de Lesseps and Florent Evain de Vendeuvre. The former was the son of Ferdinand de Lesseps, the famed developer behind the Suez Canal.[235]

Dr. Abdullah Cevdet, a founding member of the Committee of Union and Progress, promoted a renewed confidence in the suddenly infamous Adana region, calling it "the Egypt of Tomorrow" in his periodical *İçtihat*. He featured the translations of French-language articles about Cilicia published in Egypt by a certain Ohanian Efendi just before the 1909 massacres. The contents suggested that Cilicia compared favorably with Egypt across many criteria. Its soil was not salinated and was more fertile, already earning yields comparable to those of Egypt without the aid of irrigation. The Seyhan and Ceyhan Rivers, fed by the snow-covered and forested peaks of the Taurus and Anti-Taurus Mountains, contained rich organic material that further endowed the land. Feed for animals was comparatively cheap, as was manure. Perhaps most important, the political and economic context of the region was entirely different. There was no danger of the monoculture of Egypt taking over in Cilicia, thanks to the balance of wheat and cotton that prevailed. Better still, the economy of the province of Adana had not been "capitulated to foreigners" as in Egypt, exporting nearly twice what it imported. He concluded the comparison saying that the weather in Cilicia was such that two harvests might be possible if the as yet rudimentary agricultural methods of the region could be mechanized.[236]

The appraisal reflected the unique features of the ecology that defined

Cilicia during the late Ottoman period. The region had its own local capitalists, who participated in a flexible and dynamic economy that cut across many social divisions in late Ottoman society. Çukurova had its own species of cotton suited to the specificities of both the local environment and the socioeconomic context. To some extent, Cilicia was incorporated into the world economy on its own terms. In this regard, the article also contained profound contradictions. It was the would-be conservatism of Cilicia's local cultivators that had saved the region's soil from salination and perhaps protected the countryside from being further penetrated by foreign interests. Yet these "conservative" cultivators were presented as an impediment to agricultural progress. The irony of the Second Egypt paradigm was that becoming the "Egypt of tomorrow" implicitly meant that Cilicia might someday be colonized, environmentally exhausted, and rendered dependent on foreign trade not just for income but for formerly noncommercial commodities like grain.

There were many ways in which Cilicia was never really the Second Egypt at all. Yet if we regard capitalism in the terms of Jason Moore, as a way of ordering nature with its own ecology, it is clear that the capitalist reordering of the environment and life of Cilicia was well under way by the end of the Ottoman period, just as had occurred in Egypt somewhat earlier.[237] The emergent economic thought of the period largely masked certain environmental costs, making it difficult to see, for example, that the malaria suffered by workers was a consequence not of Çukurova's inherently malarial environment but rather of the transformation of labor relations and ecology that commercial agriculture brought. Just as relations of power were inseparable from questions of ecology, so too was the politics of the region intertwined with its broader environmental restructuring. In this way, Cilicia did resemble Egypt, where changes in the disease ecology introduced by temporal disruptions of capitalism and colonialism carved deep wounds into the bodies of Egyptian workers who suffered elevated incidence of horrible diseases like schistosomiasis.[238]

The history of provincial life in Cilicia up until 1914 offers many visions of possible futures past. However it is framed, it reveals that the Çukurova region of modern Turkey had late Ottoman foundations. In this regard, it had its own modern history that—while sharing in the broader phenomena of the Mediterranean at the turn of the twentieth century—nonetheless produced a distinctive socioeconomic space with its own identity and political dynamics. Had history played out differently and an independent political formation emerged in Cilicia as in other regions of the former Ottoman world, there would already be many more books about the history of this space published in the English language. The preceding chapters might have become the history of a nation-state and its making. Instead, World War I and the brief French occupation would radically alter Cilicia's political trajectory, resulting in the destruction of Cilicia as a recognizable geographical entity. Just as the region had emerged as a quintessential late Ottoman frontier, as we saw in chapter 2, and a model of commercialization in the Ottoman Mediterranean, as we have seen throughout this chapter, the experience of the war in Cilicia would in many ways be a microcosm of the dynamics that defined the social history of the war in the Ottoman Empire: mass displacement, violence, hunger, disease, and death.

{ CHAPTER 4 }

FALLOWED YEARS

War, Environment, and the End of Empire, 1914–23

In the spring of 1914, five years after horrific massacres rocked the province, tens of thousands of men and women descended on Adana in search of work. They sowed more cottonseed than had ever been planted before in a single season. With prospects for export stronger than ever, landowners were confident about returns on the loans they took to open up more land for cultivation. With the arrival of summer, well-to-do families took to the orchards and mountain *yaylas* to seek refuge from the sweltering heat, anticipating the greatest fall harvest in the region's history. Meanwhile, a provincial official back in Adana telegraphed the Ministry of Interior about the need for more attention to the joyless affair of the military draft lottery. "Since it will not be possible to conduct the drawing of numbers in July and August because the inhabitants . . . will be at the *yayla*, and doing it in their absence will be unfair to them," he reasoned, "this year the drawing of numbers should start at the beginning of June and next year in early May."[1] Both fair and prudent, this suggestion might also have reflected his own desire to head for higher ground sooner than later. By June, the *yayla* season had already begun.

Unknown to most, it would be their last normal summer at the *yayla* for many years to come. By the time everyone returned at the end of the summer, the Ottoman government was beginning the greatest mobilization for war in its history, and the fall's bumper crop of cotton would not yield the anticipated profits. Allied with the Central Powers of Germany and Austria-Hungary against the Triple Entente of Britain, France, and Russia, the Ottoman Empire soon faced invasions on all sides. All able-bodied men and work animals were needed at the fronts, and Mediterranean trade suddenly came to a halt. Over the course of the next four years and the French occupation that followed the war, Cilicia's population would be beset by scarcity, epidemic disease, death, and displacement. These would be fallowed years in the history of the Çukurova's steady economic growth and settlement. During the war years, the ecology of cotton was replaced by an ecology of total war that marched to its own rhythms. Virtually no part of the region was left untouched by its impact.

Though it was peripheral to some of the dynamics that started the war, in terms of political consequence and impact on its everyday citizens, the Ottoman Empire would arguably lose more than any other combatant state. Its consequent breakup, its colonization by European powers, and the eventual triumph of a national resistance in establishing an independent and sovereign Republic of Turkey are well charted.[2] This chapter tells the other side of that story: the impact of the war on provincial society. As recent work increasingly shows, war transformed Ottoman society in a variety of ways and touched virtually every Ottoman citizen, even those far from the battlefield.[3] For Cilicia, the years between the beginning of the war in 1914 and the establishment of the Republic of Turkey in 1923 were characterized by mass displacement and economic upheaval.

The war brought to a sudden halt the meteoric rise of cotton during the early twentieth century. Rapid agrarian expansion in the lowlands gave way to crisis as the social and economic fabric of the region unraveled under the stress of wartime conditions. Mobilization of soldiers and mass deportation of Armenian civilians created acute labor shortages. Fields lay fallow. What was sowed went unharvested. Cultivators failed to find buyers for what was harvested. They defaulted on their loans. A growing number of people unable to provide for their families grew desperate. The war also changed the ecology of the Cilicia region in qualitative terms. The paradox of mobilization was that the very disadvantages that had made it more difficult for the empire to mobilize increased the intensity of the war for Ottoman subjects.[4]

As production plummeted, the military and its commercial intermediaries played a greater role in the life of the countryside. As infectious diseases spread throughout the empire, the very nature of disease in Cilicia also changed. A virulent outbreak of malaria in 1916 found an unlikely locus at a Taurus Mountain *yayla* due to the ways in which war, railways, and their construction reshaped local ecology and patterns of mobility.

Ultimately, the war brought a new political regime to Cilicia as well, due to the increased concentration of power and resources within the military. The CUP government attempted to destroy the Cilician Armenian community and confiscate its wealth. When France assumed control of the region in 1918, it touted Cilicia as a momentous colonial venture promising renewed prosperity for the region and restitution for the Armenian community, but its brief rule proved to be merely a tragic encore of the wartime displacement and scarcity. The fall of French Cilicia also spelled the end of Armenian towns that had existed for almost a millennium. At the outset of the war, Cilicia had been a site of commercial expansion, but the industry most rapidly expanding in the region by the end of the war was humanitarianism. In many ways, the Republic of Turkey inherited Cilicia in a state that would have been unrecognizable just a decade before. The war had revealed just how fragile the prosperous, multiconfessional society of late Ottoman Cilicia had been.

Mobilization and Displacement

Whether or not Ottoman officials were as eager for war as their contemporaries in Europe, by 1914 they knew they had to be ready to move in the wake of the war in Libya (1911) and the Balkans Wars (1912–13).[5] Their empire was the structural outlier among combatant states. According to the oft-cited data of Ahmet Emin Yalman, the Ottomans possessed only a fraction of the railway line per square km found in Germany and France, and considerably less than India.[6] Large stretches of the railway meant to link the Ottoman capital to its eastern frontier in Iraq were incomplete at the outset of the war and would not be completed until its last years. A comparative lack of industrial infrastructure and railways presented a barrier to Ottoman mobilization, and the Ottoman government compensated through new laws and coercive policies that brought state and society into an unprecedented level of contact. Mobilization meant finding a way to move as quickly and efficiently as possible, but this process became violent and chaotic. Yalman would refer to these mobilization policies as "militarism gone mad."[7] What appeared from the vantage point of the military as strategic movement of people, animals, and materials was experienced by Ottoman subjects as mass displacement. Due to its geographical position, Cilicia was at the center of different, overlapping experiences of displacement resulting from the Ottoman war effort.

The first great exodus of Ottoman subjects during the war involved mobilization itself or *seferberlik*. Around 3 million Ottoman soldiers would serve during World War I. In the first year alone, approximately 50,000 of the roughly 200,000 Muslim men in the province of Adana were conscripted.[8] The largest army ever amassed in the long history of the empire would soon face crushing defeat in the snow of Sarıkamış at the hands of Russian forces in the east. It then launched a legendary defense in the muggy and malarial coasts of the Gallipoli Peninsula in 1915. The diary of Mehmed Fasih, a native of Mersin who served as an officer in Gallipoli, illustrates the many hazards soldiers found there: disease, malnutrition, constant bombardment, and omnipresent anxiety.[9] Non-Muslims and those unfit for battle could still wind up within labor battalions, digging the trenches where their compatriots fought. Around 75 percent of the men in labor battalions were Armenian. The working conditions of these battalions were usually abysmal, often as bad as or even worse than those of soldiers.[10]

From the Balkans to Basra, whether in victory or in defeat, the war left a gaping hole in the last generation to reach adulthood as Ottoman citizens. More than 700,000 soldiers were reported injured by war's end; official statistics counted more than 500,000 dead, primarily due to disease.[11] Many thousands more were carried off to the shores of other empires as prisoners of war; some never returned. A scribbled note in the archives of the Red Crescent attests to the unprecedented scale of the displacement for local communities. Hacı Süleyman, a resident of the Kars district of Çukurova created during the Reform Division's settlement activities in the 1860s, desperately tried to send 160 *kuruş* to his son Osman, captive at a British POW camp in Bellary, India.[12] Osman bore the name of the empire's founder and his father, its most celebrated sovereign. The letter remains as a small testament to the quotidian sacrifice of countless rural people for the survival of the empire up to its last year of existence.

Though the majority of soldiers and workers remained dutifully at the front, desertion was common. The archival record reflects cat-and-mouse efforts by the Ottoman government to track down deserters or "runaways [*firari*]" as well as *bakaya*, soldiers who simply did not report for duty.[13] The number of deserters rose dramatically over the course of 1917, with more than 300,000 men having deserted by December 1917.[14] In Cilicia, from the beginning of the war until July 1917, there were more than 20,000 instances of desertion (*firari* and *bakaya*), overwhelmingly by Muslims, in the İçil district (which included Mersin) alone. More than one-third had not been apprehended by the gendarmerie.[15] Reports by the gendarmerie in Adana reflect a similar and steady rise in the number of outstanding deserters, increasing by thousands each month.[16] The majority of deserters counted in the gendarmerie reports of the Adana province had not perpetrated any criminal act, but some took to the mountains to resist the state. The gendarmerie in the Amanus and Taurus regions would become locked in a struggle with growing armed bands, or *çetes*, that swelled with deserters.[17] Mass conscription was fundamental to the Ottoman war effort, but by the end of the war, desertion and brigandage among the soldiers became a major security risk in the provinces.

Parallel to the mobilization of troops, the Ottoman government undertook a sweeping effort to forcibly transfer Armenians out of Anatolia and into Northern Syria for putative security concerns. The Armenian communities of Zeytun and Dörtyol, which were occupied by the Ottoman military during the first months of 1915 over the issue of desertion, were among the first in the empire to be forcibly disarmed and deported. More than 20,000 Armenians of Zeytun were deported on April 8.[18] After an escalation of violent incidents targeting Armenians in and around the Van region, the Armenians of the city refused to disarm, and the battle for Van between the Armenian militias and the Ottoman government began on April 20.[19] Shortly after, the Ottoman authorities arrested some 2,000 Armenian politicians, intellectuals, and professionals in Istanbul on April 24, 1915, a date commonly taken to mark the beginning of the Armenian genocide.[20] Hagop Terzian, who had left Adana for the capital, was among those arrested notables, nearly all of whom were assassinated or died during their exile. By the end of 1915, the government had begun the deportation of the entire Armenian population of Anatolia in areas it still controlled. Forced to sell or relinquish their property, these families suffered from sickness, hunger, and violence on the deportation routes and in the camps of Northern Syria. More than half of the Ottoman Armenian population died during the war.[21] In an era defined by pogroms, expulsions, and mass atrocities committed by imperial nation-states in zones of warfare, expansion, and colonial exploitation, no modern state had concertedly inflicted so much suffering on so many of its own citizens in such a short period of time.

As a growing center of Ottoman Armenian life, Cilicia was devastated by the deportations. At the outset of the war, there were around 100,000 Armenians in the region (which includes Marash) along with residents from other provinces who do not show up in the statistics.[22] Between April and October 1915, most of the Armenians in Cilicia would be removed from civilian life, either serving in labor battalions or deported first to camps along the Baghdad Railway line and eventually into the Syrian desert toward the provinces of Zor and Mosul. The aforementioned Armenians of Zeytun and Dörtyol were among the first in the empire to be deported.[23] But many of Cilicia's Armenians remained for months as people from farther west passed through the province en route to Syria. Adana's governor during the early years of the war, İsmail Hakkı Bey, had stalled or ignored deportation orders from the central government, particularly in the city of Adana itself.[24] Around 20,000 Armenians were finally expelled from the city of Adana in the fall of 1915, and some 50,000 were deported from the province as a whole throughout the year.[25] Because of the close ties between Cemal Pasha and the Armenians of Adana, some were able to secure relatively favorable terms of exile in Hama and Damascus for the rest of the war period.[26] Many of the Armenians from the countryside of Cilicia ended up in caravans marched overland into the Jazira and the Syrian desert.[27]

Governor Hakkı Bey had warned that provisions for Armenian deportees, even under perfect conditions, would run out well before the journey was over, exposing them to extreme hunger and poverty as they were moved from place to place, often by foot.[28] As the caravans made their way across the empire, the telegrams concerning their movements remained matter-of-fact and often cryptic. But the accounts of survivors are not for the faint of heart. In addition to the well-known details of the pain suffered by and violence inflicted upon the deportees, their own accounts reflect the climate of fear and torment that followed them at every stage of an increasingly perilous journey. Hadjin native Hovhannes Der Manoukian recounted how the guards of his group of deportees kept along the Khabur River in the arid space between Ras al-Ayn and Deir Ez-Zor seemed to revel in the psychological torment of Armenians in the encampments, sometimes engaging in random acts of violence and at other times giving false hope of aid and survival. Hovhannes only survived to relate his account by ingratiating himself with a Chechen notable, who enlisted him as a clerk to benefit from his knowledge of Turkish.[29]

Like those Chechens settled in this part of the desert during the 1860s, the Armenians who survived often did so by adapting to local conditions.[30] As Sam Dolbee notes, "while the ruling CUP used the nature of the Jazira to kill Armenians, Armenians used the very same qualities of the Jazira to survive."[31] In the records of Armenian women and children recovered by humanitarian efforts in Aleppo, the number of individuals incorporated into Muslim families as children, wives, house servants, and shepherds in a largely pastoralist economy is striking.[32] Hagop Nazarian, a seventeen-year-old, was one of many young men with a biography along similar lines. He was taken by "an Arab" when the family his caravan was in was attacked and his parents and siblings killed. Then, "he met with a Kurd who persuaded him to follow him near Ras-el-Ain, [and] he lived by the Kurd 8 years" until he heard about the rescue home in Aleppo.[33] That captors, husbands, and adoptive parents in these records are usually identified only by ethnicity belies the intimacy and integration that survival entailed. In Hagop's case, he lived with "the Kurd" in Ras al-Ayn for longer than he had lived with his own family before deportation. Survival nonetheless was the exception in the desert. According to the statistics of Talat Pasha that have been published by Murat Bardakçı, almost 40 percent of the Armenians from the province of Adana, many of whom were permitted exile in the Levant, were either dead or unaccounted for by 1917. Their counterparts from other provinces in the empire fared much worse.[34]

As soon as Armenians were deported from the province of Adana,

Muslim refugees from the Balkan Wars were settled in their places. "When they first came the men were too weak to work, all were subject to chills and fever," American missionary Edith Cold noted, writing from Hadjin, where there were many more vacated Armenian houses than refugees to settle them. "One of the women spoke with horror at having to live in a house with such association, saying that only they knew what such suffering meant."[35] These Balkan *muhacirs* were the vanguard of a much larger refugee population that would descend on Cilicia. In addition to the prewar refugee population, tens of thousands of people fleeing the combat zone in Eastern Anatolia passed through or settled in the province of Adana. The refugees from the east were in desperate condition. An American missionary report on relief activities for Armenians and Assyrians included these predominantly Kurdish refugees in their potential purview, describing their plight in staccato prose: "Kurds—pillaged and plundered—men killed—crops not planted as before—animals taken—destitute."[36] Grigor Balakian, an Armenian bishop who hid out in the Taurus Mountains under the false identity of Herr Bernstein, a German machinist, encountered a few hundred Turkish and Kurdish refugees from Bitlis who had fled the Russian advance in December 1916.[37] They were in desperate condition, and their "camels, horses, mules, and donkeys—all reduced to skin and bones."[38]

The CUP saw the refugee crisis during the war as an opportunity for broader demographic engineering.[39] The Refugees and Tribes Directorate (Aşair ve Muhacirin Müdüriyet-i Umumiyesi) arranged for these people also to replace Armenian deportees, even before the orders had been implemented in places like Adana. This new directorate brought more coordinated Ottoman settlement policies that had long involved both immigrants and nomadic communities.[40] The policies of the Ottoman frontier had coalesced into a comprehensive population management scheme deployed the CUP to remake Anatolia. As a point of arrival between Eastern Anatolia and the imperial center, the Cilicia region was key to the orchestrated movements of refugees. In the summer of 1916, a telegram from the provincial treasurer in Adana reported the presence of more than 500 new refugees (*mülteci*) in the province. Most were settled in towns that had possessed large Armenian populations; more were sent to Sis than to Adana, and as many were sent to Hadjin and Dörtyol as to Tarsus. The provincial government sought some

5,000 lira for short-term assistance, but settlement was carried out with the hopes that many of the refugees would easily find work on the farms and in the factories of Çukurova.[41]

The process was chaotic. In some cases, the vacated houses of Armenians, intended for new refugees, had already been illegally occupied by others or partially demolished.[42] As the numbers of those coming from Eastern Anatolia grew, the Ministry of Interior also became concerned with the large number of Kurdish refugees moving into the heartland of Anatolia. In the Adana region, this meant that those refugees from the Balkans and Anatolia who were "Turks" would be permanently settled. Meanwhile, those who were "Kurds" were to remain in Adana until the end of the war and then return to their regions of origin.[43] As a result, most fell short of becoming full-fledged settlers or active members of the agrarian economy. A German officer concerned by the miserable state of Kurdish refugees at Mamure wondered, with a tone of skepticism, "Is really anything going to be organized for their reception in Adana? Will they be given land, cattle, and tools? Or will they go to pieces in misery?"[44]

By the following spring of 1917, the population of refugees in Cilicia had risen sharply.[45] There were more than 16,000 refugees (*muhacir ve mülteci*), about one-quarter of them in the district of Kozan alone. The governor of Adana requested 1 million *kuruş* to provision these refugees and the other needy people in cities like Adana and estimated that another 500,000 *kuruş* would be needed for further refugees coming from Urfa.[46] Those coming from Urfa would be estimated at almost another 10,000 individuals.[47] There, the extreme crowding of refugees was creating major issues with provisioning, and some had been blamed for crimes such as assault and the theft of cattle and onions.[48] Their exodus left these communities in a very precarious situation. By August 1917, the Adana province had received more than 30,000 *lira* in assistance for refugees and other needs. Yet they were requesting a number about ten times larger for the purpose of facilitating the active participation of refugees in the province's agriculture. The Ministry of Interior replied that such an amount was infeasible, deciding that the refugees should be given "a few *dönüms*" of land in hopes that they could grow something.[49] By June 1918, the governor was requesting approximately 50,000 *lira* to provision a local population of 18,120 refugees.[50]

The Political Ecology of War

Wartime displacements shaped the underlying conditions of a new political ecology of war. As one of the empire's most agriculturally productive and prosperous regions, Cilicia was critical to the war effort. But instead of increasing output to meet the needs of the army, its cultivators struggled to produce a fraction of what they had before the war. By the end of the war, Cilicia, much like other parts of the empire, had witnessed precipitous economic decline, extreme scarcity, and mass displacement. As the population verged on starvation under the weight of the military's demands and a blockade on imports enforced by the Entente, epidemic diseases spread throughout all ranks of society. The government sought to reduce production gaps using conscript labor, but the net result was still an agrarian collapse.

Mobilization and mass conscription in 1914 began at the end of summer, the precise moment when hands were most needed in the fields. "The condition of the people is deplorable," an American missionary wrote from Marash in August 1914. "They have no money, scant food, and famine looms up ahead. The men have been called out by the stringent new mobilization laws and hardly any are left to gather the standing grain. In a short time much of the harvest will be lost."[51] For the Ottoman government, mobilization was a rush to muster resources and accelerate the movement of people and the pace of production, but the levying of soldiers was detrimental to agriculture. Long dependent on seasonal migrants who met the high demand for labor, Cilicia was especially vulnerable to the sudden disruption. Mobilization also stipulated a requisition of all types of draft animals, and on the eve of the war the province relied on an estimated 200,000 oxen, horses, mules, donkeys, and camels.[52] To make matters worse, the Ottoman government placed a ban on agricultural exports and abrogated foreign concessions, meaning that the commercial class of Adana and Mersin was suddenly cut off from vital Mediterranean markets.

Cotton had already been planted in the spring of 1914. Local cultivators anticipated around 120,000 bales, arguably the best crop in the region's history. But because of the emergency ban on exports and the loss of labor, they were hard pressed to move any cotton they managed to harvest. Local cotton prices dropped by 50 percent due to lack of demand, and commercial revenues plummeted.⁵³ In response to the livid complaints of Cilicia's most prominent merchants and cultivators, the Ottoman government lifted the ban on cotton export in November 1914. Yet in January 1915 less than 10 percent of the fall's cotton harvest had been exported.⁵⁴ The Entente navies had blockaded the Eastern Mediterranean coast, and no ship captain dared to anchor in Mersin to unload goods. In the end, only about one-third of the cotton produced in the Adana region during 1914 could be exported, mostly by land. Roughly 10,000 more bales, or about 8–10 percent of the crop, was purchased by the military.⁵⁵

On the strength of many profitable years, landowners had assumed greater liabilities in order to grow more cotton. Unable to reap what they had sown, many began to default. In the winter of 1914–15, the case of eight landowners, who collectively possessed some 17,000 *dönüms* of primarily agricultural land, came to the Ministry of Interior. The owners ranged from elite landowning Armenian families of Adana, and Marie Sursock, a member of the Beirut-based Sursock family, to upstart rural landowners of Eastern Çukurova, such as Alaybeyzade Mehmed.⁵⁶ These cultivators had used their land as collateral on loans from the German Anatolian Cotton Company. When their payments faltered, the company came into possession of the properties. Upon understanding the scale of these landholdings, the Ottoman administration reasoned that the German company, as a foreign entity, could not assume ownership of the land.⁵⁷ In February 1915, the Ministry of Interior elected to loan Ziraat Bankası in Adana some 50,000 *lira*—roughly 10 percent of the total budget expenditures for agriculture and industry in Adana—in order to bail out the cultivators of the Cilicia region.⁵⁸ The cotton crisis of 1914–15 in Cilicia illustrated the precarious state of the sudden commercial growth in the region, which was tightly bound to credit and access to foreign markets.

While wartime conditions threatened Adana's wealthiest merchants and landowners, they had a broader impact on the normally bountiful food supply. Adana usually maintained an annual agricultural surplus of grain going into the war, allowing for export within the empire and beyond.⁵⁹ Governor İsmail Hakkı implemented a prescient policy in August 1914, delaying the mobilization of new conscripts for three months until the completion of the harvest.⁶⁰ Nonetheless, the grain harvest was comparatively small. The Adana province, particularly Eastern Çukurova, had faced crop damage due to excessive rain.[61] The fall harvest rotted in the fields in the hinterland regions toward Marash due to labor shortages.[62] Already harvested grain began to go bad due to lack of means of transport.[63] A comparison with production statistics before the war indicates a serious decline in grain production.[64] With rising concern about the food supply in Lebanon, the Ministry of Interior inquired about the amount of grain left in Adana in October 1914. The response was that Adana had only small reserves it could afford to send elsewhere.[65] Within a few months, the Lebanese population would begin starving en masse.

In March 1915, the Ministry of Commerce and Agriculture adopted measures to increase agricultural production in the empire. The principal measure was the extension of more loans to local cultivators, about 25,000 *lira* in total.[66] An additional overall concern was labor; head of the ministry Ahmed Nesimi acknowledged that at planting and harvest time cultivators faced "great difficulties" in finding workers and suggested the use of conscript labor battalions. Another aspect of the plan was to offset the labor effects of mobilization by doubling the number of mechanical reapers in the empire to 500 through imports from the United States, as well as the use of copper sulfate to ward off plant diseases. It also meant diversifying the food supply to better incorporate foods most useful for emergency provisioning, such as potatoes and maize.[67] In the Adana region, this entailed the development of a five-year plan involving expenditures in the areas of agriculture and technical training in order to raise Ottoman agriculture "to the level of Europe."[68]

The Ministry of Agriculture struggled to implement these imperatives. Signs of trouble in Adana came as the grain harvest approached in May. The government had already missed the chance to send the six labor battalions needed for planting, and it was late in scrambling to send the 15,000 hands that Adana needed for the harvest.[69] A group of eleven cultivators in Ceyhan complained to the government that neither funds nor hands were available as promised. They said that by request of the government, they had greatly expanded their area of cultivation. The year 1915 had brought them bountiful yields. But their annual produce normally relied on some 10,000 migrant workers, and meanwhile the government had not even sent the 5,000 needed for the harvest and threshing.[70] About two weeks later, with the harvest in jeopardy, arrangements were still being made.⁷¹ The frontier in Çukurova that the Ottoman government worked so hard to develop was now overextended. Meanwhile, a more efficient team of harvesters was fast descending on the region independent of Ottoman control.

During that spring of 1915, swarms of locusts began to spread throughout Greater Syria. They devoured the crops and orchards of countless villages, wreaking particular havoc in Palestine as the entire Levant descended into famine.⁷² By May, locusts had arrived in Cilicia. Airborne (*uçkun*) locusts began to appear around İslahiye and Marash, soon spreading north toward Elbistan, Sivas, Niğde, and the Cappadocia region by June of 1915. Locusts could be eliminated fairly easily while in egg or larval form by using fire or burial, but they were virtually unstoppable once they sprouted wings.⁷³ In the mountainous interior of Kozan, they engulfed some fifteen villages and destroyed much of the summer crop. Edith Cold described the battle with locusts in Hadjin, which had already been emptied of its Armenian inhabitants. "They first appeared in early June and ravaged the country till September," she wrote. "They destroyed our vineyards, and we had to fight day after day to keep them out of the Compound. When we destroyed those hatched on our premises, their places were quickly filled by armies coming down the mountain side. When I left many of the villages were suffering for the lack of food due to the locust scourge."⁷⁴ Local inhabitants in the region along with Ottoman labor battalions were eventually able to destroy most of the new generation, but not before incurring considerable losses.⁷⁵

The economic costs of conscription and the subsequent deportation of Armenians during 1915 only exacerbated the unfolding economic crisis. An American missionary noted that more than two-thirds of the businesses in Adana relied on Armenians, and that after the deportation of some 18,000 people, "the city seemed deserted."⁷⁶ In his memoirs, Damar Arıkoğlu recalled that "moving the Armenians to Syria made our Province of Adana a completely empty void [*tamtakır bir boşluk*]."⁷⁷ The province struggled to find even 15,000 hands of conscripted labor for harvest, when normal labor flows at harvest time were often many times that number. İsmail Hakkı warned that the demands of the army upon the grain supply in Adana were dangerously high. When compared with years leading up to the war, grain production was less than half.⁷⁸ This decline appears to have been much sharper than was the case in provinces closer to the capital, where total production was just 20 percent lower than prewar averages in 1915 and 27 percent lower in 1916.[79] Nonetheless, the army was requesting more than 40 percent of the wheat crop and 55 percent of the barley to provision some 20,000 military personnel and 5,000 animals. Hakkı deemed this request unreasonable, noting that "while [Adana] is renowned as an agricultural region, that renown is more for cotton than cereals."[80]

Hakkı later reported that the year's crops had not flourished and "due to present circumstances and since all of the coastlines are blockaded, the crops that could be obtained cannot be exported and have remained in all the cultivators' hands." He added that "because of the loss of commerce, the already present economic crisis in this country has doubled in severity."[81] Unable to make payments on their loans with Ziraat Bankası, more cultivators were once again on the verge of defaulting. In response to the crisis, the director of the bank announced that, as had been done during the previous year, the cultivators in Adana who were truly unable to make payments on their loans received permission to delay payment until the subsequent cotton harvest.[82]

The financial shock was reflected in nearly every aspect of local life. A close-up view of the Sursock family and its finances in Mersin and Tarsus illustrates the complexity of the economic reverberations and the gloomy fates of merchants and cultivators of the Cilicia region. The Sursocks owned many shops and properties in Mersin, which endured the conditions of the blockade and saw three of its four main piers destroyed by bombing during the war.[83] Even though the Sursocks were offering deep discounts, they had trouble collecting on their Mersin properties and agricultural land around Tarsus.[84] A frustrated letter to their main intermediary in Mersin complained of the particular trouble in collecting rents there, exclaiming, "You have lowered the rents to a very reduced price. Instead of the 4,000 *lira*, which we were collecting before the war, the rents of Mersin have been reduced to 500 *lira* of which we only collect half!!!!!"[85] The names of the tenants who paid reduced rent or failed to pay reveal much about precisely what the war did to commerce. A half-dozen of those tenants who had not paid their rent were Armenians, presumably deported from the region. Given the context, it made some strange sense that the Sursocks tried to collect on these rents from the Ottoman government.[86]

The winter of 1915–16 proved more trying than any in recent memory. "The country became miserable," Arıkoğlu recalled. "Starvation, poverty, despair. Huge crowds in front of the bakeries. People fighting with each other to get bread that was like mud, obtained with a ration card. The cries of those who could not get it. People fainting from hunger. It was becoming normal." Starvation loomed over the once thriving city of Adana. "There was no counting the people begging for bread. The streets had become the realm of the poor and hungry."[87] The American missionary hospital reported feeding roughly 150 people per day.[88] İsmail Hakkı declared as early as October that reduced harvests, coupled with the demands of the military and the overall impact of the deportations on the region's food supply, could be leading to "an acute famine [*buhranlı bir kaht*]." The province did not even have enough seed for the coming year.[89] He wrote to the Ministry of Interior to explain in numerical terms precisely how mobilization and the deportation of Armenians had crippled the province. He warned that Adana might not have even two weeks' worth of grain left, and the provincial government was scrambling to facilitate whatever planting might be possible.[90]

Meanwhile, there were major shortages of items like coffee, salt, and fuel. One American missionary claimed that people in Adana resorted to using fruit trees and the homes of deported Armenians for firewood. One of her Muslim neighbors had "all last winter used the flooring of her [own] house for cooking her food."[91] By the end of the winter in February 1916, prices of basic foodstuffs in Cilicia spiked to unprecedented levels, and the municipal government in Adana could not procure enough wheat to regulate the supply of bread.[92] The treasurer of the province reported that the price of a bushel of wheat had reached 6 *mecidiyes*, or roughly 120 *kuruş*.[93] The local going rate for a bushel before the war had been 20–25 *kuruş*.[94] The poor simply "could not buy it," and the supply of grain was becoming increasingly monopolized by a few merchants and profiteers (*muhtekirin*).[95]

Financial stress and hunger had escalated to the point that families began to pressure the government. A telegram from a certain Ayşe writing on behalf of "all the military families of Adana" demanded that the government look after their needs. "We receive a salary of 30 *kuruş* [per month] and a bushel of wheat is 6 *mecidiye* [or 120 *kuruş*]," she railed. "We and our children are being wiped out by hunger while our men are sacrificing their lives for the sake of defending their faith and the state [*din ve devlet*]."⁹⁶ Another telegram issued within a day of Ayşe's call for assistance during the winter of 1916 bears the signatures of fifteen women from Tarsus who hailed from the families of Muslim soldiers (*şehit gazi asakir-i islamiye*). They too asked for intercession, declaring that "the local businessmen do not accept banknotes. We cannot buy the things we need to buy. We will die from hunger with paper in our hands. A bushel of wheat has risen to 100 *kuruş*. We cannot find bread."⁹⁷ There are many such telegrams and petitions in the various documents and correspondence concerning provisioning in the Ottoman Empire from 1916 onward. Often penned by the wives, sisters, mothers, and daughters of Ottoman military personnel, they consistently assert their basic right to eat as part and parcel of their family's service to the war effort.⁹⁸

The introduction of paper banknotes to pay salaries had fed the turmoil. Ottoman paper currency was introduced in 1915 as one-to-one equivalent with the gold *lira*, but by the end of the war the paper version was worth less than 20 percent of the coin equivalent. An American missionary in Marash observed that "when the use of coin was forbidden, the merchants displayed their poorest goods and sold them at the highest rates, and the villagers refused to bring their grain and produce to sell. The markets practically closed, and people went hungry." Meanwhile, in Adana, paper money took hold with unusual effect. "The people hid their money and dealt only in paper," he explained, "but instead of advancing the prices of goods 400 percent, the traders advanced them 1,000 percent."⁹⁹ Inflation and lack of faith in the paper currency were worst in provinces farthest from the Ottoman capital; by August 1917, one gold *lira* would be worth 430 *kuruş* in Istanbul and 450 *kuruş* in Bursa and Izmir. Meanwhile, it was 600 *kuruş* in Adana, 555 in Beirut, and as much as 766 in Mosul.¹⁰⁰ As the conflict and Ottoman financial woes worsened, the government began to print money ad hoc, further inflating the currency. But here, Ottoman citizens tried to use the state of affairs to their advantage, hoarding their coin while paying their taxes in the much devalued but officially equal paper currency promoted by the government. Even if the government reacted by raising tax rates, it could not make up the difference.¹⁰¹

By February 1916, it was painfully clear that Ottoman provisioning practices did not meet the needs of civilian populations during wartime. Over prior decades, the state had played little role in the regulation of the food supply beyond sometimes banning exports from regions of scarcity, facilitating the movement of emergency supplies, and implementing price ceilings. Early responses to scarcity during the war, as described above, were improvised and failed to systematically address the issues that gave rise to provisioning problems. For the most part, the Ottoman administration sought to orchestrate the movement of flour and grain to places where it was critically needed. This was the initial response to the looming famine in Adana. The provincial treasurer proposed that the best solution was to sell the 80,000 kg of grain reserves belonging to the 4th Army of Syria, led by Cemal Pasha, to the local population at a moderate price.[102] After some correspondence with Cemal Pasha and the Ministry of Interior, the provincial government ended up purchasing grain from the province of Konya—the only region in a position to supply it—allowing residents of the city to purchase a meager 2 kg apiece at a reduced price.[103] An investigation of the impacts of provisioning measures on various provinces from 1916 produced ambivalent results. Whereas in Beirut, free trade had supposedly allowed profiteers to monopolize the grain supply, thereby exacerbating famine, the local government in Adana claimed that measures such as price ceilings were ultimately counterproductive and that trade should be free.[104] In other words, according to these explanations, free trade caused the famine in Lebanon, where up to one-third of the population died, whereas absence of free trade had pushed Adana toward famine.[105]

The year 1916 brought the crescendo of the agrarian crisis in the Cilicia region, but the same issues lingered and spread to other provinces during the last years of the war. Total grain yields throughout the empire continued to decline in 1917 and 1918. The amount of land cultivated with wheat, even when excluding the provinces that were zones of combat, dropped by more than 25 percent between 1914 and 1918, and total yields sank by almost half.[106] Cilicia remained in a state of intense scarcity and verged on famine at least twice in 1917 and 1918.[107] By March 1918, women in the villages of the mountains between Mersin and Silifke complained that they were unable to support their families, the poorest among them having been reduced to eating acorns gathered from the forest.[108] In his poem about mobilization for war and everything it entailed, simply titled "Seferberlik Destanı," Adana native Movses Hagopyan neatly summarized what the war looked like from the vantage point of Ottoman citizens: horrific machines engaged in a pointless struggle, resulting in senseless death and the erosion of all things that held social, spiritual, and material worth. The opening lines were: "Mobilization (*seferberlik*) has brought us much hardship / Is there any trouble that I have not lived? / Hostility has captured everyone's thoughts / Is there any nation (*millet*) still not mixed up in this?"[109]

Though the demands of war crushed the Ottoman populace and stifled production, the war nonetheless reshaped the political ecology of the empire. The role of the government and military in the agrarian sphere expanded through the deployment of labor battalions. The CUP promoted a notion of "war agriculture" from 1916 onward, increasing budgetary allocations in the agricultural sphere and equating agricultural labor with other civic duties, such as military service.[110] Provincial governments became more insistent about military aid during planting and harvest. For example, Governor İsmail Hakkı requested that during February 1916, ten to fifteen labor battalions of workers should carry out the planting and suggested the English, French, and Russian prisoners of war with agricultural skills should be forced to work as well.[111] By 1917, it had become standard in Cilicia and Syria for the province to request labor battalions at harvest time upon specific instructions of the Ministry of Agriculture.[112] Agricultural manuals published by the military emphasized the importance of mechanization and the application of new agronomical techniques in the production of wheat, corn, and other food staples.[113] Meanwhile, toward the end of the war the CUP promoted the cultivation of fairly uncommon but hardy staples through its agricultural publication *Çiftçiler Derneği Mecmuası* (The Farmers Association Magazine).[114] It also featured numerous articles on the importance of agriculture as a civic and indeed religious duty, stressing the value of women's labor during wartime.[115] The government promoted mechanization, but a 1917 review of the ongoing five-year plan for agriculture in Adana indicated that no significant increase in expenditures had been made beyond the purchase of a single sprayer (*pülverizatör*) used in protecting orchards from insects and diseases.[116]

Many of the new mercantile families in Cilicia struggled through the war. However, war also presented opportunities. Prodomos Bodosakis

Athanasiadis was a figure who profited greatly from the war. He was a Greek Orthodox merchant whose father had migrated to Cilicia from the town of Bor on the other side of the Taurus Mountains. Bodosakis had almost left for the Americas in the years leading up to the war in search of better opportunities. Yet during the war, the mill his family owned in Mersin entered into a lucrative partnership with the Ottoman military. Bodosakis expanded his milling operations to Tarsus and began supplying the army with cattle. He became the leading provisioner of the railway construction sites and the army in the Cilicia region, forging a relationship with Cemal Pasha, earning a medal from Enver Pasha, and gaining the protection of Enver's brother-in-law and Adana governor, Cevdet Bey. Even amid the deportations of Greek Orthodox civilians from the Cilicia region, Bodosakis and his many workers remained. In 1918, a conflict with Bahattin Şakir, head of the Special Organization (Teşkilat-ı Mahsusa), drove Bodosakis to Istanbul, where he purchased the Pera Palace Hotel, joining the ranks of the cosmopolitan elite.[117] Thanks to the economic conditions of war, before reaching the age of thirty Bodosakis had become one of the wealthiest natives of the Cilicia region.

In tandem with provisioning efforts, the Ottoman government adopted many policies regarding health and medicine that went beyond securing the well-being of the military. Foremost among them was a Quinine Law, adopted in 1917. The law affirmed the right of all Ottoman citizens to antimalarial medicines. Among the provisions in this law was the stipulation that quinine be purchased by the government and sold to Ottoman citizens with a standard markup of 15 percent.[118] Here too, the reach of these practices was relatively limited. This law was not the first attempt by the Ottoman government to make quinine available to citizens, but the empire did not have enough medicine. Correspondence between the Red Crescent and the Ministry of Interior reveals that even Ottoman personnel in the Cilicia region did not have reliable access to quinine sulfate during the last years of the war.[119] Mobilization did not accelerate the progress of the Ottoman struggle to limit the spread of malaria. On the contrary, the quinine law was adopted the year after the entire empire was overrun by a malaria pandemic. Cilicia was the epicenter.

1916: Year of the Mosquito

In late May 1918, a Swiss engineer by the name of Lütneger, employed by the railway at a place called Belemedik, wrote to the Ottoman Ministry of Interior for permission to return home, citing his inability to "adapt to the climate."[120] As we have seen, such a request usually referred to bouts of malaria; countless civil servants and immigrants in the Ottoman Empire had made similar requests over prior decades. Of course, change of air was often a good excuse to escape a bad situation, but what made this case unusual was that the region to which Lütneger claimed to be unable to acclimate was not particularly tropical. Tucked away between mountain peaks, Belemedik's climate was if anything alpine, and with average temperatures in June hovering around 20°C/68°F, there was no better time of year to be in a Taurus Mountain town.[121] Lütneger improbably claimed to be unable to endure one of the only microclimates in the empire that resembled his home country. Yet he was likely being truthful. He had lived through a malaria outbreak the likes of which had never before been seen in the Taurus Mountains.

Ground zero of the pandemic was indeed Belemedik, a small settlement created as a Baghdad Railway construction site. German doctors stationed there were confounded by the severity and tenacity of the variety of malaria they had apparently encountered in 1916. Additional personnel from a German tropical medicine laboratory even moved their operations to the Taurus Mountains, a seemingly unlikely location for the study of tropical medicine.[122] They found that in August 1916, "mortality caused by malaria at the hospital in Belemedik" was greater than 50 percent and remained above 20 percent until December.[123] One doctor reported that as many as 95 percent of the soldiers and workers under his care had malaria.[124] Malaria came back strong the following summer. Between August 1917 and July 1918, the hospitals in the region recorded 2,798 cases of malaria, almost 7 percent of which were fatal.[125] During that time, 36.9 percent of the blood samples at the German laboratory in the Taurus Mountains tested positive for malaria.[126] Suspicion of a uniquely virulent strain of malaria was certainly warranted, but a lead researcher, Eugene Bentmann, argued some years later that ecological causes were at the root. For almost entirely anthropogenic reasons, 1916 was, in Bentmann's words, "a year the mosquitos swarmed."[127]

Malaria was prevalent in the Ottoman Empire throughout the war. Yet the Taurus Mountains epidemic was unusual because of its environmental context. The most common anopheline malaria vectors in Cilicia, according to studies from the 1920s, belonged to the *maculipennis* complex, which did not typically reside in such chilly environs.[128] Much later studies point to *sacharovi*, a member of the *maculipennis* complex, as the dominant vector in the Cilician lowlands.[129] *Sacharovi* is among the most thermophilic species in the complex and is typically found in the coastal regions of the Mediterranean, thriving in spaces such as swamps, floodplains, and areas of commercial cultivation, such as rice paddies.[130] Under normal conditions, such mosquitos could not proliferate in the mountains. Bentmann identified another species in the Pozantı region, *Anopheles superpictus*, a species that "one hardly meets on the plain."[131] *Superpictus* mosquitos fare well in colder climates and can remain active feeders even during the winter or in relatively cool locations like Belemedik.[132] As the Adana Malaria Institute director would explain in a later study, *superpictus* could "reach distances eight or nine kilometers from its home by scaling mountains and hills."[133]

The proliferation of *superpictus* was contingent on human beings interacting with the mountain environment in such a way as to allow mosquitos to breed and feed. For most of the Ottoman period, Belemedik had been little more than a secluded summer getaway of local Tahtacıs, who moved between the Taurus Mountains and the coast west of Mersin. The Belemedik construction project changed that. It involved thousands of laborers working for years on tunnels through the valley of the Çakıt River to connect the Taurus Mountains to the Çukurova plain below. Worker health was a systemic issue at Baghdad Railway construction sites. In fact, during the first year of new railway construction in the Cilicia region, in 1911, malaria had cut through the ranks of the German railroad workers. Tunnel construction near Belemedik actually began prematurely as a summer refuge from the scourge of the plain that would salvage the lost work time.[134] The tunneling operations were far from complete at the outset of the war.[135]

The construction activities at Belemedik began to alter the landscape in a manner that would make it more conducive to mosquito reproduction. According to Bentmann, "the considerable number of trees felled during the war" in the well-wooded Taurus region triggered sudden erosion and provided more spaces for mosquitos to breed.[136] The puddles that formed on treeless ground or at the bottom of eroded slopes would have been perfectly adequate sanctuary for mosquitos. The Ottoman Ministry of Forests in the Adana province counted around 75,000 pine trees and some 10,000 oak and beech trees felled between 1915 and 1918, and most of these were in the Taurus Mountains.[137] The work sites were themselves ideal breeding ground for mosquitos. Some of the best places for mosquitos to strike were the under-construction railway tunnels, trenches, and holes the workers occupied throughout the day. Bentmann also referred to the poor location of the German automobile corps camp, which was exposed to wet, mosquito-prone terrain nearby.[138] The automobile corps circulated in the region throughout the day, conveying materials and items between Pozantı, Belemedik, and the other works sites. Men in automobiles inadvertently became some of the most efficient malaria vectors in the region. Mosquitos could hitch a ride in their cars, and malaria could do the same in their blood.

The incompleteness of the railway tunnels added another dimension to the crisis. Pozantı served as a convergence between Anatolian railways coming from the west and the Adana railway that led toward the Baghdad and Hejaz railways. At the outset of 1916, a 37 km stretch of rail between Belemedik and Dorak remained incomplete.[139] That line, which connected Pozantı in the Taurus Mountains and Yenice in the Çukurova plain below through the rail tunnels at Belemedik would not be completed until 1918. Transfer between these two lines consisted of several kilometers crossed on foot or with animals. A stretch of Decauville rail, which was of a lighter gauge than the railways to which it connected, completed the gap between the Taurus Mountains and the main line of the Adana railway. From grains and lemons to camels and humans, the combination of speedy rail going to a brutal bottleneck led to all sorts of congestion and stoppages around the Pozantı station.[140] All transport at sites between Belemedik and the plain was carried out by animals.[141]

Because it became a major transfer point, soldiers who merely stopped in the region helped bring malaria to Belemedik. Some of the men who died in Belemedik during the summer of 1916 probably succumbed to infections they contracted at the front. Postwar reports from the Ottoman military indicated more than 400,000 cases of malaria alone during the war and some 20,000 malaria-induced deaths.[142] The Ottoman fronts were among the war's worst in terms of malaria infection rates, and the Ottoman army was hit harder than any other.[143] The main Ottoman fronts during World War I put soldiers and laborers in contact with mosquito-friendly regions. Trenches were ideal breeding ground for mosquitos, and soldiers weakened by combat and malnutrition were especially vulnerable targets for the malaria parasite. Due to the layout of the railway system, almost all the soldiers headed to the Syrian and Mesopotamian fronts had to pass through places like Adana and İskenderun that people typically avoided during the summer.[144] In prior years, the Ottoman government had managed to suppress malaria among its military personnel.[145] But by 1916, it was clear that the Ottoman army was having serious issues with the supply of quinine, which could only be an effective method of prophylaxis if administered regularly to all the troops in appropriate dosages.

There were also thousands of prisoners of war in Pozantı and Belemedik during the last years of the war (see figure 4.1). The POWs were sent there from the beginning of 1916 onward largely to replace deported Armenian workers. For example, men from the POW camps in Afyonkarahisar and Çankırı were sent to work in Belemedik in February 1916.[146] One source mentions around 1,600 British and Indian soldiers sent to work in Belemedik following the deportation of the Armenians from the area in June 1916, just as the malaria epidemic was beginning to escalate.[147] They had been captured at Kut-el-Amara, 100 miles south of Baghdad, and marched all the way to the Amanus Mountains.[148] Some 13,000 such soldiers had been captured at Kut-el-Amara and sent toward the Taurus and Amanus construction sites.[149] There were also Russian POWs in Pozantı and Belemedik, already 748 of them by April 1916.[150] Though Russian prisoners in particular complained of maltreatment, the lives of the captured adversaries in Belemedik were not necessarily worse than those of Ottoman soldiers at the front. British POWs enjoyed a fair amount of freedom of movement, allowing them to organize football matches, briefly publish a newspaper called the *Belemedik Bugger*, hold memorable drinking sessions filled with *rakı* and wine, and even carouse with women in the vicinity.[151] But many of those brought to Belemedik were captured in Syria or Mesopotamia. If they had not contracted malaria at the front, where more virulent *falciparum* strains of the parasite could thrive, they would certainly have been exposed to malaria

Figure 4.1. Houses and encampments at Belemedik during World War I. The hospital is on the hill on the right. Source: Courtesy of Gunter Hartnagel.

Figure 4.2. A small graveyard on a hill overlooking Belemedik. The large headstone in the center belongs to three German military officers. The smaller headstones on the left and right belong to Armenian men. The cemetery was restored during the early 2000s. Source: Photo by author.

risk on the long journey across the empire. In the end, many POWs died of illness in Belemedik from 1916 onward (see figure 4.2).[152]

Displacement, especially the deportation of Armenians, may have played an even greater role in sustaining the malaria epidemic in the Taurus Mountains.[153] Armenians from the western region of Anatolia, from Bursa and Izmit to Ankara and Konya, were deported along the rail line between Istanbul and the Adana region during the summer of 1915. The last stop on this route was the Pozantı train station. According to Kevorkian, the number of deportees who followed this route, either by train or by foot, totaled as many as 400,000.[154] Large camps formed in the train stations between Konya and Pozantı over the course of 1915, where tens of thousands of people awaited further deportation.[155] During 1915, the camps between Konya and Pozantı saw famine and disease begin to spread throughout the Armenian population. Kevorkian states that as many as 10,000 Armenians died in the Pozantı camp during the summer and fall of 1915.[156]

While subsequent deportations to Syria were well under way by September 1915, they were carried out very gradually. An extra military detachment was sent to Pozantı in the fall of 1915 solely for the purpose of maintaining order there due to the numbers of people in the camps.[157] The movement of Armenians toward Pozantı continued over subsequent months.[158] In October 1915, there were more than 20,000 Armenian deportees in the railway stations between Eskişehir and Pozantı. But Cemal Pasha recommended they not be sent onward to the "desert [*çöl*]" until the spring due to transport issues in the Taurus Mountains during winter.[159] In a prior telegram he had warned that there were already 200,000 Armenians in Aleppo and that if an outbreak of infectious disease among the Armenians occurred, "it will be difficult to protect the 4th Army."[160] An inspection soon after revealed that there were about 6,000 Armenians around the Pozantı station, many of whom had infectious diseases, and that they had been living in stables and tents.[161]

Meanwhile, in December 1915, the governor of Konya wrote to the Ministry of Interior saying that the Armenians being sent from his area to Mosul would be moved to Pozantı.[162] In January 1916, Talat inquired about the reported 20,000 Armenians congregated in the Pozantı region. The military was reporting "the necessity of their being sent to the places they are to go caravan by caravan, stating that their provisioning in homes will not be possible, just as their transport by rail is not presently possible."[163] Well into 1916, Pozantı remained a point of centralization for Armenians awaiting an arduous journey toward the south. In the early months of 1916, a second exodus of Armenians—this time out of the Pozantı region—commenced. By the end of January, the governor of Adana notified the Ministry of Interior that there were reportedly no Armenian deportees (the term used is *muhacir*) between Pozantı, Gülek, and Tarsus, although this may not have been the case.[164]

Kevorkian indicates that the appointment of Cevdet Bey, Enver Pasha's brother-in-law, as the new governor of Adana in February 1916 facilitated a more aggressive removal of Armenians from Cilicia and the resolution of irregularities, such as the ballooning Armenian population of labor battalions.[165] Even after this, some Armenians were able to remain in the Pozantı region due to the importance of the construction projects. Armenian experts and laborers were critical to ongoing work on the railway. The aforementioned Lütneger, along with an Armenian doctor named Boyajian stationed in the area, convinced the Ottoman military official responsible for the deportations to allow the Armenians to stay.[166] By June 1916, Talat telegraphed Adana informing them that it was not possible for deported Armenian railroad workers to return to their original construction sites; however, to ensure that the construction continue quickly and without interruption, the government would be cautious about deporting Armenian workers henceforth.[167] Only a small portion of the Armenian workers in Pozantı were deported in the end, and there were around 3,000 Armenians working on the Belemedik connection between Pozantı and Dorak well into the last year of the war.[168] The slow progress of the workers likely saved many lives. But the railway work and the opportunities to escape deportation in the Pozantı region added to an unusually large conglomeration of people, many of whom suffered malnutrition and substandard living conditions.

By 1918, malaria had become deeply entangled with the Taurus Mountains environment due to anthropogenic causes associated with the war. This malaria epidemic reveals an environmental history of the war not fully captured by production statistics, rates of disease, or mortality figures. The war had also overthrown a longstanding ecology in which the mountains had served as the antidote to the malaria of the lowlands. Though the first victims of this epidemic might have been soldiers or Armenian deportees, neither mosquitos nor malaria parasites adhered to the numerous distinctions between the different groups in the Ottoman Empire. Even the Tahtacıs of the Taurus Mountains, who had for long relied on their quiet *yayla* as a refuge from disease and the state alike, would ultimately fall victim to a deadly malaria epidemic. Half of local Tahtacıs examined in April 1918 tested positive for the parasite.[169]

France in Cilicia

With the Ottoman defeat in 1918, France claimed Cilicia as an integral part of Greater Syria, which it would govern throughout the interwar period.[170] General Taillardat, the governor of the district of Kozan, declared that Cilicia was a "rich but ravaged and depopulated country" and that the first goals of the French administration would be to repopulate the countryside and forestall famine.[171] Meanwhile, the Ottoman governor of Adana wrote to the Ministry of Interior in recently occupied Istanbul requesting aid for local civil servants, who were in dire financial straits due to the continuous escalation of an "extraordinary scarcity [*gala-yı fevkalade*]."[172] The price of grain had increased to roughly fifteen times the prewar value by 1918, and though it had moderated a little with the armistice, it was still very high.[173] A doctor who arrived with an Armenian medical mission from Paris noted the epidemic proportions of malaria throughout Cilicia, conveniently citing Ottoman misrule.[174] No measure undertaken by the French administration would fundamentally change this situation during their short adventure in Cilicia. For a period lasting almost as long as the war itself, Cilicia remained a giant humanitarian disaster zone.[175]

France had not entered the region with humanitarian ambitions. Rather, Cilicia appeared ideal for agricultural development to feed a struggling manufacturing industry. Within this context, the imaginary of Cilicia as Second Egypt became more explicitly colonial. A military officer in Cilicia referred to the region as a former "Granary of Rome," a notion that had been already used as an ecological justification for French colonialism in North Africa decades prior.[176] The same ruins of Anazarbus that had justified an Ottoman civilizing mission during the 1860s now justified a colonial mandate to develop Cilicia's economy. Another writer would go on to romantically describe Cilicia as "Egypt with the Alps," a land with the productivity of Egypt coupled with the natural beauty of Europe.[177] French agronomist E. C. Achard offered data in his study of agriculture in Greater Syria showing that the region could fully meet the demands of the French textile industry, which was heavily reliant on American cotton.[178] The aforementioned French investors Lesseps and Vendeuvre still held a claim to the Çukurova Estates, once the Çukurova Imperial Farm held by Sultan Abdülhamid II, which if developed, had the potential to become one of the largest agricultural ventures in the Mediterranean.[179]

The lofty prospects for colonization clashed with the desperate realities of life in the region. The extreme decline in commerce, particularly the sale of cotton, the deportation of Adana's Armenians, and the general disappearance of laborers during the war had scaled back agriculture to the state of many decades earlier. The low point of cotton production during the war had been by all estimates significantly lower than production figures from the 1880s (see figure 4.3). In fact, agricultural production had not been so meager since before the 1860s, when the urban populations of the Cilicia region were less than half what they had become by 1914.[180]

A cornerstone of French policy in Cilicia was Armenian repatriation, which brought upwards of 100,000 Ottoman Armenians to the region by the end of 1919.[181] These repatriates were natives of the Adana province as well as Armenians from other parts of Anatolia who ended up in French territory. Repatriation was seen as complementary to the economic goals of the French administration, and it provided a solution for the large Armenian refugee population in Syria. It would also allow France to claim that Cilicia was a predominantly Christian territory and establish a political relationship with a client community presumably loyal to French rule.[182] Thousands of Armenians were already fighting with the French army, and many refugees were trying to return on their own. By October 1919, repatriation to Cilicia became mandatory for Anatolian Armenians located in most of Greater Syria.[183]

Cilicia never formally became a French mandate, but it functioned long enough as a polity to leave behind a substantial archive of administrative documentation, some of which is in Ottoman Turkish. Economic affairs

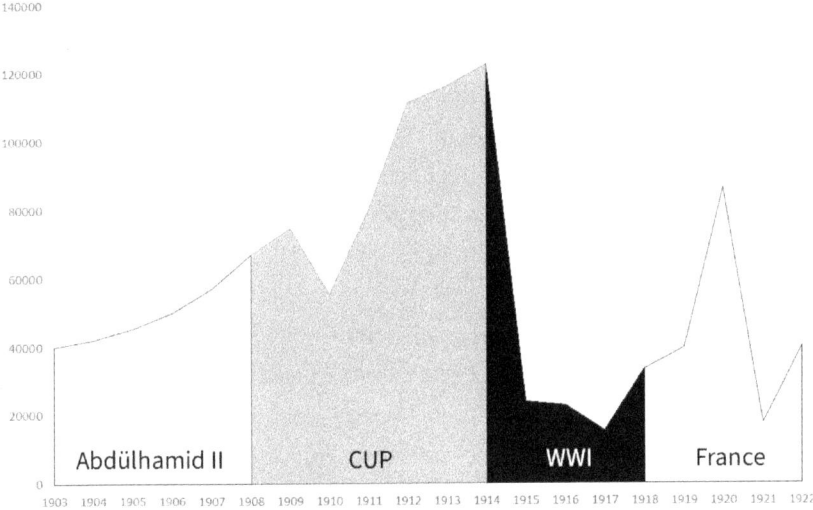

Figure 4.3. Annual cotton production of Cilicia (in bales). This graph represents cotton production estimates based on a combination of source data and does not reflect the amount of cotton sold, used, or exported in the Adana region. Sources: CADN, 8PO/1, Vol. 46, *Coton*, "La Culture de coton par la Chambre Agricole à Adana, 1341"; Achard, *Le coton en Cilicie et en Syrie*, 9; Remzi Oğuz, *Adana Ticaret Rehberi* (Istanbul: Cihan Biraderler Matbaası, 1340 [1924]), 56; *İkinci Adana Pamuk Kongresi Zabıtnamesi*, (Istanbul: Matbaa-yı Amire, 1925), 163–64. See also Polatel and Üngör, *Confiscation and Colonization*, 128. Graph by author.

returned to a semblance of normalcy during the first year of French rule, though the harvest of 1919 came up short of expectations.[184] Wheat was still over three times its prewar price, and the prices of many other items were even higher in towns like Tarsus.[185] In January 1920, the local *mutasarrıf* of Mersin asked for an emergency halt on the export of sheep and goats to protect the critically low supply of meat and milk.[186] Yet from the vantage point of the French administration, the prospects for 1920 looked promising.[187] In the countryside of Adana, Tarsus, and Mersin, planting took place on schedule.[188]

Due to the escalation of conflict in the countryside, economic crisis would soon return. Even as the French government ruled largely through the preexisting Ottoman administration in the cities, France's arrival engendered immediate conflict in the hinterland. Between 1915 and 1919, many properties of Armenians were distributed to refugees who had arrived in the wake of the deportations or simply seized by new owners.[189] Letters from repatriated Armenians in Dörtyol pointed to a messy process. Some found their old land occupied by new Muslim inhabitants, many of whom were refugees. The region's famous orange groves, which had been expanded by Armenian landowners for commercial export during the late Ottoman period, were taken over and planted with more traditional food crops, such as grapes and olives, by their new stewards.[190]

As early as the fall of 1919, French authorities were confronted by armed bands made up in part of former Ottoman soldiers carrying out acts of brigandage in the mountains, just as such groups had already done during the later years of the war. The violence caused a panic among the local Armenian population in the countryside and resulted in the flight of cotton cultivators from the villages to the cities.[191] Then during the winter of 1919–20, a small militia of a few thousand fighters, supported by some local notables in Marash, achieved the Turkish national resistance's first major victory against the French. The sudden French withdrawal left the Armenians of Marash, who were subject to mass violence throughout the siege, in an extremely vulnerable position.[192] Most of the Armenian population fled on foot, and the majority of those who left with the French died during a three-day march through the snow toward İslahiye. The number of Armenians who did not survive the siege and exodus was estimated in the thousands.[193] After the fall of Marash, fighting paralyzed the Cilicia region. A French observer noted that life was so disrupted that people could not even sleep on their roofs under the comfort of a mosquito net to escape the miserable and muggy summer nights, for fear of shelling.[194] The government did persist in trying to normalize agricultural activities, arranging the distribution of about 75,000 kg of seed for cotton planting in the spring of 1920.[195] But sowing of cotton halted at half of the anticipated capacity due to labor shortages.[196]

In June 1920, the Adana Fair opened in what must have been a somber atmosphere. Planning for the fair, which involved some of the most important businessmen and officials in the region, had begun in the fall of 1919. Various booths showcased facets of modern life in Cilicia, such as Renault tractors, wares of the Orosdi-Back department store, and the activities of an agricultural school for Turkish girls.[197] The event was meant to represent the new collaborations between international companies, the French administration, and local institutions in Cilicia. However, during the period between the fair's planning and opening, a political crisis had unfolded that would have made any visitor skeptical about the region's future. French cotton prospects in Cilicia were not panning out, due to the disruption of normal labor migrations from Eastern Anatolia and provinces to the north caused by political conflicts. Brémond suggested that this deficit could be overcome using workers imported from Northern Syria to work at set rates, with women receiving wages half of men's.[198] But none of this talk of the future was rooted in realities on the ground. In fact, the same month of the Adana Fair's opening, the French army faced another major defeat, evacuating Sis and bringing an Armenian refugee population of between 4,000 and 7,500 inhabitants with them to the cities of Adana, Tarsus, and Mersin.[199] Most would never return again to live in this city, which had been a center of Armenian ecclesiastical authority since the late thirteenth century.

The fighting that had begun in the mountainous hinterland had reached the plain by the summer of 1920, and more displacement ensued. Around 25,000 Muslims, many of them Nusayri Arabs, suddenly fled to areas beyond French control.[200] A Red Crescent doctor related how a refugee crisis among the Muslims of Adana unfolded. "Early last July, Adana's Muslim inhabitants abandoned Adana in one day fearing for their lives, leaving behind all their wealth and belongings." They spread out first in the gardens surrounding the city and then moved into the mountains. Those from Adana, Tarsus, and Mersin who had *yayla* homes in Gülek, Namrun, and Mersin took refuge there. Others found help from their "coracialists [*ırkdaşlar*]" in the villages. The poorest segment hid in caves and mountain dens. With the onset of winter, severe hardship came, "since most of the population that fled are plains people [*ova efradı*], they are not able to adapt to the weather in the mountains or the harsh climate of Konya, Bor, and Niğde." The exodus from Adana took a heavy toll on these families. Aside from hunger, the most common affliction was malaria, followed by typhus, trachoma, and numerous other diseases.[201]

The future of Cilicia had become a national struggle between local Muslims and Christians. Armenian repatriation had fueled national aspirations of the Armenian political leadership, even as France's hold on Cilicia grew more tenuous. The Armenian leadership in Cilicia declared independence in August 1920 in the midst of what appeared to be France's incremental loss of the territory.[202] Meanwhile, a group called the Cilicians Society (Kilikyalılar Cemiyeti), founded by Ali Münif Bey and other Cilicia natives in Istanbul, lobbied for the independence of Cilicia on the basis of its being a majority-Muslim region with a long history of Turkish identity.[203] An Adana notable named Hasibe Ramazanoğlu composed songs of rebellion when her family fled into the Taurus Mountains during the war. "Oh French, did you think it would be easy to take this country? / If there's any lie in my words / Announce it to the papers / Our ancestor Ramazanoğlu took Adana first," she declared in reference to her descent from the local dynasty that had ruled Cilicia before the Ottomans.[204] *Yeni Adana*, an Ottoman Turkish newspaper published out of a mountain stronghold in Pozantı, became the local mouthpiece of the resistance. The service of the Armenian Legion in the French military exacerbated this tension, although Muslim minority groups, such as Circassians and Kurds in Cilicia, were also recruited.[205] Through the association of Armenian personnel with the French military and their involvement in acts of violence against the Muslim population, the Cilician Armenian community was recast as part of the occupying force, even though their numbers were small among the overall military presence in the region.[206]

Recognizing the course of events, in September 1920, the French authorities adopted a more conciliatory approach toward the Turkish national movement, ceding much of the original occupied territory.[207] The sudden French withdrawal from the mountains spelled disaster for remaining Armenian communities in the hinterland. The inhabitants of Hadjin, estimated at around 9,000 individuals, became isolated in their Taurus Mountain villages, surrounded by rebels and teetering at the brink of starvation.[208] Some Armenian leaders had advocated the evacuation of Hadjin as early March 1920, but the plan was rejected by the French administration, which still held the district capital of Sis at that time. The decision, which did little to stem French losses, had severe consequences in Hadjin. Local fighters defended the town for a few months, but when the town fell in October 1920, it was the site of a terrible massacre.[209] Those who managed to escape joined the growing number of refugees in the towns of the lowlands, where concerned compatriots could only read with apprehension and horror as news from

Hadjin trickled onto the pages of *Giligia*, the most important Armenian newspaper in Adana.[210]

The growing humanitarian crisis was caused by armed conflict, but the commercial nature of the economy France sought to foster in Cilicia exacerbated local conditions of scarcity. In August 1920, Colonel Bremond had warned that "the grain harvest is very compromised," presaging an encore of the famine of 1916. "Meanwhile, Anatolia, which every year furnished several thousand tons of grain, will not give any, as it was not cultivated and the harvest cannot be made."[211] Nonetheless, in late September 1920 the interim Ottoman governor wrote to the French administration with a tone of incredulous alarm to express his extreme displeasure with the prospect of continued export of cereals from the region.[212] Even with the ongoing war, French administrators and some local merchants still hoped that a return to an export economy would help restore prosperity and normalcy. Yet the region no longer had grain to spare. As war and internal displacement intensified, a growing number of people were pushed toward starvation, and care for refugees and orphans became the dominant civil concern for a variety of humanitarian aid groups in Cilicia.

The aforementioned flour magnate Bodosakis returned to the scene in Adana during this period. The young man who had been one of the most important suppliers of the Ottoman army became the key figure in France's provisioning system in Cilicia. French concerns about flour and grain were not limited to supplying the military. Between April and August 1920, as Armenians fled the countryside, the French government dispensed rations to between 10,000 and 15,000 people per day in Adana, a number equivalent to roughly one-fifth of the city's permanent population. Coordinating the provisioning involved constant correspondence between the Mersin Chamber of Commerce, Bodosakis, other merchants, and the government. Yet by September 1920, the severity of the food crisis was apparent. Rations had been set at 450 g per person in April, but as the granaries became increasingly stretched, that number was reduced to 102.5 g. A French official described this amount as "just enough to prevent people from dying of hunger."[213]

The hungry and displaced population was also a sick population, but the health apparatus of the French government did not extend beyond the preexisting Ottoman institutions: four municipal hospitals in Adana (150 beds),

Mersin (25 beds), Tarsus (50 beds), and Ceyhan (25 beds) along with a hospital for women engaged in sex work.[214] Outside the cities, public health activities were severely limited. A Dr. Cemal Bey, who filed a report on the health situation in Çukurova, noted that malaria was especially rampant in the Ceyhan region, stating that many soldiers had returned from Yemen and elsewhere after the war with new strains of the parasite.[215] Quinine could be used to control malaria infections, but the French administration could not regulate the supply and distribution of medicines. The French army issued quinine to its personnel along with propaganda emphasizing that malaria and mosquitos were their "enemies" in the Levant.[216] An investigation discovered that military personnel and soldiers were selling their quinine on the black market. An interrogation of pharmacists in Adana revealed why they were tempted to do so. Quinine was extremely difficult to obtain, and the pharmacists all reported that they essentially scraped together supplies however they could by purchasing from travelers from Istanbul and Izmir. A certain Mr. Nassibi purchased his quinine from an Indian doctor, and an Armenian pharmacist simply reported that "we buy a little medicine from here and there on random occasions." Pharmacists bought quinine for 40 *lira* per kilogram.[217] The skyrocketing prices meant that antimalarial medicines were simply inaccessible to ordinary people.

Humanitarian organizations stepped in to fill the growing need for care. The Armenian Medical Mission (AMM; Հայ Բժշկական Առաքելութիւն) was sent from Paris with support from the Armenian General Benevolent Union (AGBU) to help provide public health relief for Armenian repatriates and refugees in Cilicia. Dr. Diran Ghazarossian headed the mission made up of five doctors and four nurses, who arrived in Mersin at the end of May 1919. They immediately founded a new hospital in the city of Adana and opened medical dispensaries. The AMM hospital contained sixty beds and a maternity ward. It worked almost exclusively with the Armenian community; Ghazarossian stated that the clinics welcomed the needy of other communities but did not offer free care. In addition, the AMM operated clinics in the Gulbenkian and Rolland refugee camps as well as in the Armenian neighborhoods of Adana. Two nurses visited the camps to encourage pregnant women to give birth at the hospital. The doctors of the AMM also performed house visits. The mission aimed to send doctors to Marash,

Hadjin, Dörtyol, Tarsus, Misis, and Osmaniye, but struggled to find people willing to work in the more remote areas. Approximately 25,000 patients were helped during the first months of the mission, roughly one-third being treated for malaria.[218]

Meanwhile, local Armenian women in Tarsus created "the firstborn among sister Red Crosses of Cilicia."[219] The eventual chairwoman, Zaruhi Shalvarjian, was the wife of a Tarsus factory owner. The group maintained a hospital in the city, which had treated several thousand patients by the end of 1920. Though the effort was inspired by support for the Armenian Legion, roughly 60 percent of the patients who stayed in the hospital at some point were women and girls. The Armenian Red Cross of Tarsus operated independently from the AGBU because of a falling out. The AGBU attempted to name the hospital the Benevolent Hospital (Բարեգործական Հիւանդանոց), even though the women deemed it "an institution established through our sacrifices."[220] Most of the early donors to the hospital were local Armenian women, alongside Colonel Bremond himself and a few international Armenian organizations. The largest individual donations came from Bodosakis, and the remainder of the hospital's budget—about half—was covered by the French administration.[221]

While foreign and Armenian humanitarian organizations focused their efforts on the largely displaced Christian communities, the Red Crescent began providing care to the growing number of Muslim inhabitants of Cilicia displaced by the conflict. The Cilicians Society in Istanbul lobbied the Red Crescent, which had become a relief organization in support of the Kemalists, to send a relief mission to Cilicia called the Adana Health Relief Commission (Adana İmdad-ı Sıhhi Heyeti).[222] The commission was headed by Dr. Haydar. It was made up of eight doctors, a pharmacist, four health officers, and six male and female aides, who arrived in Antalya in October 1920.[223] They established headquarters in Konya and catered mainly to the 27,480 refugees from Adana in the Konya province and another 2,686 in Pozantı.[224] During the winter of 1920–21, the Red Crescent institutions administered treatment and relief to refugees through the hospitals and dispensaries it had established. In addition to hospitals in Konya and Bor, there were dispensaries in several locations, including Konya, Ereğli, Bor, Belemedik, and Namrun. Between December 1920 and October 1921, the hospitals treated thousands of patients and the dispensaries served tens of thousands. At the Konya hospital, soldiers and officers constituted more than 90 percent of the patients.[225] But the Bor hospital and the various dispensaries were used by civilians. The five dispensaries treated more than 20,000 people for various ailments over the course of 1921.[226] Reports stated that around 80 percent of those who came to one of the dispensaries had malaria and the organization was dispensing a tremendous amount of quinine.[227]

As the crisis in the countryside escalated, the remaining areas of French control swelled with refugees. By 1921, most of the Armenian population in Cilicia had fled to Adana, Tarsus, and Mersin. Dörtyol became the only provincial stronghold where the idea of Cilicia as an Armenian homeland lived on in any meaningful sense. Due to the prevailing displacement, the harvests of 1921 were significantly worse than those of 1920. Cilicia only produced half of the food required to feed the local population.[228] Without an emergency shipment of grain in September 1921, per request of the local civilian government, a mass starvation event might have been the final chapter of France's short history in the region.[229]

In October 1921, France and the Grand National Assembly of Turkey signed the Ankara Agreement. France acknowledged Turkish sovereignty over Cilicia in exchange for recognition of the remaining French mandate territory in Syria and Lebanon. More refugees, including 17,000 Armenians fleeing violence and starvation, flocked to Adana on the eve of their departure with the fleeing French.[230] The withdrawal brought yet another wave of displacement in the form of history's first humanitarian evacuation, what Benjamin Thomas White dubbed the "grudging rescue" of Cilicia's Armenians by France.[231] Almost the entire Armenian population of Cilicia, which had been repatriated from Syria just a few years before, was hastily transferred, with most initially brought to either Dörtyol, Istanbul, or Beirut.[232] In December 1921, France transferred the holdout Armenian community in Dörtyol to Syria, principally the Sanjak of Alexandretta (Iskenderun), which would remain in French hands as a subdivision of its mandatory territories until the mid-1930s.[233]

The Treaty of Lausanne in 1923 marked an official end to the conflicts of World War I. The Republic of Turkey became the successor to the fallen Ottoman Empire. France and Great Britain divided the former Ottoman territories of the Levant under the League of Nations mandate system. Most Armenians evacuated from Cilicia with the fleeing French became nationals of Syria and Lebanon. Many lived the lives of refugees, with some of the initial camps gradually becoming neighborhoods in cities like Aleppo and Beirut. The ecclesiastical authority of Cilicia, formerly based in Sis, reconstituted itself in Antelias, Lebanon. Many Armenians migrated farther to places like Soviet Armenia, the Americas, and France as the Cilician diaspora spread. Between 1940 and 1960, diaspora communities compiled three different memory volumes authored and funded by the former residents of three central Armenian settlements of Cilicia that stretched back to the medieval period: Hadjin, Sis, and Zeytun. The books were published in Los Angeles, Beirut, and Buenos Aires, respectively.[234]

The Greek Orthodox population, which had played a crucial role in the mercantile networks of Adana and Mersin, was also expelled from the Cilicia region by the exchange of populations that accompanied the peace agreement between Greece and Turkey. In Greece, they arrived near the bottom of the social ladder, although Prodromos Bodosakis Athanasiadis would become one of the richest men in the country, building on his prior experience to become a major arms manufacturer during the 1930s.[235] Of all the lessons to come out of the war, what Bodosakis learned was probably the worst. But his own life story joined a rich corpus of oral history and memoirs of exchanged people from Cilicia who became Greek. Their testimonies contained textured depictions of local life in Cilicia and the coexistence of its different ethnoreligious communities during the prosperous final decades of Ottoman rule. Perhaps it was in exile that these new migrants most appreciated the intercommunal world that once thrived in the Ottoman provinces.

Cilicia's diverse communities did not remember the First World War in the same way, but there were elements of shared experience. One of the many songs from the Ottoman period that the Avşars of the Taurus Mountains passed across generations was the "Song of the Seventeener." It opens with the lines: "The trumpets sound / 'Let the soldiers come' they cry / The Seventeener has become a soldier / They gather them to die."[236]

Born in 1901–2, or the *rumi* year of 1317, the "seventeeners" were barely adolescents at the outset of World War I, but they had been conscripted into an increasingly disastrous venture by its end. The feeling that young men were simply gathered up to die conveyed a sense of futility about the war. Far from an exception, this song belonged to an entire genre of laments that rural people in Anatolia preserved about soldiers who were taken before their time.[237] What Cilician Armenians experienced during the genocide was distinct, but in many senses, they too felt they had been cruelly gathered up to die. The memories of deportation, massacre, and exile remain defining features of Armenian national consciousness a century after the war's end.

The senseless suffering of the war and many other examples presented in this chapter give the same impression that Movses Hagopyan sought to achieve in his song about *seferberlik*: a world turned upside-down. Residents of the once prosperous city of Adana used their furniture and beloved summer orchards as firewood. The Tahtacıs who once lived off timber in the Taurus Mountains were reduced to eating acorns. Soldiers became brigands, and brigands became heroes. Armenian boys lived the lives of Arab and Kurdish shepherds in the deserts of Syria. Armenian women became members of Muslim families, and sometimes remained as such decades after the war's end, guarding the secrets of their origins. Survival often entailed such inversion, and in fact, the war inverted many relationships. Conscript laborers were removed from village life only to tend the fields of others. The cotton merchants of Adana and Mersin went bankrupt as flour replaced the old white gold of late Ottoman Cilicia. And those unfortunate enough to spend the summer of 1916 in the Taurus Mountains died of malaria in the very place they would normally go to escape it.

The war also offended any basic sense of moral economy. Decent people suffered, but profiteers thrived. Merchants hoarded grain and benefited from the skyrocketing prices of basic foodstuffs. At every stage of Armenian deportation, from the hurried departure to the struggle for survival in the Syrian desert, there were opportunities for others to profit. When the Ottoman Empire finally collapsed, France claimed stewardship of the Cilicia region with dreams of cheap cotton and little regard for, or even knowledge of, the concerns of its inhabitants. Its soldiers sold the medicine France gave them, which was meant to protect them from the epidemic that war had produced, to those inhabitants at exorbitant prices. Nonhuman profiteers also abounded. Mosquitos and the malaria parasites they carried thrived and even expanded their reach into mountain spaces normally spared the summer scourge. Typhus-carrying lice hitched a ride on displaced people throughout the empire, and airborne locusts beat local villagers to the harvest of precious wheat amid famine conditions.

Ultimately, the grotesque reality of wartime Cilicia contorted the images of its history. Songs that the Avşars preserved about their Armenian neighbors did not reflect a sense of shared struggle or past. Most of what survives are accounts of atrocities committed by Armenians, bandits like Çöllo, who "took from the Armenian and gave to the poor," and heroes of the independence war.[238] Such stories could already be found in the ethnomusicological research of Wolfram Eberhard from decades prior, though he noted that portrayals of Armenians in Turkish folklore were at least more nuanced and varied than in the standard national memory of the early republican period.[239] That nuance was likely lost with the last generation to actually share the mountains with Armenian neighbors.

Armenian memory literature is similarly short on fond depictions of intercommunal life. The experience of the Armenian genocide eclipsed Cilicia's history as a place where many different communities lived side by side for centuries. However, in the memory books the last generation of Ottoman Armenians made about their lost towns and villages, there were still a few vestiges of that world. One was the "Song of Kozanoğlu," the only leader who never really surrendered to the Ottoman government during the forced settlement campaigns of the 1860s. As the tale of Kozanoğlu's defiant stand went: "Mighty Kozanoğlu, whose fame is so great, said 'I will not leave my place.'" The displaced Armenians of Hadjin, the last mountain town to fall in 1920, had not forgotten him generations later.[240] As late as 1953, an Armenian interlocutor in California bragged to Eberhard that his ancestors had fought alongside mighty Kozanoğlu.[241] In other iterations of the poem, Armenians who fought with Kozanoğlu stand in as protagonists, showing how, just as in the case of people forced to settle during the 1860s, the lament of an individual became a frame for accounts of a collective experience.[242] Ultimately, Armenians in diaspora preserved the memory of Kozanoğlu for separate reasons than their former Turkish neighbors did—only their reasons were not so different at all. Kozanoğlu had become more relevant than ever. His stand against the Ottoman government and his refusal to accept exile resonated in new ways after what Armenians endured throughout the war years.

The war's many refugees were part of a longer history. Their experiences of exile and survival were entangled with the still unfolding displacement of Muslims during the Balkan Wars a few years prior, as well as the many waves of *muhacirs* who arrived at Ottoman shores going back to the Crimean War of the 1850s. Many in Cilicia were themselves, or were descended from, such migrants, just as many came from the pastoralist communities subject to forced sedentarization during the 1860s. To what extent were those who experienced and observed the devastation of World War I conscious of the historical experience of death and displacement they shared with prior generations? When during the war Besim Atalay (see chapter 2), wrote a history of Marash, equating the forced sedentarization, or *iskân,* of Cilicia's tribes with annihilation (*imha*), did he not see any connection with what was happening to the Armenians of Marash under the wartime orders of "relocation and resettlement" (*sevk ve iskân*)?

The historiography of the Ottoman world has long been divided by the contentious war period in which Cilicia was so pivotal. Yet its history reveals much about what came before and after. With regard to the developments of the late Ottoman frontier, we can better see through the lens of World War I why the costly "defensive modernization" of the Ottoman Empire occurred and yet how it also remained incomplete. The reforms of the Tanzimat period had been intended to strengthen the region's relationship with the Ottoman state and by extension strengthen the empire. However, that relationship proved destructive for people in the region when it came time for the Ottoman Empire to mobilize the new society it had built. The destruction of Cilicia during the war also revealed the fragility of the cosmopolitan societies created by late Ottoman reform and commercialization. On one hand, the local reverberations of political conflicts made it untenable for Muslims and Christians to imagine a future together. On the other, the sudden disruption of commercial traffic and networks of migrant workers completely undermined economic life. There was nothing resilient about an economy built on cotton export, cycles of credit, and a volatile labor supply. When that economy buckled under the pressure of war and demands of mobilization, it exposed a growing segment of the population, ranging from wealthy merchants to wage workers who were dependent on the market for their livelihoods.

During the war, the state became concerned with matters that had hitherto remained largely outside its domain. Whether in use of labor battalions for agricultural purposes or provisioning efforts, the military became a major force in the regulation of the food supply. In seeking to put quinine in the blood of every individual, the Ottoman government had become involved in a new biological dimension of war. When the state failed, humanitarian organizations emerged to address the severe impact of war on civilian populations. For international humanitarians, Cilicia was at the center of novel developments in how their moral mandate was conceptualized as service to humanity itself.[243] But for local actors, whether agents of the Red Crescent or Armenian aid workers, Cilicia underscored the centrality of humanitarianism for national movements. Public health and nationalism would remain wedded after the war. And although the Republic of Turkey would never again be involved in a conflict approaching such a magnitude, the national rhetoric employed the language of war and mobilization in a number of fields, including agricultural modernization, medicine, and environmental policy.

Though the war represented a rupture in the history of late Ottoman Cilicia and produced new conditions, its history also reveals dimensions that were enduring. Despite the utter destruction of the cotton industry during the war, cotton would reclaim its central position in the region afterward. Just as Çukurova was a settlement frontier during the late Ottoman period, the interwar period would be characterized by new attempts to resettle a countryside depopulated by the war and its impacts. The war did not derail the region from its basic historical trajectory. Emboldened by new technologies, the early republican state gave science a prominent place in governance, adopting a technocratic approach as a key pillar of its nation-making agenda and extending the legacy of the late Ottoman frontier more than a century after the Tanzimat experiment began. As science emerged as a dominant way of knowing and ordering the environment, Çukurova, a borderland region narrowly snatched from the claws of colonial encroachment, would become a laboratory of the new nation.

(CHAPTER 5)

A MODERN LIFE OF TRANSHUMANCE

Change and Continuity in the Republic of Turkey, 1923–56

With the breakup of the Ottoman Empire, Cilicia's Amanus Mountains were no longer the geographical center of an empire but rather the border region of a new nation-state: the Republic of Turkey. An area that had been strategically important enough to send an army to reform it during the 1860s had no less political value to the new government formed by the Republic People's Party (CHP). An early report by an official in the region about its future contained what Ankara might have seen as an odd recommendation. Among the reforms or "revolutions [*inkilap*]" envisioned was the creation of "a modern life of transhumance [*fenni bir yaylacılık hayatı*]."[1] What the official who wrote the report intended was a 20 km road between the city of Osmaniye—a creation of Cevdet Pasha's Reform Division—and the "natural wonders" that were the *yaylas* of the nearby mountains. He contended that by facilitating transhumance, "the fight against malaria and tuberculosis would begin to yield fruitful results in a more reduced time span."[2] Whereas the seasonal migration of pastoralists had once been marked as an impediment to an Ottoman civilizing mission—and the report noted that tens of thousands of such nomads still roamed the region unmonitored—it nonetheless touted the value of producing a modernized version of the old and enduring practice as part of the national project. The notion of modern transhumance illustrated the protean nature of modernity as a concept when left to the imagination of state actors operating on localized ecological understandings.

Seasonal migration never took an official place within Turkey's modernization agenda. Such movements were incompatible with the resurrection of commercial agriculture in Çukurova, which was slow to recover in the wake of World War I and the ensuing global depression. Transhumance also had little to do with state-of-the-art biomedical knowledge about malaria and mosquitos. Instead, the local medical establishment would become more involved in monitoring and controlling the bodies, homes, and agrarian spaces of rural communities, as Adana became a laboratory for malaria research and treatment. Health officials had begun mass medical examinations even before the first national census in 1927. Yet even in doing so, they were obliged to accommodate longstanding practices that were ostensibly obsolete, conducting examinations in the fall after everyone's return from the *yayla*.[3] In order to carry out the measures necessary to control and monitor malaria, the doctors first had to wait for people to return from the places where they already had sought refuge from the disease for centuries. This seasonal ritual of migration followed by testing in the fall would carry on for decades, as the public health apparatus of the Turkish government extended its reach in the countryside. When antimalaria efforts were reinvigorated following World War II, the practice was still the same.[4]

The state narrative during the interwar period of one-party rule emphasized that the Republic of Turkey had made a firm break with the Ottoman period. Early republican imagery cast Turkey as a young, fledgling nation, and the government instituted reforms in matters of law, language, and dress meant to send the message that its recent Ottoman history was relegated to a distant past.[5] This chapter, in keeping with a more recent historiographical trend, challenges the notion of the early republican period as a fundamental break in Turkey's history, rather seeing it as a continuation of a much longer transformation that began during the late Ottoman period. Although war disrupted commercial and social life, the major themes and ecological relationships that came to define life before the war continued as the republican government inherited the late Ottoman frontier.

There was, however, change, reflected in the state's growing embrace of science as a means of remaking the population and environment.[6] Adana became a center of both agricultural and medical experimentation, and efforts to engineer the environment and develop new ways of improving upon it produced what Seçil Binboğa describes as "experimental nature."[7] The expansion of public health activities during the interwar period became part and parcel of a larger project of subject-making, and the laboratory of the Turkish countryside served as a site for new attempts at harnessing nature through infrastructure projects, mechanization of agriculture, experimentation with seed, and modification of the landscape. At the same time, Cilicia's oldest ritual—the annual summer retreat to the *yaylas* of the Taurus and Amanus Mountains—underwent a metamorphosis. The extension of railways and automobiles into the mountains allowed locals to move through space in a new way, making the "modern life of transhumance" a reality for the region's elite. Rather than malaria or livestock, leisure defined a new love affair with the mountains among the elite and professional classes of the modern lowland cities. Yet economic conditions continued to erode the livelihoods of those who once called the mountains theirs: the pastoralists who had long moved between the *yayla* and the plains with their flocks. These groups would come to be seen as bearers of authentic Turkish culture. But their storied history of traversing the land of Anatolia could provide linguistic and cultural links between the natural geography and the modern nation, only after they had been pushed to the furthest margins of local society.

Exchanging Peasantries

The Republic of Turkey was founded on the idea of a national revolution that rejected much of the Ottoman past. In 1928, the republican government adopted a new Latin alphabet for the Turkish language. Various vestiges of the Ottoman era were suppressed or erased.[8] Each citizen was eventually issued a new surname conforming to the Turkish language reforms that purged the vocabulary of many Arabic and Persian words.[9] And in the Cilicia region, erasing the traces of the region's non-Muslim past was also integral. Sis, the former center of Armenian ecclesiastical life, was renamed Kozan. Hadjin became Saimbeyli. Zeytun became Süleymanlı. The city of Marash became "Kahramanmaraş," earning the honorific of "heroic" to signify the role it played in the expulsion of the French from Cilicia. Even that name was soon erased. Remzi Oğuz, the author of the first significant study of the region after the war, adopted it for the sake of continuity. He explained in his historical overview that "we use the name Cilicia in place of the Adana province [*Adana vilayeti*] because political configurations are always changing."[10] However, this was the last time the name appears in a significant publication from the republican period to describe the contemporary Adana region. Having gained an association with the French occupation and a memory of Armenian Cilicia that few wished to maintain, the toponym Cilicia—much like the Ottoman Empire itself—was banished to the past.

By the mid-twentieth century, Çukurova would emerge as the new name for the geography once known as Cilicia. This shift reflected the completion of what began during the late Ottoman period. Once referring to a sparse, uncultivated lowland used as winter pasture by nomads, the name Çukurova came to refer an entire socioeconomic region comprising the now densely cultivated plain and its mountainous hinterland. The republican project in Çukurova was not about charting a completely new vision for the countryside, however. Instead, it cemented the trajectory established with settlement and commercialization during the late Ottoman period, placing the village at the center of the national project and using technology to improve it. It was a project of exchanging the image of the fragmentary Ottoman peasantry in Cilicia, which included Turkish, Kurdish, Arab, Armenian, Greek, Circassian, Chechen, Cretan, Balkan, and other communities, for an archetype of the modern Turkish villager. Comparisons to Egypt were gone. Çukurova was the nation: *Memleket Çukurova'da*, as Adana's education ministry would title its main periodical. And in many ways, it would become the agricultural engine for all of Turkey, a gateway to the eastern Anatolian frontier for Ankara and Istanbul, and a gateway to prosperity and urban life for migrants from the east.

At the outset of the republican period, the Adana region was less populated than it had been in 1914 due to wartime mortality and the exile of most of its non-Muslim population. Combined with the population figures of the 1920s and 1930s, data indicate a resumed shift in center of gravity from the mountains to the lowlands. Former centers of Armenian and Greek population *in the mountains*, like Hadjin and Feke, witnessed an overall decline, some in a proportion greater than the initial non-Muslim percentage of the population. By contrast, the coastal town of Dörtyol (formerly

Çokmerzimen), also about one-third Christian before the war, grew quickly during the early republican period.¹¹ By the 1930s, its population had returned to prewar levels. In his 1939 study of the region's villages, Taha Toros, who would become one of the republic's major historians, claimed that "it would not at all be realistic to imagine the coming economic development of the plain occurring for the mountain villages."¹² The mountains belonged to the past; the villages of Çukurova, which had emerged mainly during the late nineteenth century, were the future of the regional economy. The early republican period also saw a slowdown in the late Ottoman trend of urbanization. The growth of Çukurova's cities, with the notable exception of Ceyhan, was negligible. Even though the district of Adana grew by 20 percent over that period, the official population of the city itself only grew by a few thousand.¹³ Meanwhile, the districts of the Upper Çukurova plain grew as much as or more than the district of Adana. Ceyhan grew by more than 40 percent.

The early republican project was intensely rural in that it was concerned with securing the participation and cooperation of villagers from an early stage. For example, Dr. Muhittin, the Red Crescent inspector in the Adana province during the late 1920s, insisted on the value of visiting "even the villages" to solicit donations and membership.¹⁴ "I will try to go, even if by animal," he declared at one point, when the small and muddy roads in Eastern Çukurova prevented passage during his tour.¹⁵ His interest in the villages was more ideological than financial. Among the struggling rural communities of the Çukurova region, he was often met with optimism if not sizeable donations.¹⁶ In the village of Mercimek near the Ceyhan River, he encountered a village of migrants from Rumeli who reacted warmly to his solicitations, saying they had always seen kindness from the Red Crescent.¹⁷ But beyond enlisting the support of villagers, Dr. Muhittin's reports called on the Red Crescent to hitch itself to the agrarian economy of the Çukurova region by mandating stamps on major agricultural produce: 5 *kuruş* on every bale of cotton, 1 *kuruş* on every sack of grain, and a stamp on every orange.¹⁸

Early republican politicians affirmed both the economic and cultural value of the village, which rose in discursive significance, especially during the 1930s in the wake of financial crisis.¹⁹ According to Asım Karaömerlioğlu, peasantism in Turkey assumed the form of concrete policies. The politics of peasantism inverted the prior relationship between the Ottoman state and rural people. The Tanzimat state treated the rural sphere as a source of anxiety about the question of civilization. The republican discourse still contained a strong degree of condescension but invested rural people with qualities deemed valuable and worth cultivating for the national project. The creation of the People's Houses (Halk Evleri) in 1932 and the beginning of the short-lived but highly influential Village Institutes program during the late 1930s were two important examples of the peasantist mentality at play.[20] A wide array of public health programs, including those aimed at village midwives, also became part of this project.[21] As Sibel Bozdoğan has shown, architects claiming to be "agents of civilization" even designed model villages aimed at projecting modernity into agrarian spaces, as an interest in modernist architecture grew throughout the 1930s.[22] This trend grew in part from the populism and romanticism that took hold among nationalists from the late Ottoman period onward, notably Ziya Gökalp, who saw peasants as the repository of national culture.[23] The periodical of the local education ministry in the Adana region, which was rebranded as *Memleket Çukurova'da* after the alphabet reform of 1928, published frequent pieces on the history of Adana, the culture of its rural and pastoralist communities, romantic poetry about the region's geography, and lists of vocabulary from the local Turkish dialects.

As the republican government heaped special focus onto the countryside of the lowlands, it also renewed attempts at settlement efforts that resembled the policies of the late Ottoman period. During World War I, the Cilicia region had received thousands of refugees from the Balkans and Eastern Anatolia. With the exchange of populations between Turkey and Greece, Cilicia received another 20,000 migrants by 1930.[24] The first came from Serres in Greek Macedonia.[25] Other important regions of origin for migrants to Adana included Demirhisar, Crete, and Elassona.[26] These individuals, referred to as exchangees, or *mübadils*, were settled usually in clusters based on place of origin. The process was messy. *Yeni Adana* published quite a few stories dealing with a range of irregularities and corruption regarding the settlement of new migrants and the distribution of land.[27] The *mübadils* and other immigrants in these stories appeared at times as helpless victims and at others as scheming swindlers seeking to capitalize on a unique historical opportunity.[28] A particularly convoluted story of two non-*mübadil* men from Macedonia who defrauded the exchange commission to obtain lands in Çukurova formerly owned by Kosmo Simyonoğlu exemplified the haphazard and muddled process of redistributing properties.[29] While some rumors smacked of spite toward newcomers, all evidence suggested potential abuse of the system on the part of every class of individual involved amid unresolved ambiguities. In some cases, wealthy businessmen bought up the as yet unused documents of *mübadils* to accrue property and benefits.[30] In 1935, *Yeni Adana* featured an announcement from Finans Bank clarifying that land deeds for immigrants did not feature the small logo of an airplane, presumably indicating that counterfeit documents fitting that description were being produced.[31]

Much less discussed than the issues surrounding the population exchanges was a crucial period of land-grabbing during and immediately after the war that laid a muddy foundation for the early republican property regime. Immediately after the deportation of Adana's Armenians in 1915, the Ottoman government had begun to confiscate Armenian properties; according to Talat Pasha's notebook, almost 700 buildings and adjacent properties were confiscated during the war.[32] These houses, shops, factories, and farms were part of the abandoned properties, or *emval-i metruke*, which with the establishment of the republic were to be distributed to new migrants in addition to what was left behind by their Greek Orthodox inhabitants headed to Greece with the population exchange. But by the time *mübadils* began to be formally settled, much of this property had already been taken over.[33] Üngör and Polatel have translated a document indicating that a large number of houses in and around the city of Adana from the abandoned properties were by 1924 in the possession of civil servants and military personnel, from teachers and doctors to policemen and army officers.[34]

Just as the Ottoman government had done for previous migrants, the new Turkish government built villages and distributed land in the sparsely populated sections of the Çukurova plain. For most of the 1920s, many of the villages ruined in the war had not yet been put back together. In September 1924, a decision signed by Mustafa Kemal indicated that due to the large amount of destruction in the countryside during the French occupation of Cilicia, most of the houses were uninhabitable. It ordered the construction of 808 *huğs*, large huts built from reeds, cane, clay, mud, animal skin, and other materials common to the Çukurova region.[35] The republican government eventually set aside 1 million *lira* to rebuild villages in the east to facilitate the return of refugees, and in June 1929, the parliament authorized the dispensation of about 50,000 *lira* to rebuild villages in Adana.[36] Aslı Çomu's research in the Köy Hizmet Genel Müdürlüğü archives shows that many migrants were settled in *huğs* or in common houses called *iktisadihanes* that held up to four families. Some of these sites of *huğ* construction, such as the Bedros Farm and the disputed Tılan Farm near Sis, were former Armenian properties.[37] Demand for the construction of *huğ* settlements in Çukurova exceeded supply, and as Çomu points out, *huğs* built at an average price of 167 *lira* apiece could not be seen as an overall viable expense in most cases.[38] Ultimately, many settlers would have to shoulder the financial burden of their own settlement.

The preexisting ecology posed a further barrier to rebuilding settlements. A few thousand *mübadils* refused to settle near Kozan (formerly Sis) because of an inability to adapt to the climate, in familiar reference to the malarial environment of the plain.[39] These newcomers, just like Ottoman-era migrants from the Caucasus and the Balkans, suffered from issues of acclimation. The agricultural economy of the Adana region also differed significantly from that of the home regions, where orchards and tobacco farming were the more common. In one instance, migrants from Crete in Adana were given vineyards in keeping with their general way of life back on the island.[40] But much of the former properties of Greeks and Armenians that became part of the settlement policies had been used for growing cotton, a commercial crop unfamiliar to many migrants and not well suited for small-time farming.

Despite demographical upheaval, the property regime of the Ottoman period did not change substantially during the early republican period. According to Taha Toros, 93 percent of the villagers in Çukurova owned land in 1939. This statistic in isolation made Çukurova appear like a giant village where everyone had a share of the wealth. The only caveat was that this landowning majority did not farm in the strictest sense. "The 93% of villagers who own property employ a large number of laborers to plow, sow, and harvest their land," Toros remarked. And the labor was not supplied by that small 7 percent, who were "also increasingly tending towards becoming landowners," but rather by workers who came from "the Eastern provinces [*şark vilâyetleri*]" to work in Çukurova every year.[41] The villagers of the early republican period in Çukurova made their livings just as did the cultivators of the late Ottoman period. Çukurova was no longer a plain of nomads, and the livelihood of its villagers was predicated on cheap itinerant labor.

A handful of newcomers did become incredibly wealthy. A young man from Kayseri settled in the Çukurova region upon hearing, in the words of one biographer, "that there was much bread to be had in Adana" following the hurried departure of the Cilician Armenian population.[42] Over subsequent decades, that same young man, Hacı Ömer Sabancı, would build a small cotton kingdom for himself that was poised to become a commercial empire during the post–World War II period. The story of the Sabancı fortune did have a rags-to-riches aspect, one that in many ways defined the crucible of native capitalism that was late Ottoman and early republican Adana. One did not need to be elite to become wealthy in Çukurova. Yet, it is clear that being relatively local came with an advantage. Of the five major businessmen in Çukurova whom American officials saw as potential partners for industrial development during the 1950s, three—Hacı Ömer Sabancı (Sabancı Holding), Emin Özgür (Milli Mensucat), and Ömer Başeğmez—had been born in Kayseri and were not yet adults at the time of World War I. The other two, Şadi Eliyeşil (founder of Çukurova Holding, 1923) and İsmail Sürmeli, were from notable families of Tarsus that expanded their wealth immediately following the war period.[43] According to Çomu, it was newcomers "adjusted" to the socioeconomic environment, such as Kayseri businessmen eager to work with other Kayseri businessmen of the Adana region, who initially prevailed during the republican period.[44]

For most new immigrants, seasonal workers, and recently sedentarized pastoralists, working up the social ladder in Çukurova was not easy. Migrant workers faced an especially steep climb along with body-breaking labor and abysmal living conditions. Articles reminiscent of *Bereketli Topraklar Üzerinde*, Orhan Kemal's famous novel that portrayed farm and factory work in Adana, were frequent in *Yeni Adana* newspaper.[45] One 1929 headline reading "It Seems He Wanted to Kill Himself" described an unemployed migrant worker from Elazığ who nearly died after diving into the well near the fortress gate at the end of the Stone Bridge over the Seyhan River in Adana.[46] Two years later, on the other side of the Stone Bridge, another such worker was found dead under the shade of a tree in the Karşıyaka neighborhood where laborers often lodged. The cause of death was reportedly poverty (*sefalet*). "Because it was not known who or from where he was, his friends will be found and his identity will be ascertained" was all the information the article provided.[47] Ten days earlier, the headline "Farmers Are Unable to Pay the Cost of Labor" had adorned the front page of the same newspaper.[48] Everyone involved in the market-oriented agricultural economy bore risks. But when revenues failed to meet expectations, it was ultimately the seasonal workers and their families who stood to lose the most.

At the 1925 cotton congress held in Adana, labor was one of the principal topics that had been discussed.[49] In order to regulate the volatile labor market, a labor commission was created in Adana to negotiate and manage the relationship between employers and agricultural workers. The commission lasted until the late 1930s, when it was abolished by governor of Adana Tevfik Hadi Baysal.[50] The head of the commission was chosen by the Chamber of Agriculture (Ziraat Odası) in Adana, and the other members included two representatives of producer interests from the chamber, two worker representatives elected by a committee of fifteen *elçibaşıs*, a gendarme officer, the police commissioner, and two government representatives.[51] While the employer side hoped the commission would ensure easier access to labor, the main issues of workers concerned minimum wage set at 4 *lira* per week, limitation of work hours, and access to medical care in the likely event of falling ill.[52] Meanwhile, local law enforcement was concerned with regulating and monitoring the movement of workers and issuing ID cards to men and women employed on farms in the Adana region during the agricultural high seasons.[53]

Estimates of about 30,000 workers arriving in Çukurova at harvest time suggest a reduced flow of workers in comparison with the prewar period, though their points of origin were similar.[54] Labor shortages were common, in which case landowners were obliged to go out to the surrounding villages and pay a higher wage to carry out the harvest.[55] High profits were ultimately contingent on sustained economic underdevelopment of provinces farther east. Hilmi Uran noted this issue in his 1925 report on agricultural labor in Adana, saying that since work opportunities were set to rise in regions where workers came from, it would be harder to find people who would come to Çukurova "just to earn 3–5 *kuruş*."[56] However, the economic disparity between the predominantly Kurdish east and the highly commercialized and increasingly industrialized Çukurova region did not fade with time.[57]

The nature of migrant labor in Adana exacerbated an emerging social divide between "Turks" and the non-Turkish migrants who worked in Çukurova during a period of state-driven formation of Turkish national identity. Beginning in the mid-1920s, *Yeni Adana* began to run pieces demanding that Arabic not be spoken in the public places of Adana, Tarsus, and Mersin, and calling on the residents of the region to speak only Turkish.[58] This conformed to the broader language policy of the republic, including the Citizen! Speak Turkish (Vatandaş! Türkçe Konuş) campaign that sought to enforce linguistic homogeneity in Turkish and even made publicly speaking other languages a punishable offense.[59] Many of the seasonal laborers in Çukurova were Arab or Kurdish, while the urban residents of the area generally spoke Turkish, irrespective of divergent family origins. In addition to agricultural workers, immigrants were also constructed as not fully Turkish, as most spoke a language other than Turkish at home.[60]

There were important differences between seasonal migrant workers and immigrants. Immigrants were given homes and even enrolled in courses for Turkish language to facilitate their social integration.[61] Migrant laborers meanwhile resided in the most underserviced provinces. In regions such as Adana, linguistic difference would come to represent not so much distinctive ancestral or racial origins but rather social class, as assimilation and economic integration were intertwined with the use of Turkish.[62] It is telling that while most of the farmhands in Çukurova during the early republican period were Arab and Kurdish, many of the various farm managers, overseers, cafe owners, and cooks who were charged with the daily management and supervision of workers were themselves from immigrant backgrounds, and while by no means economically privileged, occupied a higher rung on the social ladder. At the same time, this trend signaled an interesting shift. Whereas Arab and Kurdish workers were relative newcomers in late Ottoman Cilicia, through their involvement in agricultural labor, they increasingly became the quintessential rural inhabitants of early republican Çukurova.[63]

With the withdrawal of the French, agriculture had immediately resumed.[64] During the interwar period, Adana's principal crops remained constant: wheat, cotton, barley, oats, and sesame. The ratio of food staples to commercial crops also remained consistent. Roughly one-third of the cultivated area was devoted to cotton in any given year, and most of the rest to cereals. During the 1920s, wheat yields were initially reduced, and the overall area devoted to cotton in 1927 was about two-thirds of what it had been before the war.[65] Despite a decrease in output, Çukurova's significance had grown within the Turkish cotton sector. In 1927, about 70 percent of the cotton produced in Turkey came from Adana, Mersin, and Cebel-i Bereket.[66]

Throughout the 1920s and 1930s, agricultural production was inconsistent, due primarily to the shakiness of the global market for export. The destinations for the region's cotton exports—just as in the Ottoman period—were not at the centers of the global textile industry. In the 1920s, Italy emerged as a major trade outlet for Turkish goods. Former Anatolian Greeks who settled in Trieste helped forge new connections with the textile factories there.[67] Frustrated French diplomats in Mersin and Adana watched as the Soviet Union, Spain, and Germany also increased their share of the Adana cotton market.[68] By the mid-1930s, Germany was far and away the leading importer of Çukurova cotton. In a 1935 article, Hilmi Ozansoy declared that Germany "would always be" Adana's foremost trade partner, indicating that Bremen and Hamburg imported 63,475 and 47,457 bales of their cotton, respectively, while the next biggest foreign buyer was Trieste at 4,108 bales.[69] By the 1930s, Adana had its own business periodical entitled *Adana Tecim Gazetesi*, published three times a month with information about the latest trends in cotton cultivation not only in the region but across the world, as well as other matters of economic importance. Like the other newspapers in Çukurova, it reported on the continually shifting prices so that cultivators could plan their planting and time their release to the market based on anticipated demand.

Hilmi Ozansoy regularly published the figures of the Adana Chamber of Commerce concerning production in the region. In 1934, Turkey implemented its first five-year plan, which either had the impact of stimulating agriculture or, at the very least, stimulating agricultural statistics.[70] Ozansoy bent the truth on production by not accounting for significant changes in the boundaries of the Adana (Seyhan) province to encompass the rapidly growing Cebel-i Bereket within data published in a special issue of *Adana*

Tecim Gazetesi for the twelfth anniversary of the republic.[71] When controlling for Ozansoy's error, an uptick in cultivation appears to have begun in 1930 when, following a poor year, the area of cultivation shot up to about 175 percent of what it had been in 1927 and 1928. *Memleket Çukurova'da* reported strong harvests that year.[72] But 1932 and 1933 were quite possibly the worst years for agricultural production since before 1927.[73] During the five-year plan, Adana enjoyed harvests of around 100,000 bales once again, and harvests increased for the remainder of the decade. If the data for 1936 are accurate, that year represented a level of agricultural production that was unprecedented during the late Ottoman period.

Citrus production in Çukurova had exploded during the last decades of the Ottoman period, due mainly to the expansion of groves by Armenian villagers around Dörtyol (formerly Çokmerzimen). Their produce rivaled the oranges and lemons of Jaffa, which had risen to international renown.[74] By the end of the Ottoman period, the area exported around 60 million oranges, but those groves went untended after the evacuation of Dörtyol's Armenians with the French in 1921, and cultivation was not revived until the end of the 1920s.[75] However, by 1935, citrus production around Dörtyol had more or less returned to prewar levels.[76]

Population growth was certainly a key factor in rising agricultural numbers, but the overall increase in production and cultivation was also aided by mechanization. Beginning in 1924, experimentation with mechanical seeders allowed farmers in Çukurova to plant more and faster, facilitating the additional cultivation of some 15,000 *dönüms* in that first year.[77] In 1927, Turkey had 15,711 agricultural machines in operation, and more than 2,000 of them were in the Çukurova region (Adana, Mersin, and Cebel-i Bereket).[78] An article discussing the mechanization of agriculture from *Memleket Çukurova'da* from 1930 commented on the sharp rise in the number of machines.[79] The use of Fordson tractors in plowing became a standard operating expense of the region's cultivators.[80]

In 1930, the Adana cotton breeding station (*pamuk ıslâh istayonu*) in Taşçı Köyü opened for the purpose of experimenting with and honing new strains of cotton.[81] At the time, there were a few different foreign strains in use, such as the subsidy (*iane*) Upland variety, as well as Lightning Express, Rowden, a number of variations on Cleveland, and Batr. 508, a drought-resistant cultivar from the Caucasus. However, 85 percent of the cotton in Çukurova remained of the local *yerli* variety.[82] In the earliest statistics of the republican period, *yerli* cotton cultivation not only greatly exceeded foreign cotton cultivation; its average price was actually higher.[83] But during the intervening decade, the Turkish government became more proactive about promoting American breeds. The annual cotton congresses held in Adana brought together government officials and cultivators to discuss approaches to collective issues, such as seed choice.[84] Turkish agronomists looked to emulate the cotton cultivation techniques of the American South, conducting investigative trips to Georgia and Texas.[85]

During the 1930s, the cotton breeding station promoted variants of the Upland variety.[86] Changing the dominant cultivar in Çukurova required a coordinated effort by local government and trade organizations, because cross-pollination undermined the purity of foreign strains.[87] In 1933, the Cleveland variety was chosen as the new favorite by the Adana Chamber of Commerce, and by 1936, the Turkish government mandated that only Cleveland cotton be planted between the Seyhan and Ceyhan rivers.[88] Yet within a few years, Cleveland suffered the same fate as many prior experimental cultivars, and during World War II, Çukurova cultivators completely reverted to *yerli*.[89] In turn, the government imposed even stricter regulations on cultivators and promoted the Acala variety of Upland cotton, mandating its use in 1942.[90] In 1944, 80 percent of the cotton planted in Çukurova was Acala.[91] However, these efforts were also short-lived. By the 1950s, the Çukurova *yerli* predominated once again.[92] Technological conditions had enabled the adoption of potentially more profitable strains of cotton in the Adana region, and both state and cultivators were largely in agreement. Yet in the case of *yerli* cotton, it would seem the plant itself resisted its own replacement by overwhelming new strains through cross-pollination and offering unmatched compatibility with the local environmental conditions.

The Nation's Laboratory

Public health was integral to the early republican government's policy in the countryside, and malaria was the primary public health issue. It was not uncommon at that time for the majority of people in a particular region, from Bursa to Ankara to Mardin, to suffer from malaria during the summer.[93]

The war period had brought serious epidemics, and soldiers returning from the southern fronts brought with them tropical strains of the more deadly *falciparum* species of malaria. Even the new capital of Ankara, a small city surrounded by swamps, was a profound symbol of the centrality of malaria in the national project.[94] Yet no province suffered more from malaria than Adana, and over the course of the interwar period, Adana would become a major center for malaria research and treatment as Turkey declared war on the nation's most widespread disease. The national health program made strides in limiting malaria's spread and mortality, but the disease remained firmly entrenched. In the meantime, medicine became an instrument through which the consent of citizens was cultivated, and the authority of experts was legitimated. By virtue of its central position in Turkey's malaria program, the Çukurova region became a laboratory of the new nation.

During the first years of the republic, the Turkish government in Ankara established an agenda for improving public health and combating the effects of malaria.[95] The organizations that laid the groundwork for reestablishing a health service in Turkey were some of the same types of aid institutions that had arisen during the late Ottoman period and had become the lifeline for millions of refugees and prisoners of war during World War I. In 1926, the Rockefeller Foundation, a philanthropic partner of Near East Relief (one of the main institutions caring for Armenian refugees in the Middle East), conducted a detailed study of health programs as a potential donor and logistical partner for the health ministry of the Turkish government. The report, written by Ralph Collins, a graduate of Johns Hopkins University who had worked on the issue of malaria in Florida and would eventually return to Ankara to teach at the School of Public Health in 1935, devoted considerable space to the province of Adana.[96] During 1927–28, the Red Crescent also performed a thorough inspection of a large number of provinces in Anatolia, with a special emphasis on the Cilicia region, in order to solidify the networks of funding and relief in the countryside.[97] In both studies, the importance of malaria as the most widespread and serious health issue in Turkey was affirmed.

The budget of the malaria control centers throughout Turkey would rise from 576,000 TL (Turkish *lira*) in 1925 to 808,000 TL in 1936.[98] Between 1925 and 1937, some 18 million medical examinations were conducted.

More than 62,000 kg of quinine was distributed throughout the country.[99] Though willing to receive donations from abroad, the Ankara government maintained a high degree of medical sovereignty, balancing its needs for funding and expertise with control of its own programs.[100] Yet at the same time, Turkish doctors readily engaged with global debates and developments regarding medicine and public health, frequently going abroad for special training. *Sıhhiye Mecmuası*, released monthly by the Ministry of Public Health, featured official announcements, nationwide statistics, and an array of articles written by Turkish doctors, sometimes reporting experiences in their local districts but often reporting recent findings from English, French, or German publications. Malaria experts would be periodically sent abroad for additional training throughout the interwar period.[101] Early issues of *Sıhhiye Mecmuası* featured articles about malaria in the Mediterranean, including a translation of an article by Lucien Raynaud, a health inspector in Algeria, about the ambitious malaria control efforts in Italy.[102]

The struggle with malaria was highly symbolic within the new nationalist discourse. In the Rockefeller report filed by Ralph Collins was a striking photograph meant to attest to the importance and benevolence of the prospective Rockefeller-Turkey partnership. Standing in a swamp outside a village near Adana, a row of boys appeared naked, the thick tan-lines on their necks revealing that they had been disrobed for the purposes of representation, ostensibly to show the swollenness of their spleens. The photograph served in part to show the stakes of Rockefeller's support. As for the boys, they were nameless sufferers, "examples of splenomegaly from malaria."[103] Turkish health officials were willing participants in this spectacle, but for their own reasons. One of the boys in the picture also appeared in *Sıhhiye Mecmuası* as the poster child of antimalarial efforts in the Adana region. Here, he had a name: Ramazan, the son of Mahmut, not a boy in the strictest terms but a twenty-three-year-old whose distended belly stood between his body and proper manhood. According to Adana region malaria specialist Ekrem Tok's triumphant report, Turkish doctors delivered on their promise to make Ramazan a man; a photograph taken just three years after Collins's visit shows Ramazan standing on the dry land of a newly drained swamp, fully clothed and proudly clutching his own two-year-old son (see figure 5.1).[104] Ramazan's story elegantly illustrated the difference between international humanitarianism and national public health in Turkey. For institutions like Rockefeller, the Pasteur Institute, and the League of Nations, it did not matter who Ramazan was. For the new Turkish health corps, Ramazan was a citizen with a name. His body was the body of the nation, and in the wake of a fallen empire, rejuvenated and civilized bodies were what the republic promised.

Adana quickly became a center of the Turkish malaria control efforts that brought together international expertise and local initiative. In the summer of 1925, a special malaria commission was formed in Adana. It was led by Ekrem Tok, a young doctor who had trained with one of Europe's premier parasitologists, Emile Brumpt, whose work with the Rockefeller Foundations and the Pasteur Institute in Paris was well known. Brumpt devoted a considerable portion of his career to researching the spread of malaria in the Middle East.[105] Tok would later rise to become the head of Turkey's health ministry. In September 1925, Tok was issued a diplomatic passport so that he could attend the First International Malaria Conference in Rome.[106] It was a Eurocentric affair. The only delegate from the former Ottoman Empire allowed to speak at the conference was Dr. Ahmed Hilmy Bey from Egypt, although the League of Nations commissioned the aforementioned German doctor Bentmann to supplement the proceedings with a report on malaria in Turkey and the Belemedik epidemic of World War I (see chapter 4).[107] The conference nonetheless energized malaria control programs throughout the world. Tok and his commission in Adana worked to test and treat as many malaria patients as they could, leading up to the establishment in 1928 of the Adana Malaria Institute (Adana Sıtma Enstitüsü), which Tok would initially head.

Adana was a logical site for a malaria institute. It was a modern city with a good railroad network. The province also had a large rural population living close by in Çukurova. With its hot, humid climate and malarial reputation, Adana was for the Republic of Turkey what the tropics were for European empires and their colonial laboratories. It was also true that in the countryside of the Adana region, malaria was as rife as anywhere in Turkey. As Dr. Tok explained in an extended report in the *Sıhhiye Mecmuası* from 1929, malaria dominated the postwar landscape. "In the year we began the campaign and the years leading up to it, malaria had truly come to be the most

Figure 5.1. Ramazan and son on the land of reclaimed swamp in Mercin, three years after the visit of Ralph Collins and Ekrem Tok. Source: *Sıhhiye Mecmuası*, November 1929, 1299.

important problem in the Adana region," he remarked. "In the cities and the villages, there were thousands of people with malaria who lay in the shade of every tree."[108] In 1925, more than 50 percent of the people tested in the city of Adana turned up positive for malaria. The problem was even worse in the villages, where more than 90 percent of the villagers in the Adana district and about 85 percent in the villages around Mersin and Tarsus had malaria. Meanwhile, the spleen indices for districts of Eastern Çukurova such as İslahiye and Payas reflected a level of malaria so deeply entrenched that Tok characterized it as hyperendemic. All in all, more than 30,000 people in the Adana province were examined for malaria, with about two-thirds of that number receiving treatment.[109]

By the time of the establishment of the Adana Malaria Institute in 1928, a standardized approach to monitoring and controlling malaria infections was in place. The most important part of this process was a general examination carried out by local doctors in malaria control areas every spring and again every fall.[110] The gendarmerie was called upon to compel villagers to attend the annual examinations for malaria.[111] Malaria detection involved checking and measuring swelling of the spleen and sometimes conducting blood tests.[112] Between 1925 and 1929, almost half of the population in the Adana province was tested for malaria either by spleen measurement or blood sample.[113] From April 1934 to the end of March 1935, some 300,000 examinations were done in Adana.[114] From August 1935 to the end of July 1936, that figure was almost 400,000.[115] Although many people were probably examined multiple times, these numbers were equal to or greater than the entire population of the Adana province. After taxation, military service, and school enrollment, medical examinations for malaria and other diseases were probably the most common form of state-society interaction in the early republican period, and certainly among the most intimate.

Even more intimate perhaps was the inspection of homes for extermination of mosquitos. Personnel armed with toxic Paris green insecticide went from house to house spraying for mosquitos. Between 1926 and 1929, an average of some 17,000 houses per year in the province of Adana were inspected and treated.[116] These inspections required the antimalaria teams to scrutinize the darkest corners of the domestic sphere where mosquitos might lurk, forcing Turkish citizens to open their homes to the gaze of state officials. The monitoring of citizens and mosquitos was intertwined, but outright compulsion was not the only means of access. The malaria control team employed nurses who participated in every aspect of the examinations and treatment, facilitating access to women and families. Most were literate and, when they visited families, would instruct them about necessary precautions for malaria and help them understand the contents of the treatment instruction cards that were distributed throughout the countryside. Other trusted officials, such as the village head, or *muhtar*, and teachers, played a role in disseminating information about malaria and distributing free quinine.[117]

Dispensaries offering basic medicines and care to local populations were opened in Adana, Tarsus, Mersin, and Ceyhan, mainly for the purpose of distributing quinine. In Adana, two of the three dispensaries were solely for malaria, and the same was true for Tarsus.[118] The dispensary in Mersin dealt with a wide range of ailments and was used by more women than men.[119] In

1929, the Red Crescent in Adana reported that 95 percent of the "hundreds" of people who came to its dispensaries each day had malaria.[120] From August 1935 to July 1936, more than 1,700 kg of quinine was dispensed in the province of Adana.[121] The function of the dispensaries, malaria clinics, and hospitals run by the Health Ministry in the Adana region was not only to provide treatment but also to teach the local population about the correct use of medicine and thereby enlist them in a program of self-treatment. One of the frequent complaints of doctors was that people did not take their medicines at proper intervals or did not complete courses of quinine once their fevers subsided.[122] While quinine may have had a relatively quick impact in terms of alleviating the symptoms, completion of a weeks-long treatment regimen was necessary to ensure the complete elimination of parasites. Similarly, prophylactic use of quinine required taking medicine at three-day intervals throughout a months-long malaria season that began in April and sometimes lasted through November. To facilitate the self-administration of these complicated treatment regimens, the malaria commissions issued instruction cards for both prophylactic and curative quinine use that patients could use to ensure that their medicine was taken at the proper interval (see figure 5.2). These cards served not only as means of encouraging proper quinine use but also as didactic tools that engendered a sense of self-discipline. Adhering to the quinine prophylaxis regimen would have certainly been a novel form of medical precaution within most families.

The Adana Malaria Institute was also a training center for the broader national public health apparatus. A critical aspect of public health policy was the mandatory two-year service of all medical school graduates for the purpose of guaranteeing health services in rural regions.[123] Every fall, as the Adana Malaria Institute began a new round of examinations, medical students and doctors from throughout the country traveled there in order to participate. In 1929, for example, the team included some fifty military and civilian doctors in training from every corner of Turkey who arrived for a month's worth of classes and activities.[124] By 1939, the number of interns at the Malaria Institute rose to one hundred.[125] During the spring and fall, the villages of Çukurova became open-air laboratories for physicians and nurses in training. While the Adana Malaria Institute was a novel institution, many public health practices carried over from the late Ottoman period.

		كنين				كنين	برنجی هفته
	كنين				كنين		ایكنجی هفته
كنين				كنين			اوچنجی هفته
			كنين				دردنجی هفته
		كنين				كنين	بشنجی هفته
	كنين				كنين		آلتنجی هفته
كنين				كنين			یدنجی هفته
			كنين				سكزنجی هفته
	كنين				كنين		طقوزنجی هفته
	كنين				كنين		اونجی هفته
كنين				كنين			اون برنجی هفته
			كنين				اون ایكنجی هفته

١ — هر قارت بر شخص اچوندر .

٢ — هر خانه بر كون مخصوصدر . كنين یازیلی اولان كونلرده كنين آلنجق بوش اولان كونلرده آلنمایجقدر .

٣ — كنين كونلرنده قاچ قومبریه آلندیسه او خانه اوزرینه او عددده چیزكی چكیله جكدر.

Figure 5.2. Quinine card for prophylaxis, c. 1924. Caption reads: "1. Each card is for one individual. 2. Every box belongs to a day. The days where 'quinine' is written, quinine should be taken. On the empty days, it should not. 3. However many pills are taken on quinine days, that number of slashes should be drawn on that box." Source: CA, 490–1-0–0 1464/6/1, 78.

For example, traveling doctors were employed in a host of activities, ranging from the treatment of syphilis and trachoma to the vaccination of humans and animals. A significant component of the traveling doctor's work was not just treatment but also surveillance. The traveling doctors kept detailed records of malaria cases in their region of activity and reported on the presence of potential mosquito breeding grounds along with the rates of malaria in the regions visited. In addition to local villagers, the traveling doctor was required to monitor the health situation of migrant laborers, especially those working in the rice paddies.[126]

Lilo Linke, a German reporter residing in London as an exile, published an account of her travels in Turkey during the 1930s, entitled *Allah Dethroned*. She offered insights into not just the impacts of Turkey's modernization policies in the countryside but also the mentality underlying the Kemalist project.[127] One of the people she interviewed was Dr. Fehmi, the head of the Adana malaria control station during the 1930s. Fehmi said that when he had first arrived in the 1920s, the people "wanted to stone" him. He was just another meddling government official, no better than a tax collector. But he claimed, according to Linke, that he had quickly won over the people and was now regarded as a "demi-god." He explained his method of convincing villagers of the necessity of modern medicine. "I talked with them in their own language," he said. "I asked them what they did when a dog attacked them, and when they answered: 'We throw stones at it and run for a stick,' I said: 'Well, and what is malaria but a million mad dogs raging in your blood, and what is quinine but a stick to beat them?'—And when they hesitated, I said: 'Can't Allah make animals of any size he pleases? Or are you so blasphemous as to doubt because your stupid eyes can't see them?'"[128]

The familiar bluster of a relatively minor government official might rightly call into question the veracity of Fehmi's rendition. Yet this type of hyper-vernacularization of scientific knowledge appears throughout Turkish medical literature of the period. Appealing to faith to convince patients of the power of medical knowledge was not unusual.[129] As the work of Emine Evered and Kyle Evered demonstrates, the didactic language employed by Turkish doctors during the interwar period was integral to the "biopolitics of public health education." Turkish antimalarial campaigns were inextricable from a broader political project that wielded a civilizational discourse emphasizing the extent to which the problem of malaria was embedded in the lifestyles and environments of Turkish peasants.[130] The Health Ministry's sometimes patronizing rhetoric deployed clear civilizational dichotomy between the urban and modern republican and the backward peasant. Propaganda informing villagers about how to protect themselves from malaria also served to establish the hegemony of the knowledge and methods of the Health Ministry and the supremacy of the doctor.

The early republican government sometimes utilized the press to disseminate its understanding of malaria and its prevention. Throughout July 1929, for example, instructions about avoiding malaria and the danger of mosquitos graced the front page of *Yeni Adana* newspaper.[131] A 1927 publication by the Ministry of Public Health offered advice about how to avoid malaria. It was likely intended to be read aloud in rural settings, as the text began with the salutation, "Villagers! Fellow Countrymen! [*Köylüler! Hemşeriler!*]." It warned villagers to use quinine (*sulfato*) and to protect their homes from mosquitos by installing screens or sleeping under nets.[132] Aside from print, state officials organized lessons on malaria in classrooms as well as organized events such as "malaria theater" using the familiar puppet characters Karagöz and Hacıvat.[133]

Public health education required not only disseminating reliable scientific information about malaria epidemiology and prevention but also convincing ordinary citizens that their own understandings of disease were false. A 1928 manual with instructions about health for village teachers asserted that "the biggest harm is that we consider malaria to be an unimportant disease. When we hear that someone we know has caught a feverish illness, this wish immediately flies to the tip of our tongue: 'hopefully it is malaria, it will come and pass.'" The same manual indicated that "there is a mistaken belief and opinion that has settled and taken root not only among our villagers who remain ignorant (*cahil kalmış*) but also among those who are rather literate about malaria being transmitted by air or water." The manual declared that even someone who has been told how malaria is transmitted "five minutes earlier" will go on to say that "the air of such and such village is malarial" or "of course someone who drinks any old water they encounter will get malaria."[134]

As another publication emphasized, "malaria is only transmitted by mosquitos. That which causes malaria in humans is neither the impact of weather [*hava çalması*], nor bad water, nor junk food."¹³⁵ A later malaria publication used almost the same formulation: "In the past, some people thought that malaria happened because of eating junk food [*abur cubur şeyler*] like raw fruit, green salads, melon and watermelon on an empty stomach. Some also believed that the bad odors coming from swamps or the jinns and fairies found in swampy areas brought malaria. Even now there are people who believe such things."¹³⁶ While public discourses about malaria were dominated by the propaganda of the Health Ministry, government doctors did have to compete in a wider market of information about and solutions for malaria. Numerous advertisements for medicines or consumer insecticides appeared regularly in the newspapers and medical journals, and not all products marketed to malaria sufferers conformed to the Health Ministry's general stance on how to approach the disease.¹³⁷ A running advertisement in *Yeni Adana* newspaper for Sıhhat brand *rakı*, the new alcoholic beverage of choice in Turkey, declared that "those who fear malaria should drink Sıhhat *rakı* regularly."¹³⁸ The brand name of Sıhhat may have meant "health," but the Ministry of Public Health would likely have disagreed with this prescription. In fact, doctors regularly warned that drinking alcohol would impede the recovery of patients.¹³⁹

At the malaria control center in Adana, Linke described a striking procession of children who passed through for screening. "Most of the children were well-trained through previous experiences," she observed. "In most of the cases it was sufficient to press the belly of the child in order to detect any enlargements of the spleen, and he could quickly dismiss the child with a slight slap on its bottom. But a few of the children, to the extreme envy of their friends, had to give a drop of their blood. It was then put on a glass slide to be sent away to the Adana laboratory. These children who had thus suffered were clearly the heroes of the day." Fatma, "a slender girl of about nine," was one such stubborn patient. "'Tamam, Fatma, tamam—finished,' said Dr. Hamit a little impatiently, already waiting for the next child. Fatma began to sob: 'Doctor bey, efendim, please—why don't you prick my finger?' 'There's nothing wrong with you!' 'Oh, yes—I am very ill!' . . . Dr. Fehmi intervened: 'I think Fatma should have her blood tested.' She looked at him as grateful and delighted as if he had given her happiness for the rest of her life. When Faruk Bey took a drop of her blood, she kept so quiet and the children watched her in such admiring silence that in that moment of tension nothing but the loud baa of a sheep from the stable downstairs could be heard. After she had made sure that she got a glass-slide all to herself, she shot off to inform her mother of the honour she had received." Linke also noted the preference of locals for the head doctor Fehmi. The other doctors were mere country doctors there to administer treatment. "Dr. Fehmi was much more. He was the medicine-man whose influence extended far beyond easily definable limits into the mystic spheres of the soul and governmental power itself."[140]

In asserting their authority, doctors and public health officials could claim political backing and expert knowledge, but the problem with these claims was that their proscriptions and prescriptions were not necessarily supported by results. While overall annual malaria rates in Turkey dipped to around 15 percent in the late 1920s, they rose a few points during the 1930s, and in 1936 and 1937 were above 20 percent. From July through October of most years, it was routine for more than 30 percent of individuals examined in Adana to exhibit the presence of a malaria infection in their spleen. Between 1935 and 1937, several newspaper articles from the Adana region referred to the perception that malaria was on the rise.[141] In September 1935, *Türksözü* reported that malaria had spread to "every home" and that in comparison with the few years preceding, had become "more virulent [*daha salgın*]."[142] Malaria was worse in summer 1936. During July, 90 percent of the people who went to the doctors of Adana were found to have malaria. In the villages, malaria devastated local populations, proving especially lethal for children and preventing agricultural workers from carrying out their normal tasks. An article in *Yeni Adana* reported that one farmer had fled to the city of Adana, bringing sixteen of his own malaria-stricken workers in a single truck. The article noted that, given the development of the malaria control apparatus in the Çukurova region, "it is a very strange thing for this disease to show this much fierceness."[143]

For the officials involved with malaria control in Çukurova, the resurgence must have been somewhat disconcerting, though it was likely not the consequence of flawed science. Some of the conditions that may have influenced the malaria epidemics of the mid-1930s were environmental factors that had always influenced malaria parasite and mosquito reproduction. Both 1935 and 1936 were exceptionally rainy years, and stagnant water—particularly the water left behind by frequently overflowing rivers—was always one of the main contributors to relative prevalence of malaria.[144] Yet another important factor must have been the continued rise in agricultural activity and the movements of seasonal laborers, who were especially vulnerable to malaria infections. The malaria epidemics of the late 1930s coincided precisely with a sharp increase in cultivation, in part due to the five-year plan implemented in 1934. The amount of cultivated area in Çukurova was significantly greater than what it had been in 1927. This might have cleared swamps, but it also put more people in contact with agricultural spaces. As one writer opined in *Yeni Adana*, rampant malaria was natural among workers who spent the summer in the fields exposed to the elements and working under the hot sun.[145]

The resurgence of rice cultivation may provide one vivid example of how new agriculture impacted malaria rates. In the lowlands near Marash, Osmaniye, Kozan, and İslahiye, cultivators during the early republican period began to exploit the swampy and indeed malarial geography of Çukurova by developing lucrative rice plantations. Between 1932 and 1935, the number of hectares planted with rice in Çukurova more than tripled.[146] During the late 1930s, the press in Adana commented on the promising prospects of rice paddies in the region.[147] In order to offset the impacts of rice cultivation, a new regulation was passed in 1936 that sought to ensure better drainage and the maintenance of proper distance between rice cultivation areas and significant settlement areas.[148] These laws also included regulations about the working conditions of rice laborers, such as forbidding work before sunrise or after sunset.[149]

While these factors might have exacerbated the risk of malaria in the face of control efforts, occasional references in letters to the Adana press also offer clues about slippages in public health infrastructure. The government may have handed out large quantities of free quinine, but that did not mean it always reached everyone when necessary. An anonymous letter to *Yeni Adana* in August 1929 claimed that for all the antimalarial efforts in Adana, the people of remote villages—80 percent of whom suffered from malaria—did not have access to quinine. They were too poor to afford the medicine, and the local dispensaries in their regions reported that they had run out of supplies.[150] The work of Taha Toros on villages in Adana during the mid-1930s confirmed that villagers had trouble accessing and purchasing medication.[151] Medical care remained unevenly distributed throughout the Çukurova region, with those most in need often least likely to have access. Similarly, *Yeni Mersin* newspaper reported in September 1935 that, despite denizens of the city having gladly paid 1 *lira* each for drainage efforts that year, drainage work had never begun.[152]

Biomedical knowledge offered a coherent alternative framework for understanding malaria, but selling that knowledge required a combination of education, political force, and persuasion that involved achieving results. Yet state and peasant were not in the end blamed for the failures of malaria control measures. Instead, nature itself, whether in the heavy and foul air of old or the new specter of the mosquito, continued to be represented as the ultimate source of illness. And in articulating a clear understanding of nature as a force to be harnessed or enemy to be subdued, public health campaigns extended into a much broader struggle with nature that moved to the center of nationalist political, economic, and cultural discourses.

Militant Ecology

One day in late spring 1929, an unusual rain fell on the Adana region. When the clouds dispersed, people began to report that it had "rained fish." Indeed, small fish were found in holes and puddles throughout the city, provoking alarm among local inhabitants as rumors spread. But Adana Malaria Institute director Ekrem Tok explained the phenomenon to the press. Fish had been dispersed into small bodies of water all over the province so that they might eat the mosquito larvae that inevitably formed in the wake of rainstorms during the warm months of the year.[153] He had recently written an article on the uses of fish like the gambusia, pioneered in part by his mentor, Professor Brumpt, as well as the presence of some local species of mosquito-eating fish in the irrigation canals and small bodies of water in Osmaniye and İslahiye. The Adana aquarium was working hard to study and develop these miracle fish.[154] They had been transplanted to many bodies of water on purpose, and if not by flooding, perhaps they found their way to some of the smaller puddles by hungry birds having dropped their prey mid-flight.

Mosquitofish were not the only foreign entity to turn up in the waters of Adana that year. As Tok also explained, the malaria control centers throughout the province had begun oiling even the smallest ponds and puddles with the arrival of the spring rains. Between April and June of 1929, 8,060 kg of diesel oil—that is, almost 2,400 gallons—was poured into various bodies of water to prevent the development of mosquito larvae on the water's surface.[155] This represented a major increase when compared with the roughly 3,000 kg used for the same purpose in 1925.[156] But much more ambitious interventions were promised in the years to come. As Tok indicated, significant amounts of wetland drainage had already occurred in the area around Mersin, and more was promised in the east of the province around Osmaniye and İslahiye, where swamps had defied previous attempts at elimination.[157]

While led by physicians trained primarily in medicine, the campaign against malaria became an environmental struggle through the expanding arena of public health. The standard name for the antimalarial campaign was the Sıtma Mücadelesi. In the early republican context, the word *mücadele*, which means "combat," "fight," or "struggle," evoked the Milli Mücadele, or "National Struggle," that led to the foundation of an independent Turkish state following World War I. Not only malaria, but in fact several other diseases, namely, syphilis, tuberculosis, and trachoma, were also the targets of an official *mücadele*. After World War II, the term would become Sıtma Savaşı, meaning "War on Malaria." Particularly in official documentation and the press, malaria control, as well as many other public health and social welfare programs, were represented in this way. Much like national malaria programs elsewhere, the militant language of antimalarial campaigns mirrored a broader pairing of citizens and soldiers that emerged in the interwar period in Turkey.[158]

One of the directors of the Adana Malaria Institute conceptualized his mission as a war against mosquitos. "The secret to success in the fight with malaria: First and foremost, to know the adversary, to understand its way of life, its temperaments, its friends and its enemies."[159] Later representations of mosquitos depicted them as a looming menace or as dive bombers attacking innocent villagers.[160] Malaria control efforts were framed as attacking the mosquito wherever it might be found. Oiling or petrolage, for example, which entailed pouring large amounts of diesel and raw petroleum into puddles, ponds, and swamps, was effective in reducing the mosquito population to the extent that it eliminated spaces where mosquitos could breed. A thin layer of oil on the surface of water prevents mosquitos from laying eggs and suffocates newly hatched mosquito larvae. However, this method was costly and required constant labor. In the Adana province, the malaria control teams carried out petrolage every fifteen days during the spring and fall, and every ten days during the peak mosquito breeding periods of the summer.[161] The use of Paris green was another method used to kill mosquitos in the region.[162] Paris green released from airplanes over swamps, a method of mosquito control that the early republican government experimented with, could also be effective at killing mosquitos and their larvae.[163] A growing number of facets of the natural world were presented as threats, adversaries to be fought and indeed conquered. Much of this discourse centered on pesky animals, from mosquitos and locusts to pigs and dogs, and their extermination.[164]

Within this context, draining swamps remained the most powerful symbol of the war on the mosquito, and during the 1920s and 1930s, enormous stretches of wetland in Turkey were desiccated under the auspices of the Sıtma Mücadelesi. About 1,100 km of drainage canals—more than the distance between Istanbul and Adana—were opened throughout Turkey in a decade between 1927 and 1937. In that same time frame, 300 square kilometers of swamps and wetlands was drained.[165] The most ambitious desiccation project in the Adana region was the draining of the Karabucak south of Tarsus. The great lagoon, which had existed for centuries, was eliminated through an experimental program involving the plantation of eucalyptus. As in many places throughout the world, the eucalyptus was touted as a healthful tree that would assist in draining marshy land and in afforestation.[166] The French company that built the Adana railway during the 1880s planted trees at each station for decorative purposes, but the Karabucak project was the first serious eucalyptus-based antimalaria project in Turkey.[167] The decision for eucalyptus planting at Karabucak was signed by Mustafa Kemal Atatürk in December 1937.[168] The initial plans projected some 30 square kilometers of trees to replace largely uncultivated marshes.[169] Local women were employed on the eucalyptus farm to raise young trees that could be planted in the swamp. The final form of Karabucak eucalyptus forest occupied 855 hectares, or 8.55 square kilometers, roughly halfway between Tarsus and the sea.[170] A newspaper article from 1939 encapsulated the sentiment of the project with a defiant headline: "Karabucak Swamp Is Living Its Last Moments."[171]

The Karabucak forest soon became a laboratory for eucalyptus planting in other parts of Turkey; the first practical manual in Turkish on growing eucalyptus was published by the eucalyptus region chief of Tarsus in 1947.[172] Mary Gough, an American who traveled in the area during the 1950s, remarked upon the commonness of eucalyptus trees on farms and throughout the countryside, as well as along the railway, so that "the eucalyptus trees could almost, in Cilicia, be called station fittings."[173] A map in Saatçioğlu and Pamay's 1958 study of eucalyptus in Karabucak and the rest of Çukurova listed more than sixty sites of eucalyptus cultivation scattered throughout the Adana-Tarsus-Mersin region, as well as surrounding the cities of Ceyhan, Kozan (formerly Sis), Kadirli (formerly Kars-ı Zülkadriye), Bahçe, Osmaniye, Dörtyol, Payas, İskenderun, Kırıkhan, Reyhanlı, Antakya, and Arsus.[174]

The emergence of modernist discourses about fighting, harnessing, and transforming nature were also reflected in the aftermath of another Seyhan River flood, in December 1936.[175] After a few days of heavy rain in Çukurova and the Taurus Mountains, the Seyhan River had, as was so often its wont, broken the dams and overflowed into the city. The flood lasted for days. In the countryside, torrents had engulfed the agricultural spaces of the Yüreğir Plain. A Seyhan River flood was nothing out of the ordinary, but the scale of this disaster was particularly devastating. As usual, the comparatively poor neighborhood of Karşıyaka, located on the lower eastern banks of the river, was hit the hardest. In one gruesome accident, eighteen people drowned under the debris of their collapsed house.[176] In and around the city, more than 1,000 such buildings were toppled, and more than 100 people and 891 animals, including 419 goats, perished in the turbid waters.

There had been numerous floods in the past years, though none of the same magnitude as the flood of 1936.[177] For the press in Adana, which had warned of the dangers of the frequently flooding rivers in the past, the 1936 flood was a moment of trepidation but also vindication. Ahmet Remzi Yüreğir, the editor of *Yeni Adana*, had published multiple articles on the "harms [*zararlar*]" of rivers, saying that "while in other countries, a great benefit is obtained from rivers, our rivers only bring great harm."[178] Not to be outdone, *Türksözü* scolded past naysayers with the headline "What Will Those Who Disclaimed Us Saying 'There Is No Danger from the Seyhan' Say Now?"[179] Many articles followed in the weeks after the flood. One author likened the flood to the French occupation of Cilicia, saying "a comprehensive plan is necessary for Adana's second liberation."[180] Another labeled the flood just the latest assault by nature (*tabiatın bu yeni tecavüzü*).[181]

The national press in Turkey had a similar reaction. Writing from Ankara, Kâmuran Bozkır declared that "Adana has suffered an attack of nature."[182] Ahmet Emin Yalman, whose writing on World War I has so singularly influenced the historiography, expressed a similar sentiment: "We have lost a decisive battle in our war with nature." The Turkish press almost unanimously called for a retaliatory response to this "assault of nature." Falih Rıfkı Atay wrote in *Ulus* that the Seyhan River had killed people and destroyed their homes, and that "we will take revenge on it with dams and barrages and all the weapons of concrete and steel." Yalman wrote that "the most unambiguous measure of civilization" was success in the fight with nature.[183] In similar fashion, Kâmuran Bozkır stated that "a civilized human is a human who can harness nature."[184] Nevzad Güven of *Türksözü* commented that "nature, in the hands of civilization, gradually takes on the friendliness of a domesticated animal."[185] One author even published a poem in *Yeni Adana* declaring war on the Seyhan, warning it "to know its limits."[186]

The growing scale of the damage caused by the Seyhan floods was primarily a consequence of the changes in human relationships with the river throughout Çukurova's transformation and Adana's growth. Politicians and journalists mainly called for large-scale irrigation strategies, better and bigger dams, and any measures that could tame the wild waters of Çukurova and make the region safe for the widespread cultivation that had sprung up over the course of less than a century. In particular, the construction of a large irrigation network in Çukurova, which began in 1938, was touted with great optimism.[187] The plan involved eventually raising the level of the Seyhan River above Adana to 30.25 m using a dam to regulate water flow and irrigate the surrounding areas.[188] The irrigation works were set to provide water to a large swath of agricultural space to the west of Adana. The construction of a 16 km irrigation canal required the expropriation of properties on the left (west) side of the Seyhan River.[189] The highly involved construction was still going on at the outbreak of World War II in the fall of 1939. With the canals complete, work for the mechanical regulator of the barrage, the construction of which had been contracted to a German company for 2.4 million *lira*, began in October 1939. The project was set to be completed during the 1941 fiscal year.[190] The barrage was completed in June 1942.[191] The Seyhan Barrage was not the first and would not be the last of its kind. It was the latest iteration of attempts to control the waters of the Seyhan River that stretched back into the Ottoman past. Yet the developments surrounding it reflected a defining cultural trend of the interwar period. Modern medicine, science, and technology did not necessarily possess the means to eliminate malaria or to control the rivers. But in the decades leading up to World War II, the scale of both technology and the technocratic imagination allowed attempts to willfully transform the environment of an unprecedented magnitude.

During World War II, Turkey remained neutral, although British prime minister Winston Churchill did his best to court President İsmet İnönü during a January 1943 meeting in a railroad car under the shade of eucalyptus trees at the train station in Yenice, just 15 km from Tarsus.[192] Nonetheless, the Turkish government used the exceptional conditions to expand its domestic power and declared martial law. The war period was filled with want. The disruption of trade cut Turkey off from many basic import items, sending prices skyward. The purchasing power of workers dropped by more than 40 percent.[193] In the towns, bread and other items were dispensed via ration cards.[194] In the hinterland, the early 1940s were remembered as years of scarcity among the Avşars. The concurrent drought compelled villagers to scrounge for goat weed in the mountains to keep their animals alive through the winter.[195] Cultivators who relied on the small number of individuals who owned machines complained of exorbitant price hikes. The cost of cultivation also rose due to labor and transportation shortages; despite rising yields, the cost of cotton production more than doubled between 1940 and 1942.[196] Perhaps as a sign of discontent, cultivators in Adana resumed wearing the formerly banned baggy pants of the region, the *karadon*—in the words of the British consul in Adana, they were "reverting to the comfortable habits of their forefathers," much to the chagrin of local journalists.[197] Meanwhile, malaria infections raged with new vitality throughout Turkey. Tropical strains of malaria spread all over the country during the war.[198] Quinine could not be imported, and as a result, Turkish citizens were left without the treatment and medicines they normally used to ward off the disease.[199] A tenacious malaria epidemic in Karataş, which the health ministry eventually brought under control, illustrated the extent to which malaria was still entrenched in Çukurova.[200]

The government responded to wartime issues by declaring war on the economic crisis, instituting a more heavy-handed economic policy to regulate the food supply and increase production.[201] It distributed draft animals to farmers in need.[202] It became the purchaser of all cotton produced as of 1941, giving cultivators some security, though production greatly exceeded demand, and in many of the war years, large amounts of cotton remained in stock.[203] In February 1942, the government called for "agricultural mobilization [*ziraat seferberliği*]" to increase planting of wheat that even encompassed schoolchildren, who sowed 26 decares of agricultural land in the Çukurova region that year.[204] Agricultural production ramped up with tighter control over the decisions of cultivators, and over prices and the supply of goods. State rhetoric declared that the country was in the midst its own agricultural war. The government supplied aid to try to boost agriculture and spent millions of *lira* on equipment and seed.[205] Wartime agricultural mobilization was unable to resolve all of the economic problems. But in taking on an increased role in economic life—just as the CUP government had done during World War I—İnönü's CHP government solidified economic prosperity not just as a goal but also as a national struggle. The militarization of ecology during the 1930s and the war period had paved the way for future environmental interventions that had very recently been unimaginable.

Gentrification of the Summer Pasture

While public health, infrastructure, and even economic development veered toward a militant discourse about the environment during the 1930s, other nationalist environmental imaginaries glorified Anatolia's pristine nature. The mountains and their summer *yaylas* served as the object of adoration in bourgeois circles as the summer retreat persisted as local practice. In a 1936 newspaper article, Taha Toros profiled what seemed to be two very different forms of transhumance: the longstanding seasonal migration of pastoralists, on one hand, and the new family vacation culture of the *yayla* resort town, on the other. Toros cast the latter group as categorically different, explaining that they "go to the Taurus mountains not to make their living but to slake their weariness."[206] As the natural beauty of the *yayla* and clean air of the Taurus Mountains were combined with modern amenities and forms of transport, the *yayla* became the place where middle-class people could be in touch with nature, the Anatolian geography, and the lifestyles of the region's "traditional" inhabitants. Yet at the same time, those bearers of tradition—the pastoralists who had long moved between the mountains and the plains— found their way of life threatened by economic change and political policies. The rise of modern transhumance, which was accompanied by the rise of the "last nomad" trope, represented the gentrification of the summer pasture.

The early republican period witnessed the ascendance of a new kind of urban transhumant: the *yaylacı*, meaning "summerer" or "yayla-goer." In contrast to the conventional transhumance model, the *yaylacı* did not spend the entire warm season in the mountains. The length of one's stay at the *yayla* was dictated by the amount of time they could afford to spend on vacation.[207] Generally speaking, large-scale movement from the city toward the *yayla* would begin at some point during mid- to late June and continue over the subsequent months.[208] In early July 1937, *Türksözü* reported that 25 percent of Adana's inhabitants had moved to the *yayla* for the summer and that on the weekends, the city was desolate.[209] During August, cities like Adana would be almost entirely empty, with everyone on vacation.[210] Activity would begin to pick up gradually by September, and with the first days of fall and the arrival of cool breezes from the north (*poyraz*), usually by the end of September, many inhabitants would begin to return, although *yayla* season normally lasted into October.[211]

By the 1920s, Adana was linked to Pozantı and the villages of the Taurus Mountains not only by railways but also by paved roads frequented by automobiles and buses. This drastically reduced travel times and increased access to the *yayla*. Local newspapers in Çukurova published reviews and the latest news on developments in *yaylas* near Adana and Tarsus as well as around Osmaniye on the other side of the plain.[212] Of all the *yaylas* profiled, the village of Bürücek received the most attention. At the outset of the decade, it had been a small settlement of around forty to fifty houses. By 1936, there were more than 400 houses along with various hotels.²¹³ By 1939, the number of homes had risen to 600.²¹⁴ *Yeni Adana* reported that it had become the choicest *yayla* in the Taurus Mountains. Bürücek's rise was not solely due to its natural beauty and cool mountain air. It also happened to be located on a paved road through the Gülek Pass just 7 km from Pozantı, a town easily reachable by train, thanks to the Belemedik tunnel projects of the World War I period.²¹⁵ The trip between Bürücek and Pozantı was just twenty minutes.²¹⁶ Daily minibus services between Pozantı and Bürücek were advertised in *Yeni Adana* beginning in 1930.²¹⁷ By 1936, there was a special train designated for bringing people from Adana directly to Bürücek on Saturdays during the summer, and similar service for return to Adana early Monday morning just in time to start the work week.²¹⁸ Coverage in *Yeni Adana* stated that whereas "the *yaylacıs* of old once traveled three days and three nights by camel, the *yaylacıs* of today reach Bürücek in four or five hours."²¹⁹ The expansion of rail and motor transport allowed men to spend the work week in the lowlands and the weekend at the *yayla* with their families.

The modern *yayla* specialized in offering the aesthetics of a mountain village with all the amenities that a respectable Adana family might seek. One article claimed that Bürücek was the simultaneous product of nature (*tabiat*) and civilization (*medeniyet*). There was good security in the town, which had its own gendarmerie, making it "safer than Switzerland." ²²⁰ The *yayla* even had its own governing council, which became filled with professionals from the city. Bürücek had a telephone connection, a rarity at the time. Alongside its natural beauty, one admirer noted that "Bürücek is benefiting from its very civilized means [*çok medeni vasıtaları*]."²²¹ Whereas the men once dressed in the conservative, religious garb (*sarıklı, kavuklu*) of clerics, now there were businessmen, farmers, artisans, civil servants, teachers, writers, doctors, pharmacists, and industrialists.²²² Bürücek became a space of conspicuous consumption for elite and aspiring families. When the building craze began in the village, people competed to build higher and higher up on the *yayla*.²²³ Although many *yaylacıs* from Adana owned homes at Bürücek, the many more who could not afford to do so could have a taste of the high life by renting a home or booking a room in hotels such as the Pine Palace.²²⁴ Due to its ease of access, Bürücek was attracting not only residents of the

Çukurova region but also well-to-do vacationers from all over Turkey, especially Ankara and Istanbul.[225] "Even Americans and Jews," one article stated, were coming to the newly found summer paradise.[226]

Bürücek was only one of many *yaylas* to thrive amid a climate of bourgeois transhumance during the early republican period. The much older and larger *yayla* town of Namrun presented a similar appearance. Around the time of the French occupation, Namrun was a town of a few hundred houses.[227] However, a 1929 article in *Yeni Adana* indicated that Namrun had become a town of some 2,000 households.[228] By 1948, Namrun had a summer population of more than 25,000, with 5,000 to 10,000 people from Adana making the trip at some point during the *yayla* season.[229] Changing infrastructure and lifestyles caused people to view the local geographies in a new light.[230] For example, the area of Karaisalı was, in the eyes of Dr. Muhittin Nuri, the Red Crescent inspector of the Çukurova region, an extremely poor town with more than 150 abandoned houses as of 1927.[231] But during the 1930s, *Yeni Adana* ran articles that spoke positively of the charming simplicity and natural beauty of Karaisalı, which had good access to *yaylas* and orchards, and was "one of Turkey's towns where death is sparse, air is clean, and forest is plentiful."[232] An article about the potential virtues of Bor, a town just on the other side of the Taurus Mountains, as a *yayla* resort reflected the concerns of *yaylacıs* in Çukurova. Like Karaisalı, Bor was relatively poor, but it possessed much of the natural beauty of other Taurus Mountain *yaylas*, was easy to access, and less crowded and less expensive than other locations, such as Bürücek. Moreover, the social atmosphere in Bor would be relatively comfortable for city folk as there were many educated people in the town and an excellent library.[233]

Residents of the Çukurova region continued to associate the *yayla* with health.[234] In one article about Namrun, an author declared that "I believe that on summer days those who come to Namrun even for one day will have added ten years to their lives."[235] Likewise, *Türksözü*'s profile of Bor as a potential space for *yayla* development mentioned the resurgence of malaria epidemics as the primary factor pushing those who could afford it into the mountains for as long as possible during the summer.[236] However, the sudden growth of *yayla* resorts like Bürücek gave rise to some complications. Bürücek suffered from severe water issues. There was limited drinking water at the *yayla*, and the influx of families quickly began to contaminate the water supply to the point that it was not potable.[237] The local council in Bürücek, the meetings of which were sometimes attended by hundreds of people, worked to make sure that the water supply was protected as a collective resource.[238] But at the same time, the problem of wastewater there may have contributed to the rise of a mosquito problem at the *yayla*.[239] In fact, there were even complaints of widespread malaria in Bürücek during the late 1930s, just as in most of Çukurova.[240] The allure of the *yayla* still appealed to older conceptions of the relationship between climate and health. Yet while the Taurus Mountain air might have offered a modicum of comfort, the new, punctuated form of transhumance offered almost no protection from malaria.

These changes also transformed the *yayla* as a socioeconomic space, as aspects of the new, middle-class household were transported to the summer home. The "modern" *yayla*, which became a space of leisure, did not presumably involve much labor for men, who made their livings in the city. For them, the *yayla* was a place of rest and relaxation, where they could socialize with other men who spent the summer in the small towns or villages. But to a large extent, women were still tasked with many of the household duties that would follow the family wherever it moved throughout the year. In this regard, another important point of difference regarding the modern form of transhumance and the rise of the *yayla* resorts pertained to class. Going to the *yayla* may have been easier, but economic conditions also made it pricier. Agricultural workers and their families especially were deprived of the cool mountain air during the summer, as they could not afford to rent a place at the *yayla* or for that matter leave their wage-paying jobs to take a summer vacation. A regular commentator in *Yeni Adana* reminded readers of how summer was especially hard on the working class of Adana, saying, "Let's think of those who plow fields, make hay, and thresh grain in the hellish daytime heat. These poor souls have neither a bathtub nor a shower. Never mind that, they are deprived of even the shade or cold water that would give the slightest bit of relief."[241]

The emergence of a modern, bourgeois transhumance was accompanied by romantic literature about nature frequently centered on the *yayla* and summer spaces.[242] Local authors in Çukurova also composed short travel accounts in the newspapers of region that allowed space for reflection on the national geography.²⁴³ *Memleket Çukurova'da* devoted considerable space to literary pieces that fixated on the beauty of mountain landscapes in Anatolia. A poem entitled "Anadolu (Anatolia)" offered a deified portrayal of the national geography:

> Violets in the mountains, the sap of forest trees
> All who enter sink deep into its airs that are free [*hür*]
> They call this homeland [*yurt*] paradise, it's full of history
> Its rivers are heroic fighters [*gazi*], every cascade a soldier
> There is a sweetness in its air, the soul its wind does enter
> It is a place to be worshipped: Anatolia is a temple²⁴⁴

The notion that the geography of the nation would be an object of admiration reflected the ways in which romantic nationalist discourse intersected at natural spaces. *Yayla* poetry appears to have been a veritable craze among the middle class and elite. In his memoirs, Damar Arıkoğlu included a long poem of his about the *yayla* resort of Bürücek, depicting it as a space of intense personal nostalgia in a section concerning his "feelings [*duygular*]" about his country.²⁴⁵ For early republican writers, the mountains embodied the coveted natural beauty of Anatolia that elicited feelings of love be they for another person or for the nation. Pastoral romance was nothing new in itself, but the intimate relationship between the adoration of nature and the territorialization of early republican nationalism represented a new development in Turkish literature.

While the mountains maintained their defiant character in early republican discourses, they came to represent not a threat to the state but rather the heritage of the Turkish nation. As a result, their historical inhabitants—Yörük and Türkmen pastoralists—also received new attention as bearers of the national culture.²⁴⁶ In publications like *Memleket Çukurova'da*, the new compositions of local writers, some of whom were students, were often printed side by side with rediscovered excerpts of folk poetry by the most prominent Turkish bards of Ottoman Cilicia, such as Karacaoğlan and Dadaloğlu. In claiming ownership of Dadaloğlu's words, early republican writers also claimed ownership of defiant lyrics that had once been directed at state attempts at forced settlement. Just as these works of poetry served as a model to be emulated by young writers of the nation, the editors of

Memleket Çukurova'da chose excerpts that spoke to nationalist geographies of the period. Running sections on poetry about mountains in the words of the folk poets followed by contemporary odes to different mountains in the region such as Bulgar Dağı and Binboğa served to establish continuity between the literary geographies of the Anatolian Turkish past and the national present.[247]

Pastoralist populations in Anatolia also became subjects for a variety of social scientists engaged in the academic study of Turkishness. One of the first early republican intellectuals in Adana to work extensively on pastoralists of the Çukurova region was Ali Rıza Yalgın. Born in the Ottoman Balkans, Yalgın worked as an educator in the Adana region beginning in the 1920s. During that time, he made many excursions to travel with pastoralist communities that summered in both the Taurus and Amanus Mountains. His accounts and findings were published in newspapers such as *Türksözü* and then subsequently in book form. In Yalgın's writings, these tribal communities that migrated in and out of the Çukurova region appeared as a repository of tradition. He recorded any new folk song or lament that he encountered when traveling with pastoralists in the mountains, but he also solicited evidence of the familiar folk poets of the national repertoire and variations on popular folk tales, such as "Dede Korkut" and "Alageyik." Yalgın searched not only for new raw material to incorporate into a national corpus but also for traces of familiar literary material that attested to a deeper shared past between different Turkic communities in Anatolia.[248]

The members of Taurus Mountain tribes could also be instrumentalized as discursive constructs of ideal Turkishness that intersected with discourses about social categories such as gender. Müfide Hasan detailed an encounter with some Tahtacı women during a train ride through Pozantı, in a short travel account published in *Yeni Adana*. "The lumberjacks in the Taurus were strong, powerful women," she remarked. Her account was published with a photograph of a woman, not apparently taken by Hasan herself, but rather chosen as an exemplar of the rugged Turkish women of the Tahtacı tribes that lived on the forests of the Taurus.[249] Interestingly, the photograph had appeared in Yalgın's publications.[250]

Turkish geographer Cemal Arif Alagöz conducted field research in the Taurus Mountains during the summer of 1937. The subject of Alagöz's research was the emerging European concept of transhumance, which he translated as *yaylacılık,* or "being a *yayla*-goer." He spent a twenty-four-day excursion in the Taurus Mountains, accompanied by German geographer Herbert Louis and Niyazi Çıtakoğlu, both Ankara University colleagues, encamped with some shepherds at different *yaylas* of the region. In April 1938 Alagöz gave a presentation entitled "Transhumance in Anatolia [*Anadoluda Yaylâcılık*]," based on his field research the previous summer, to an audience at the Ankara Halkevi. The theme of his presentation was the extent to which transhumance and pastoralism were an integral part of the Anatolian geography. He began the talk by emphasizing that, in comparison with European countries, in Turkey sheep and goats were much more common than cattle. Sheep were not only more numerous than cattle but also more highly valued; he noted that in Anatolia "they say 'oh he's a rich man, he has farms and so many thousand sheep.' Whereas in France, wealth for the Savoy villager is cattle." Nonetheless, Alagöz was keen to emphasize that Turkish transhumance was part of a broader practice in many parts of the world, from Argentina to the Alps.

For Alagöz, who was educated in France, Anatolian transhumance was a natural feature of Mediterranean geographies, which possessed what he referred to as a "transitional climate [*intikal iklimi*]" between the tropics and Europe. He stated that all of the peoples of the Mediterranean had been "compelled by the climate" to practice transhumance. The word that Alagöz used to express the notion of "transhumant" was *yaylacı*, a concept that linked the movements of transhumant pastoralists with the practices of *yayla*-goers or *yaylacıs* of Adana and the other towns in the Çukurova plain. Alagöz constructed a parallel between the lifestyles of Yörük and Türkmen tribes in Anatolia and the broader Turkish population's practice of "urban transhumance." He noted that just as the pastoralist communities he studied engaged in seasonal migration, the inhabitants of Adana, Tarsus, and Mersin also had their own *yaylas* in Bürücek, Gülek, Tekir, Gözne, and Namrun.

Alagöz represented the transhumant pastoralists of the Taurus Mountains as intimately attuned to nature in quotidian but seemingly superficial ways. "These transhumants [*yaylacılar*], who are very close to nature, do not use matches and light their cigarettes by igniting tinder," he marveled in one passage. The pastoralists of the Taurus Mountains lived in black tents made from the hair of their goats and produced their own cheese and yogurt while living on the *yayla*. While engaging in light romanticism about pastoralist proximity to nature, Alagöz also waded into the murky distinction between transhumance (*yaylacılık*) in Anatolia and the nomadism (*göçebelik*) practiced by communities in Africa, Iraq, Iran, and the Arabian Peninsula who "wander after their flocks from pasture to pasture." He claimed that "it is easily understood that nomadism and transhumance are not the same thing." Nomadism was, "geographically speaking, the result of a manner of raising animals," whereas transhumance was formed through the practice of "sending or bringing animals to elevated areas and from there to low regions with a mild climate." The key difference was the degree of settlement and human agency involved in these distinct lifestyles. Nomads supposedly wandered after flocks, whereas transhumants moved with them deliberately. In other words, "the nomad has no fixed village, is not tied to the land, does not practice agriculture, and even if they do, it has a unique character. As for the transhumant, they move between specified villages and specified mountain pastures on specified routes."[251]

The distinction between nomadism and transhumance had implicit racial connotations in Turkey. The transhumant population of Alagöz's study consisted of those who were properly considered Turkish or from "the Turkish race."[252] The racial component of early republican interest in Yörüks, Türkmens, and the pastoralists of Anatolia was more explicitly stated in a 1941 study published by Alagöz's colleague at Ankara University, an anthropologist named Kemal Güngör. His analysis of the Yörük populations of Southern Anatolia included not only information about way of life, economy, folklore, and traditions, but also extremely detailed anthropometric measurements from the various tribes he studied during field research in 1938–39.[253] The studies of Alagöz and Güngör occurred during a pivotal moment in history that required qualifying transhumance with ethnic or racial modifiers. As Soner Çağaptay notes, "the word nomad in the republican jargon was a euphemism for the Kurds, and the occasional Roma."[254] The definition of transhumance employed by Alagöz rendered Turkish pastoralists essentially similar to all other Turkish citizens in origin, no more distant than the Parisian was from the Alpine villager. This distinction in turn rationalized the settlement laws aimed at Kurdish populations, conceptualized as the settlement of nomads who were deviant within the national culture and therefore a threat.[255] The Dersim rebellion of 1937–38 was the culmination of such policies. In Dersim, the army waged war with largely pastoralist communities who resisted the 1934 Settlement Law and other measures aimed at pacifying Kurdish communities in Anatolia. The consequent military campaign was brutal. It employed aerial bombing, killing large numbers of people and displacing most of the population.[256]

Although the Turkish pastoralist was a useful foil in this context, the romanticization of groups like Yörüks and Türkmens in Anatolia occurred only after these communities were sedentarized and rendered governable. At the outset of the republican period, nomadic pastoralism in Cilicia was alive and well. Wartime depopulation in the mountains may have led to an expanded availability of pasturage during the first decades of the republican period.[257] Güngör's 1941 study exhibited the transhumant geographies of ten pastoralist tribal communities (*aşiret*) that could be identified in the Çukurova region. All ten of these communities summered in the Taurus Mountains, with about half of their *yaylas* clustered west of the railway near Pozantı and the rest farther to the northeast past Niğde and near the vicinity of the recently depopulated area of Hadjin (Saimbeyli). Notably, only two of these ten communities, the Karahacılı and Bahşiş tribes, were mentioned in Langlois's estimates of tribal populations in Cilicia during the 1850s. As a member of the Aydınlı tribe would explain to a reporter for *Engizek* newspaper, communal subdivisions and their shifting names were the consequence of peaceful fragmentation that occurred as groups split up to find new pasture.[258]

The migrations of pastoralists were not dictated only by weather but rather by the availability and depletion of pastures at different elevations and different points throughout the year. As such, the expansion of agriculture and the creation of an ascendant class of large landholders during the late Ottoman period fueled a creeping process of dispossession. For example, during Yalgın's travels in the Taurus Mountains in 1928, he spoke to members of the Bahşiş tribe, who had maintained approximately the same *yayla* since the late eighteenth century. They complained of difficulties in finding winter pasture. "The Bahşiş tribe has no land [*toprak*] or winter pasture [*kışlak*]," he remarked. "This tribe winters in rented locations south of Adana. As they poured out their bitter sorrows, they began to discuss how they had until now remained without home or hearth, and how they wanted so much to settle."[259] A local official in Misis reported a similar phenomenon in the villages to Red Crescent inspector Muhittin Nuri during the 1920s. There, the villagers rented out some of their property to pastoralists coming down from the Taurus Mountains during the winter.[260] The registration of land was a policy intended to create more landed agriculturalists and raise agricultural yields, but in effect, it created the opportunity for new landlords to generate revenue from unused land that was valuable to pastoralists. In this regard, the major factors influencing the settlement of migratory populations were not only government pressure or economic incentive but also the economic constraints that the sudden introduction of private property in the Çukurova region placed on landless pastoralists. Particularly while in and around the lowlands, the pastoralists in Bates's study from the 1970s rented pasture from villagers and landlords in the regions through which they passed.[261]

Even if they held a special place within nationalist discourses, Turkish pastoralists were still expected to become regular villagers, and they were subject to piecemeal settlement policies. In 1931, members of the Aydınlı, Karakeçili, Horzun, Sarıkeçili, and Tekeli tribes—about 210 families representing about 1,500 people—were placed in villages in the Niğde province, far from Çukurova, in the location of their summer *yaylas*.[262] In 1934, with the promulgation of the infamous 1934 Settlement Law, more members of these communities were given land in Çukurova. Sixty-two families representing 280 individuals from the Karatekeli tribe were given land, some 2,750 *dönüms*, at their winter quarters near Kadirli.[263] Members of the Tekeli and Horzun tribes—179 households of 988 people—were given land in more hilly regions of Karaisalı and Feke, while another 79 Tekeli people were settled on vacant lands at Deveciuşağı near Yumurtalık.[264] As Alagöz noted at the end of his study of transhumance, a 1937 law that put forests and *yaylas* under military control—a measure inextricable from the context of the Dersim rebellion—was sure to limit the grazing capacity of pastoralists. He predicted that "transhumance in Anatolia will inevitably decline."[265]

The relatively few who had not sedentarized became something of a curiosity, embodied by the "last nomads" trope that has lingered for decades in the Çukurova region. For example, in 1947, journalist Alaattin Benal published an interview he conducted with an elderly man and a young man who were members of the Aydınlıs. The pair elaborated upon their various lifestyles and how they wintered near İslahiye and summered at Pınarbaşı, which had been in the settlement sites of the Avşars almost a century prior. They belonged to different *aşirets*, which were among ten or eleven tribes under the umbrella of Aydınlı. The two complained about government policies, saying that "the state banned goats, so now most of us raise sheep," and adding, "May God not destroy our state [*Allah devletimize zeval vermesin*]," to express roughly the opposite sentiment. When asked whether they would settle if given land, the young man said, "We can't stay still, that's what we're used to. We would feel like they tied us down. If only pasture was as plentiful as it used to be, thankfully we have no other problem."[266]

While the slow erosion of pastoralist communities and ways of life in Anatolia is well documented, it is worth noting that settling such communities also had far-reaching impacts on mountain landscapes. Sedentarization of pastoralists seems to have accelerated deforestation in the Taurus Mountains. Citing studies of tree root structures, McNeill indicates that "fuel needs of the villages (made up of recently settled nomads) caused the deforestation."[267] Spending the winter in the mountains came at an environmental cost. He notes that "the foothills of the Cilician Taurus have also eroded down to the rock, and sediments have washed down to the plain of Adana, expanding it into the Mediterranean." The formation of new land out in the sea within the deltas of Çukurova was very rapid between the 1930s and 1950s.[268] For roughly a century, nomads and pastoralists had been blamed for the supposed degradation of mountain landscapes. But it appears that it was when their communities were finally settled into village life that the mountains they once roamed witnessed the most pronounced period of ecological change.

In 1948, President İsmet İnönü flew over the Çukurova region to observe the damage of yet another Seyhan River flood. Afterward, he called for a comprehensive plan that included flood control, irrigation, and even hydroelectric power. "No matter how money much it will cost," he wrote, "the government must venture it all."[269] Less than a decade later, under the technocratic consensus of the early republican period and the new, democratically elected government of İnönü's rival Adnan Menderes, the hydroelectric Seyhan Dam was completed. It was the first of many hydroelectric projects of the World Bank, funded by an initial loan from the IBRD of $25 million.[270] The construction began in 1953 and was completed on schedule in 1956. In addition to increasing the amount of water available for irrigation, it supplied electricity to the city of Adana. Standing 50 m tall, the dam also created a large reservoir north of the city. One article in *Demokrat*, the organ of the ruling party of the same name, declared "The Hollow Plain is becoming a Golden Plain [*Çukurova Altınova oluyor*]."[271] Another writer admonished the critics of the Demokrat Party, saying, "Today the Seyhan Barrage will open, and as it gives its first hydroelectric current, we will feel the electricity of all of our feelings, our 'free' feelings, and a deep peace and satisfaction."[272]

A century after the reforms reached Cilicia, the region had essentially become a living production of Tanzimat-era science fiction called Çukurova. The old neighborhoods of Adana looked about the same, but the people who resided there had new names. The same was true in Tarsus, where exotic trees from the other side of the planet had overtaken the large lagoon that had rested just south of the city since time immemorial. For malaria, there were now pills made from bark that also came from *the other* other side of the planet that killed invisible parasites in the blood. Of course, residents of Çukurova still fled the summer heat, rocketing in locomotives and automobiles to ancestral *yaylas*. In the lowlands, giant machines farmed plantations in the former wilderness, but the seed they sowed was still for the most part the good old *yerli* that had risen to global prominence during the cotton boom of the 1860s. The farmers, who had only heard tell of how their ancestors lived, sang "the Song of Kozanoğlu atop their tractors, like the song of a former, foreign world."[273]

The region's material context had changed considerably, but many of the fundamental political concerns were the same. Just as İnönü had used an aerial survey to articulate a hydraulic vision similar to that of Ziya Pasha and other Tanzimat-era politicians who saw Çukurova as the Egypt of the future, aerial bombing over Dersim roughly a decade earlier had been used to pursue a policy of tribal pacification and resettlement in a region that had been within the purview of Cevdet's Reform Division during the 1860s. Just as factions within the Tanzimat bureaucracy battled over the future of the liberal experiment, so too did the Demokrat Party and its adversaries; the fate of Menderes was not dissimilar from that of Sultan Abdülaziz, the latter deposed and found dead under mysterious circumstances and the former tried and executed by a military junta. The more things changed, the more they stayed the same. The march of progress was full of familiar refrains.

Just as the forcibly settled pastoralists sang songs that cursed their swampy environs, a new generation of bards was still producing politically charged songs about malaria. A song by Aşık Bayram published in the Marash-based newspaper *Engizek* described how the powerful rice industry had caused malaria to spread among the locals: "We were surrounded on all sides by impassable swamps / The water has become poisonous and undrinkable / It's hard to get by and we can't go to the *yaylas* / We are all suffering as if doomed to torment / It's impossible to sleep with the cries of the sick / We've been weakened by the bites of mosquitos / We can't even drink from our own streams . . . Is there no brave soul to remove this rice paddy / Someone to bring a smile to the innocent children / The one who kills a ricefarmer is a hero / He'll fly straight to heaven like the wind." This was just one of many poems from the Çukurova region featured in a book entitled *Isıtma ve Çeltik* (Malaria and Rice) by Dr. Şerif Korkut.[274] Korkut presented malaria not merely as a disease, but also as an issue of social justice nested in the political economy of the rice paddy.[275] He was certainly influenced by the socialist and peasantist currents of his era, but the poems about malaria he included in his work, which mirrored the folk poetry of prior generations stretching back to Dadaloğlu and beyond, suggested a genealogy of political critique deeply embedded in local history.

Power relations in Çukurova had changed. Ankara was present in the daily lives of rural people in ways that the Ottoman officials in Gülhane could only have imagined at the declaration of the Tanzimat in 1839. And when it came to matters of agriculture, health, and environment, science had finally attained the primacy foretold by Tanzimat-era technocrats. Yet the persistence of malaria and its relationship with settlement and commercial agriculture forged a powerful continuity. After all, Ibrahim Pasha had drained the swamps of İskenderun, but they came back. Cevdet Pasha had claimed that cultivation would eliminate malaria, but it seemed to make it worse. The Committee of Union and Progress had promised quinine to every Ottoman citizen, only to watch malaria penetrate even deeper into Ottoman society during World War I. Annual examinations, complex pill regimens, mosquito-eating fish, and toxic chemicals had been promoted by the Adana Malaria Institute, but a malaria-free summer remained more an aspiration than an actual attainable goal in the imaginations of many.[276]

Then, within a few decades, that too changed. DDT, a powerful insecticide pioneered during World War II, became available to Turkey in almost limitless quantities in part thanks to the US Marshall Plan for postwar rebuilding. In the years after the war, Ekrem Tok, the former head of Adana's malaria program, led Turkey's health ministry. From the late 1940s onward, homes were inspected for mosquitos and sprayed for DDT on a systematic basis. Airplanes were used to douse wetlands and fields with the chemical.[277] By 1950, the number of malaria cases in Turkey was half of what it had been in 1945.[278] Less than 10 percent of people tested positive for malaria, and during the first half of the 1950s those rates dropped below 5 percent. By the late 1950s, the number of people being tested and treated for malaria was just a fraction of what it had been a decade prior.[279] In 1960, just 1 percent of people in Çukurova suffered a malaria infection. There were practically no cases of malaria in Çukurova as of 1965.[280] During the late 1970s, there was a brief resurgence. In 1977, there were 94,000 cases of malaria in Çukurova, mostly among the enormous migrant worker population.[281] But today, malaria rates in Çukurova are effectively zero. Mosquito eradication coupled with surveillance and proactive medical interventions made malaria the least of anyone's concerns. Its omnipresence had once influenced how people in the region ordered time itself; before long, there might be few left who ever experienced it.

Once the threat of malaria was removed from daily life, Çukurova was a different place. The village population of the Adana province (excluding urban) grew by almost 70 percent between 1945 and 1960. The growth was highest in the districts of Ceyhan, Kozan, and Kadirli, the regions of Çukurova that had become the late Ottoman frontier of immigrant and tribal settlement but where malaria had historically been most pervasive.[282] Meanwhile, the importation of affordable agricultural machinery meant that animals began to disappear even from the villages. The number of oxen in Çukurova dropped by 85 percent between 1948 and 1952.[283] Instead of worrying about feeding their animals or having them requisitioned by the military, one-third of villagers in Çukurova reported issues with frequent breakdowns of equipment and trouble obtaining repairs.[284] Amid this rapid growth, land became scarce, and people flocked to the cities of the region. By 1970, around 60,000 Çukurova residents had taken up residence in Istanbul, Ankara, and other cities, while Çukurova received 200,000 new residents primarily from the Eastern Anatolian provinces of Elazığ, Diyarbakır, Erzurum, Gaziantep, and Van.[285] In 1935, Adana had fewer than 80,000 inhabitants and Mersin just over 20,000. By 1965, Adana's population was approaching 300,000 and Mersin was larger than Adana had been decades earlier. Ceyhan's population quadrupled over that period.[286] Today, the urban populations of Adana and Mersin approach 2 million and 1 million, respectively. There are many lesser cities in Çukurova that rival old Anazarbus at its height.

For government supporters, Çukurova embodied "the Turkish miracle." Yet throughout this period, Çukurova was the fulcrum of Turkey's Marxist literary tradition that critiqued what was unfolding. Beginning in the 1950s, authors like Yaşar Kemal and Orhan Kemal put workers, peasants, and pastoralists at center stage in Turkey's national literature. They were keen observers of the negative consequences of state-making, capitalism, and conflict for ordinary people in the region. Orhan Kemal's 1954 novel *Bereketli Topraklar Üzerinde* would stand as an iconic representation of Çukurova from a worker's perspective, and before long, this new world shaped by capital and cotton would itself become a timeless image. In the 1979 film adaptation of the novel, the final frame featured a quotation attributed to Orhan Kemal from 1968, in which he said, "I checked and Çukurova is still the Çukurova of *Bereketli Topraklar Üzerinde*. It has been this way for a thousand years," or in other words, Çukurova was the same as it had always been.[287]

This book has documented considerable changes in the history of Çukurova over the past millennium, perhaps most notably the elimination of malaria that occurred within the last decades of Orhan Kemal's lifetime. So how could he argue that Çukurova was still the same?

Perhaps the enduring quality that Kemal found was the continuous reiteration of certain themes and rhythms over time: the eternal heat of summer, the annual arrival and departure of seasonal workers, and the weekly bargaining over goods and labor. The constant immigration, whether from the Caucasus, Crete, the Balkans, or Eastern Anatolia. Despite land changing hands many times, continuity could be found in the unequal property relations that emerged during the earliest periods of sedentarization and commercialization, and followed workers to the farm and the factory floor. These features were not entirely new, even on the timescale of a millennium. Cilicia had welcomed migrants throughout history, and it had always been shaped by movement between the mountains and the lowlands. The two largest local communities of the region at the outset of the nineteenth century—the Armenians and the Türkmens—had once been newcomers. But the mainstays of their way of life had largely been in place as early as the Hittite period. Rome had invaded Cilicia for supposed security reasons, designating the groups that controlled the mountains as pirates and outlaws, just as their Ottoman successors did during the 1860s, prompting Dadaloğlu's famous retort that "the mountains are ours." Did enslaved Cilicians of the Roman period also maintain their own songs about the mountains while tending the estates of absentee landowners in far-off Sicily or in the shadow of their ancestral highlands on the plantations of Anazarbus?

Whether or not they did, "the mountains are ours" was a refrain that would have been intelligible to those people, just as it was to people in Turkey more than a century after the forced settlement campaigns. The poetry of Dadaloğlu became part of a national folklore corpus in Turkey, which means it eventually entered popular music.[288] Dadaloğlu's legacy is now found scattered among piles of 45 rpm records of *arabesk* songs and the nostalgic hits of Turkish cinema's Yeşilçam era. The refrain "the mountains are ours" had passed to Mehmet Ruhi Su, an accomplished musician believed to have been an orphan of Armenian origin brought to Adana during World War I. Ruhi Su used the poetry of bards like Dadaloğlu to express his political sentiments in a more accessible format after his opera career in Turkey was cut short by a jail sentence under accusations of communism. Likewise, Cem Karaca's rock rendition of "the mountains are ours" was one of his many songs with subversive undertones used in similar allegations that drove him into exile during the 1970s.[289] Artists from that period also performed songs about

Kozanoğlu, and Yılmaz Güney, himself the child of migrants to Çukurova who settled in Yenice, performed the role of Kozanoğlu in one of his earliest films, eventually going on to become an acclaimed director known for his portrayals of Anatolian westerns, gangsters, the working class, and the experience of Turkey's Kurdish communities.[290] These artists reached the height of their popularity during the period of relatively open political expression in Turkey that preceded the 1980 coup. It is no accident that when pop culture and mass media took the lid off Turkey's political memory, echoes of the past were waiting to be heard.

In the summer of 2013, "the mountains are ours" echoed back during another period of political expression remembered simply as "Gezi." The impending demolition of the Gezi Park in Taksim Square in Istanbul catalyzed protests throughout Turkey about a range of grievances that somehow converged on the controversial commercialization of a public space. The park became a commune for activists, who endured a siege by the police throughout much of June. One of the activist Facebook groups shared a map of the occupied Gezi Park in the center of Istanbul on which makeshift barricades had been labeled using the names of historical figures synonymous with resistance. The barricade blocking the road to the Gezi Park near Ataturk Library bore Dadaloğlu's name; in the center of the map, the author had written, "the decree is the Sultan's, but Gezi is ours."[291]

For anyone who knows the history of this allusion, it would read as more than a play on words. It was a powerful example of how a sentiment could travel across time and space between people who never knew one another but knew something of a shared experience. The original declaration "the mountains are ours" represented more than a localized tribal rebellion against Ottoman rule. It was a battle over two competing visions of the future: one in which the people who lived on the land and knew it intimately should define their relationship with that land and another in which that relationship should be subservient to the needs of the state and the desires of those with the money or power to influence it. Though the battle between Dadaloğlu's people and the Ottoman state lasted just a few years, those competing visions of the future have never ceased to clash. And though I have studied many centuries of significant changes in the place they called home, I still find the repetition of this refrain to hold the most compelling lesson from its history.

ACKNOWLEDGMENTS

Thank you for reading my first published book. After years immersed in archives, newspapers, memoirs, folk songs, and novels, each with their own story to tell, I learned what Yaşar Kemal had long said: Çukurova is inexhaustible. The most difficult part was choosing which stories to include in the manuscript, which paths to follow, and what to cut. Each foray into the sources turned up new characters with stories worth telling. The more I learned, the more value I saw in each one. But this book has a character limit, and I have left numerous stories untold. I hope that both my insights and shortcomings will be useful to future authors who explore those stories. I would like to thank Kate Wahl, Caroline McKusick and the folks at Stanford University Press for taking on this project, and I owe a special debt of gratitude to the four peer reviewers who read this manuscript at SUP. They played a fundamental role in choices about the final form of this book.

The Unsettled Plain is the product of work that took place at many institutions. At Le Moyne College, Keith Watenpaugh and Meredith Terretta helped me turn my enthusiasm for history into a viable plan for graduate study. At Georgetown University, the encouragement and mentorship of Judith Tucker and John McNeill were invaluable. Sylvia Wing Önder, Gabor Agoston, Mustafa Aksakal, Salim Tamari, Osama Abi Mershed, Rochelle Davis, Alison Games, and Aparna Vaidik also offered important guidance during various stages of my training. This project received funding from the SSRC-IDRF and Mellon/ACLS-DCF, and I benefited from multiple FLAS scholarships for language study, the ARIT summer scholarship for Turkish language at Boğaziçi University, and a CASA scholarship for one year of Arabic study at Damascus University.

At Yale University's Program in Agrarian Studies, I broke out of my regional bubble under the mentorship of James C. Scott and Kalyanakrishnan Sivaramakrishnan. At the Harvard Academy for International and Area Studies, I developed the current shape of the manuscript through an author conference chaired by Sunil Amrith and attended by Emine Evered, Reşat Kasaba, Myrna Santiago, Meltem Toksöz, and Sam White, who suggested a new organization reflected in this published version. I also thank Melani Cammett, Kathleen Hoover, Bruce Jackan, Ian Miller, and Ajantha Subramanian for their support during two years at the Harvard Academy. Polina Ivanova added significant material and insight to chapter 1 as a research assistant at Harvard, including Greek archival sources that would otherwise have been inaccessible to me. During my first years teaching at University of Virginia, I finished the manuscript with encouragement from many colleagues, especially Joshua White, Fahad Bishara, Erin Lambert, Jennifer Sessions, and Samhita Sunya. I completed the final rounds of revisions on this book in Charlottesville, under the trying conditions of the COVID-19 pandemic, and the final copy edits on a cool October day in Istanbul.

Institutional support over the years is only a small part of what made this book happen. Friends and colleagues going back to my early years of study played the biggest role in my intellectual development. Sam Dolbee, Graham Pitts, and Seçil Yılmaz were particularly important collaborators on research and writing throughout the formative period of this work. Their feedback and contributions to the book are immense. Sam has commented on many iterations. I also thank Önder Eren Akgül and Nicholas Danforth for feedback on large portions, as well as Susanna Ferguson for reading a comical number of versions of the introduction.

I have many others to thank for various contributions, whether help with sources, advice, ideas, or comments on writing: Oscar Aguirre-Mandujano, Yiğit Akın, Taylan Akyıldırım, Elçin Arabacı, Reem Bailony, Seçil Binboğa, Edna Bonhomme, Kellen Bucher, Eda Çakmakçı, Aurora Camaño, Lâle Can, Rishad Choudhury, Graham Cornwell, Jennifer Derr,

Sultan Doughan, Jeffery Dyer, Madeleine Elfenbein, Hülya Eraslan, Mehtap Ergenoğlu, Harika Zöhre Eryılmaz, Kyle Evered, Zachary Foster, Ella Fratantuono, Matthew Ghazarian, Eric Gratien, Robert Greeley, Zoe Griffith, Huma Gupta, Can Gümüş, Emrah Safa Gürkan, David Gutman, Timur Hammond, Julia Harte, Kerem Mert İspir, Amy Johnson, Lori Jones, Cemal Kafadar, Melike Kara, Özlem Karasandık, Mehmet Kentel, Elektra Kostopoulou, Harun Küçük, Ümit Kurt, Selim Kuru, Tyler Kynn, Noora Lori, Michael Christopher Low, Nidhi Mahajan, Sandrine Mansour, Lawrence McMahon, Alan Mikhail, Owen Miller, Sona Mnatsakanyan, Taylor Moore, Nada Moumtaz, Emily Neumeier, Hande Özkan, Nilay Özlü, Burçak Özlüdil-Altın, Şuşan Özoğlu, Maryam Patton, Michal Polczynski, Dan Pontillo, Jim Ryan, Zeynep Güler Sabancı, Akın Sefer, Elyse Semerdjian, Nir Shafir, Vahé Tachjian, Kenan Tekin, Elizabeth Thompson, Alp Eren Topal, Abdullah Uğur, Songül Ulutaş, Arianne Urus, Leili Vatani, Raffi Joe Wartanian, Heghnar Watenpaugh, Elizabeth Williams, Akif Yerlioğlu, Dilan Yıldırım, Emrah Yıldız, Murat Yıldız, Naz Yücel, and Majed Zouba.

There are many unsung heroes not mentioned here. These include archivists and librarians, some of whom I never even met, though they tirelessly supplied us with material over the years. I am especially indebted to the highly professional staff at the Ottoman Archives in Istanbul between the years 2011 and 2017. I would also like to recognize the interlibrary loan staff at Georgetown University who served up rare books as fast as I could consume them. Even further behind the scenes are those who worked on the digitization projects that have transformed how we conduct research over the span of this work's completion, as well as often anonymous editors of Wikipedia who have made the work of both exploration and fact-checking easier.

Finally, I thank my mother, Julie Gratien, for taking time out of her well-deserved retirement to work on the art for this book. It means a lot to have her be part of this study after devoting so much of my own life to it. I hope this will be one in the line of many new histories of the Çukurova region yet to be written, and I look forward to the work of those who follow the paths left uncharted in this manuscript. I am honored and humbled by its readers.

ARCHIVES AND LIBRARIES

Archives and libraries consulted for primary sources cited in this book are listed alphabetically by country. Published primary and secondary sources are fully cited in the notes.

Armenia
Hayastani Azgayin Gradaran (National Library of Armenia), Yerevan
Matenadaran (Mesrop Mashtots Institute of Ancient Manuscripts), Yerevan

France
Archives de l'Institut Pasteur (Pasteur Institute Archives), Paris
Bibliothèque interuniversitaire de Santé (Interuniversity Health Library), Paris
Bibliothèque nationale de France (National Library of France), François-Mitterrand, Paris
Bibliothèque Nubar de l'UGAB (Nubarian Library of the AGBU), Paris
Centre des archives diplomatiques (Diplomatic Archives Center), La Courneuve
Centre des archives diplomatiques, Nantes
Gallica, gallica.bnf.fr

Greece
Kentro Mikrasiatikon Spoudon (Centre for Asia Minor Studies), Athens

Lebanon

American University in Beirut
Phoenix Center for Lebanese Studies, Université Saint-Esprit de Kaslik

Switzerland

Archive of the League of Nations and United Nations, Geneva

Turkey

Atatürk Kitaplığı (Ataturk Library), Istanbul
Cumhuriyet Arşivi (Republican Archives), Ankara
Osmanlı Arşivi (Ottoman Archives), Istanbul
Beyazıt Devlet Kütüphanesi (Beyazıt State Library), Istanbul
Süleymaniye Yazma Eser Kütüphanesi (Süleymaniye Library), Istanbul
Taha Toros Arşivi (Taha Toros Archive), openaccess.marmara.edu.tr/handle/11424/120957
Türk Kızılay Arşivi (Red Crescent Archive), Ankara
Türkiye Büyük Millet Meclisi (Grand National Assembly of Turkey), tbmm.gov.tr

United Kingdom

British National Library, London
The National Archives, Kew

United States

American Board of Commissioners for Foreign Missions Papers, Harvard University
GoogleBooks, books.google.com
HathiTrust, hathitrust.org
Internet Archive, archive.org
Library of Congress, loc.gov
National Archives and Records Administration, College Park, MD
Rockefeller Archive Center, Sleepy Hollow, NY

ABBREVIATIONS AND ACRONYMS

ABC	American Board of Commissioners for Foreign Missions Papers
AGBU	Armenian General Benevolent Union
AK	Atatürk Kitaplığı
ALON-UNOG	Archive of the League of Nations and United Nations
AUB	American University in Beirut
BN	Bibliothèque Nubar de l'UGAB
BNF	Bibliothèque François-Mitterrand
CA	Başbakanlık Cumhuriyet Arşivi
CADC	Centre des archives diplomatiques, La Courneuve
CCC	Correspondance commerciale et consulaire
CADN	Centre des archives diplomatiques, Nantes
1SL/1/V, 126–361	Territories Ennemis Occupés, Zone Nord—Cilicie
8PO	Adana et Mersine, Consulaire
CHP	Cumhuriyet Halk Partisi (Republican People's Party)
CUP	Committee of Union and Progress (İttihat ve Terakki)
H.	Hicri (date in Islamic hijri calendar)

IBRD		International Bank for Reconstruction and Development
IP		Archives de l'Institut Pasteur
KMS		Kentro Mikrasiatikon Spoudon
NARA		National Archives and Records Administration, College Park
	RG 166	Records of the Foreign Agricultural Service
OA		Osmanlı Arşivi, Istanbul
	A	Sadâret (Grand Vizierate)
	AMD	Âmedî Kalemi
	DVN	Divan Kalemi
	NZD	Nezâret ve Devâir
	BEO	Bab-ı Ali Evrak Odası
	C	Cevdet
	AS	Askeriye
	DH	Dahiliye Nezâreti (Ministry of Interior)
	EUM	Emniyet-i Umumiye (Directorate of Security)
	HMŞ	Hukuk Müşavirliği (Legal Council)
	İD	İdare
	İ-UM	İdare-i Umumiye
	MUİ	Muhaberat-ı Umumiye İdaresi
	SN-THR	Sicill-i Nüfus Tahrirat Kalemi
	ŞFR	Şifre (Encoded Telegram)
	TMIK-S / M	Tesri-i Muamelat ve Islahat Komisyonu
	UMVM	Umur-ı Mahalliye ve Vilayat Müdürlüğü
	EK	Ek (Supplement)
	HR	Hariciye Nezâreti (Ministry of Foreign Affairs)
	HR-HMŞ-İŞO	Hukuk Müşavirliği İstişare
	İM	İstanbul Murahhaslığı
	SFR (3)	Londra Sefareti (London Embassy)
	SYS	Siyasi
	TO	Tercüme Odası (Translation Office)
	HRT	Harita (Map)
	İ	İrade (Decree)
	DA	Divan-ı Ahkam-ı Adliye (Court of Cassation)

	DUİT	Dosya Usulü
	MMS	Meclis-i Mahsus
	MF	Maarif Nezâreti (Ministry of Education)
	MHM	Mühimme Kalemi
	MKT	Mektubî Kalemi
	MVL	Meclis-i Vala (Supreme Council)
	NF	Nafia (Public Works)
	NFS	Nüfüs (Population)
	ŞD	Şûrâ-yı Devlet (Council of State)
	T	Ticaret (Trade)
	UM	Umum/Umumi
	VRK	Evrâk (Documents)
	Y	Yıldız (Yıldız Palace)
	A-HUS	Sadâret Hususî Maruzâtı
	EE	Esas Evrakı
	MTV	Mütenevvi Maruzat Evrakı
	PRK-KOM	Perakende Evrakı Komisyanlar Maruzatı
	PRK-UM	Perakende Evrakı Umumi
	RES	Resmi Maruzat
RAC		Rockefeller Archive Center
SYEK		Süleymaniye Yazma Eser Kütüphanesi
TKA		Türk Kızılay Arşivi
TNA		The National Archives, Kew
	FO	Foreign Office
USEK		Phoenix Center, Université Saint-Esprit de Kaslik

NOTES

Introduction

1. Fethi Ahmet Canpolat and Selçuk Hayli, *Pınarbaşı İlçe'sinin (Kayseri) beşeri ve iktisadi coğrafyası* (Istanbul: Hiperlink, 2019), 66.

2. The Turkish word *mucuk* is of Armenian origin. Robert Dankoff, *Armenian Loanwords in Turkish* (Wiesbaden: Otto Harrassowitz, 1995), 108.

3. All information pertaining to "The Lament of Ömer" in Ahmet Z. Özdemir, *Öyküleriyle Ağıtlar* (Ankara: Kültür Bakanlığı, 1994), 263–64. The stories behind folk songs, much like the lyrics themselves, usually circulate in multiple versions. Özdemir cites three men from the area as the source for his explanation and lyrics. An alternate understanding of the lament appears in a Facebook post featuring a video of a live performance of the song by Aşık İmami. According to the caption, Ömer and his father Durmuş had both gone to Adana together to earn money for the wedding, and the lament was in Durmuş's voice rather than Ömer's mother's voice. Shared in Radyo Avşar'ın Sesi (7 January 2012), facebook.com/watch/?v=2299766023987.

4. Yaşar Kemal, *Çukurova Yana Yana* (Istanbul: Yeditepe Yayınları, 1955), 13.

5. See Gilles Deleuze and Félix Guattari, *A Thousand Plateaus: Capitalism and Schizophrenia*, trans. Brian Massumi (Minneapolis: University of Minnesota Press, 1987); Guy Debord, *The Society of the Spectacle* (New York: Zone Books, 1994).

6. See Avner Wishnitzer, *Reading Clocks, Alla Turca: Time and Society in the Late Ottoman Empire* (Chicago: University of Chicago Press, 2015); Dale Tomich, "The Order of Historical Time: The Longue Durée and Micro-History," in *The Longue Durée and World-Systems Analysis*, ed. Richard E. Lee and Immanuel Wallerstein (New York: State University of New York Press, 2012); Reinhart Koselleck, *Sediments of Time: On Possible Histories*, trans. Sean Franzel and Stefan Ludwig-Hoffmann (Stanford: Stanford

University Press, 2018); Henri Lefebvre, *Rhythmanalysis: Space, Time, and Everyday Life* (London: Continuum, 2004).

7. Anna Lowenhaupt Tsing, *The Mushroom at the End of the World: On the Possibility of Life in Capitalist Ruins* (Princeton: Princeton University Press, 2017), 22.

8. See Donald R. Wright, *The World and a Very Small Place in Africa* (Armonk, NY: M. E. Sharpe, 1997).

9. Olçay Önertoy, "Yaşar Kemal ve Çukurova," *Türk Dili* 375 (March 1983): 147.

10. See Yaşar Kemal, *Memed, My Hawk* (New York: Pantheon, 1961).

11. "'Çukurova'sını yazmayan hiçbir yazar büyük romancı olamaz,'" *Milliyet*, 3 October 2012.

12. Yaşar Kemal, *Ağıtlar: Folklor derlemesi* (Istanbul: YKY, 2004), 19–47.

13. Ahmet Taner Kışlalı, "Demokrasi, Roman, Dil, Eğitim, Sanat, Politika Üzerine," *Haftaya Bakış*, 22–28 March 1987, via yasarkemal.net. See also Ali Taş, "Yaşar Kemal Çukurova Ödülü," *Yeni Adana*, 15 June 2020.

14. See Yiğit Akın, *When the War Came Home: The Ottomans' Great War and the Devastation of an Empire* (Stanford: Stanford University Press, 2018), 1; Nazan Maksudyan, *Ottoman Children and Youth during World War I* (Syracuse, NY: Syracuse University Press, 2019), 10–11.

15. Suraiya Faroqhi, "A Study of Rural Conflicts: Gegbuze/Gebze (District of Üsküdar) in the Mid-1700s," in *Ottoman Rural Societies and Economies: Halcyon Days in Crete VIII*, ed. Elias Kolovos (Rethymno: Crete University Press, 2015), 10.

16. J. R. McNeill, "The State of the Field of Environmental History," *Annual Review of Environment and Resources* 35, no. 1 (2010): 347.

17. Alan Mikhail, *Under Osman's Tree: The Ottoman Empire, Egypt, and Environmental History* (Chicago: University of Chicago Press, 2017), 199. See also Sam White, *The Climate of Rebellion in the Early Modern Ottoman Empire* (Cambridge: Cambridge University Press, 2011); Nükhet Varlık, *Plague and Empire in the Early Modern Mediterranean World: The Ottoman Experience, 1347–1600* (Cambridge: Cambridge University Press, 2016); Yaron Ayalon, *Natural Disasters in the Ottoman Empire: Plague, Famine, and Other Misfortunes* (Cambridge: Cambridge University Press, 2014). For reflections on the emerging field, see Onur İnal, "Environmental History as an Emerging Field in Ottoman Studies: An Historiographical Overview," *Osmanlı Araştırmaları* 38 (2011): 1–25; Elizabeth Williams, "Environmental History of the Middle East and North Africa," in *The Oxford Handbook of Contemporary Middle-Eastern and North African History*, ed. Jens Hanssen and Amal N. Ghazal (Oxford: Oxford University Press, 2017); Christopher S. Rose, "The History of Public Health in the Modern Middle East: The Environmental-Medical Turn," *History Compass* 19, no. 5 (2021).

18. Faisal Husain, *Rivers of the Sultan: The Tigris and Euphrates in the Ottoman Empire* (New York: Oxford University Press, 2021); Michael Christopher Low, *Imperial Mecca: Ottoman Arabia and the Indian Ocean Hajj* (New York: Columbia Univer-

sity Press, 2020); Zozan Pehlivan, "El Niño and the Nomads: Global Climate, Local Environment, and the Crisis of Pastoralism in Late Ottoman Kurdistan," *Journal of the Economic and Social History of the Orient* 63, no. 3 (2020): 316–56; Onur İnal and Yavuz Köse, *Seeds of Power: Explorations in Ottoman Environmental History* (Winwick, UK: White Horse Press, 2019); Samuel Dolbee, "The Locust and the Starling: People, Insects, and Disease in the Late Ottoman Jazira and After, 1860–1940," PhD diss., New York University, 2017; Camille Lyans Cole, "Precarious Empires: A Social and Environmental History of Steam Navigation on the Tigris," *Journal of Social History* 50, no. 1 (2016): 74–101; Graham Auman Pitts, "Fallow Fields: Famine and the Making of Lebanon," PhD diss., Georgetown University, 2016; Onur İnal, "A Port and Its Hinterland: An Environmental History of Izmir in the Late-Ottoman Period," PhD diss., University of Arizona, 2015. See also Caterina Scaramelli, *How to Make a Wetland: Water and Moral Ecology in Turkey* (Stanford: Stanford University Press, 2021).

19. Robert Kern, "Ecocriticism: What Is It Good For?" *Interdisciplinary Studies in Literature and Environment* 7, no. 1 (2000): 11 cited in Enrico Cesaretti, *Elemental Narratives: Reading Environmental Entanglements in Modern Italy* (University Park: Penn State University Press, 2020), 12.

20. Thomas Albert Perreault, Gavin Bridge, and James McCarthy, *The Routledge Handbook of Political Ecology* (New York: Routledge, 2015), 7.

21. Jim Igoe, *Conservation and Globalization* (South Melbourne, Australia: Wadsworth Cengage Learning, 2013), 2.

22. See Alfred W. Crosby, *Ecological Imperialism: The Biological Expansion of Europe, 900–1900* (Cambridge: Cambridge University Press, 1986).

23. Diana K. Davis, *The Arid Lands: History, Power, Knowledge* (Cambridge, MA: MIT Press, 2016). See also James Fairhead and Melissa Leach, *Misreading the African Landscape: Society and Ecology in a Forest-Savanna Mosaic* (Cambridge: Cambridge University Press, 1996).

24. Jason W. Moore, *Capitalism in the Web of Life: Ecology and the Accumulation of Capital* (New York: Verso, 2016).

25. See John Robert McNeill and Peter Engelke, *The Great Acceleration: An Environmental History of the Anthropocene since 1945* (Cambridge, MA: Harvard University Press, 2016); Christian Parenti and Jason W. Moore, *Anthropocene or Capitalocene? Nature, History, and the Crisis of Capitalism* (Oakland, CA: PM Press, 2016).

26. Amitav Ghosh, *The Great Derangement: Climate Change and the Unthinkable* (Chicago: University of Chicago Press, 2017).

27. Bathsheba Demuth, *Floating Coast: An Environmental History of the Arctic* (New York: W.W. Norton, 2019).

28. Myrna I. Santiago, *The Ecology of Oil: Environment, Labor, and the Mexican Revolution, 1900–1938* (Cambridge: Cambridge University Press, 2006). See also Casey

Marina Lurtz, *From the Grounds Up: Building an Export Economy in Southern Mexico* (Stanford: Stanford University Press, 2019).

29. Debjani Bhattacharyya, *Empire and Ecology in the Bengal Delta: The Making of Calcutta* (Cambridge: Cambridge University Press, 2019). See also Sunil S. Amrith, *Crossing the Bay of Bengal: The Furies of Nature and the Fortunes of Migrants* (Cambridge, MA: Harvard University Press, 2013); Iftekhar Iqbal, *The Bengal Delta: Ecology, State and Social Change, 1840–1943* (Basingstoke, UK: Palgrave Macmillan, 2010).

30. Prasenjit Duara, "Transnationalism and the Challenge to National Histories," in *Rethinking American History in a Global Age*, ed. Thomas Bender (Berkeley: University of California Press, 2002), cited in Arbella Bet-Shlimon, *City of Black Gold: Oil, Ethnicity, and the Making of Modern Kirkuk* (Stanford: Stanford University Press, 2019), 8.

31. James Belich, *Replenishing the Earth: The Settler Revolution and the Rise of the Anglo-World, 1783–1939* (Oxford: Oxford University Press, 2009).

32. See John F. Richards, *The Unending Frontier: An Environmental History of the Early Modern World* (Berkeley: University of California Press, 2003).

33. Mostafa Minawi, *The Ottoman Scramble for Africa: Empire and Diplomacy in the Sahara and the Hijaz* (Stanford: Stanford University Press, 2016); Matthew H. Ellis, *Desert Borderland: The Making of Modern Egypt and Libya* (Stanford: Stanford University Press, 2018); Ebubekir Ceylan, *The Ottoman Origins of Modern Iraq: Political Reform, Modernization and Development in the Nineteenth-Century Middle East* (London: I. B. Tauris, 2011); Nora Elizabeth Barakat, "An Empty Land? Nomads and Property Administration in Hamidian Syria," PhD diss., University of California, Berkeley, 2015; Isacar Bolanos, "Environmental Management and the Iraqi Frontier during the Late Ottoman Period, 1831–1909," PhD diss., Ohio State University, 2019.

34. Thomas Kuehn, *Empire, Islam, and Politics of Difference: Ottoman Rule in Yemen, 1849–1919* (Leiden: Brill, 2011).

35. See Reşat Kasaba, *A Moveable Empire: Ottoman Nomads, Migrants, and Refugees* (Seattle: University of Washington Press, 2009); Isa Blumı, *Ottoman Refugees, 1878–1939: Migration in a Post-Imperial World* (London: Bloomsbury, 2013); David Cuthell, "The Muhacirin Komisyonu: An Agent in the Transformation of Ottoman Anatolia 1860–1866," PhD diss., Columbia University, 2005; Ella Fratantuono, "Migration Administration in the Making of the Late Ottoman Empire," PhD diss., Michigan State University, 2016.

36. Blumı, *Ottoman Refugees*, 5.

37. Milen V. Petrov, "Tanzimat for the Countryside: Midhat Paşa and the Vilayet of Danube, 1864–1868," PhD diss., Princeton University, 2006.

38. Frederick Walter Lorenz, "The 'Second Egypt': Cretan Refugees, Agricultural Development, and Frontier Expansion in Ottoman Cyrenaica, 1897–1904," *International Journal of Middle East Studies* 53, no. 1 (2021): 89–105.

39. Eugene L. Rogan, *Frontiers of the State in the Late Ottoman Empire: Transjordan, 1850–1921* (Cambridge: Cambridge University Press, 1999).

40. Vladimir Hamed-Troyansky, "Circassian Refugees and the Making of Amman, 1878–1914," *International Journal of Middle East Studies* 49, no. 4 (2017): 605–23; Yücel Terzibaşoğlu, "Landlords, Nomads and Refugees: Struggles over Land and Population Movements in North-Western Anatolia [1877–1914]," PhD diss., University of London, 2003; Ebubekir Ceylan, "Carrot or Stick? Ottoman Tribal Policy in Baghdad, 1831–1876," *International Journal of Contemporary Iraqi Studies* 3, no. 2 (2009); Yonca Köksal, "Coercion and Mediation: Centralization and Sedentarization of Tribes in the Ottoman Empire," *Middle Eastern Studies* 42, no. 3 (2006): 469–91; Yasemin Avcı, "The Application of Tanzimat in the Desert: The Bedouins and the Creation of a New Town in Southern Palestine (1860–1914)," *Middle Eastern Studies* 45, no. 6 (2009): 969–83; Dawn Chatty, *Displacement and Dispossession in the Modern Middle East* (Cambridge: Cambridge University Press, 2010); Norman N. Lewis, *Nomads and Settlers in Syria and Jordan, 1800–1980* (Cambridge: Cambridge University Press, 1987).

41. Ümit Kurt, *The Armenians of Aintab: The Economics of Genocide in an Ottoman Province* (Cambridge, MA: Harvard University Press, 2021), 3. See also Mehmet Polatel and Ümit Üngör, *Confiscation and Colonization: The Young Turk Seizure of Armenian Property* (London: Continuum, 2011); Ryan Gingeras, *Sorrowful Shores: Violence, Ethnicity, and the End of the Ottoman Empire, 1912–1923* (Oxford: Oxford University Press, 2009).

42. Heather J. Sharkey, *A History of Muslims, Christians, and Jews in the Middle East* (Cambridge: Cambridge University Press, 2017), 243–89.

43. Nicholas Doumanis, *Before the Nation: Muslim-Christian Coexistence and Its Destruction in Late Ottoman Anatolia* (Oxford: Oxford University Press, 2013).

44. See Greg Grandin, *The End of the Myth: From the Frontier to the Border Wall in the Mind of America* (New York: Henry Holt, 2019), 72.

45. Meltem Toksöz, *Nomads, Migrants, and Cotton in the Eastern Mediterranean: The Making of the Adana-Mersin region 1850–1908* (Leiden: Brill, 2010). More historiography of Çukurova and the Adana region is cited throughout the notes.

46. See Işık Tamdoğan, "Çukurova" (2013), in *Encyclopaedia of Islam*, 3rd ed., ed. Kate Fleet, Gudrun Krämer, Denis Matringe, John Nawas, and Everett Rowson. An interesting indication of the meaning conveyed by this name can be found in the case of a playbill for the Turkish translation of the German opera *Tiefland*, which itself was based on the Catalan play entitled *Terra baixa*, both names referring to "lowlands." The Turkish translator, an opera actress named Saadet (Alp) İkesus rendered the title as "Çukurova." AK, Muhsin Ertuğrul (ME)-Evr 10292, "Çukurova operası rol dağılımı" (1951).

47. W. F. Albright, "The Origin of the Name Cilicia," *American Journal of Philology* 43, no. 2 (1922): 166–67.

48. See William Cronon, *Nature's Metropolis: Chicago and the Great West* (New York: W. W. Norton, 1991).

49. See, for example, Conevery Bolton Valenčius, *The Health of the Country* (New York: BasicBooks, 2004); M. A. Urban, "An Uninhabited Waste: Transforming the Grand Prairie in Nineteenth Century Illinois, USA," *Journal of Historical Geography* 31, no. 4 (2005): 647–65; David Blackbourn, *The Conquest of Nature: Water, Landscape, and the Making of Modern Germany* (New York: W. W. Norton, 2006).

50. *P. vivax* and *P. falciparum* have distinct evolutionary histories. Recent research suggests that *falciparum* first infected human communities through a relatively late cross-species transmission (past 10,000 years) from gorillas, whereas *vivax* is much older. Dorothy E. Loy et al., "Out of Africa: Origins and Evolution of the Human Malaria Parasites *Plasmodium falciparum* and *Plasmodium vivax*," *International Journal for Parasitology* 47, nos. 2–3 (2017): 87–97.

51. See John Robert McNeill, *Mosquito Empires: Ecology and War in the Greater Caribbean, 1620–1914* (Cambridge: Cambridge University Press, 2010).

52. James L. A. Webb, *Humanity's Burden: A Global History of Malaria* (Cambridge: Cambridge University Press, 2009), 1.

53. McNeill, *Mosquito Empires*, 6.

54. See Alexander M. Nading, *Mosquito Trails: Ecology, Health, and the Politics of Entanglement* (Berkeley: University of California Press, 2015).

55. Michael Watts, *Silent Violence: Food, Famine, and Peasantry in Northern Nigeria* (Berkeley: University of California Press, 1983).

56. Katerina Gardikas, *Landscapes of Disease: Malaria in Modern Greece* (Budapest: Central European University Press, 2018).

57. Arabinda Samanta, *Malarial Fever in Colonial Bengal, 1820–1939: Social History of an Epidemic* (Kolkata: Firma KLM, 2002); Timothy Mitchell, *Rule of Experts* (Berkeley: University of California Press, 2002), 13–53; Margaret Humphreys, *Malaria: Poverty, Race, and Public Health in the United States* (Baltimore: Johns Hopkins University Press, 2001); Sandra M. Sufian, *Healing the Land and the Nation: Malaria and the Zionist Project in Palestine, 1920–1947* (Chicago: University of Chicago Press, 2007). As Anne Marie Moulin notes, "colonialism has contributed to combating a fire which it had in great part kindled." Anne Marie Moulin, "Tropical without the Tropics: The Turning-Point of Pastorian Medicine in North Africa," in *Warm Climates and Western Medicine: The Emergence of Tropical Medicine, 1500–1900*, ed. David Arnold (Amsterdam: Rodopi, 1996), 173. See also Webb, *Humanity's Burden*, 121–23.

Chapter 1

1. The complete first two verses are as follows: *Yaz olur da temmuz olur Adana / Aşkolsun da sılasına gidene / Büyük bahçe yanındaki selvi fidana / Yaz olur da temmuz olur od olur / Hep sinekler bir alıcı kurt olur / Yavru sen gidersen yüreğime dert olur / Allı tur-*

nam kalk gidelim yaylaya. Ahmet Sükrü Esen, Pertev Naili Boratav, and Fuat Özdemir, *Anadolu Türküleri* (Ankara: T. C. Kültür Bakanligi, 1999), 189–90. My more dramatic interpretation of "*sen gidersen* [if you go]" as "if you die" is based on Yaşar Kemal's invocation of the line elsewhere as "*sen ölürsen* [if you die]." Kemal, *Çukurova Yana Yana*, 32.

2. The collection of Ahmet Şükrü Esen edited by Pertev Naili Boratav contains a list of songs with references to the concept of *sıla*. Ahmet Sükrü Esen, *Anadolu Türküleri*, 333–34.

3. Jérôme Cler notes the paradox of the symbolic importance of the *yayla* within the music of transhumant village communities in Western Anatolia today. Although these communities are permanently settled in the plains, their songs that feature transcendent or eternal time are for the *yayla*, whereas the songs of the plains are replete with the theme of exile. Jérôme Cler, *Yayla: Musique et musiciens de villages en Turquie méridionale* (Paris: Geuthner, 2011), 139.

4. Grigor Galustean, Մարաշ կամ Գերմանիկ եւ հերոս Զէյթուն (New York: Marashi Hayrenakts'akan Miowt'iwn, 1934), 550.

5. Karen Barkey, *Empire of Difference: The Ottomans in Comparative Perspective* (Cambridge: Cambridge University Press, 2008), 12–14.

6. See Süha Göney, *Adana Ovaları* (Istanbul: Istanbul Üniversitesi, 1976).

7. OA, HRT-h 486 (1287 [1870/1]).

8. By the measures of Turkish studies from the 1970s, the city of Adana has on average 195 summer days (high of 25°C/77°F or greater) and over 136 tropical days (high of 30°C/86°F or greater) per year. The neighboring provinces of İçel and Hatay (Antakya) by contrast experience 61.5 and 89.5 tropical days per year, respectively. *Çukurova Bölgesi: Bölgesel gelisme, Şehirleşme ve Yerleşme Düzeni* (Ankara: Bölge Planlama Dairesi, 1970), 15–16.

9. See OA, A-MKT-MHM 523/51, Mehmed Necib to Sadaret, Adana (16 Teşrinievvel 1319 [29 October 1903]). Ottoman agronomists sometimes placed Cilicia in its own clime (*iklim*), referred to as the Adana or "Taurus (Toros)" region, distinct from that of Syria or other parts of Anatolia. SYEK, *Ziraat-ı Umumiye*, 7793/630, Yazma Bağışlar, 2386, 8–9.

10. Hüseyin, *Memalik-i Osmaniye'nin Ziraat Coğrafyası* (Istanbul: Mihran Matbaası, 1303 [1888]), part 2, 14–15.

11. Կիլիկիա․ փորձ աշխարհագրութեան արդի Կիլիկիոյ (St. Petersburg: I. Libermani, 1894), 35.

12. TNA, FO 78/4938, Barnham to Salisbury, Aleppo (6 June 1898).

13. *Ziraat-ı Umumiye*, 8–9.

14. H. P. Poghosean, Համռնի ընդհանուր պատմութիւն եւ շրջակայ Գոզան Տաղի հայ գիւղերը (Los Angeles: Bozart Press, 1942), 7.

15. For example, one author described the Armenian communities within Cilicia as having completely different cultures and politics depending on their belonging to ei-

ther the mountains or the plains. Krikor Koudoulian, *Հայ լեռը: կարմիր դրուագներ Կիլիկիոյ աղէտէն* (Constantinople: T. Toghramachean, 1912), 28–29.

16. Paolo Desideri, "Strabo's Cilicians," *Anatolia Antiqua* 1, no. 1 (1991): 299–304.

17. For visual representation of migration routes, see Andrew Gordon Gould, "Pashas and Brigands: Ottoman Provincial Reform and Its Impact on the Nomadic Tribes of Southern Anatolia, 1840–1885," PhD diss., University of California, Los Angeles, 1973, 31.

18. See Victor Langlois, *Voyage dans la Cilicie et dans les montagnes du Taurus: éxécuté pendant les années 1852–1853* (Paris: Duprat, 1861), 19–25.

19. Andrew Gordon Gould, "Lords or Bandits? The Derebeys of Cilicia," *International Journal of Middle East Studies* 7, no. 4 (1976): 490–91.

20. A population register from the 1860s counted just sixteen households in Çokmerzimen. OA, NFS-d 3703. See also Minas Gocayean, *Պատմութիւն Շորր-Մարզպանի: (Շէորբ- Եոյ); գիւղարագար մը Կիլիկիոյ մէջ* (Los Angeles: Los Ancelesi Cork-Marzpani Hayrenakcakan Miowtiwn, 2005).

21. Kemal H. Karpat, *Ottoman Population, 1830–1914: Demographic and Social Characteristics* (Madison: University of Wisconsin Press, 1985), 124.

22. This work will not deal extensively with the transformation of the Aintab region, which itself would merit an entire study. Ümit Kurt describes Aintab as being on the borders of Cilicia and Syria. Although the city's overall links to Aleppo were more salient, the Armenians of Aintab were thoroughly integrated into the communal dynamics of the broader Cilician Armenian community. Kurt, *The Armenians of Aintab*, 30.

23. See Işık Tamdoğan-Abel, "Les modalités de l'urbanité dans une ville ottomane: Les habitants d'Adana au XVIIIème siècle d'après les registres des cadis," PhD diss., EHESS, Paris, 1999.

24. Stefan Winter, *A History of the 'Alawis: From Medieval Aleppo to the Turkish Republic* (Princeton: Princeton University Press, 2016), 224.

25. For an overview, see Gisela Procházka-Eisl and Stephan Procházka, *The Plain of Saints and Prophets: The Nusayri-Alawi Community of Cilicia (Southern Turkey) and Its Sacred Places* (Wiesbaden: Harrassowitz Verlag, 2010).

26. Mübeccel Kıray, "Social Change in Çukurova: A Comparison of Four Villages," in *Turkey: Geographic and Social Perspectives*, ed. Peter Benedict, Erol Tümertekin, and Fatma Mansur (Leiden: Brill, 1974), 179; cited in Toksöz, *Nomads, Migrants, and Cotton*, 19; Haim Gerber, *The Social Origins of the Modern Middle East* (Boulder, CO: L. Rienner, 1987), 87; Faruk Tabak, *The Waning of the Mediterranean, 1550–1870: A Geohistorical Approach* (Baltimore: Johns Hopkins University Press, 2008), 220.

27. Marco Polo, *The Travels of Marco Polo: The Complete Yule-Cordier Edition*, vol. 1 (New York: Dover Publications, 1993), 41.

28. Mary Momdjian, "Halabis and Foreigners in Aleppo's Mediterranean Trade," in *Aleppo and Its Hinterland in the Ottoman Period*, ed. Mafalda Ade and Stefan Winter

(Leiden: Brill, 2020), 109–29; Alison Games, *The Web of Empire: English Cosmopolitans in an Age of Expansion, 1560–1660* (Oxford: Oxford University Press, 2008), 47–80.

29. In addition to what follows, see Aaron David Abraham Shakow, "Marks of Contagion: The Plague, the Bourse, the Word and the Law in the Early Modern Mediterranean, 1720–1762," PhD diss., Harvard University, 2009, 258–62. See also Lori Jones, "The Diseased Landscape: Medieval and Early Modern Plaguescapes," *Landscapes* 17, no. 2 (2016): 108–23.

30. Sébastien Brémond, *Viaggi fatti nell'Egitto superiore et inferiore*, trans. Giuseppe Corvo (Rome: P. Moneta, 1679), 269.

31. Pedro Teixeira, *Relaciones de Pedro Texeira* (Amberes: Hieronymo Verdussen, 1610), 194.

32. William Biddulph, *The travels of foure English men and a preacher into Africa, Asia, Troy, Bythinia, Thracia, and to the Black Sea* (London: Felix Kyngston, 1612), 39.

33. Henry Teonge, *The Diary of Henry Teonge* (London: Routledge, 2005), 112.

34. Andrew Archibald Paton, *The Modern Syrians* (London: Longman, Brown, Green & Longmans, 1844), 215.

35. OA, İ-DH 244/14880, no. 1.

36. Nükhet Varlık, "'Oriental Plague' or Epidemiological Orientalism? Revisiting the Plague Episteme of the Early Modern Mediterranean," in *Plague and Contagion in the Islamic Mediterranean*, ed. Nükhet Varlık (Kalamazoo, MI: Arc Humanities Press, 2017).

37. Paton, *The Modern Syrians*, 215. See F. Harrison Rankin, *The White Man's Grave: A Visit to Sierra Leone in 1834* (London: R. Bentley, 1836).

38. Aaron Shakow, "'Oriental Plague' in the Middle Eastern Landscape: A Cautionary Tale," *International Journal of Middle East Studies* 42, no. 4 (2010): 660–62.

39. Badr al-Dīn Muḥammad al-Ghazzī, *al-Maṭāliʿ al-Badriyya fī'l-Manāzil al-Rūmiyya* (Abu Dhabi: Dar al-Suwaidi, 2004), 89.

40. Al-Ghazzī, *al-Maṭāliʿ*, 93.

41. Nir Shafir, "The Road from Damascus: Circulation and the Redefinition of Islam in the Ottoman Empire, 1620–1720," PhD diss., University of California, Los Angeles, 2016, 244. See also Helen Pfeifer, "Encounter after the Conquest: Scholarly Gatherings in 16th-Century Ottoman Damascus," *International Journal of Middle East Studies* 47, no. 2 (2015): 219–39.

42. Al-Ghazzī, *al-Maṭāliʿ*, 98.

43. Helen Pfeifer, *Empire of Salons: Conquest and Community in Early Modern Ottoman Lands* (Princeton: Princeton University Press, 2022), 97–132.

44. Vere Monro, *A Summer Ramble in Syria, with a Tartar trip from Aleppo to Stamboul*, vol. 2 (London: R. Bentley, 1835), 147.

45. Monro, *A Summer Ramble in Syria*, 158–59.

46. Monro, *A Summer Ramble in Syria*, 263–64.

47. Monro, *A Summer Ramble in Syria*, 268–70.

48. It is spelled alif-ya-lam-mim-ta marbuta (aylah) in Leiden MS Or. 1602, fols. 11v–12r, and Belfour rendered it as "Eilat" in his translation. Bulus al-Halabi and Francis Cunningham Belfour, *The Travels of Macarius, Patriarch of Antioch Vol. 1* (London: Valpy, 1836), 5. Thanks to Polina Ivanova for providing the relevant folios.

49. Hafiz Mehmet Zilla Evliya Çelebi, *Evliya Çelebi seyahatnamesi 3. kitap, Topkapi Sarayı Bagdat 305 yazmasinin transkripsiyonu, dizini* (Istanbul: Yapi kredi, 1999), 29.

50. Mehmed Edib, *Itinéraire de Constantinople à la Mecque*, trans. Thomas Xavier Bianchi (Paris: Everat, 1840), 19.

51. BNF, Supplément Turc, 1276, Mehmed Adib, *Bahjat al-Manazil*, 9a.

52. Edib, *Itinéraire de Constantinople à la Mecque*, 24.

53. Evliya Çelebi, *Evliya Çelebi seyahatnamesi 3. kitap*, 32.

54. See Cevdet Türkay, *Başbakanlık arşivi belgeleri 'ne göre Osmanlı İmparatorluğunda oymak, aşiret ve cemâatlar* (Istanbul: İşaret Yayınları, 2012); Faruk Sümer, *Oğuzlar, Türkmenler: tarihleri, boy teskilâtı, destanları* (Ankara: Ankara Üniversitesi Basimevi, 1967).

55. The variant *yaylak* is not used in modern Turkish but is common in Ottoman texts. The words *yayla* and *yaylak* have different connotations; however, in Ottoman documentation from the nineteenth century, these terms appear to be interchangeable or overlapping, sometimes appearing with the same meaning even within the same document. For example, see OA, İ-MMS 60/2843, no. 3 (26 Şevval 1295 [23 October 1878]); see also accounts of Evliya Çelebi. For the *yaylaq* in Iran, see Daniel T. Potts, *Nomadism in Iran: From Antiquity to the Modern Era* (Oxford: Oxford University Press, 2014); Arash Khazeni, *Tribes and Empire on the Margins of Nineteenth-Century Iran* (Seattle: University of Washington Press, 2010). Scholars who study the history of pastoralism and herding tend to classify transhumance as only one of many seasonally migratory patterns of raising livestock. Anatoly Khazanov distinguishes between the term "transhumance," which arises from a European context, and "yaylag pastoralism," that is, migration between a *yaylak* (summer pasture) and *kışlak* (winter pasture). Khazanov is correct in his assertion that the "yaylag pastoralism" practiced by herders in many parts of Central Asia or Iran are very different from the model of Alpine transhumance in that it entailed much longer distance migration, different sets of livestock, and often a lack of fixed villages. But in Ottoman Anatolia, the nature of pastoralism much more closely resembled European equivalents in terms of geographical similarities and relative distances of migration, commensurable with the notion of transhumance, even if its terminology resembles Khazanov's "yaylag pastoralism." Anatoly M. Khazanov and Julia Crookenden, *Nomads and the Outside World*, 2nd ed. (Cambridge: Cambridge University Press, 1994), 23–24. In the case of Cilicia, Suavi Aydın equates these practices with transhumance while acknowledging that different kinds of pastoralism have historically been practiced in the region. Suavi Aydın, "Toroslarda Yaylacılık ve Çukurova'nın Önemi," *Kebikeç* 21 (2006): 111–34. Andrea Duffy's label of "Mediterranean

pastoralism" in this region is one framework that encompasses the diversity of herding strategies and avoids the fraught over-classification that typified much of the earlier scholarship. *Nomad's Land: Pastoralism and French Environmental Policy in the Nineteenth-Century Mediterranean World* (Lincoln: University of Nebraska Press, 2019), xxii. See also J. Malcolm Wagstaff, *The Evolution of Middle Eastern Landscapes: An Outline to A.D. 1840* (Totowa, NJ: Barnes & Noble, 1985).

56. Ali Riza Yalgın, *Cenupta Türkmen Oymakları*, vol. 1, ed. Sabahat Emir (Ankara: Kültür ve Türizm Bakanlığı, 1977), 51; Cemal Arif Alagöz, *Anadoluda Yaylâcılık* (Ankara: Ankara Halkevi, 1938), 18–19; Daniel G. Bates, *Nomads and Farmers: A Study of the Yörük of Southeastern Turkey* (Ann Arbor: University of Michigan, 1973), 8–20.

57. Alagöz, *Anadoluda Yaylâcılık*, 23.

58. On "avoidance," see Webb, *Humanity's Burden*, 14–15.

59. Webb, *Humanity's Burden*, 3.

60. Alan Mikhail, "The Nature of Plague in Late Eighteenth-Century Egypt," *Bulletin of the History of Medicine* 82, no. 2 (2008): 249. For views of miasma in the Ottoman context, see Miri Shefer-Mossensohn, *Ottoman Medicine: Healing and Medical Institutions, 1500–1700* (Albany: SUNY Press, 2009), 170–79.

61. Ibrahim Atalay, Recep Efe, and Münir Öztürk, "Effects of Topography and Climate on the Ecology of Taurus Mountains in the Mediterranean Region of Turkey," *SBSPRO Procedia* 120 (2014): 147.

62. Change of air was not solely understood as a solution to malaria; it covered a range of ailments, especially fevers, and people did not necessarily differentiate between diseases when seeking summer respite in the mountains. Nükhet Varlık describes the "seasonal signature" of annual plagues that emerged in Ottoman cities and sometimes provided a powerful impetus for people to flee the city for the *yayla* during the warm months much as they did for malaria. Varlık, *Plague and Empire*, 18.

63. OA, MVL 310/45 (9 Şevval 1273 [2 June 1857]).

64. William Burckhardt Barker and William Ainsworth, *Cilicia, Its Former History and Present State* (London: R. Griffin, 1862), 115. See also Կիլիկիա: փորձ աշխարհագրութեան արդի Կիլիկիոյ, 34. Also, OA, İ-MVL 472/21365, no. 5/2; MVL 643/6, no.1; MVL 776/2.

65. Misak Keleshean, *Սիս-մատեան: պատմական, բանասիրական, տեղեկագրական, ազգագրական եւ Հարակից պարագաներ* (Beirut: Hay Chemaran, 1949), 406. See also Galustean, *Մարաշ կամ Գերմանիկ*, 327.

66. Keleshean, *Սիս-մատեան*, 81. See also H. Ter Ghazarean, *Հայկական Կիլիկիա: տեղագրութիւն* (Antelias: Kat'oghikosut'ean Hayots' Metsi Tann Kilikioy, 2006), 311.

67. Poghosean, *Զմառնի քաղհանուր պատմութիւնը*, 236–37.

68. Buzand Yeghiayean, *Ատանայի հայոց պատմութիւն* (Antelias: Katoghikosutean Hayots Kilikioh, 1970), 741. American missionaries looking to expand their

work in the Cilicia region established an Adana/Hadjin mission, with Hadjin as the summertime base of operations, upon realizing that few people stayed in Adana during the warm months. ABC 641/232, Coffing to Anderson (7 June 1860).

69. KMS, Kilikia KL 5 (Tarsus), Mousis Christofidis. Research at KMS and translations by Polina Ivanova.

70. KMS, Kilikia KL 5 (Tarsus), Kostas Rafoulis.

71. KMS, Kilikia KL 7 (Hristiankioi), Georgos Dimitriadis.

72. KMS, Kilikia KL 18 (Taşucu).

73. KMS, Kilikia KL 9 (Alakilise).

74. KMS, Kilikia KL 14 (Mara).

75. Feyzullah İzmidi, *Sıtma: Maraz-ı Merzagi* (Istanbul: Tanin, 1329 [1911]); Tevfik Rüştü, *Sıtma'ya Karşı Muharebe* (Selanik: Rumeli Matbaası, 1326 [1910]).

76. Özdemir, *Öyküleriyle Ağıtlar*, 129.

77. KMS, Kilikia KL 6 (Iskilic), Mosises Christofides (26 February 1968).

78. Poghosean, Հասարիի ընդհանուր պատմութիւն, 224.

79. KMS, KL 3A, Tsalikoglou, Emmanouil, *Avtobiografia* (Athens: typewritten manuscript, 1957), 80; Keleshean, Սիս-մատեան, 406. See the Houshamadyan website (houshamadyan.org) for articles about folk medicine for Hadjin, Sis, and Marash.

80. Mustafa Ekmekçi, "Sıtma! Bu iti tutma," *Cumhuriyet*, 21 April 1991.

81. Kemal Özbayrı and Hatice Gonnet, *Tahtacılar ve Yörükler* (Paris: A. Maisonneuve, 1972), 30–31; Alagöz, *Anadoluda Yaylâcılık*, 18–19; Yaşar Kemal, *Binboğalar Efsanesi* (Istanbul: YKY, 1971; 2004), 17–18.

82. See Ethel Sara Wolper, "Khidr and the Politics of Place," in *Muslims and Others in Sacred Space*, ed. Margaret Cormack (Oxford: Oxford University Press, 2012); Doumanis, *Before the Nation*, 76–78; Elena Marushiakova and Vesselin Popov, "The Vanished Kurban," in *Kurban in the Balkans*, ed. Biljana Sikimic and Petko Hristov (Belgrade: Institut des études balkaniques, 2007).

83. KMS, Kilikia KL 6 (Iskilic), Mosises Christofides.

84. It is worth mentioning that the Nusayri Arab inhabitants of Cilicia did not celebrate Hıdırellez, though the figure of Hızır was an important aspect of their sacred geography, nor is it clear that they participated in the same rhythm of transhumance. For more on the Nusayris of Cilicia, see Procházka-Eisl and Procházka, *The Plain of Saints and Prophets*. In correspondence with Gisela Prochazka-Eisl, she confirmed that Hıdırellez was not an aspect of the Nusayri calendar in Cilicia.

85. Tarsus, Anazarbus, Elaeussa, Corycus, Pompeiopolis (Soli), Adana, Augusta, Mallus, Zephyrium, Mopsuestia, Aegeae, Epiphaneia, Alexandria ad Issum, Rossos, Irenopolis, Flaviopolis, and Castabala Hierapolis. Jennifer Tobin, *Black Cilicia: A Study of the Plain of Issus during the Roman and Late Roman Periods* (Oxford: Hedges, 2004), 8. Remarkably, the cities of Adana and Tarsus have retained the same names and ap-

proximate locations (though their centers have shifted) since at least the Hittite period. Paolo Desideri and Anna Margherita Jasink, *Cilicia: dall'età di Kizzuwatna alla conquista macedone* (Florence: Le Lettere, 1990), 7.

86. See Michael Gough, "Anazarbus," *Anatolian Studies* 2 (1952): 85–150.

87. John Julius Norwich, *Sicily: A Short History, from the Greeks to Cosa Nostra* (London: John Murray, 2016), 43; Aaron L. Beek, "The Pirate Connection: Roman Politics, Servile Wars, and the East," *TAPA* 146, no. 1 (2016): 99–116.

88. Kyle Harper, *Slavery in the Late Roman World, AD 275–425: An Economic, Social, and Institutional Study* (Cambridge: Cambridge University Press, 2016), 98.

89. See James C. Scott, *Against the Grain: A Deep History of the First Civilizations* (New Haven: Yale University Press, 2017); Davis, *The Arid Lands*.

90. Robert Sallares, *Malaria and Rome: A History of Malaria in Ancient Italy* (Oxford: Oxford University Press, 2002), 251–52.

91. A. Asa Eger, *The Islamic-Byzantine Frontier: Interaction and Exchange among Muslim and Christian Communities* (New York: I. B. Tauris, 2016), 2–3.

92. Eger, *The Islamic-Byzantine Frontier*, 161–62.

93. Eger, *The Islamic-Byzantine Frontier*, 259–61.

94. Aurora E. Camaño, "Towards a Social Archaeology of Forced Migration: Comparing Memory, Myth and Place-Making in Medieval Armenian Cilicia," in *Homo Migrans: Modeling Mobility and Migration in Human History*, ed. Meghan Daniels (Albany, NY: SUNY Press, 2022).

95. See Angus Donal Stewart, *The Armenian Kingdom and the Mamluks: War and Diplomacy during the Reigns of Het'um II (1289–1307)* (Leiden: Brill, 2001); Jacob G. Ghazarian, *The Armenian Kingdom in Cilicia during the Crusades: The Integration of Cilician Armenians with the Latins, 1080–1393* (London: Routledge, 2014). Also Vahram, *Vahram's Chronicle of the Armenian Kingdom in Cilicia during the time of the Crusades*, trans. Karl Friedrich Neumann (London: Oriental Translation Fund, 1831).

96. Smbat Sparapet, Տարասանագիրք, ed. A. G. Galstian (Erevan: Aipetrat, 1958), 14.

97. Nina G. Garsoïan, "The Early-Medieval Armenian City: An Alien Element?" *JANES* 16, no. 1 (1984).

98. Krikor Koudoulian, Հայ լեռը, 14; Léon M. Alishan, *Sissouan, ou l'Arméno-Cilicie: Description géographique et historique, avec cartes et illustrations* (Venice: S. Lazare, 1899), 25.

99. A. S. Ktsoyan, "Սալարիան Հայաստանում հնագույն ժամանակներից մինչև սովետական շրջանը," PhD diss., Haykakan SSṘ Gitut'yunneri Akademia, 1949; Alishan, *Sissouan*, 25. See Mkhit'ar Herats'i, Մխիթարայ Բժշկապետի Հերացւոյ ջերմանց մխիթարութիւն (Venetik: I. Tparani Srboyn Ghazaru, 1832), 90–132; in Russian translation: Mkhit'ar Herats'i, *Утешение при лихорадках*, trans. G. G. Harut'yunyan and L. A. Oganesov (Erevan: Tipografiia Ministerstva Kul-

tury Arm. SSR, 1955), 162–98. Thanks again to Polina Ivanova. Studies have found higher degrees of Alpha-Thalassemia mutations, which are associated with genetic resistance to malaria, in the Province of Adana when compared with other regions of Turkey, suggesting a long presence of malaria in the region. Sevcan Tuğ Bozdoğan et al., "Alpha-Thalassemia Mutations in Adana Province, Southern Turkey: Genotype-Phenotype Correlation," *Indian Journal of Hematology and Blood Transfusion* 31, no. 2 (2015): 223–28.

100. See S. Peter Crowe, "Patterns of Armeno-Muslim Interchange on the Armenian Plateau in the Interstice between Byzantine and Ottoman Hegemony," in *Islam and Christianity in Medieval Anatolia*, ed. A. C. S. Peacock, Bruno De Nicola, and Sara Nur Yıldız (London: Routledge, 2019), 77–105.

101. Smbat the Constable's law code, written in 1265, for example, mentions Turkic pastoralists in a larger section about the possible damages of livestock to agricultural land. Smbat Sparapet, Դատաստանագիրք, 169–70.

102. Enver Kartekin, *Ramazanoğulları Beyliği tarihi* (Istanbul: Doğuş Matbaasi, 1979), 40; Aydın, "Toroslarda Yaylacılık ve Çukurova'nın Önemi," 116.

103. Yılmaz Kurt and M. Akif Erdoğru, *Adana Evkaf Defteri*, vol. 4 (Ankara: Türk Tarih Kurumu, 2000).

104. İsmail Altınöz, *Dulkadir Eyâletinin Kuruluşu ve Gelişimi* (Kahramanmaraş: Ukde, 2009), 41–52; Refet Yinanç, *Dulkadir Beyliği* (Ankara: Türk Tarih Kurumu, 1989), 80–105.

105. Tabak, *The Waning of the Mediterranean*, 124–25.

106. Rhoads Murphey, *Regional Structure in the Ottoman Economy: A Sultanic Memorandum of 1636 A.D. concerning the Sources and Uses of the Tax-Farm Revenues of Anatolia and the Coastal and Northern Portions of Syria* (Wiesbaden: O. Harrassowitz, 1987), 7. See Halil İnalcik, "Rice Cultivation and the çeltükci-re'âyâ System in the Ottoman Empire," *Turcica* 14 (1982): 69–141.

107. See Huri İslamoğlu and Suraiya Faroqhi, "Crop Patterns and Agricultural Production Trends in Sixteenth-Century Anatolia," *Review (Fernand Braudel Center)* 2, no. 3 (1979): 423–24.

108. İslamoğlu and Faroqhi, "Crop Patterns and Agricultural Production Trends in Sixteenth-Century Anatolia," 418–19.

109. See Suraiya Faroqhi, "Ottoman Cotton Textiles: The Story of a Success That Did Not Last, 1500–1800," in *The Spinning World: A Global History of Cotton Textiles, 1200–1850*, ed. Prasannan Parthasarathi and Giorgio Riello (Delhi: Primus Books, 2012), 89–104.

110. See Geoffrey Parker, *Global Crisis: War, Climate Change and Catastrophe in the Seventeenth Century* (New Haven: Yale University Press, 2014).

111. White, *The Climate of Rebellion*, 229–48. See also Oktay Özel, *The Collapse of Rural Order in Ottoman Anatolia: Amasya, 1576–1643* (Leiden: Brill, 2016).

112. Simeon, *The Travel Accounts of Simeon of Poland*, trans. George A. Bournoutian (Costa Mesa, CA: Mazda Publishers, 2007), 271–72.

113. Tabak, *The Waning of the Mediterranean*, 190–91.

114. Shakow, "Marks of Contagion," 262–64.

115. John McNeill, *The Mountains of the Mediterranean World: An Environmental History* (Cambridge: Cambridge University Press, 1992), 345.

116. Tabak, *The Waning of the Mediterranean*, 14–16; McNeill, *The Mountains of the Mediterranean*, 86–92.

117. For an overview, see Bruce McGowan, "The Age of the Ayans, 1699–1812," in *An Economic and Social History of the Ottoman Empire, 1300–1914*, ed. Halil Inalcik and Donald Quataert (Cambridge: Cambridge University Press, 1994), 637–758. See also Cemal Kafadar, "The Question of Ottoman Decline," *Harvard Middle Eastern and Islamic Review* 4, nos. 1–2 (1997–98).

118. Barkey, *Empire of Difference*; Michael E. Meeker, *A Nation of Empire: The Ottoman Legacy of Turkish Modernity* (Berkeley: University of California Press, 2002), 185.

119. Ali Yaycioglu, *Partners of the Empire: The Crisis of the Ottoman Order in the Age of Revolutions* (Stanford: Stanford University Press, 2016).

120. Gould, "Lords or Bandits?" 485–506. See also Işık Tamdoğan, "La mobilité comme compétence dans la société ottomane: Nomades de la Çukurova et travailleurs migrants à Üsküdar au XVIIIè siècle," in *Le monde de l'itinérance en Méditerranée de l'Antiquité à l'époque moderne*, ed. Claudia Moatti, Wolfgang Kaiser, and Christophe Pébarthe (Bordeaux: De Boccard, 2009), 192–97.

121. Langlois, *Voyage dans la Cilicie*, 21–23.

122. OA, A-MKT-MHM 437/34, no. 2 (19 Zilkade 1285 [3 March 1869]). See also Yılmaz Kurt, "Menemencioğulları ile ilgili Arşiv Belgeleri I," *Belgeler* 21, no. 25 (2000).

123. Menemencioğlu Ahmed, *Menemencioğulları Tarihi*, ed. Yılmaz Kurt (Ankara: Akçağ, 1997).

124. The name Mustuk, a nickname in place of his given name Mustafa, is also found in the spelling of Mıstık in the region today. Foreign sources often spelled his name as "Mustook," and Ottoman sources used variations that could be transliterated as Mustuk or Musdık.

125. Ahmet Cevdet, *Tezâkir*, vol. 3, ed. Cavid Baysun (Ankara: Türk Tarih Kurumu, 1986), 131; Mehmet Akif Terzi, *Gâvurdağı'nın Bulanık tarihindeki sır perdesi* (Istanbul: Doğu Kütüphanesi, 2010), 192.

126. Gould, "Lords or Bandits?" 489.

127. See Heghnar Zeitlian Watenpaugh, *The Missing Pages: The Modern Life of a Medieval Manuscript from Genocide to Justice* (Stanford: Stanford University Press, 2020), 79–115. Also Erdal İlter, *Ermeni mes'elesinin perspektifi ve Zeytûn isyânları (1780–1880)* (Ankara: Türk Kültürünü Arastirma Enstitüsü, 1988).

128. Gould, "Lords or Bandits?" 491.

129. Gould, "Lords or Bandits?" 495.

130. Poghosean, Հայոց ընդհանուր պատմություն, 146–50; Langlois, *Voyage dans la Cilicie*, 11, 19. Abdurrahman Münir Kozanoğlu depicts the family as a Turkish tribe that played an important role in the "Turkification (Türkleşme)" of Anatolia, in *Kozanoğulları* (Istanbul: Bakış Müessesesi, 1983). By contrast, the Armenian writer Aghasi argued that many of the tribal lineages in Cilicia descended from, had shared customs with, and therefore had close relations with Armenians in the Taurus Mountains. Aghasi and Arshag Chobanian, *Zeïtoun: Depuis les origines jusqu'à l'insurrection de 1895* (Paris: Éditions du Mercure de France, 1897), 60.

131. Kasaba, *A Moveable Empire*, 14–35.

132. OA, C-AS 872/37389 (27 Zilkade 1225 [24 December 1810]). This is hardly surprising given that according to the estimates of Langlois, the tribes of Cilicia possessed more than 20,000 camels in the 1850s, with nomadic communities holding the largest camel concentrations. Langlois, *Voyage dans la Cilicie*, 21–23. Wheeled transport was not widely used in the region until the arrival of immigrants from the Caucasus. Roger Owen, *The Middle East in the World Economy, 1800–1914* (London: Methuen, 1981), 121.

133. On the complex origins of the Ottoman state, and its relationship with both pastoral nomads and preexisting agrarian state structures, see Cemal Kafadar, *Between Two Worlds: The Construction of the Ottoman State* (Berkeley: University of California Press, 1995); Rudi Paul Lindner, *Nomads and Ottomans in Medieval Anatolia* (Bloomington: Indiana University Press, 1983).

134. Rhoads Murphey, "Evolving versus Static Elements in Ottoman Geographical Writing between 1598 and 1729, Perspectives and Real-Life Experience of 'the Northern Lands' (Taraf al-Shimalli) over 130 Years," in *Ottoman Bosnia: A History in Peril*, ed. Markus Koller and Kemal H. Karpat (Madison: University of Wisconsin Press, 2004). Cited in White, *The Climate of Rebellion*, 46. See also Kemal H. Karpat and Robert W. Zens, *Ottoman Borderlands: Issues, Personalities, and Political Changes* (Madison: Center for Turkish Studies, University of Wisconsin, 2003).

135. White, *The Climate of Rebellion*, 48.

136. Cengiz Orhonlu, *Osmanlı imparatorluğunda aşiretlerin iskânı* (Istanbul: Eren, 1987), 53–85.

137. Mustafa Soysal, "Die Siedlungs und Landschaftsentwicklung der Çukurova: mit besonderer Berücksichtigung der Yüregir-Ebene," PhD diss., Fränkische Geographische Gesellschaft, 1976, 38–39.

138. Kasaba, *A Moveable Empire*, 86.

139. Gould, "Pashas and Brigands," 38.

140. OA, A-MKT-UM 385/69, no. 2 (22 Cemaziyelevvel 1276 [5 December 1859]).

141. Gould, "Pashas and Brigands," 38.

142. Toksöz, *Nomads, Migrants, and Cotton*, 20.

143. Albert Hourani, *Europe and the Middle East* (Berkeley: University of California Press, 1980), 189.

144. For an overview of Cilicia from the Hittite to Hellenic periods, see Desideri and Jasink, *Cilicia* (Florence: Le Lettere, 1990). For a study that covers the region "up until" the Ottoman period, see Ahmet Ünal and Serdar Girginer, *Kilikya-Çukurova ilk çağlardan Osmanlar dönemi'ne kadar Kilikya'da tarihi coğrafya, tarih ve arkeoloji* (Istanbul: Homer, 2007).

Chapter 2

1. Ahmet Cevdet, *Marûzât*, ed. Yusuf Halaçoğlu (Istanbul: Çağrı Yayınları, 1980), 182.

2. Kemal, *Binboğalar Efsanesi*, 71.

3. Pieces of this song have been collected in different versions by various researchers. The version quoted here is based on the earliest published version I found. Pertev Naili Boratav, *Çukurova'da folklor derlemeleri* (Ankara: Türk Tarih Kurumu, 1947), 268–69. For commentary on other versions, see İsmail Görkem, *Yeni bilgiler ışığında Dadaloğlu: bütün şiirleri* (Istanbul: E Yayınları, 2006), 410–12; Mehmet Fuat, *Dadaloğlu: yaşamı, düşünce dünyası, sanatçı kişiliği, seçme şiirleri* (Istanbul: YKY, 2002), 48–49; Ahmet Z. Özdemir, *Avşarlar ve Dadaloğlu* (Ankara: Dayanışma Yayınları, 1985), 244–45. For translation, see Gould, "Pashas and Brigands," 211.

4. Kuntay Gücüm, *İmparatorluğun "Liberal" Yılları (1856–1970)* (Istanbul: Tarih Vakfı, 2015); Roderic H. Davison, *Reform in the Ottoman Empire, 1856–1876* (Princeton: Princeton University Press, 1963).

5. Davison, *Reform in the Ottoman Empire, 1856–1876*, 98–99; Huri Islamoğlu, "Property as a Contested Domain: A Reevaluation of the Ottoman Land Code of 1858," in *New Perspectives on Property and Land in the Middle East*, ed. Roger Owen (Cambridge, MA: Harvard University Press, 2000), 3–63; E. A. Aytekin, "Agrarian Relations, Property and Law: An Analysis of the Land Code of 1858 in the Ottoman Empire," *Middle Eastern Studies* 45, no. 6 (2009): 935–51. Islamoğlu argues that the 1858 Land Code was an attempt to move into the contested domain of property, a shift typical of states during that era. Gerber presents a discussion of the 1858 Land Code's impact in different parts of the empire, including Çukurova. Gerber, *The Social Origins of the Modern Middle East*, 67–90. See also Peter Sluglett and Marion Farouk-Sluglett, "The Application of the 1858 Land Code in Greater Syria: Some Preliminary Observations," in *Land Tenure and Social Transformation in the Middle East*, ed. Tarif Khalidi (Beirut: American University of Beirut, 1984); Tosun Arıncanlı, "Property, Land, and Labor in Nineteenth-Century Anatolia," in *Landholding and Commercial Agriculture in the Middle East*, ed. Çağlar Keyder and Faruk Tabak (Albany: State University of New York Press, 1991).

6. Petrov, "Tanzimat for the Countryside"; Ceylan, *The Ottoman Origins of Modern Iraq*.

7. On the development of the Egyptian army, see Khaled Fahmy, *All the Pasha's Men: Mehmed Ali, His Army, and the Making of Modern Egypt* (Cambridge: Cambridge University Press, 1997). See also Eve Troutt Powell, *A Different Shade of Colonialism: Egypt, Great Britain, and the Mastery of the Sudan* (Berkeley: University of California Press, 2003).

8. Owen, *The Middle East in the World Economy*, 60.

9. Gould, "Pashas and Brigands," 41–45.

10. Hikmet Özdemir, *Salgın hastalıklardan ölümler, 1914–1918* (Ankara: Türk Tarih Kurumu, 2005), 51–54. For more on Ottoman involvement in the Crimean War, see Candan Badem, *The Ottoman Crimean War, 1853–1856* (Leiden: Brill, 2010).

11. The image of a female warrior named Kara Fatma recurs throughout the history of late Ottoman and early republican Anatolia. See Zeynep Kutluata, "Geç Osmanlı ve Erken Cumhuriyet Dönem'inde Toplumsal Cinsiyet ve Savaş: Kara Fatma(lar)," *Kültür ve Siyasette Feminist Yaklaşımlar* 2 (February 2007).

12. OA, İ-DH 308/19638 (5 Muharrem 1271 [28 September 1854]).

13. Adolphus Slade, *Turkey and the Crimean War* (London: Smith, Elder & Co., 1867), 186–88; Félix Mornand Joubert, *Tableau historique, politique et pittoresque de la Turquie et de la Russie* (Paris: Paulin & Le Chevalier, 1854), 109–10. For more, see Cezmi Yurtsever, *Çukurova Türkmenleri* (Adana: Çukurova Yayınları, 2007), 30–41.

14. See Chris Gratien, "The Mountains Are Ours: Ecology and Settlement in Late Ottoman and Early Republican Cilicia, 1856–1956," PhD diss., Georgetown University, 2015, 96–135.

15. Victor Langlois, *Les Arméniens de la Turquie et les massacres du Taurus* (Paris: J. Claye, 1863); Aghasi and Chobanian, *Zeïtoun*.

16. Gould, "Pashas and Brigands," 56. See Ussama Makdisi, *The Culture of Sectarianism: Community, History, and Violence in Nineteenth-Century Ottoman Lebanon* (Berkeley: University of California Press, 2000), 96–145.

17. Toksöz, *Nomads, Migrants, and Cotton*, 41–55. The records of the Egyptian government contain documentation pertaining to farms in Çukurova during and immediately after the Egyptian occupation of the 1830s. See AUB, Asad Rustum Collection, Box 3 1/10, letter from Mehmed Arif regarding farm of Ahmed Pasha.

18. For more, see Stephan Astourian, "Testing world-system Theory, Cilicia (1830's–1890's): Armenian-Turkish Polarization and the Ideology of Modern Ottoman Historiography," PhD diss., University of California, Los Angeles, 1996. For brief discussion of the US Civil War and its global impact, see C. A. Bayly, *The Birth of the Modern World, 1780–1914: Global Connections and Comparisons* (Malden, MA: Blackwell, 2004), 161–65.

19. Orhan Kurmuş, "The Cotton Famine and Its Effects on the Ottoman Empire," in *The Ottoman Empire and the World-Economy*, ed. Huri Islamoğlu-İnan (Cambridge: Cambridge University Press, 1987), 163.

20. The French consul of Aleppo reported 15,000 bales of cotton produced in 1861, 34,000 bales in 1862, and 63,500 bales in 1863. CADC, CCC, 1793–1901, Alep 33 (1863–66), 61, Bertrand to de Lhuys (20 July 1864). Citing British records, Gould indicates a roughly sixfold increase in Çukurova cotton production from 1860 to 1865. Gould, "Pashas and Brigands," 195.

21. Kurmuş, "The Cotton Famine and Its Effects on the Ottoman Empire," 165; Stephan Astourian, "The Silence of the Land: Agrarian Relations, Ethnicity, and Power," in *A Question of Genocide*, ed. Ronald Grigor Suny, Fatma Müge Göcek, and Norman Naimark (Oxford: Oxford University Press, 2011), 69.

22. OA, A-MKT-MVL 144/58 (16 Şevval 1278 [16 April 1862]); A-MKT-MHM 256/79 (4 Ramazan 1279 [23 February 1863]); 257/97 (27 Ramazan 1279 [18 March 1863]).

23. OA, A-MKT-MHM 299/36 (26 Zilkade 1280 [3 May 1864]); 328/84, no. 1 (8 Mart 1281 [20 March 1865]).

24. Some argue that the policies pursued by the Russian military during the 1860s in the Caucasus amounted to ethnic cleansing or genocide, as the Russian Empire was consciously thorough in their removal of Muslim populations from certain problem areas. For discussion, see Willard Sunderland, *Taming the Wild Field: Colonization and Empire on the Russian Steppe* (Ithaca, NY: Cornell University Press, 2004), 151–55; Gary Hamburg, "A Commentary on the Two Texts in Their Historical Context" in Thomas Sanders et al., *Russian-Muslim Confrontation in the Caucasus: Alternative Visions of the Conflict between Imam Shamil and the Russians, 1830–1859* (London: RoutledgeCurzon, 2004), 154–57; Walter Richmond, *The Circassian Genocide* (New Brunswick, NJ: Rutgers University Press, 2013).

25. See Ella Fratantuono, "Producing Ottomans: Internal Colonization and Social Engineering in Ottoman Immigrant Settlement," *Journal of Genocide Research* 21, no. 1 (2019): 1–24; Başak Kale, "Transforming an Empire: The Ottoman Empire's Immigration and Settlement Policies in the Nineteenth and Early Twentieth Centuries," *Middle Eastern Studies* 50, no. 2 (2014): 252–71.

26. Cuthell, "The Muhacirin Komisyonu," 18–20.

27. Cuthell, "The Muhacirin Komisyonu," 260. Hakan Kırımlı states that about 300,000 Crimean Tatars and Nogays alone departed for the Ottoman Empire between 1856 and 1865. Hakan Kırımlı, *Türkiye'deki Kırım Tatar ve Nogay köy yerleşimleri* (Istanbul: Tarih Vakfı, 2012), 31. Hilmi Bayraktar offers a number of scholarly estimates of post–Crimean War *muhacir* populations with totals ranging from 600,000 to 1 million, in "Kırım Savaşı Sonrası Adana Eyaleti'ne Yapılan Nogay Göç ve İskânları (1859–1861)," *Bilig* 45 (2008): 49–50.

28. Here this is presumably due to the fact that many *muhacirs* would have had difficulty communicating in Turkish. OA, İ-MVL 439/19468 (17 Rebiulahir 1277 [2 November 1860]).

29. OA, MVL 662/51 (11 Receb 1280 [22 December 1863]). For more, see Vladi-

mir Hamed-Troyansky, "Imperial Refuge: Resettlement of Muslims from Russia in the Ottoman Empire, 1860–1914," PhD diss., Stanford University, 2018, 198–258.

30. OA, İ-MVL 586/26367, no. 6, Zülkifl Ağa to Meclis-i Vala (27 Haziran 1276 [9 July 1860]).

31. See OA, İ-MVL 586/26367.

32. OA, A-MKT-UM 492/93 (12 Safer 1278 [19 August 1861]).

33. Ձկյթուևի պատմագիրք (Buenos Aires: Tp. Ararat, 1960), 344–45. It stands to reason that the number of Circassians killed was embellished for dramatic effect.

34. Gould, "Pashas and Brigands," 73–106.

35. Cevdet, Tezâkir, 3, 108.

36. For example, a group of some 300 Tecirli households led by Palalı Hasanoğlu Süleyman Agha defied settlement orders and retreated into Gavurdağı, protected by 200 fighters from the village of Haruniye before being subdued. OA, A-MKT-MHM 336/3, no. 1 (19 Mayıs 1281 [31 May 1865]).

37. "Hakkımızda devlet etmiş fermanı / Ferman padişahın, dağlar bizimdir," in Cahit Öztelli, Köroğlu ve Dadaloğlu (Istanbul: Varlık Yayınevi, 1953), 81. Some versions may differ slightly, as the songs of Dadaloğlu were transmitted orally and not written down for several decades. One of the earliest mentions of a Dadaloğlu song appears to have been by Ahmed Besim Atalay, who interviewed peasants in the Çukurova region around the time of World War I. Besim Atalay, Maraş Tarihi ve Coğrafyası (Istanbul: Matbaa-yi Âmire, 1332 [1916], 1339 [1923]), 70–71. By the 1920s, the poems of Dadaloğlu began to appear in publications such as Memleket Çukurova'da. See also Wolfram Eberhard, Minstrel Tales from Southeastern Turkey (Berkeley: University of California Press, 1955); Haşim Nezihi Okay, Köroglu ve Dadaloğlu (Istanbul: May Yayınları, 1970); Faik Türkmen, Mufassal Hatay Tarihi (Antakya: Iktisat Basımevi, 1939); Boratav, Çukurova'da folklor derlemeleri; Taha Toros, Dadaloğlu: XIX. asır Çukurova sazşairi (Adana: Yeni Adana Basımevi, 1940). For translations, see Gould, "Pashas and Brigands," 209–11.

38. See Günil Ayaydın Cebe, "İskâna Direnen Kimlik: Dadaloğlu'nun Coğrafyası," Milli Folklor 23, no. 90 (2011): 60–69.

39. Andrew Gordon Gould, "The Burning of the Tents," in Humanist and Scholar: Essays in Honor of Andreas Tietze, ed. Heath Lowry and Donald Quataert (Istanbul: Isis Press, 1993), 71–85.

40. Cevdet, Marûzât, 147.

41. Cevdet, Tezâkir, 3, 188; Poghosean, Համփի բնդհանուր պատմութիւն, 529.

42. Gould, "Lords or Bandits?" 499.

43. "General Report by Mr. Consul J. H. Skene on North Syria under the New Organization of the Turkish Provinces," in Commercial Reports Received at the Foreign Office from Her Majesty's Consuls in 1868 (London: Harrison & Sons, 1868).

44. Cited in Toksöz, *Nomads, Migrants, and Cotton*, 21.
45. OA, HRT-h 486 (1287 [1870/1]).
46. Camille Favre and B. Mandrot, *Voyage en Cilicie* (Paris: C. Delagrave, 1878), 21.
47. Soysal's study includes a map and list of settlements from the period in question with estimates of foundation date and the communities settled therein. Soysal, "Die Siedlungs und Landschaftsentwicklung der Çukurova," 58–61.
48. Bayraktar, "Adana Eyaleti'ne Yapılan Nogay Göç ve İskânları," 50–51. One source indicated that by spring of 1861, just over 15,000 *muhacirs* had been settled. OA, A-MKT-NZD 359/43, no. 4 (Mart 1277 [March 1861]).
49. OA, İ-MVL 586/26367 no. 11 (5 Safer 1277 [23 August 1860]).
50. TNA, FO 222/7/1, 1880 no. 12, Bennet to Goschen, Adana (15 December 1880).
51. Toksöz, *Nomads, Migrants, and Cotton*, 65.
52. Gould, "Pashas and Brigands," 130.
53. Langlois, *Voyage dans la Cilicie*, 18–23.
54. For example, Langlois listed the population of Adana at around 150,000, but this figure does not make much sense alongside Karpat's statistics for the 1880s and 1890s based on census data, which gave the Adana province a population of approximately 400,000. Karpat, *Ottoman Population*, 124–27. If the estimates of Langlois only counted men, then the data make more sense, in which case the tribal population might have been much higher.
55. Hilmi Bayraktar, "Kırım ve Kafkasya'dan Adana Vilayeti'ne Yapılan Göç ve İskânlar (1869–1907)," *Türkiyat Araştırmaları Dergisi* 22 (2007): 414.
56. TNA, FO 424/106, pp. 395–96, Chemerside (1 October 1879); Soysal, "Die Siedlungs und Landschaftsentwicklung der Çukurova," 58–61.
57. Bayraktar was unable to arrive at a figure. Bayraktar, "Kırım ve Kafkasya'dan Adana Vilayeti'ne Yapılan Göç ve İskânlar (1869–1907)," 415.
58. The figure of 16,351 comes from a document that contains a list of provinces and the number of refugees. OA, Y-PRK-KOM 1/5 (15 Teşrinisani 1294 [27 November 1878]). However, it is unclear if the figures in question pertain to the 1877–78 migrants or are intended to include prior waves. This and other estimates are cited in Bayram Şen, "Empires from the Margin: Bosnian Muslim Migrants between the Ottoman Empire and the Austro-Hungarian Empire—Petitions of the Returnees," in *Emigrants and Minorities: The Silenced Memory of the Russo-Ottoman War 1877–1878*, ed. Dominik Gutmeyr (Sofia: Balkanistic Forum, 2015), 16.
59. C. Favre and B. Mandrot, *Voyage en Cilicie 1874* (Paris: Librairie Charles Delagrave, 1878), 16.
60. TNA, FO 222/7/1, 1880 no. 12, Bennet to Goschen, Adana (15 December 1880). Lt. Ferdinand Bennet traveled in Cilicia and other parts of Anatolia between 1879 and 1882 on a mission to report the impacts of provincial reform and chart the geography of the interior. His records at the British National Archives are

under the codes FO 222/7/1, 222/8/2, and 222/8/3. See Gould, "Pashas and Brigands," 165–66.

61. TNA, FO 222/7/1, 1880 no. 12, Bennet to Goschen, Adana (15 December 1880).

62. Favre and Mandrot, *Voyage en Cilicie*, 40.

63. OA, ŞD 2117/55, no. 4 (24 Rebiulahir 1293 [19 May 1876]).

64. TNA, FO 424/132, p. 110, Bennet to Dufferin (22 March 1882).

65. Gould attempted to evaluate the demographic impact of settlement on the first generation after the Reform Division by comparing *salname* data from the 1860s and the 1890s, finding that while most districts increased significantly in population, the population in Kars, Sis, and Karaisalı decreased substantially between 1868 and 1890. This was despite an increase in the number of villages. Gould, "The Burning of the Tents," 82. The figures provided by Gould, while conceivably accurate, are based on imperfect data. The data, to the extent we may rely on them, do indicate low to zero population growth in certain regions of tribal settlement, and given that many immigrants had also been settled in those areas, the general conclusion that high mortality and low birth rates in those areas prevailed appears accurate. See *Salname-i vilâyet-i Adana* for years H. 1287, H. 1293, and H. 1294; Cengiz Eroğlu, Murat Babuçoğlu, and Mehmet Köçer, *Osmanlı vilayet salnamelerinde Halep* (Ankara: Global Strateji Enstitüsü, 2007), 174–84; Karpat, *Ottoman Population*, 124–27; Vidal Cuinet, *La Turquie d'Asie* (Paris: Leroux, 1891), 2:5.

66. As Gould notes, even if the Avşars were not counted in these statistics due to their being settled outside of the boundaries of the Adana province, the numbers still reflect a 22 percent decrease. Gould, "The Burning of the Tents," 84.

67. TNA, FO 222/7/1, 1880 no. 12, Bennet to Goschen, Adana (15 December 1880).

68. TNA, FO 424/106, pp. 395–96, Chemerside (1 October 1879).

69. OA, İ-ŞD 40/2123, no. 2 (12 Ramazan 1295 [28 August 1878]).

70. E. J. Davis, *Life in Asiatic Turkey* (London: Edward Stanford, 1879), 103.

71. Davis, *Life in Asiatic Turkey*, 79.

72. Favre and Mandrot, *Voyage en Cilicie*, 23.

73. Henry C. Barkley, *A Ride through Asia Minor and Armenia* (London: Murray, 1891), 195.

74. Cholera first entered Cilicia during the second global cholera pandemic when Mehmed Ali's army invaded Syria in 1832. Edmond de Cadalvène and Émile Barrault, *Histoire de la guerre de Méhemed-Ali contre la Porte ottomane en Syrie et en Asie Mineure* (Paris: Arthus Bertrand, 1837), 168–70, 95, 202. Also TNA, FO 78/316, p. 98, Herry to Palmerton (20 May 1837), and p. 209, Herry to Palmerton (13 October 1837).

75. See Michael Christopher Low, "Empire and the Hajj: Pilgrims, Plagues, and

Pan-Islam under British Surveillance, 1865–1908," *International Journal of Middle East Studies* 40, no. 2 (2008): 269–90.

76. CADC, CCC, Alep 33, pp. 138, Bertrand to de Lhuys (22 June 1865), 141, Bertrand to de Lhuys (12 August 1865), and 144, Bertrand to de Lhuys (22 August 1865).

77. CADC, CCC, Alep 33, p. 176, Bertrand to de Lhuys (12 October 1865).

78. Cevdet, *Marûzât*, 165–68.

79. Şevket Pamuk, "The Ottoman Empire in the 'Great Depression' of 1873–1896," *Journal of Economic History* 44, no. 1 (1984): 107–18.

80. OA, A-MKT-MHM 466/45 (21 Şaban 1290 [2 October 1873]); 469/30 (9 Şevval 1290 [18 November 1873]).

81. Özge Ertem, "Eating the Last Seed: Famine, Empire, Survival and Order in Ottoman Anatolia in the late 19th Century," PhD diss., European University Institute, 2012, 13.

82. OA, ŞD 243/24 (29 Receb 1289 [20 September 1872]).

83. Davis, *Life in Asiatic Turkey*, 186; *Report upon the Commercial Relations of the United States with Foreign Countries for the Year Ending September 30, 1874* (Washington, DC: Government Printing Office, 1875), 1129.

84. "The Asia Minor Famine," *New York Times*, 1 January 1875.

85. Davis, *Life in Asiatic Turkey*, 169.

86. "Famine in Asia: A Record of Suffering," *New York Times*, 26 July 1875.

87. OA, A-MKT-UM 500/82, Ahmed to Sadaret (17 Rebiulevvel 1278 [22 September 1861]).

88. The three doctors were paid 1,000 kuruş each plus travel expenses and one was asked to remain as country doctor after the disease passed in December 1865. OA, A-MKT-MHM 345/363 (17 Cemaziyelevvel 1282 [2 November 1865]); İ-DH 543/37810 (19 Receb 1282 [9 December 1865]).

89. OA, İ-ŞD 40/2123, no. 2 (12 Ramazan 1295 [28 August 1878]). While touring Çukurova, E. J. Davis contracted a debilitating fever that left him bedridden in Mersin. He secured some quinine at an exorbitant price, but he soon understood that it was diluted or of a low quality. Davis, *Life in Asiatic Turkey*, 464–66. For an overview of health institutions in Adana during this period, see Özlem Karasandık, "Çağdaşlaşma Sürecinde Adana (1839–1876)," PhD diss., Ankara University, 2012, 121–34.

90. Davis, *Life in Asiatic Turkey*, 187.

91. Ertem, "Eating the Last Seed," 74.

92. Ertem, "Eating the Last Seed," 174.

93. These loans were used to pay prior debts and meet the government's large budget deficit. Murat Birdal, *The Political Economy of Ottoman Public Debt: Insolvency and European Financial Control in the Late Nineteenth Century* (New York: Palgrave Macmillan, 2010), 28.

94. Birdal, *The Political Economy of Ottoman Public Debt*, 39.

95. OA, ŞD 2114/22, no. 1 (16 Rebiulevvel 1287 [4 June 1870]).

96. C. Luxemburger et al., "Effects of Malaria during Pregnancy on Infant Mortality in an Area of Low Malaria Transmission," *American Journal of Epidemiology* 154, no. 5 (2001): 459–65.

97. Patrick E. Duffy and Michal Fried, "Pregnancy Malaria throughout History: Dangerous Labors," in *Malaria in Pregnancy: Deadly Parasite, Susceptible Host*, ed. Patrick E. Duffy and Michal Fried (London: Taylor & Francis, 2001), 1–26.

98. TNA, FO 222/7/1, 1880 no. 12, Bennet to Goschen, Adana (15 December 1880).

99. TNA, FO 424/106, pp. 395–96, Chemerside (1 October 1879).

100. OA, ŞD 2117/55, no. 4 (24 Rebiulahir 1293 [19 May 1876]).

101. Gould translates as "Day of Judgement" ("Pashas and Brigands," 210).

102. TNA, FO 222/7/1, 1880 no. 12, Bennet to Goschen, Adana (15 December 1880).

103. Atalay, *Maraş Tarihi ve Coğrafyası*, 71–72. See Ali Birinci, "Besim Atalay'ın Hayatı ve Eserleri," *Türk Yurdu* 101, no. 295 (2012).

104. See Richard L. Chambers, "The Education of a Nineteenth-Century Ottoman Âlim, Ahmed Cevdet Paşa," *International Journal of Middle East Studies* 4, no. 4 (1973): 440–64; Christoph K. Neumann, *Araç tarih amaç Tanzimat: Tarih-i Cevdet'in siyasi anlamı*, trans. Meltem Arun (Istanbul: Tarih Vakfı, 2000); Ahmed Şimşirgil and Ekrem Buğra Ekinci, *Ahmed Cevdet Paşa ve Mecelle* (Istanbul: Marmara Üniversitesi, 2007).

105. See Kenan Tekin, "Reforming Categories of Science and Religion in the Late Ottoman Empire," PhD diss., Columbia University, 2016.

106. For a thorough discussion, see Alp Eren Topal, "Order as a Chronotope of Ottoman Political Writing," *Contemporary Levant* 5, no. 1 (2020): 24–32. See also Cornell H. Fleischer, "Royal Authority, Dynastic Cyclism, and 'Ibn Khaldunism' in Sixteenth-Century Ottoman Letters," *Journal of Asian and African Studies* 18, nos. 3–4 (1983): 198–220; Bruce B. Lawrence, *Ibn Khaldun and Islamic Ideology* (Leiden: Brill, 1984).

107. Ahmed Cevdet, *Tarih-i Cevdet*, vols. 1–2 (Istanbul: Matbaa-yı Osmaniye, 1309 [1891]), 15.

108. Neumann, *Araç tarih amaç Tanzimat*, 176–83.

109. Neumann, *Araç tarih amaç Tanzimat*, 138–39.

110. Cevdet, *Tezâkir*, 3, 108.

111. Cevdet, *Tezâkir*, 3, 111–12.

112. Cevdet, *Tezâkir*, 3, 107.

113. Cevdet, *Tezâkir*, 3, 168.

114. Cevdet, *Marûzât*, 173.

115. OA, A-MKT-MHM 391/84 (24 Cemaziyelahir 1284 [23 October 1867]); Cevdet, *Tezâkir*, 3, 112.

116. The deliberate juxtaposition of *şenlik* and *vahşet* with their dual meanings illustrates the paradox of "wilderness" as both opportunity and hazard.

117. Cevdet, *Tezâkir*, 3, 170.

118. For an example of this logic, see OA, ŞD 2114/18, no. 4 (18 Şaban 1286 [10 November 1869]).

119. Cevdet, *Marûzât*, 179.

120. Cevdet makes this link explicitly in *Marûzât*, 140–41. Alexander and his exploits in Cilicia became a common feature of European travel writing on Cilicia. See John Macdonald Kinneir, *Journey through Asia Minor, Armenia and Koordistan* (London: J. Murray, 1818), 131–44; Langlois, *Voyage dans la Cilicie*, 51; E. J. Davis, *Life in Asiatic Turkey*, 493–94.

121. OA, Y-EE 142/7, no. 12 (6 Muharrem 1282 [1 June 1865]).

122. OA, Y-EE 142/7, no. 14 (16 Muharrem 1282 [11 June 1865]).

123. OA, Y-EE 142/7, no. 10 (22 Muharrem 1282 [17 June 1865]).

124. Cevdet, *Marûzât*, 182.

125. OA, MVL 707/87 (14 Safer 1282 [9 July 1865]).

126. Ibn Khaldun, *The Muqaddimah: An Introduction to History*, trans. Franz Rosenthal (New York: Pantheon Books, 1958), 2:246.

127. Cevdet, *Marûzât*, 182.

128. Davis, *Life in Asiatic Turkey*, 71.

129. İzmidi, *Sıtma*, 17.

130. *Sեղեկագիր Հայ Բշկական Առաքելութեան (Կիլիկիա) Մայիս—Օգոստոս 1919* (Paris: Imprimerie Turabian, 1920), 36.

131. Selim Deringil, "'They Live in a State of Nomadism and Savagery': The Late Ottoman Empire and the Post-Colonial Debate," *Comparative Studies in Society and History* 45, no. 2 (2003): 311–42; Ussama Makdisi, "Rethinking Ottoman Imperialism: Modernity, Violence and the Cultural Logic of Ottoman Reform," in *The Empire in the City: Arab Provincial Cities in the Ottoman Empire*, ed. Jens Hanssen and Thomas Philipp (Würzburg: Ergon in Kommission, 2002), 29–48.

132. Duffy, *Nomad's Land*, 41.

133. Special thanks to Mehtap Ergenoğlu for sharing unpublished oral history research on Atlılar with me in 2013.

134. Kemal, *Çukurova Yana Yana*, 14.

135. OA, A-MKT-MHM 223/3 (14 Zilhicce 1277 [23 June 1861]).

136. There is also a "Çukurova" breed that is a cross between the Uzunyayla horses and the Cilicia region's species of Arabian horse. Bonnie L. Hendricks, *International Encyclopedia of Horse Breeds* (Norman: University of Oklahoma Press, 1995), 145, 430. See Hamed-Troyansky, "Imperial Refuge," 198–258.

137. Cevdet, *Tezâkir*, 3, 157.

138. Özdemir, *Öyküleriyle Ağıtlar*, 303; Cevdet, *Tezâkir*, 3, 188.

139. OA, A-MKT-UM 519/54 (11 Cemaziyelevvel 1278 [14 November 1861]).

140. Atalay, *Maraş Tarihi ve Coğrafyası*, 72.

141. The document in question is dated to 1876 but refers to events occurring in years prior. OA, ŞD 2117/55, no. 4 (24 Rebiulahir 1293 [19 May 1876]).

142. OA, ŞD 2118/60, No 3 (10 Mayıs 1295 [22 May 1879]).

143. OA, İ-MMS 60/2843, no. 3 (26 Şevval 1295 [23 October 1878]). For a complete translation, see Gratien, "The Mountains Are Ours," 211–14.

144. Cevdet's writings display some prejudice against the Kurdish tribes in Cilicia; he describes the Turkish tribes as "the much lesser of two evils [*çok ehven*]." Cevdet, *Marûzât*, 120.

145. OA, ŞD 2118/4, no. 1 (16 Cemaziyelevvel 1295 [18 May 1878]).

146. OA, DH-HMŞ 27/68 (5 Cemaziyelevvel 1334 [10 March 1916]). Late in the Ottoman period public health officials established formal health precautions for the foundation of new villages, singling out swamps as the primary source of health issues such as malaria commonly faced by new settlers. *Yeni tesis olunacak köylerde nazar-ı dikkate alınacak esasat-ı sıhhiye* (Istanbul: Ahmed İhsan ve Şürekası, 1914), 4–5.

147. On enslavement in *muhacir* households, see Ceyda Karamursel, "Transplanted Slavery, Contested Freedom, and Vernacularization of Rights in the Reform Era Ottoman Empire," *Comparative Studies in Society and History* 59, no. 3 (2017): 690–714.

148. OA, ŞD 2117/25, no. 1 (7 Rebiulahir 1290 [4 June 1873]).

149. OA, ŞD 2114/18, no. 4 (18 Şaban 1286 [10 November 1869]); Toksöz, *Nomads, Migrants, and Cotton*, 72.

150. OA, HRT-h 486 (1287 [1870/1]).

151. Davis, *Life in Asiatic Turkey*, 141.

152. TNA, FO 424/106, p. 2 (27 October 1879). Tellingly, Lieutenant Bennet noted in 1880 that "as a rule the Circassians are credited with all lawless acts." TNA, FO 222/7/1, 1880 no. 1, Bennet to Goschen, Kaiserieh (16 June 1880).

153. OA, ŞD 2889/13, no. 3 (4 Cemaziyelevvel 1295 [25 April 1878]); CADC, CCC, Alep 35, Destrées to Waddington (31 August 1878), 283; Poghosean, *Հուշեր քաղաքական պատմության*, 532. For the complete interrogations of local officials and notables involved in the second Kozanoğlu rebellion, see OA, İ-DH 775/63109.

154. Kemal, *Ağıtlar*, 27.

155. James C. Scott, *Seeing Like a State* (New Haven: Yale University Press, 1998), 1.

156. Kasaba, *A Moveable Empire*, 86.

157. *Salname-i vilâyet-i Adana* (H. 1294 [1877]), 106.

158. See Sunderland, *Taming the Wild Field*; Benjamin Claude Brower, *A Desert Named Peace: The Violence of France's Empire in the Algerian Sahara, 1844–1902* (New York: Columbia University Press, 2009); Lucy Riall, *Sicily and the Unification of Italy: Liberal Policy and Local Power, 1859–1866* (Oxford: Oxford University Press, 1998).

159. Mike Davis, *Late Victorian Holocausts: El Niño Famines and the Making of the Third World* (London: Verso, 2001).

160. See George Custer, "Expedition to the Black Hills" (Washington, DC: US Senate, 1874).

161. See Osama Abi-Mershed, *Apostles of Modernity: Saint-Simonians and the Civilizing Mission in Algeria* (Stanford: Stanford University Press, 2010).

162. Toksöz, *Nomads, Migrants, and Cotton*, 20.

Chapter 3

1. Damar Arıkoğlu, *Hâtıralarım* (Istanbul: Tan, 1961), 14–15; Orhan Kemal, *Eskici Dükkânı* (Istanbul: Cem Yayınevi, 1973), 190. Rain prayers were often official business in the Ottoman Empire. See OA, A-MKT-MHM 296/21, no. 3 (18 Şevval 1280/14 Mart 1280 [27 March 1864]); Y-MTV 3/71 (19 Cemaziyelevvel 1297 [16 April 1880]).

2. "Yağmur ve dua," *Yeni Adana*, 15 April 1937. See also M. Kaya Bilgegil, *Ziyâ Paşa üzerinde bir araştırma* (Erzurum: Atatürk University Press, 1970), 293; Taha Toros, *Şair Ziya Paşanin Adana Valiliği* (Adana: Yeni Adana Basımevi, 1940).

3. OA, ŞD 2118/35, map (1878).

4. OA, DH-MKT 1312/11 (25 Mayıs 1286 [6 June 1870]).

5. OA, HR-TO 556/15 (25 Şubat 1294 [9 March 1879]).

6. OA, ŞD 2118/35, no. 15 (5 Şubat 1294 [17 February 1879]); no. 16 (15 Şubat 1294 [27 February 1879]); Bilgegil, *Ziyâ Paşa*, 291, cited in Gould, "Pashas and Brigands."

7. OA İ-ŞD 45/2413, no. 9 (21 Şubat 1294 [5 March 1879]).

8. OA, İ-ŞD 45/2413, no. 14 (16 Kanunusani 1294 [28 January 1879]).

9. OA, A-MKT-MHM 485/40, no. 3 (17 Mart 1296 [29 March 1880]); Bilgegil, *Ziyâ Paşa*, 319–20. Nazan Çiçek, *The Young Ottomans* (London: I. B. Tauris, 2010), 45; İsmail Habip, "Meşhur Şair Ziya Paşanın Adana Valiliği," *Memleket Çukurova'da*, 1931, 5.

10. See Davis, *Life in Asiatic Turkey*, 30; Şerafeddin Mağmumi, *Bir Osmanlı Doktoru'nun Anıları*, ed. Cahit Kayra (Istanbul: Boyut, 2001), 174; Yusuf Ziya, *Tabsıra yahut Adana Temaşası* (Adana: Adana Vilayet Matbaası, 1314 [1898]), 10; Koudoulian, *Zuy ltnp*, 12; Frederic Macler, "La Cilicie: Porte Maritime de l'Arménie," *L'Acropole* 1, no. 2 (November 1920); Hagop Terzian, Աստանայի կեանքը (Constantinople: Z. N. Perperean, 1909), 8.

11. Toksöz, *Nomads, Migrants, and Cotton*, 15.

12. Toksöz, *Nomads, Migrants, and Cotton*, 204.

13. On second nature, see Richard William Judd, *Second Nature: An Environmental History of New England* (Amherst: University of Massachusetts Press, 2014); Cronon, *Nature's Metropolis*, xvii.

14. See Alan Mikhail, *Nature and Empire in Ottoman Egypt: An Environmental History* (Cambridge: Cambridge University Press, 2011).

15. Toksöz, *Nomads, Migrants, and Cotton*, 46–48. This project apparently led to the

contamination of the Cydnus River, leaving its waters nonpotable. Davis, *Life in Asiatic Turkey*, 40.

16. Doughty Wylie, *Report for the Year 1908 on the Trade of the Province of Adana* (London: Harrison & Son, 1909), 3; cited in Toksöz, *Nomads, Migrants, and Cotton*, 137. *1325 senesi Asya ve Afrika-yı Osmani Ziraat İstatistiği* (Istanbul: Matbaa-ı Osmaniye, 1327 [1911]); *Memalik-i Osmaniye'nin 1329 senesine mahsus Ziraat İstatistiği* (Istanbul: Ticaret ve Ziraat Nezareti, 1330 [1914]).

17. Ottoman statistics categorize these products as *sanaiye*, a classification distinct from grains, legumes, and orchards. The only other provinces to allocate even 10 percent of their cultivated land to such commercial crops in 1909 were Istanbul (13.6%), Beirut (10%), and the small Sancak of Jerusalem (10.1%). *1325 senesi Asya ve Afrika-yı Osmani Ziraat İstatistiği*, ث.

18. *Reports from Her Majesty's Consuls*, vol. 4 (London: Harrison & Sons, 1877), 965; Lamberto Vannutelli, "Cenni sulla produzione del cotone in Asia Minore," *Bolletino della Società geografica italiana* 7 (August 1906): 863; A. F. Townshend, *Trade of the Vilayets of Aleppo and Adana for the Year 1903* (London: Foreign Office, 1904), 24; Wylie, *Report for the Year 1908*, 16. Toksöz indicates that the largest recipient of Çukurova cotton was Germany after the establishment of the German Cotton Society of the Levant in 1906. Toksöz, *Nomads, Migrants, and Cotton*, 153.

19. Sven Beckert, *Empire of Cotton: A Global History* (New York: Knopf, 2014), xi.

20. For a more thorough overview of late Ottoman Çukurova's political economy, see Toksöz, *Nomads, Migrants, and Cotton*, 85–188.

21. *1325 senesi Asya ve Afrika-yı Osmani Ziraat İstatistiği*, ج-د.

22. Toksöz, *Nomads, Migrants, and Cotton*, 190.

23. For discussion of different types of empty land in the late Ottoman Empire, see Barakat, "An Empty Land?" 29–54. On early debates about *mevat* land and the *çiftlik*, see Halil İnalcık, "The Emergence of Big Farms, Çiftliks: State, Landlords, and Tenants," and Gilles Veinstein, "On the Çiftlik Debate," both in *Landholding and Commercial Agriculture in the Middle East*, ed. Çağlar Keyder and Faruk Tabak (Albany: State University of New York Press, 1991).

24. For a detailed study of how this played out in Ottoman Transjordan, see Martha Mundy and Richard Saumarez Smith, *Governing Property: Law, Administration, and Production in Ottoman Syria* (London: I. B. Tauris, 2007), 66–79.

25. Toksöz, *Nomads, Migrants, and Cotton*, 64. In his discussion of Aleppo, Bruce Masters equates the land grabs that occurred under this law with the homesteads of the United States from the same period. Bruce Masters, "The Political Economy of Aleppo in an Age of Ottoman Reform," *Journal of the Economic and Social History of the Orient* 53, nos. 1–2 (2010): 309. See also Meltem Toksöz, "Modernisation in the Ottoman Empire: The 1858 Land Code and Property Regimes from a Regional Perspective," in *Ottoman Rural Societies and Economies*, ed. Elias Kolovos (Rethymno: Crete University Press, 2015), 381–98.

26. Davis, *Life in Asiatic Turkey*, 148.

27. Barkley, *A Ride through Asia Minor and Armenia*, 191.

28. Toksöz, *Nomads, Migrants, and Cotton*, 136.

29. *Mevat* signified uncultivated land that was not possessed by anyone with a deed and not within earshot of a town or village. See Atıf Bey, *Arazi Kanunname-i Hümayunu Şerhi*, 2nd ed. (Istanbul: Matbaa-i Hayriye ve Şürekâsı, H. 1330 [1911–12]), 43–46, 327–37. Also F. Ongley and Horace E. Miller, *The Ottoman Land Code* (London: W. Clowes & Sons, 1892), 54. For global comparison, see Vittoria Di Palma, *Wasteland: A History* (New Haven: Yale University Press, 2014).

30. Announcements of the new amendment were sent out to all the provinces of the empire. For an example of the language, see OA, T-NF-VRK 31/20 (8 Kanunuevvel 1298 [20 December 1882]).

31. USEK, Sursock 18022, 19232, 19249. See Kristen Alff, "Levantine Joint-Stock Companies, Trans-Mediterranean Partnerships, and Nineteenth-Century Capitalist Development," *Comparative Studies in Society and History* 60, no. 1 (2018): 150–77.

32. Toksöz, *Nomads, Migrants, and Cotton*, 144.

33. OA, Y-PRK-UM 6/77 (22 Cemaziyelevvel 1301 [20 March 1884]); DH-MKT 1587/4 (21 Cemaziyelevvel 1306 [23 January 1889]); DH-MKT 2715/1 (2 Zilhicce 1326 [22 January 1909]); DH-İD 160-2/56, no. 5 (11 Şubat 1324 [24 February 1909]); Toksöz, *Nomads, Migrants, and Cotton*, 163. Bennet predicted that Abidin Pasha would not profit from acquisition of these lands because they were prone to flooding. TNA, FO 222/8/2, 1882 no. 3, Bennet to Dufferin, Adana (6 February 1882).

34. OA, BEO 4341/325518, no. 2–3 (29 Kanunusani 1330 [11 February 1915]).

35. Toksöz, *Nomads, Migrants, and Cotton*, 145.

36. For example, on the provincial level, Diyarbekir displayed one of the highest concentrations of large (50 *dönüms* or more) landholdings in the Ottoman land survey, and alongside the provinces of Mosul, Baghdad, and Basra (not covered in the survey), it was the leading rice-producing region of the empire. See *1325 senesi Asya ve Afrika-yı Osmani Ziraat İstatistiği*; *Memalik-i Osmaniye'nin 1329 senesine mahsus Ziraat İstatistiği*.

37. See *Pirinç Ziraatı Kanunnamesi* (Istanbul: Matbaa-yı Amire, H. 1328 [1910/11]), 4.

38. OA, DH-İ-UM 79/62, no. 1 (1 Kanunusani 1331 [1 January 1916]).

39. Ercan Göl, "Cumhuriyet Döneminde (1923–1950) Maraş'ın Sosyo-Ekonomik Yapısı ve Gelişimi," MA thesis, Sütçü İmam University, 2006, 45.

40. Toksöz, *Nomads, Migrants, and Cotton*, 63–64.

41. Toksöz, *Nomads, Migrants, and Cotton*, 93.

42. Toksöz, *Nomads, Migrants, and Cotton*, 91.

43. Toksöz, *Nomads, Migrants, and Cotton*, 132; Meltem Toksöz, "Family and Migration: The Mavromatis Enterprises and Networks," *Cahiers de la Méditerranée* (2011): 359–82.

44. Toksöz, *Nomads, Migrants, and Cotton*, 110–11.

45. Toksöz, *Nomads, Migrants, and Cotton*, 168–72. Abidin Pasha is cited as the first person to import a steam plow to Cilicia, which he intended for use on his own land. Lieutenant Bennet remarked that the governor had "rubbed his hands in glee as he talked of the possibility of working all night by the light of the moon." TNA, FO 222/8/2, 1881 no. 24, Bennet to Dufferin (6 December 1881). A brochure for the plow manufacturer that Abidin Pasha ordered from, as well as his correspondence, is extant in the Ottoman archives. OA, HR-SFR (3) 282/31.

46. Toksöz, *Nomads, Migrants, and Cotton*, 176.

47. TNA, FO 222/8/2, pp. 58–60, "Report on the Vilayet of Adana" (6 February 1882).

48. For a smattering of labor flow estimates in chronological order: Davis, *Life in Asiatic Turkey*, 172; TNA, FO 222/8/2, no. 3 Bennet to Dufferin, Adana (6 February 1882); OA, HR-SFR (3) 282/31, no. 52 (11 February 1885); Mağmumi, *Bir Osmanlı Doktoru'nun Anıları*, 174; Ziya, *Tabsıra yahut Adana Temaşası*, 18. OA, İ-DH 1386/33, no. 7 (30 Nisan 1317 [13 May 1901]); A-MKT-MHM 523/51 (16 Teşrinievvel [29 October 1903]); DH-MKT 2801/54, no. 1 (17 Rebiulevvel 1327 [26 March 1909]). Terzian, *Ատանայի կեանքը*, 6; W. J. Childs, *Across Asia Minor on Foot* (London: W. Blackwood, 1917), 343.

49. Georges Tsapalos and Pierre Walter, *Rapport sur le domaine impérial de Tchoucour-Ova* (Paris: Villeneuve-Saint-Georges, 1912), 19–20.

50. Davis noted that around 40 percent of the workers were Nusayris (*Life in Asiatic Turkey*, 172).

51. OA, A-MKT-MHM 328/84, no. 1 (8 Mart 1281 [20 March 1865]); DH-MKT 2843/31 (30 Mayıs 1325 [13 June 1909]).

52. OA, İ-DA 8/194 (14 Cemaziyelahir 1287 [11 September 1870]); DH-MKT 330/45 (12 Receb 1312 [27 December 1895]); ŞD 633/18, no. 4 (7 September 1893); TNA, FO 222/7/1, 1881 no. 3, Bennet to Goschen, Adana (22 January 1881). British intelligence indicated that the Afghans and Indians in Çukurova "have immigrated to escape from British rule." *A Handbook of Asia Minor*, vol. 4 (London: Naval Staff, Intelligence Dept., 1918), 43–44.

53. They may be related to the deployment of enslaved or corvée laborers from Nubia and Sudan by the Egyptian occupation of the 1830s or the broader Ottoman slave trade. However, sources about such people from late Ottoman Çukurova simply refer to the presence of a small rural population. References are common in European sources but without much detail. See TNA, FO 222/8/2, p. 55, "Report on the Vilayet of Adana" (6 February 1882); Childs, *Across Asia Minor on Foot*, 340. A British source refers to people living in "Ethiopian-style" huts in the Ceyhan region. *A Handbook of Asia Minor*, 4:42. Ehud Toledano argues that enslavement was not a major dimension of Çukurova's agrarian economy, but does not resolve the question of this community's origins in "Where Have All the Egyptian Fallahin Gone?" in *Mersin, the Mediterranean*

and Modernity: Heritage of the Long-Nineteenth Century, ed. Tülin Selvi (Mersin: Mersin University, 2002), 21–28.

54. OA, HR-HMŞ-İŞO 207/28, no. 1, Ali Münif to Sadaret (15 Kanunuevvel 1329 [28 December 1913]). See also Lâle Can, *Spiritual Subjects: Central Asian Pilgrims and the Ottoman Hajj at the End of Empire* (Stanford: Stanford University Press, 2020), 149–74.

55. OA, DH-İD 80/26 (9 Haziran 1330 [22 June 1914]).

56. OA, DH-MKT 1712/31, no. 1 (14 March 1890); DH-MKT 2074/36, no. 1 (10 Nisan 1312 [22 April 1896]), no. 2 (13 Nisan 1312 [25 April 1896]).

57. OA, ŞD 2124/28 (6 Cemaziyelahir 1310 [14 December 1892]); Hilmi Uran, *Adana Ziraat Amelesi* (Adana: Türksözü, 1925), 13–14.

58. Uran, *Adana Ziraat Amelesi*, 15.

59. Arıkoğlu, *Hâtıralarım*, 16; Uran, *Adana Ziraat Amelesi*, 20–21.

60. Mağmumi, *Bir Osmanlı Doktoru'nun Anıları*, 175.

61. See OA, BEO 3599/269906, no. 2 (22 Cemaziyelahir 1327 [27 June 1909]).

62. Uran, *Adana Ziraat Amelesi*, 10.

63. Uran, *Adana Ziraat Amelesi*, 10. Gisela Procházka-Eisl and Stephan Procházka indicate that "Ibrahim Pasha's labor regulations [during the 1830s] were the first and last ones" (*The Plain of Saints and Prophets*, 40).

64. Wylie, *Report for the Year 1908*, 14. The first meal came after about an hour of work in the morning and consisted of a loaf of bread. The "pilav break," during which workers were given a bowl of bulgur or barley, came in the late morning. The next break, known as the "ass break [*göt soluğu*]," came at the high heat of the afternoon and was intended solely for sitting. Alongside an optional prayer break in the afternoon, a roughly forty-five-minute break for a meal occurred at lunch. The workers would generally eat a loaf of bread with barley soup, compote, or ayran. There was usually a water boy on hand in the fields during work hours. Uran, *Adana Ziraat Amelesi*, 7–10.

65. KMS, Kilikia KL 6 (Iskilic), Mosises Christofides (26 February 1968).

66. OA, ŞD 2124/28 (13 Kanunuevvel 1308 [25 December 1892]); 2124/29 (14 Kanunuevvel 1308 [26 December 1892]); ŞD 2124/30 (22 Kanunuevvel 1308 [3 January 1893]); TNA FO 222/8/2, no. 3 Bennet to Dufferin, Adana (6 February 1882).

67. Donald Quataert makes a similar observation about miners in the Black Sea region. Donald Quataert, *Miners and the State in the Ottoman Empire: The Zonguldak Coalfield, 1822–1920* (New York: Berghahn Books, 2006).

68. Egypt's first modern cotton strain was a variety known as Jumel developed by a French engineer by the same name from a variant of *Gossypium barbadense*, a long-staple variety from the Americas. Richard G. Percy, "The Worldwide Gene Pool of Gossypium barbadense L. and Its Improvement," in *Genetics and Genomics of Cotton*, ed. Andrew H. Paterson (New York: Springer, 2009), 56–57.

69. Wylie, *Report for the Year 1908*, 12–13; Kemal, *Pamuk Ziraati* (Istanbul: Hilâl Matbaası, 1931), 3–4, 22–23; Toksöz, *Nomads, Migrants, and Cotton*, 157.
70. Terzian, Ատանայի կեանքը, 10.
71. Kemal, *Pamuk Ziraati*, 22–23.
72. Barkley, *A Ride through Asia Minor and Armenia*, 180.
73. Terzian, Ատանայի կեանքը, 9–10.
74. OA, A-MKT-MHM 727/21 (6 Safer 1312 [9 August 1894]).
75. Toksöz, *Nomads, Migrants, and Cotton*, 156–57.
76. Davis, *Life in Asiatic Turkey*, 56–57.
77. Wylie, *Report for the Year 1908*, 13.
78. Wylie, *Report for the Year 1908*, 14.
79. Arshakuhi Teodik, Ամիս մը ի Կիլիկիա: ձգտումը նօթեր (Istanbul: Ter-Nersesean, 1910), 58.
80. Wylie, *Report for the Year 1908*, 11.
81. Terzian, Ատանայի կեանքը, 10.
82. Further study of these effects in Cilicia would be a useful complement to prior work on the impacts of commercialization in the late Ottoman Mediterranean. See Judith E. Tucker, *Women in Nineteenth-Century Egypt* (Cambridge: Cambridge University Press, 1985); Akram Fouad Khater, *Inventing Home: Emigration, Gender, and the Middle Class in Lebanon, 1870–1920* (Berkeley: University of California Press, 2001); David Gutman, *The Politics of Armenian Migration to North America, 1885–1915: Sojourners, Smugglers and Dubious Citizens* (Edinburgh: Edinburgh University Press, 2019).
83. "The Mersina, Tarsus and Adana Railway: reprinted from the Times, May 19th, 1884," *Bristol Selected Pamphlets* (1884): 4.
84. See Henri Lefebvre, *The Production of Space*, trans. Donald Nicholson-Smith (Malden, MA: Blackwell, 2007); Manu Goswami, *Producing India: From Colonial Economy to National Space* (Chicago: University of Chicago Press, 2004).
85. All census data from Karpat, *Ottoman Population*.
86. See Songül Ulutaş, *19. yüzyılda Tarsus'ta ekonomik ve sosyal yaşam (1856–1914)* (Tarsus: Tarsus Ticaret ve Sanayi Odası, 2015).
87. In the table, especially in the case of Adana, these numbers refer to official "permanent" population and do not consider floating population or seasonal fluctuations. Most sources distinguish between these two categories. These estimates are derived from a large body of narrative and official sources that, when read alongside each other, provide a fairly accurate picture of relative population. For published works, see Kinneir, *Journey through Asia Minor, Armenia and Koordistan*; Davis, *Life in Asiatic Turkey*; Favre and Mandrot, *Voyage en Cilicie*; Gould, "Pashas and Brigands," 199; "The Mersina, Tarsus and Adana Railway: reprinted from the Times, May 19th, 1884"; Vidal Cuinet, *La Turquie d'Asie* (Paris: Leroux, 1890–94); Mağmumi, *Bir Osmanlı Doktoru'nun Anıları*;

Ziya, *Tabsıra yahut Adana Temaşası*; Terzian, Առաճայի կևակրդ; Childs, *Across Asia Minor on Foot*; *A Handbook of Asia Minor*, vol. 4; Pierre H. André, *La Cilicie et le problème ottoman* (Paris: Gauthie-Villars & Cie., 1921); Gabriel Bie Ravndal, *Turkey: A Commercial and Industrial Handbook* (Washington, DC: Government Printing Office, 1926); *Türkiye Nüfusu* (Ankara: Türk Ocakları merkez heyeti, 1928); *Adana Cumhuriyetten Evvel ve Sonra* (Ankara: Ulus Basımevi, 1937); *Çukurova Bölgesi: Bölgesel gelişme, Şehirleşme ve Yerleşme Düzeni* (Ankara: Bölge Planlama Dairesi, 1970). Ottoman *salnames* also sometimes contain population estimates for cities and towns. For archival sources, TNA, FO 222/8/2, FO 371/3418; OA, HR-SFR (3) 282/31 (20 October 1881).

88. OA, DH-UMVM 114/37, no. 4 (24 Teşrinisani 1332 [5 December 1916]); İ-DH 551/38360, no. 1 (9 Mayıs 1282 [22 May 1866]).

89. See McNeill, *The Mountains of the Mediterranean*, 2–7.

90. David Harvey, *Spaces of Capital: Towards a Critical Geography* (New York: Routledge, 2001), 123.

91. *Salname-i vilâyet-i Adana* (H. 1294 [1877]).

92. TNA, FO 195/1930, p. 9, Massy to Currie, Mersina (1 April 1896).

93. Wylie, *Report for the Year 1908*, 12.

94. OA, DH-TMIK-S 69/49 (12 Receb 1325 [8 August 1907]).

95. Around Ceyhan, 88 percent of cultivator households owned more than 50 *dönüms* of land. In the Sancak of Cebel-i Bereket, the households surveyed indicated a similar figure of 74 percent. *1325 senesi Asya ve Afrika-yı Osmani Ziraat İstatistiği*.

96. Gould, "Pashas and Brigands," 183–89. See also Toksöz, *Nomads, Migrants, and Cotton*, 160–68.

97. Gould, "Pashas and Brigands," 180–82.

98. OA, DH-MKT 1289/55 (10 Şaban 1326 [24 August 1908]).

99. *A Handbook of Asia Minor*, 4:87.

100. Yaşar Kemal, *İnce Memed* (Istanbul: Çağlayan Yayınevi, 1955).

101. Gould, "Pashas and Brigands," 166.

102. OA, ŞD 2601/35, no. 5 (3 Temmuz 1308 [15 July 1892]), 2.

103. OA, ŞD 2601/35, no. 12 (7 Teşrinievvel 1308 [19 October 1892]).

104. McNeill, *The Mountains of the Mediterranean*, 247.

105. McNeill, *The Mountains of the Mediterranean*, 291.

106. OA, T-d 2210.

107. McNeill, *The Mountains of the Mediterranean*, 344.

108. The name Aydınlı does not appear in Langlois's original survey of the Cilicia region from the 1850s. Similarly, the name does not appear in the writings of Ahmed Cevdet from the period of settlement. An early reference to the Aydınlıs comes from Lieutenant Bennet, who mentioned them among various tribal groups in Cilicia. TNA, FO 222/8/2, p. 55, "Report on the Vilayet of Adana" (6 February 1882). The earliest reference that I have

found in the Ottoman archives is a telegram referring to a report about different minority communities in the Adana region that includes a description of the Aydınlıs. OA, DH-ŞFR 172/28 (11 Mart 1311 [23 March 1895]). It is hard to get a clear estimate of the Aydınlı population. In 1907, the *mutasarrıf* of Kozan reported around 2,000 Aydınlıs in the vicinity of Hadjin during the summer, but this would have been only one segment of their total population. He also noted that their households (*hane*) were made up of at least eight to ten people each. OA, DH-TMIK-M 258/17, no. 1 (30 Temmuz 1323 [12 August 1907]).

109. OA, DH-MKT 943/8, no. 1, Bahri Pasha to Dahiliye (23 Şubat 1320 [8 March 1905]).

110. The group killed a police corporal in one of these skirmishes. OA, Y-MTV 217/7 (2 Muharrem 1319 [9 April 1901]).

111. OA, DH-MKT 943/8, no. 2 (8 Muharrem 1323 [2 March 1905]).

112. OA, DH-TMIK-M 258/17, no. 1 (30 Temmuz 1323 [12 August 1907]).

113. OA, DH-TMIK-M 258/17, no. 7 (7 Teşrinisani 1323 [20 November 1907]).

114. OA, ŞD 2139/6, no. 12 (11 Şevval 1328 [2 October 1910]). In 1916, one nomadic group of forty-eight families of the Aydınlıs in the district of Tecirli was larger than half of the villages there. OA, DH-UMVM 114/37, no. 4 (24 Teşrinisani 1332 [5 December 1916]).

115. Ziya, *Tabsıra yahut Adana Temaşası*, 13–14, 17, 23.

116. Townshend, *Trade of the Vilayets of Aleppo and Adana*, 17.

117. *A Handbook of Asia Minor*, 4:715.

118. TNA, FO 195/2162, no. 1, Townshend to O'Conor (1 January 1904); Wylie, *Report for the Year 1908*, 4.

119. Childs, *Across Asia Minor on Foot*, 341.

120. OA, Y-PRK-UM 1/86 (23 Rebiulevvel 1297 [5 March 1880]); Y-A-HUS 290/21 (5 Şaban 1311 [11 February 1894]); DH-İD 44-2/1 (22 Ca 1329 [21 May 1911]); DH-MKT 2801/55 (13 Rebiulahir 1327 [2 July 1909]); Abdüllatif, *Orman ve Maden ve Ziraat Mecmuası*, vol. 9 (Istanbul: Estepan Matbaası, 1894). Lieutenant Bennet had recommended the expansion of eucalyptus cultivation in the Adana province during the 1880s. TNA, FO 222/8/2, no. 3, Bennet to Dufferin, Adana (6 February 1882). A financial report for Adana from 1903 also mentions the planting of trees to improve the area. OA, A-MKT-MHM 523/51 (16 Teşrinievvel [29 October 1903]).

121. For a global picture, see Diana K. Davis, *Resurrecting the Granary of Rome: Environmental History and French Colonial Expansion in North Africa* (Athens: Ohio University Press, 2007), 102–4; Jared Farmer, *Trees in Paradise: A California History* (New York: W.W. Norton, 2013); Carolyn Merchant, *Reinventing Eden: The Fate of Nature in Western Culture* (New York: Routledge, 2003).

122. OA, DH-MKT 1312/11 (25 Mayıs 1286 [6 June 1870]).

123. OA, DH-MKT 1478/56 (4 Cemaziyelevvel 1305 [18 January 1888]). The Ottoman government generally displayed a reluctance to enter into contracts with foreign

engineers and developers in Cilicia. See OA, ŞD 502/32 (4 Muharrem 1297 [18 December 1879]); DH-MKT 1235/78 (19 Muharrem 1326 [22 February 1908]); Toksöz, *Nomads, Migrants, and Cotton*, 95–96, 138–39.

124. See İbrahim Oğuz, *Tarsus şer'iyye sicillerine göre Mersin kentinin kuruluş öyküsü* (Mersin: Mersin Ticaret ve Sanayi Odası, 2006).

125. Toksöz, *Nomads, Migrants, and Cotton*, 95. See OA, A-DVN-MVL 24/3, no. 1 (5 Kanunusani 1298 [17 January 1883]) for complete terms of the contract.

126. See Chris Gratien, "The Ottoman Quagmire: Malaria, Swamps, and Settlement in the Late Ottoman Mediterranean," *International Journal of Middle East Studies* 49, no. 4 (2017).

127. Barker and Ainsworth, *Cilicia*, 114; Childs, *Across Asia Minor on Foot*, 449.

128. OA, A-MKT 76/26 (24 Rebiulahir 1263 [11 April 1847]); A-DVN 27/39 (10 Receb 1263 [2 July 1847]); MVL 241/25, no. 2 (12 Zilkade 1267 [8 September 1851]); A-AMD 34/16 (13 Safer 1268 [8 December 1851]); İ-DH 255/15722 (11 Şevval 1268 [29 July 1852]); A-MKT-UM 290/31 (1273 [1857]).

129. OA, İ-ŞD 1/31 (15 Zilhicce 1284 [8 April 1868]); Y-EE 35/94 (25 Cemaziyelevvel 1289 [31 July 1872]); ŞD 2215/65 (23 Şevval 1296 [10 October 1879]); DH-MKT 53/26 (13 Safer 1311 [26 August 1893]); BEO 2805/210320 (20 Safer 1324 [15 April 1906]); BEO 2724/204240 (20 Şevval 1320 [20 January 1903]); DH-MKT 2659/5 (21 Şevval 1326 [10 January 1904]).

130. OA, DH-İD 44–2/18, no.4 (24 Temmuz 1328 [6 August 1912]).

131. Toksöz, *Nomads, Migrants, and Cotton*, 23.

132. See OA, DH-MKT 1444/98 (18 Zilhicce 1304 [7 September 1887]); BEO 252/18871 (24 Muharrem 1311 [7 August 1893]); BEO 729/54656 (27 Receb 1313 [13 January 1896]); MF-MKT 436/31 (7 Şevval 1316 [18 February 1889]); DH-MKT 481/29 (7 Muharrem 1320 [26 April 1902]); DH-MKT 1169/32 (9 Rebiulevvel 1325 [22 April 1907]); DH-İD 6/29 (2 Safer 1330 [22 January 1912]).

133. OA, HRT-h 2042.

134. Barkley, *A Ride through Asia Minor and Armenia*, 179.

135. OA, DH-MKT 2352/92 (30 Muharrem 1318 [30 May 1900]); BEO 2246/168435 (15 Şevval 1321).

136. OA, DH-TMIK-M 249/44 (4 Cemaziyelahir 1325 [15 Temmuz 1907]).

137. OA, MF-MKT 567/33, no. 1 (23 Nisan 1317 [6 May 1901]); no. 2 (25 Nisan 1317 [8 May 1901]).

138. OA, DH-MKT 1760/79 (28 Muharrem 1308 [13 September 1890]).

139. The fevers were commonly understood to be over by November. Barkley, *A Ride through Asia Minor and Armenia*, 177.

140. Mağmumi, *Bir Osmanlı Doktoru'nun Anıları*, 175.

141. Hagop Babigian and Hagop Sargisyan, Ատանայի եղեռնը (Constantinople: K. Ardzagang, 1919), 18–20.

142. OA, BEO 3599/269906, no. 2 (22 Cemaziyelahir 1327 [27 June 1909]).

143. Davis, *Life in Asiatic Turkey*, 172.

144. Mağmumi, *Bir Osmanlı Doktoru'nun Anıları*, 177.

145. Mağmumi, *Bir Osmanlı Doktoru'nun Anıları*, 175.

146. Poghosean, Հաաքին քնհանուր պատմութիւն, 236–37.

147. İzmidi, *Sıtma*, 14. This proverb resembles a Khorasani saying alluding to the pitfalls of digging irrigation ditches (*karez*): "snake charmers, lion tamers and karez diggers very seldom die in their beds." Peter Christensen, *The Decline of Iranshahr: Irrigation and Environments in the History of the Middle East, 500 B.C. to A.D. 1500* (Copenhagen: Museum Tusculanum Press, 1993), 120.

148. This verse occurs with regard to later migrant life in Istanbul on a record by Seyfettin Sucu, an *arabesk* performer from Urfa who worked as a laborer in Adana before launching his musical career ("Anzılha," 45rpm [Istanbul: Urfa'nın Sesi, 1970]).

149. "Bir Tıb Mucizesi," *Yeni Adana*, 13 March 1956.

150. Murphey, *Regional Structure in the Ottoman Economy*, 7.

151. See Joost Jongerden and Jelle Verheij, *Social Relations in Ottoman Diyarbekir, 1870–1915* (Leiden: Brill, 2012). See also Chris Gratien, "The Rice Debates: Political Ecology in the Ottoman Parliament," in *Seeds of Power: Explorations in Ottoman Environmental History*, ed. Onur İnal and Yavuz Köse (Winwick, UK: White Horse Press, 2019), 211–18.

152. OA, DH-MUİ 13–3/10, no. 5 (2 Eylül 1325 [15 September 1909]).

153. See OA, DH-İD 99/6, no. 2 (16 Mayıs 1327 [29 May 1911]). See also *A Handbook of Asia Minor*, 4:712.

154. *Pirinç Ziraatı Kanunnamesi*, 4.

155. For an overview of quinine and its use in the Ottoman Empire, see Feza Günergun and Şeref Etker, "From Quinaquina to 'Quinine Law': A Bitter Chapter in the Westernization of Turkish Medicine," *Osmanlı Bilim Araştırmaları* 14, no. 2 (2013): 41–68.

156. Rengin Dramur, "Bursalı Hekim Ali Münşi'nin Kınakına risalesi," in *Bursa Halk Kültürü Sempozyumu (1.: 2002: Bursa)* (Bursa: Uludağ University, 2002), 51–55.

157. By the early twentieth century, Feyzi Pasha declared that "there is practically nobody who does not know that quinine is the medicine for malaria." İzmidi, *Sıtma*, 7.

158. *Sıhhiye Mecmuası*, vol. 11 (1911), 1095–1100.

159. Webb, *Humanity's Burden*, 112–14.

160. OA, DH-MKT 1660/113 (29 Muharrem 1307 [25 September 1889]).

161. OA, BEO 1115/83604 (5 Zilhicce 1315 [27 April 1898]); 1116/83691 (6 Zilhicce 1315 [28 April 1898]); 2195/164582 (23 Receb 1321 [15 October 1903]).

162. Nermin Ersoy, *Doktor Feyzullah İzmidi* (Kocaeli, Turkey: self published, 1998), 35. See also Davis, *Life in Asiatic Turkey*, 464–70.

163. An early indication of this phenomenon comes in 1876 from a request by

the Kaymakam of Mount Lebanon for immediate shipments of free medicine for the poor of the region, indicating that the poorest inhabitants of the mountain and particularly the Druze would otherwise suffer from malaria that year. OA, ŞD 262/53 (14 Cemaziyelahir 1293 [7 June 1876]).

164. The American Board of Commissioners for Foreign Missions opened a major hospital in Adana only after the massacres in 1909, but American missionaries were known for administering medical treatment among the populations they encountered long before that. Some were physicians themselves. See Cyril Haas, *Eight Months' Work in a Turkish Hospital* (New York: Marshall Brothers, 1912).

165. On the overlap of medicine and the notions of family and "care" in rural Turkey, see Sylvia Wing Önder, *We Have No Microbes Here: Healing Practices in a Turkish Black Sea Village* (Durham, NC: Carolina Press, 2007).

166. OA, ŞD 2116/27, no. 1 (14 Rebiulahir 1290 [30 May 1873]).

167. OA, ŞD 2120/46, no. 7 (20 Teşrinisani 1296 [2 December 1880]).

168. OA, ŞD 2116/27, no. 1 (14 Rebiulahir 1290 [11 June 1873]).

169. On the longer history of charity in the Ottoman Empire, see Amy Singer, *Charity in Islamic Societies* (Cambridge: Cambridge University Press, 2008).

170. OA, DH-MKT 2489/64 (7 Safer 1319 [26 May 1901]); DH-MKT 2517/48 (15 Rebiulahir 1319 [19 July 1901]). For more see Seçil Yılmaz, "Love in the Time of Syphilis: Medicine and Sex in the Ottoman Empire, 1860–1922," PhD diss., City University of New York, 2016.

171. OA, BEO 1713 128442 (19 Cemaziyelahir 1319 [3 September 1901]).

172. For more, see Ceren Gülser İlikan Rasimoğlu, "The Foundation of a Professional Group: Physicians in the Nineteenth Century Modernizing Ottoman Empire (1839–1908)," PhD diss., Boğaziçi University, 2012.

173. OA, A-MKT-UM 500/3 (13 Rebiulevvel 1278 [16 November 1861]); A-MKT-MHM 357/81 (23 Muharrem 1283 [7 June 1866]); DH-MKT 1551/12 (30 Muharrem 1306 [6 October 1888]); ŞD 269/42 (22 Şevval 1295 [19 October 1878]); Y-A-RES 6/41 (13 Şaban 1297 [21 July 1880]).

174. Mağmumi, *Bir Osmanlı Doktoru'nun Anıları*, 173–77.

175. OA, DH-MKT 1811/85 (12 Receb 1308 [21 February 1891]).

176. Arıkoğlu, *Hâtıralarım*, 42.

177. Terzian, *Ստամպայի կեանքը*, 32.

178. See Bedross Der Matossian, *Shattered Dreams of Revolution: From Liberty to Violence in the Late Ottoman Empire* (Stanford: Stanford University Press, 2014); Michelle U. Campos, *Ottoman Brothers: Muslims, Christians, and Jews in Early Twentieth-Century Palestine* (Stanford: Stanford University Press, 2011); Palmira Brummett, *Image and Imperialism in the Ottoman Revolutionary Press, 1908–1911* (Albany: SUNY Press, 2000); Aykut Kansu, *Politics in Post-Revolutionary Turkey, 1908–1913* (Leiden: Brill, 2000).

179. Terzian, *Ատանայի կեանքը*, 33.

180. Arıkoğlu, *Hâtıralarım*, 55; Terzian, *Ատանայի կեանքը*, 31.

181. See Teodik, *Ամիս մը ի Կիլիկիա*, 166–93.

182. *Կիլիկիոյ որբախնամ Վեհը. Յամձնածողով: Ստեկւագիր* (Constantinople: Kazmatun O. Arzuman, 1911), 41.

183. OA, DH-MKT 2813/75 (3 Mayıs 1325 [16 May 1909]).

184. Cemal Pasha's army was particularly credited with liberating the encircled villagers of Hadjin. See Rose Lambert, *Hadjin and the Armenian Massacres* (New York: Revell, 1911).

185. For a selection of published works on the massacres, see Raymond H. Kévorkian, *La Cilicie (1909–1921): Des massacres d'Adana au mandat français* (Paris: Revue d'histoire arménienne contemporaine, 1999); Bedross Der Matossian, "From Bloodless Revolution to Bloody Counterrevolution: The Adana Massacres of 1909," *Genocide Studies and Prevention* 6, no. 2 (2011): 152–73; Meltem Toksöz, "Multiplicity or Polarity: A Discursive Analysis of Post-1908 Violence in an Ottoman Region," in *Untold Histories of the Middle East*, ed. Amy Singer, Christoph K. Neumann, and Selçuk Akşin Somel (New York: Routledge, 2011); Hrachik Simonyan, *Destruction of Armenians in Cilicia, April 1909*, trans. Melissa Brown and Alexander Arzoumanian (London: Gomidas Institute, 2012); Tetsuya Sahara, *What Happened in Adana in April 1909?: Conflicting Armenian and Turkish Views* (Istanbul: Isis Press, 2013); Garabet Çalyan, Artin Arslanyan, and Hagop Babigyan, *1909 Adana Katliamı: Üç rapor*, ed. Ari Şekeryan and Taner Akçam (Istanbul: Aras, 2015); Yücel Güçlü, *Armenian Events of Adana in 1909: Cemal Pasa and Beyond* (Lanham, MD: Hamilton Books, 2018).

186. Doumanis, *Before the Nation*, 43.

187. A telegram from the governor of Bitlis to the Interior Ministry discussed an indecipherable letter originating from Dagestan in the North Caucasus: "Although it is written with Ottoman letters, it was not possible to transmit the letter with an encoded telegram because it is written in a language unknown here." OA, Y-PRK-DH 11/63 (17 Şaban 1318 [10 December 1900]). As Vladimir Hamed-Troyansky has shown, continued connection to points of emigration, as well as return migration, was common among migrants from the Caucasus. See Hamed-Troyansky, "Imperial Refuge," 320–485.

188. OA, A-MKT-MHM 523/51, no. 1 (16 Teşrinievvel 1319 [29 October 1903]); H. Yüksel Hançerli, *Giritli mübadillerin son durağı: Çukurova* (Adana, 2007).

189. Gough, "Anazarbus," 89.

190. CADN, 1SL/1/V, 287, vol. 1. I have chosen this district because it had relatively few Armenians before the war. Thus, the deportation of Armenians and the process of repatriation likely had a comparatively small impact on the demographic makeup of this particular district, making the data more readily pertinent for understanding the late Ottoman period.

191. A 2018 *Anadolu Ajansı* article and video featured interviews with the inhabitants of the village called Forlar, in apparent reference to the Fur people of Western Sudan's Darfur region. İsmihan Özgüven, "Çukurova'nın Afrikalıları," *Anadolu Ajansı*, 15 January 2018, https://www.aa.com.tr/tr/yasam/cukurovanin-afrikalilari/1031214.

192. TNA, FO 222/7/1, 1880 no. 2, Bennet to Goschen, Kaiserieh (3 August 1880); 1881 no. 10, Bennet to Goschen, Marash (11 May 1881).

193. See Houri Berberian, *Roving Revolutionaries: Armenians and the Connected Revolutions in the Russian, Iranian, and Ottoman Worlds* (Oakland: University of California Press, 2019).

194. See Janet Klein, *The Margins of Empire: Kurdish Militias in the Ottoman Tribal Zone* (Stanford, CA: Stanford University Press, 2011).

195. See Ramazan Hakkı Öztan, "Tools of Revolution: Global Military Surplus, Arms Dealers and Smugglers in the Late Ottoman Balkans, 1878–1908," *Past & Present* 237, no. 1 (2017): 167–95.

196. See Owen Miller, "Sasun 1894: Mountains, Missionaries and Massacres at the End of the Ottoman Empire," PhD diss., Columbia University, 2015; Jelle Verheij, "Diyarbekir and the Armenian Crisis of 1895," in *Social Relations in Ottoman Diyarbekir, 1870–1915*, ed. Joost Jongerden and Jelle Verheij (Leiden: Brill, 2012), 94.

197. Concerning Diyarbekir, Verheij argues that rural Kurds and Hamidiye regiments had little role ("Diyarbekir and the Armenian Crisis of 1895," 134).

198. Selim Deringil, "'The Armenian Question Is Finally Closed': Mass Conversions of Armenians in Anatolia during the Hamidian Massacres of 1895–1897," *Comparative Studies in Society and History* 51, no. 2 (2009): 344–71.

199. Gutman, *The Politics of Armenian Migration*, 100.

200. Toksöz, *Nomads, Migrants, and Cotton*, 145–46; Owen Robert Miller, "Conjuncture, Contingency, and Interpreting Violence in Late Ottoman Cilicia," MA thesis, Columbia University, 2008. See also OA, A-MKT-MHM 616/32, no. 1 (13 Teşrinisani 1311 [25 November 1895]).

201. Astourian, "The Silence of the Land," 55–81.

202. There were also tense moments around Hadjin, but the violence did not escalate. The British consul said that among officials in the Adana region, the *kaymakam* of Hadjin, who was a Circassian, was good and well liked. TNA, FO 195/1930, p. 63, Massy to Currie (17 July 1896). In the mid-1890s, there are many general reports of brigandage in Cilicia, some violence aimed at Armenians and some not. TNA, FO 195/1930, p. 93, Massy to Currie, Hadjin (3 September 1896). See OA, A-MKT-MHM 613/25; DH-MKT 411/76. See also TNA, FO 195/1930, p. 27, Christie (ABCFM) to Christmann, Mersin (25 February 1896).

203. OA, DH-ŞFR 196/21, Faik to Dahiliye, Adana (29 Temmuz 1312 [10 August 1896]).

204. OA, DH-ŞFR 200/37, Hayri to Dahiliye, Yarpuz (19 Teşrinievvel 1312 [31 October 1896]).

205. Wolfram Eberhard, "Nomads and Farmers in Southeastern Turkey: Problems of Settlement," *Oriens* 6, no. 1 (1953): 37–38.

206. OA, DH-MKT 2006/33 (6 Rebiulevvel 1310 [28 September 1892]).

207. OA, ŞD 2130/14, no. 2 (4 Safer 1319 [22 May 1901]).

208. See Erhan Alpaslan and Toroshan Özdamar, *Osmanlı arşiv belgelerine göre Çukurova (Anavarza) çiflikât-ı hümâyûn-u askerisi* (Istanbul: Hiperlink, 2019). Also OA, DH-MKT 226/32 (13 Şevval 1311 [19 April 1894]); 2345/125 (16 Muharrem 1318 [16 May 1900]); 2393/11 (25 Rebiulahir 1318 [22 August 1900]).

209. For a rough map, see end of Tsapalos and Walter, *Rapport sur le domaine impérial de Tchoucour-Ova*.

210. OA, A-MKT-MHM 529/13, no. 12 (7 Rebiulahir 1325 [7 May 1907]).

211. Bedross Der Matossian, "Ethnic Politics in Post-Revolutionary Ottoman Empire: Armenians, Arabs, and Jews during the Second Constitutional Period (1908–1909)," PhD diss., Columbia University, 2008, 449–50.

212. OA, A-MKT-MHM 529/13, no. 12 (7 Rebiulahir 1325 [7 May 1907]).

213. OA, BEO 3521/264057 (13 Mart 1325 [26 March 1909]).

214. OA, BEO 3318/248781, no. 4–7 (17 Haziran 1324 [30 June 1908]); DH-MKT 2640/26, no. 7 (23 Eylül 1324 [6 October 1908]); 2672/71 (17 Teşrinisani 1324 [30 November 1908]); ŞD 2137/27, no. 1, Bilal to Şura-yı Devlet, Aziziye (3 Eylül 1323 [16 September 1907]).

215. Toksöz, *Nomads, Migrants, and Cotton*, 145, 55–56. See also TNA, FO 195/1930, p. 105 (7 November 1896); FO 195/2095, no. 28, Massy to Conor, Adana (21 May 1901); Der Matossian, "Ethnic Politics in Post-Revolutionary Ottoman Empire," 452–68.

216. Simonyan, *Destruction of Armenians in Cilicia*, 104.

217. Koudoulian, Հայ լեռը, 43. See Klein, *The Margins of Empire*, 107–14.

218. Der Matossian, "Ethnic Politics in Post-Revolutionary Ottoman Empire," 467–71.

219. Babigian and Sargisyan, *Ատանայի եղեռնը*, 18–20.

220. TNA, FO 195/2306, p. 109 (21 April 1909).

221. OA, DH-ŞFR 413/110, Zihni to Dahiliye, Adana (13 May 1325 [26 May 1909]).

222. OA, DH-MKT 2843/31 (30 Mayıs 1325 [13 June 1909]).

223. İlkay Yılmaz, *Serseri, Anarşist ve Fesadın Peşinde: II. Abdülhamid dönemi güvenlik politikaları ekseninde mürur tezkereleri, pasaportlar ve otel kayıtları* (Istanbul: Tarih Vakfı, 2014).

224. OA, DH-TMIK 210/56 (7 Şevval 1323 [22 November 1905]).

225. OA, ŞD 2126/7, no. 2, Rıza to Askeri (8 Ağustos 1310 [20 August 1894]); no. 3, Faik to Sadaret, Adana (11 Eylül 1310 [23 September 1894]).

226. See Gutman, *The Politics of Armenian Migration*.

227. For example, in September 1870, a dagger-wielding man assaulted a police corporal on the streets of Adana. The stabbing became an international affair when it turned out he had come to Adana for work from the other side of the border with Iran. OA, İ-DA 8/194 (14 Cemaziyelahir 1287 [11 September 1870]).

228. See Blumı, *Ottoman Refugees*, 40–41.

229. Bet-Shlimon, *City of Black Gold*, 5.

230. Teodik, *Ամեն տեղ ի Կիլիկիա*, 66–71.

231. Toksöz, *Nomads, Migrants, and Cotton*, 198.

232. Childs, *Across Asia Minor on Foot*, 343.

233. See Hilmar Kaiser, "Baghdad Railway Politics and the Socio-economic Transformation of the Çukurova," PhD diss., European University Institute, 2001, 248–94.

234. OA, DH-İD 183-2/7, no. 2, 4 Teşrinisani 1329 (17 November 1913).

235. See OA, HR-SYS 2272/8; Tsapalos and Walter, *Rapport sur le domaine impérial de Tchoucour-Ova*.

236. Abdullah Cevdet, "Adana: Mısır-ı Ferda," *İçtihad*, 15 Haziran 1327 [29 June 1911]; Abdullah Cevdet, "Adana Ferda'nın Mısırdır," *İçtihad*, 1 Haziran 1327 [15 June 1911].

237. See Moore, *Capitalism in the Web of Life*.

238. Jennifer L. Derr, *The Lived Nile: Environment, Disease, and Material Colonial Economy in Egypt* (Stanford: Stanford University Press, 2019), 99–126.

Chapter 4

1. OA, DH-İD 206/10, no. 8 (25 Mayıs 1330 [7 June 1914]).

2. See Eugene L. Rogan, *The Fall of the Ottomans: The Great War in the Middle East* (New York: Basic Books, 2015).

3. Çiğdem Oğuz, *Moral Crisis in the Ottoman Empire: Society, Politics, and Gender during World War I* (London: I. B. Tauris, 2021); Nazan Maksudyan, *Ottoman Children and Youth during World War I* (Syracuse, NY: Syracuse University Press, 2019); Yiğit Akın, *When the War Came Home* (Stanford: Stanford University Press, 2018); Elif Mahir Metinsoy, *Ottoman Women during World War I* (Cambridge: Cambridge University Press, 2017); Yücel Yanıkdağ, *Healing the Nation: Prisoners of War, Medicine and Nationalism in Turkey, 1914–1939* (Edinburgh: Edinburgh University Press, 2014); M. Talha Çiçek, *War and State Formation in Syria: Cemal Pasha's Governorate during World War I, 1914–1917* (London: Routledge, 2014).

4. Akın, *When the War Came Home*, 51.

5. For good discussion of the Ottoman Empire's geopolitical position during World War I, see Mustafa Aksakal, *The Ottoman Road to War in 1914: The Ottoman Empire and the First World War* (Cambridge: Cambridge University Press, 2008). Also Mustafa Aksakal, "The Ottoman Empire," in *Empires at War: 1911–1923*, ed. Robert Gerwarth and Erez Manela (Oxford: Oxford University Press, 2014), 18–19. The Ottoman Em-

pire began mobilization in August 1914 as preparation for a state of "armed neutrality" before joining the war. M. Şükrü Hanioğlu, *A Brief History of the Late Ottoman Empire* (Princeton, NJ: Princeton University Press, 2008), 177.

6. Ahmet Emin Yalman, *Turkey in the World War* (New Haven: Yale University Press, 1930), 85.

7. Yalman, *Turkey in the World War*, 107.

8. OA, DH-İ-UM 59–2/1 31, nos. 12–13, Hakkı to Dahiliye (30 Teşrinisani 1331 [13 December 1915]).

9. Mehmed Fasih, *Kanlısırt Günlüğü: Mehmed Fasih Bey'in Çanakkale anıları*, ed. Murat Çulcu (Istanbul: Arba, 1997). Salim Tamari offers substantial treatment of this diary in *Year of the Locust: A Soldier's Diary and the Erasure of Palestine's Ottoman Past* (Berkeley: University of California Press, 2011), 13–17.

10. Erik Jan Zürcher, *The Young Turk Legacy and Nation Building* (London: I. B. Tauris, 2010), 171–72.

11. Yalman, *Turkey in the World War*, 253.

12. TKA, 817/16, Hacı Süleyman to Hilal-ı Ahmer, Kars-ı Zülkadriye (29 July 1917).

13. See Mehmet Beşikçi, *The Ottoman Mobilization of Manpower in the First World War* (Leiden: Brill, 2012).

14. Zürcher, *The Young Turk Legacy*, 177.

15. OA, DH-EUM-6-Şb 19/64, no. 5 (8 October 1917).

16. OA, DH-EUM-6-Şb 11/31, no 2 (6 Teşrinisani 1332 [19 November 1916]); 20/10, no. 13 (8 July 1917); 19/64, no. 6 (12 October 1917); DH-EUM-6-Şb 28/66, no. 5. (9 November 1917).

17. See OA, DH-EUM-6-Şb 2/4, no. 8, Adana gendarmerie to Dahiliye (7 Eylül 1331 [20 September 1915]); 27/25, no. 9, Haleb Mülkiye Müfettişi Şekib to Dahiliye (15 September 1917).

18. Raymond H. Kévorkian, *The Armenian Genocide: A Complete History* (London: I. B. Tauris, 2011), 250.

19. Kévorkian, *The Armenian Genocide*, 319–35.

20. There is not space to cover exactly what different historians have meant by the term "genocide" or how different authors have defined the case of the Armenian genocide. For a select list of works on the subject in English that address the question of genocide directly, see Ronald Grigor Suny, *"They can live in the desert but nowhere else": A History of the Armenian Genocide* (Princeton, NJ: Princeton University Press, 2015); Fatma Müge Göçek, *Denial of Violence: Ottoman Past, Turkish Present, and Collective Violence against the Armenians, 1789–2009* (Oxford: Oxford University Press, 2015); Taner Akçam, *The Young Turks' Crime against Humanity: The Armenian Genocide and Ethnic Cleansing in the Ottoman Empire* (Princeton, NJ: Princeton University Press, 2012); Uğur Ümit Üngör, *The Making of Modern Turkey: Nation and State in Eastern Anatolia,*

1913–50 (London: Oxford University Press, 2011); Ronald Grigor Suny, Fatma Müge Göçek, and Norman M. Naimark, *A Question of Genocide: Armenians and Turks at the End of the Ottoman Empire* (Oxford: Oxford University Press, 2011); Donald Bloxham, *The Great Game of Genocide: Imperialism, Nationalism, and the Destruction of the Ottoman Armenians* (Oxford: Oxford University Press, 2005).

21. For a work that attempts to offer a comprehensive overview of these measures, see Kévorkian's *The Armenian Genocide*, which treats the deportation phases in district by district, leading to significant repetition but creating a very thorough catalog of available information about the particularities of each locale. Kévorkian, *The Armenian Genocide*, 265–698. Actual figures regarding mortality of Armenians during World War I vary widely and have been hotly debated and politicized. See Justin McCarthy, *Muslims and Minorities: The Population of Ottoman Anatolia and the End of the Empire* (New York: New York University Press, 1983), 130; Fuat Dündar, *Crime of Numbers: The Role of Statistics in the Armenian Question* (New Brunswick, NJ: Transaction, 2010), 153. Another issue involved in the ambiguity is that of conversion to Islam in order to escape deportation. Some scholars have argued that a significant percentage of the Armenian population, as much as 5–10 percent, converted for that purpose, and that it appears many Armenian soldiers converted during the war for similar reasons. Zürcher, *The Young Turk Legacy*, 173. Kevorkian also mentions mass forced conversion in Syria under the government of Cemal Pasha in *The Armenian Genocide*, 681–82. The CUP was concerned that conversion was being used as a survival strategy. For example, Talat Pasha issued a telegram in July 1915 saying, "It is becoming understood that some of the deported Armenians are being left in their places due to their embrace of Islam [*ihtida etmeleri*] and even that some civil servants are serving as an intermediary for them." He stressed repeatedly that "it is absolutely not permissible to make exceptional treatment with regard to converts [*mühtediler*]." OA, DH-ŞFR 54A/49 (7 Temmuz 1331 [20 July 1915]). See also Sato Moughalian, *Feast of Ashes: The Life and Art of David Ohannessian* (Stanford: Stanford University Press, 2020), 105–27.

22. This figure is based on the prewar Ottoman census and is therefore a conservative estimate. Karpat, *Ottoman Population*, 172–73, 86–87.

23. Kévorkian, *The Armenian Genocide*, 585–90.

24. Kévorkian, *The Armenian Genocide*, 594. İsmail Hakkı had spent the summer in Marash—as Adana governors so often did—where he received a telegram from Talat Pasha in August 1915 requesting again that all Armenians who had not been sent off to be deported, should be sent. OA, DH-ŞFR 54A/271 (22 Temmuz 1331 [4 August 1915]). Ali Münif Bey claimed that he himself was dispatched to Adana to see to the initial deportations personally; *Ali Münif Bey'in hâtıraları*, ed. Taha Toros (Istanbul: Isis, 1996), 77–79. See Akçam, *The Young Turks' Crime against Humanity*, 19–20. There were many prominent figures in the Ottoman Empire by the name of İsmail Hakkı, which has been the source of confusion in some of the historiography. The İsmail Hakkı in

question was born in Prishtina in 1872 and the son of an Ottoman officer, Emin Bey. Previous to Adana, he had served as an official in Bitlis, a point of origin for many of the workers in Çukurova, and he published a lengthy report on the Kurdistan region. Hakkı, *Raporlarım* (Adana: Osmanlı Matbaası, 1914); Yıldıray Yıldırım, "Bir Devlet Adamı Olarak İsmail Hakkı Bey ve Adana Valiliği Dönemindeki Faaliyetleri (1914–1916)," in *II. Uluslararası Multidisipliner Çalışmaları Kongresi (4–5 Mayıs 2018, Adana-Türkiye)*, ed. Erdem Çanak and M. Fatih Sansar (Ankara: Akademisyen Kitabevi, 2018), 92.

25. ABC 16.19.5, Reel 672, p. 292A, "The Exiling of the Armenians: Adana District"; Kévorkian, *The Armenian Genocide*, 595. Also: OA, DH-EUM-2-Şb 73/48, no. 1, Hakkı to Dahiliye, Adana (15 Eylül 1331 [28 September 1915]); DH-İ-UM 59–2/1 31, nos. 12–13, Hakkı to Dahiliye (30 Teşrinisani 1331 [13 December 1915]).

26. See Kévorkian, *The Armenian Genocide*, 594, 674. The catholicos of Sis wrote to Cemal Pasha for help as the Cilician Armenians were first being deported in the summer of 1915. Zakaria Bzdigean, Կիլիկեան Կսկիծներ *(1903–1915)* (Beirut: Tparan Hrazdan, 1927), 194. American missionaries commented that the Armenians of Adana appeared to be in much better shape than those of most other provinces and that there was an unusual number of men in their caravans. ABC, 16.9.5, Reel 670, p. 145A, "Miss Frearson's Experience and Observations in Turkey"; Reel 672, p. 292A, "The Exiling of the Armenians: Adana District."

27. By July 1915, the Catholicos of Sis counted more than 13,000 Cilician Armenians from other rural towns and villages who had arrived in Aleppo as well as Al-Bab and Manbij to the northeast. Among them were over 4000 Armenians from Hadjin alone. Կիլիկեան Կսկիծներ, 193. The incremental deportation of Armenians from the Cilicia region continued over the following months. A rather thorough report on the Christian population of the Adana province and a chart indicating the number of Armenians deported as of September 1915 reflects the state of affairs at that time, although more deportations would occur subsequently. OA, DH-EUM-2-Şb 73/48, no. 1, Hakkı to Dahiliye, Adana (15 Eylül 1331 [28 September 1915]).

28. OA, DH-İ-UM 59–2/1 31, nos. 23–25, Hakkı to Dahiliye (24 Eylül 1331 [7 October 1915]).

29. BN, Papiers Andonian, Déportation des Arméniens de Rassoulein, p. 8 "Հաճընցի Հովհաննէս Ս. Մանուկեանի պատմութիւնը." For more accounts from this region, see Khatchig Mouradian, *The Resistance Network: The Armenian Genocide and Humanitarianism in Ottoman Syria, 1915–1918* (East Lansing: Michigan State University Press, 2021), 121–38. See also Marc Nichanian, "Testimony: From Document to Monument," in *The Armenian Genocide: Cultural and Ethical Legacies*, ed. Richard G. Hovannisian (New Brunswick, NJ: Transaction, 2007), 41–64.

30. On Chechen settlement in Ras al-Ayn, see Dolbee, "The Locust and the Starling," 128–40.

31. Samuel Dolbee, "The Desert at the End of Empire: An Environmental History of the Armenian Genocide," *Past & Present* 247, no. 1 (2020): 203.

32. See ALON-UNOG, Records of the Nansen International Refugee Office, 1920–47, "Registers of Inmates of the Armenian Orphanage in Aleppo," for more than 1,000 case files of orphans in Aleppo, most of whom had spent years in Muslim households of Northern Syria even after the war ended.

33. ALON-UNOG, Records of the Nansen International Refugee Office, 1920–47, "Registers of Inmates of the Armenian Orphanage in Aleppo," no. 927 (admission date 22 January 1926).

34. Murat Bardakçı, *Talât Paşa'nın evrak-ı metrûkesi: sadrazam Talât Paşa'nın özel arşivinde bulunan Ermeni tehciri konusundaki belgeler ve hususî yazışmalar* (Istanbul: Everest Yayinlari, 2008). Ara Sarafian has published an analysis of the figures detailed in Bardakçı's work, in English. On the province of Adana, see Ara Sarafian, *Talaat Pasha's Report on the Armenian Genocide, 1917* (London: Taderon Press, 2011), 44; Vahé Tachjian, *La France en Cilicie et en Haute-Mésopotamie: Aux confins de la Turquie, de la Syrie et de l'Irak (1919–1933)* (Paris: Karthala, 2004), 63.

35. ABC, 16.9.5, Reel 670, p. 96A, Edith Cold, "Exile of the Armenian People of Hadjin and Vicinity" (16 December 1915).

36. ABC, 16.9.5, Reel 670, "Relief Work."

37. Grigoris Balakian, *Armenian Golgotha*, trans. Peter Balakian and Aris G. Sevag (New York: Alfred A. Knopf, 2009), 320.

38. Balakian, *Armenian Golgotha*, 335.

39. Ümit Üngör refers to the transport of Kurdish populations during the war as an explicit policy of deportation that began in 1916 immediately after the deportations of Armenians had concluded. This policy was in Üngör's formulation an attempt to bring about further ethnolinguistic homogeneity in Eastern Anatolia by removing other, non-Turkish elements. *The Making of Modern Turkey*, 110. See also Akın, *When the War Came Home*, 177; Fuat Dündar, *Modern Türkiye'nin Şifresi: İttihat ve Terakki'nin etnisite mühendisliği, 1913–1918* (Istanbul: İletişim, 2008); Kasaba, *A Moveable Empire*, 135–39.

40. For example, see OA, DH-ŞFR 54/95, Ali Münif to Suriye (9 Haziran 1331 [22 June 1915]). For more on the logic of these policies, see Akçam, *The Young Turks' Crime against Humanity*, 50–53.

41. OA, DH-ŞFR 528/31, Provincial Treasurer Ahmed Besim to Dahiliye, Adana (27 Temmuz 1332 [9 August 1916]).

42. OA, DH-ŞFR 528/12 Şükrü General Director of Muhacirin in Adana to Dahiliye, Adana (24 Temmuz 1332 [6 August 1916]).

43. OA, DH-SN-THR 77/47, no. 1, Nüfus to Dahiliye (14 November 1917).

44. Üngör, *The Making of Modern Turkey*, 116.

45. Some files about the *muhacirs* who came to Adana during the war period may also be found in the archives of the republican period (CA). For example, some *muhacirs*

were settled in the predominantly Christian villages near the city of Adana, such as Hristiyanköyü, İncirlik, and Şeyh Murad in 1916. CA, 272-0-0-11 8/6/4, no. 2 Cevdet to Dahiliye, Adana (23 Mart 1332 [5 April 1916]).

46. OA, DH-ŞFR 547/7, Cevdet to Dahiliye, Adana (1 March 1917).

47. OA, DH-ŞFR 549/92, Cevdet to Dahiliye, Adana (28 March 1917).

48. OA, DH-ŞFR 74/25, Talat to Urfa Mutasarrıflığı (3 March 1917).

49. OA, DH-ŞFR 79/71, Dahiliye to Adana Province (8 August 1917).

50. OA, DH-ŞFR 587/151, Nazım to Dahiliye, Adana (22 June 1918).

51. ABC, 16.9.5, Reel 672, no. 343, Woodley to Barton, Marash (29 August 1914).

52. *Memalik-i Osmaniye'nin 1329 senesine mahsus Ziraat İstatistiği*.

53. OA, BEO 4340/325451, no. 3 (25 Kanunusani 1330 [7 February 1915]); "Supplement to Commerce Reports," in *Daily Consular and Trade Reports* (Washington, DC: US Chamber of Commerce, 1915), 8.

54. OA, BEO 4340/325451, no. 3 (25 Kanunusani 1330 [7 February 1915]).

55. OA, MV 196/121, (11 Şubat 1330 [24 February 1915]); "Supplement to Commerce Reports," 8.

56. Toksöz, *Nomads, Migrants, and Cotton*, 180.

57. OA, BEO 4341/325518, no. 3 (29 Kanunusani 1330 [11 February 1915]); MV 196/135 (13 Rebiulahir 1333 [15 Şubat 1330/28 February 1915]).

58. OA, MV 196/124 (9 Rebiulahir 1333 [11 Şubat 1330/24 February 1915]); *Adana vilayetinin 1330 senesi muvazene-i hususiyesinin masraf müfredatı* (Adana: Adana Vilayet Matbaası, 1330 [1914–15]), 3.

59. CADN, 1SL/1/V, 304, "Description des produits agricoles et autres produits exportés du Vilayet Adana pendant l'année 1913" (11 April 1919); *Memalik-i Osmaniye'nin 1329 senesine mahsus Ziraat İstatistiği*, 36. Doughty Wylie's 1909 report on agriculture in Adana indicated that most of Adana's wheat remained in the Ottoman Empire and that 25 percent of the barley and 75 percent of the oats went to Britain. Wylie, *Report for the Year 1908*, 15.

60. OA, DH-ŞFR 436/25, Hakkı to Dahiliye (27 Temmuz 1330 [9 August 1914]).

61. "Supplement to Commerce Reports," 8.

62. ABC, 16.9.5, Reel 672, no. 343, Woodley to Barton (2 October 1914).

63. OA, DH-ŞFR 445/25, Hakkı to Dahiliye, Adana (7 Teşrinievvel 1330 [20 October 1914]).

64. "Supplement to Commerce Reports," 8; *Memalik-i Osmaniye'nin 1329 senesine mahsus Ziraat İstatistiği*, 315.

65. OA, DH-ŞFR 46/60 (9 Teşrinievvel 1330 [22 October 1914]).

66. OA, DH-SYS 123-09/21-08, no. 30 (18 Mart 1331 [31 March 1915]).

67. OA, DH-SYS 123-09/21-08, no. 29 (3 Mart 1331 [16 March 1915]).

68. OA, DH-UMVM 82/61, no. 4 (17 Kanunusani 1331 [30 January 1916]).

69. OA, DH-İ-UM 59–1/1–20, no. 4, Ahmed Nesimi to Dahiliye (27 Cemaziyelahir 1333/29 Nisan 1331 [12 May 1915]).

70. OA, DH-İ-UM 59–1/1–20, no. 11, Mücteba et al to Dahiliye (26 Nisan 1331 [9 May 1915]).

71. OA, DH-İ-UM 59–1/1–20, no. 9 (9 Receb 1333/10 Mayıs 1331 [23 May 1915]).

72. Though the 1915 famine and locust invasion are intertwined in popular memory, as Graham Pitts notes, the locusts alone were not the most important factor in Lebanon's wartime famine. Pitts, "Fallow Fields," 45–53. See also Elizabeth Williams, "Economy, Environment, and Famine: World War I from the Perspective of the Syrian Interior," in *Syria in World War I: Politics, Economy, and Society*, ed. M. Talha Çiçek (New York: Routledge, 2016); Zachary J. Foster, "The 1915 Locust Attack in Syria and Palestine and Its Role in the Famine during the First World War," *Middle Eastern Studies* 51, no. 3 (2015): 370–94.

73. See Ertan Gökmen, "Batı Anadolu'da Çekirge Felaketi (1850–1915)," *Belleten* 74, no. 269 (April 2010).

74. ABC, 16.9.5, Reel 670, p. 96A, Edith Cold, "Exile of the Armenian People of Hadjin and Vicinity" (16 December 1915).

75. OA, DH-İ-UM 56/2, no. 3 (24 Mayıs 1331 [6 June 1915]); 56/4, no. 5 (2 Haziran 1331 [15 June 1915]).

76. ABC, 16.9.5, Reel 669, Chambers to Barton (31 October 1915).

77. Arıkoğlu, *Hâtıralarım*, 69.

78. These numbers should only be taken as approximations. *1325 senesi Asya ve Afrika-yı Osmani Ziraat İstatistiği*; *Memalik-i Osmaniye'nin 1329 senesine mahsus Ziraat İstatistiği*. See also OA, DH-İ-UM-EK 10/28, no. 1 (20 Ağustos 1331 [2 September 1915]).

79. Şevket Pamuk, "The Ottoman Economy in World War I," in *The Economics of World War I*, ed. S. N. Broadberry and Mark Harrison (Cambridge: Cambridge University Press, 2005), 120. The fact that Germany and the other allies of the Ottomans were experiencing similar agrarian woes may have been a major exacerbating factor. Vedat Eldem, *Harp ve mütareke yıllarında Osmanlı İmparatorluğu'nun ekonomisi* (Ankara: Türk Tarih Kurumu, 1994), 39.

80. OA, DH-İ-UM-EK 10/28, no. 1 (20 Ağustos 1331 [2 September 1915]).

81. OA, DH-İ-UM-EK 10/92, no. 2 (22 Ağustos 1331 [4 September 1915]).

82. OA, DH-İ-UM-EK 10/92, no. 3 (14 Eylül 1331 [27 September 1915]).

83. TNA, FO 925/41301.

84. USEK, Sursock, 19249/197, to Durry (31 May 1915); 260, to Durry (15 May 1916); 272, to Durry (29 September 1916).

85. USEK, Sursock, 19249/283, to Durry (2 May 1917).

86. USEK, Sursock, 19249/302, to Durry (24 April 1918); 335 (12 September 1918); 19249/295–96 (2 August 1918); 328 (31 July 1918).

87. Arıkoğlu, *Hâtıralarım*, 69. Üngör and Polatel refer to this quotation and provide many other details about the specific economic impacts of the deportation of Armenians on the economy and life of the Adana region (*Confiscation and Colonization*, 107–32).

88. ABC 16.9.5, Reel 671, p. 7, Haas to Barton (9 October 1915).

89. OA, DH-İ-UM 59–2/1 31, no. 23–25, Hakkı to Dahiliye (24 Eylül 1331 [7 October 1915]).

90. OA, DH-İ-UM 59–2/1 31, nos. 12–13, Hakkı to Dahiliye (30 Teşrinisani 1331 [13 December 1915]).

91. ABC 16.9.5, Reel 672, p. 292A, Elizabeth Webb, "The Exiling of the Armenians: Adana District."

92. OA, DH-İ-UM 98–2/1–51, no. 4, Hakkı to Dahiliye, Adana (15 Kanunusani 1331 [28 January 1916]).

93. OA, DH-ŞFR 667/43 (27 Kanunusani 1331 [9 February 1916]).

94. *1325 senesi Asya ve Afrika-yı Osmani Ziraat İstatistiği*, 14; *Memalik-i Osmaniye'nin 1329 senesine mahsus Ziraat İstatistiği*, 36.

95. OA, DH-ŞFR 667/43 (27 Kanunusani 1331 [9 February 1916]).

96. OA, DH-İ-UM 88–3/4–26, no. 10, Ayşe to Dahiliye, Adana (31 Kanunusani 1331 [13 February 1916]).

97. OA, DH-İ-UM-EK 15/51, no. 2, Münire et al to Dahiliye, Tarsus (30 Kanunusani 1331 [12 February 1916]).

98. See Yiğit Akın, "War, Women, and the State: The Politics of Sacrifice in the Ottoman Empire during the First World War," *Journal of Women's History* 26, no. 3 (2014): 12–35; Metinsoy, *Ottoman Women during World War I*, 63–84.

99. ABC, 16.9.5, Reel 672, p. 394A, E. C. Woodley, "The Currency Situation in Turkey, 1914–1919."

100. Şevket Pamuk, *A Monetary History of the Ottoman Empire* (Cambridge: Cambridge University Press, 2000), 223.

101. ABC, 16.9.5, Reel 672, p. 394A, E. C. Woodley, "The Currency Situation in Turkey, 1914–1919."

102. OA, DH-ŞFR 667/43 (27 Kanunusani 1331 [9 February 1916]).

103. OA, DH-İ-UM-EK 15/57 (1 Şubat 1331 [14 February 1916]); DH-UMVM 136/20 (3 Şubat 1331 [16 February 1916]).

104. OA, DH-İ-UM 98–2/1–51, no. 31, Azmi to Dahiliye, Beirut (11 Nisan 1332 [24 April 1916]).

105. I was unable to determine what role, if any, remittances from the United States or elsewhere played in the economy of Cilicia during the war. See Graham Auman Pitts, "The Ecology of Migration: Remittances in World War I Mount Lebanon," *Arab Studies Journal* 26, no. 2 (2018): 103–30.

106. Eldem, *Harp ve mütareke yıllarında Osmanlı İmparatorluğu'nun ekonomisi*, 37.

107. Cemal Pasha warned in October 1917 of impending famine in Adana if a new governor was not sent. OA, DH-ŞFR 569/42, Cemal to Dahiliye, Adana (22 October 1917). Cemal Pasha and Cevdet Bey had some major disagreements regarding provisioning methods during the prior year. OA, DH-İ-UM-EK 36/68 (16 July 1917). See also OA, DH-İ-UM 13–1/2–37, no. 2, Mustafa Sırrı to Dahiliye (27 January 1918).

108. OA, DH-İ-UM 20–02/2–50 (6 March 1918).

109. Yeghiayean, Ստանայի հայոց պատմութիւն, 821. The poem is in Armeno-Turkish.

110. Yalman, *Turkey in the World War*, 129–30.

111. OA, DH-İ-UM 59–2/1 39, no. 2 (13 Kanunuevvel 1331 [26 December 1915]).

112. OA, DH-ŞFR 76/136, Mustafa Sırrı to Syria, Beirut, Aleppo, Adana, Jerusalem, and İçil (15 May 1917).

113. Mehmed Esad, *Fenni ve Ameli Orduda Ziraat* (Istanbul: Matbaa-ı Askeriye, 1333 [1917]).

114. Hüseyin Tayfur, "Patates Ziraatı," and Y. Sami, "Mısır Ziraatı," both in *Çiftçiler Derneği Mecmuası* 1, no. 6 (1 March 1917).

115. *Çiftçiler Derneği Mecmuası* 1, no. 4 (11 December 1916): 58–59; M. N., "Bahçede," *Çiftçiler Derneği Mecmuası* 1, no. 9 (15 June 1917): 136–38.

116. OA, DH-UMVM 82/61, no. 8 (17 March 1917).

117. Mogens Pelt, "Remembering Home: Christians, Muslims and the Outside World in Late-Ottoman Cilicia and Cappadocia," in *Contested Memories and the Demands of the Past*, ed. C. Raudvere (Cham, Switzerland: Palgrave Macmillan, 2017), 81–105.

118. OA, İ-DUİT 81/9, no. 2 (4 April 1917). See Z. Koylu and N. Doğan, "Birinci dünya savaşı sırasında Osmanlı devleti'nde sıtma mücadelesi ve bu amaçla yapılan yasal düzenlemeler," *Türkiye Parazitolojii Dergisi* 34, no. 3 (2010).

119. OA, DH-EUM-SSM 27/36, no. 9 (3 October 1917); no. 2 (1 July 1918).

120. OA, DH-EUM-SSM 22/36, no. 3 (27 May 1918).

121. For example, a French writer covering the history of the French occupation in Cilicia described the region as "Egypt with the Alps," referring to the well-watered Çukurova plain and the nearby snow-capped Taurus Mountains. Paul Du Véou, *La Passion de la Cilicie, 1919–1922* (Paris: Paul Geuthner, 1937), 312.

122. RAC, RG 1.1, Series 805, Box 1, Folder 1, Ralph Collins, "Public Health in Turkey" (1926), 64–65; Helmut Becker, "I. Dünya Savaşında (1914–1918) Osmanlı Cephesinde Askerî Tababet ve Eczacılık (Alman Kaynaklarına Göre)" (Istanbul University, 1983), 49–54.

123. This does not mean that malaria mortality in the entire area was 50 percent, but rather solely among the patients who were taken into care at the special military

hospital in Belemedik. Ernest Basso and Eugen Bentmann, *Deux rapports sur le paludisme en Asie Mineure, en Syrie et en Palestine* (Geneva: League of Nations, 1925), 21.

124. H. Flebbe, "Ueber die Malaria im Taurus (Kleinasian)," *Deutsche Medizinische Wochenschrift* 45, no. 5 (April 1919): 126.

125. Becker, "I. Dünya Savaşında (1914–1918) Osmanlı Cephesinde Askerî Tababet," 51.

126. Basso and Bentmann, *Deux rapports sur le paludisme*, 21.

127. Basso and Bentmann, *Deux rapports sur le paludisme*, 19.

128. Ekrem Tok, "Adana mıntakasında Sıtma mücadelesi," *Sıhhiye Mecmuası* 5, nos. 31–32 (November 1929): 1302.

129. O. Demirhan and M. Kasap, "Bloodfeeding behavior of Anopheles sacharovi in Turkey," *Journal of the American Mosquito Control Association* 11, no. 1 (1995).

130. Norbert Becker, *Mosquitoes and Their Control* (Berlin: Springer, 2010), 170–77. Robert Sallares refers to *sacharovi* as the second leading malaria vector in the Mediterranean. Sallares, *Malaria and Rome*, 35. Sandra Sufian refers to *Anopheles sacharovi* as the foremost malaria vector in Palestine. Sufian, *Healing the Land and the Nation*, 76.

131. Basso and Bentmann, *Deux rapports sur le paludisme*, 24.

132. Becker, *Mosquitoes and Their Control*, 185.

133. Rafet Ahmet Pek, *Sıtma Notları* (Adana: Türksözü, 1945), 34. A study of malaria in Iran noted that *Anopheles superpictus* was found at altitudes greater than 2,000 m. M. A. Oshaghi et al., "The Anopheles superpictus Complex: Introduction of a New Malaria Vector Complex in Iran," *Bulletin de la Société de pathologie exotique* 101, no. 5 (2008): 429.

134. Jonathan S. McMurray, *Distant Ties: Germany, the Ottoman Empire, and the Construction of the Baghdad Railway* (Westport, CT: Greenwood Press, 2001), 88–89.

135. McMurray, *Distant Ties*, 118.

136. Basso and Bentmann, *Deux rapports sur le paludisme*, 24.

137. CADN, 1SL/1/V, 204, vol. 5—Comptabilité de la Foire d'Adana 1920 & Forêts—mines: Ecole d'agriculture, "Muharebe zamanında vukubulan katiyat miktarı."

138. Basso and Bentmann, *Deux rapports sur le paludisme*, 19.

139. McMurray, *Distant Ties*, 118.

140. See OA, DH-ŞFR 459/57, Hakkı to Dahiliye, Adana (15 Kanunusani 1330 [25 January 1915]); DH-ŞFR 484/105, Hakkı to Dahiliye, Adana (7 Ağustos 1331 [20 August 1915]); DH-İ-UM-EK 21/84, Trablusşamlı Hacı Ahmed Şakir to Dahiliye, Dersaadet (24 Eylül 1332 [7 October 1916]).

141. McMurray, *Distant Ties*, 121.

142. Yalman, *Turkey in the World War*, 253.

143. Bernard J. Brabin, "Malaria's Contribution to World War One: The Unexpected Adversary," *Malaria Journal* 13, no. 497 (2014).

144. Zürcher, *The Young Turk Legacy*, 176.

145. *Sıhhiye Mecmuası*, vol. 11 (1911), 1095–1100.

146. OA, HR-SYS 2221/4, Besim Ömer to Hariciye (20 Kanunusani 1331 [2 February 1916]).

147. Joseph O'Neill, *Blood-Dark Track: A Family History* (London: Granta Books, 2000), 309. Balakian referred to Russian, French, and Italian POWs celebrating a somber New Year at Belemedik in 1917 (*Armenian Golgotha*, 324–25). See also OA, DH-EUM-25/28 (8 November 1917).

148. Hilmar Kaiser, "The Baghdad Railway and the Armenian Genocide, 1915–1916: A Case Study in German Resistance and Complicity," in *Remembrance and Denial: The Case of the Armenian Genocide*, ed. Richard G. Hovannisian (Detroit: Wayne State University Press, 1998), 89. There were also many Italian prisoners working on the tunnels. OA, DH-EUM-5-Şb 49/24 (25 November 1917).

149. McMurray, *Distant Ties*, 122.

150. OA, HR-SYS 2221/8, no. 1, Bauer to Hariciye (4 Nisan 1331 [17 April 1916]). See also OA, HR-SYS 2221/4.

151. Kate Ariotti, "Australian Prisoners of the Turks: Negotiating Culture Clash in Captivity," in *Other Fronts, Other Wars? First World War Studies on the Eve of the Centennial*, ed. Joachim Bürgschwentner, Matthias Egger, and Gunda Barth-Scalmani (Leiden: Brill, 2014), 151. For mention of *Belemedik Bugger*, see Graham Seal, *The Soldiers' Press: Trench Journals in the First World War* (New York: Palgrave Macmillan, 2013), 228.

152. See TNA, FO 383/456/13209 (21 January 1918); 40368 (29 January 1918); OA, HR-SYS 2249/57, no. 2, Légation des Pays-Bas to Hariciye, Pera (8 November 1918); Don Kindell and Gordon Smith, *Royal Navy Roll of Honour: World War I, 1914–1918*, vol. 2 (Penarth: Naval-History.Net, 2009), 275. Michael White mentions a group of Australian POWs who fled Belemedik but were forced to turn themselves in when hunger and illness got the best of them; *Australian Submarines: A History* (Canberra: AGPS Press, 1992), 73.

153. For more see Kaiser, "The Baghdad Railway and the Armenian Genocide," 67–112.

154. Kévorkian, *The Armenian Genocide*, 501, 49, 80. Four thousand residents of Zeytun were expelled toward Central Anatolia in April 1915. They passed Pozantı during their forced march from their mountain village near Marash through the Çukurova plain and beyond Tarsus up into the Taurus Mountains, where they continued onward to Konya (571).

155. Kévorkian, *The Armenian Genocide*, 580.

156. Kévorkian, *The Armenian Genocide*, 977.

157. OA, DH-ŞFR 488/52, Hakkı to Dahiliye, Adana (27 Ağustos 1331 [9 September 1915]).

158. For example, the governor of Konya reported sending 1,050 Armenians in

fourteen train cars in October 1915. OA, DH-ŞFR 494/57, Samih to Dahiliye, Konya (10 Teşrinievvel 1331 [23 October 1915]).

159. OA, DH-ŞFR 495/45, Cemal to Dahiliye, Kudüs (17 Teşrinievvel 1331 [30 October 1915]).

160. OA, DH-ŞFR 493/119, Cemal to Dahiliye, Kudüs (3 Teşrinievvel 1331 [16 October 1915]).

161. OA, DH-ŞFR 496/21, İsmail to Dahiliye, Adana (23 Teşrinievvel 1331 [5 November 1915]).

162. OA, DH-ŞFR 502/81, Samih Rıfat to Dahiliye, Konya (12 Kanunuevvel 1331 [25 December 1915]).

163. OA, DH-ŞFR 60/69, Talat to Adana, Konya, and Niğde (7 Kanunusani 1331 [20 January 1916]).

164. OA, DH-ŞFR 506/115, Hakkı to Dahiliye, Adana (13 Kanunusani [26 January 1916]).

165. Kévorkian, *The Armenian Genocide*, 688. The Armenians remaining in the Cilicia region included the labor battalions around the Amanus tunnels, where Cevdet reported that some 10,000 Armenians were present and that while prior estimates might have been exaggerated, he believed that there was "a further number of Armenian families that have taken refuge in various places with the protection of railroad officials and are still hidden from the sight of the police." OA, DH-ŞFR 521/31, Cevdet to Dahiliye, Adana (15 Mayıs 1332 [28 May 1916]).

166. Kévorkian, *The Armenian Genocide*, 689.

167. OA, DH-ŞFR 65/59, Talat to Adana (9 Haziran 1332 [22 June 1916]).

168. Kévorkian, *The Armenian Genocide*, 687.

169. Basso and Bentmann, *Deux rapports sur le paludisme*, 22.

170. Tachjian, *La France en Cilicie*, 27.

171. BN, Archives Privées du Général F. Taillardat, vol. 1, no. 16, "Notes et directive générale sur les projets français en Cilicie," 358.

172. OA, DH-ŞFR 607/53 (24 December 1918).

173. ABC, 16.9.5, Reel 672, p. 372, Woodley to Barton (22 December 1918). Bread was almost 12 *kuruş* per kilogram in the countryside as of March 1919, and 1 kg of wheat cost 10 *kuruş*. CADN, 1SL/1/V, 204, vol. 2, Adana—affaires économiques, 29 March 1919.

174. *Տեղեկագիր Հայ Բշկական Առաքելութեան (Կիլիկիա)*, 36.

175. For historical studies of France in Cilicia, see Tachjian, *La France en Cilicie* (Paris: Karthala, 2004); Robert F. Zeidner, *The Tricolor over the Taurus: The French in Cilicia and Vicinity, 1918–1922* (Istanbul: Turk Tarih Kurumu Basımevi, 2005). See also Ruben Sahakyan, *Թուրք-Ֆրանսիական հարաբերությունները և Կիլիկիան (1919–1921)* (Yerevan: Hayastani Gitut'yunneri Akademia, 1970); Yücel Güçlü,

Armenians and the Allies in Cilicia, 1914–1923 (Salt Lake City: University of Utah Press, 2010).

176. André, *La Cilicie et le problème ottoman*, 11. André would later serve in Madagascar and Indochina. See Tachjian, *La France en Cilicie*, 22; Davis, *Resurrecting the Granary of Rome*, 2-6.

177. Du Véou, *La Passion de la Cilicie*, 312.

178. E. C. Achard, *Le coton en Cilicie et en Syrie* (Paris 1922), 1. An article in the *New York Times* about the economic prosperity that peacetime would bring stated that "Asia Minor and Mesopotamia could grow enough cotton to supply the world." "Good Turkish Prospects: Best among Them Is Said to Be the Growing of Cotton," *New York Times*, 22 September 1918.

179. Decades later, Lesseps still held to these claims, serving a jail sentence during the late 1940s for apparently having offered these lands to the Nazis as an aircraft base with which to attack the Suez Canal during World War II. "People," *Time*, 13 January 1947.

180. CADC, CCC, 1793–1901, Alep 33 (1863–66), Bertrand to de Lhuys (20 July 1864), 61. Colonel Brémond described cotton as having been "partly abandoned" during the war. CADN, 1SL/1/V, 304, vol. 1—Mersin—Affaires économiques, 22 August 1919.

181. Garabet K. Moumdjian, "Cilicia under French Administration," in *Armenian Cilicia*, ed. Richard G. Hovannisian and Simon Payaslian (Costa Mesa, CA: Mazda Publishers, 2008), 461. Vahram Shemmassian offers a different perspective on Armenian repatriation using the US archives, which indicate less than 50,000 repatriates to Cilicia in 1919. Vahram L. Shemmassian, "Repatriation of Armenian Refugees," in *Armenian Cilicia*, 456.

182. See Sam Kaplan, "Documenting History, Historicizing Documentation: French Military Officials' Ethnological Reports on Cilicia," *Comparative Studies in Society and History* 44, no. 2 (2002); "Territorializing Armenians: Geo-Texts and Political Imaginaries in French-Occupied Cilicia, 1919–1922," *History and Anthropology* 15, no. 4 (2004).

183. Shemmassian, "Repatriation of Armenian Refugees," 446.

184. CADN, 1SL/1/V, 304, vol. 1—Mersin—Affaires économiques, 22 August 1919.

185. ABC, 16.9.5, Reel 670, p. 452, Christie to Peet (30 August 1919).

186. CADN, 1SL/1/V, 304, vol. 1—Mersin—Affaires économiques, 26 January 1920.

187. CADN, 1SL/1/V, 304, vol. 1—Mersin—Affaires économiques, 22 August 1919.

188. Paul Bernard, *Six mois en Cilicie* (Aix-en-Provence: Editions du Feu, 1929), 30.

189. There were still 4,500 Kurdish refugees and 2,740 Balkan *muhacirs* in Cilicia around 1919. Tachjian, *La France en Cilicie*, 64.

190. CADN, 1SL/1/V, 277, vol. 1—Finance, Djebel Bereket, Köşkeryan to Bremond, Dörtyol (30 June 1919); unidentified to Bremond, Dörtyol (10 November 1919).

191. ABC 16.9.5, Reel 669, p. 408, Chambers to Peet (23 October 1919).

192. For more see Tachjian, *La France en Cilicie*, 117–30.

193. Keith David Watenpaugh, *Bread from Stones: The Middle East and the Making of Modern Humanitarianism* (Oakland: University of California Press, 2015), 91–92.

194. Bernard, *Six mois en Cilicie*, 63.

195. CADN, 1SL/1/V, 304, vol. 1—Mersin—Affaires économiques, 6 March 1920.

196. CADN, 1SL/1/V, 304, vol. 1—Mersin—Affaires économiques, 30 March 1920.

197. CADN, 1SL/1/V, 204 vol. 4—Comptabilité de la Foire d'Adana 1920.

198. CADN, 1SL/1/V, 304, vol. 1—Mersin—Affaires économiques, 16 April 1920.

199. Bernard, *Six mois en Cilicie*, 44–45; Tachjian, *La France en Cilicie*, 136.

200. Tachjian, *La France en Cilicie*, 151.

201. TKA, 1123/16.1.

202. Tachjian, *La France en Cilicie*, 152–57.

203. Yeğenağa, *Ali Münif Bey'in hâtıraları*, 95–100; Niyazi Ramazanoğlu, *La Province d'Adana: Aperçu historique ethnographique et statistique* (Constantinople: Société anonyme de papeterie et d'imprimerie, 1920).

204. Muzaffer Sümbül, "Ramazanoğlu Ailesinden Bir Ozan: Hasibe Ramazanoğlu," Çukurova University.

205. Tachjian, *La France en Cilicie*, 86–89.

206. See Zeidner, *The Tricolor over the Taurus*, 123–36.

207. Tachjian, *La France en Cilicie*, 56.

208. BN, Archives Privées du Général F. Taillardat, vol. 1, no. 6, 24 December 1919, "Rapport de F. Taillardat sur la région de Sis," 160.

209. Tachjian, *La France en Cilicie*, 136–37.

210. A fairly complete collection of *Giligia* (Կիլիկիա) is available between the Armenian National Library and the Mesrop Mashtots Institute of Ancient Manuscripts, or Matenadaran, in Yerevan.

211. CADN, 1SL/1/V, 304, vol. 3—Mersin—Affaires économiques, 1 August 1920.

212. CADN, 1SL/1/V, 204, vol. 2—Affaires économiques—no. 2129/991, Abdul Rahman to Capitrel (29 September 1920).

213. CADN, 1SL/1/V, 326, vol. 1, "Rapport sur le fonctionnement du Service des Rapartriments et de l'Assistance aux Déportés" (7 September 1920), 10.

214. CADN, 1SL/1/V, 208, vol. 3—Santé, "Oganization Provisoire des services de la Santé Hygiène et Assistance Publique dans les T.E.O. Zone Nord (Cilicie)," 5.

215. CADN, 1SL/1/V, 208, vol. 3—Santé, "Rapport de M. le Docteur Djemal Bey, Mèdecin Chef du Vilayet d'Adana concernant l'état sanitaire dans le Vilayet."
216. CADN, 1SL/1/V, 208, vol. 2—Santé, "La Paludisme voilà l'ennemi."
217. CADN, 1SL/1/V, 204, vol. 1, "Sur la question de la vente de quinine" (21 September 1921).
218. Տեղեկագիր Հայ Բշկական Առաքելութեան (Կիլիկիա), 5–18.
219. Հայ կարմիր խաչը Կիլիկիոյ մէջ (Istanbul: H. M. Aznavor, 1921), 15.
220. Հայ կարմիր խաչը Կիլիկիոյ մէջ, 30.
221. Հայ կարմիր խաչը Կիլիկիոյ մէջ, 117–23.
222. Originally referred to as Adana-Konya Heyet-i İmdadiyesi. Murat Uluğtekin, M. Gül Uluğtekin, and Ceren Aygül, *Osmanlı'dan Cumhuriyet'e Hilal-i Ahmer icraat raporları, 1914–1928* (Ankara: Türk Kızılay Derneği, 2013), 142–43.
223. Uluğtekin, Uluğtekin, and Aygül, *Hilal-i Ahmer icraat raporları, 1914–1928*, 143.
224. TKA, 1123/15.2–3.
225. TKA, 1123/16.5.
226. TKA, 1123/16.5.
227. TKA, 150/84.60; 150/84.42 (30 July 1921).
228. CADN, 1SL/1/V, 204, vol. 2—Affaires économiques, no. 36 Dufieux to High Commission (1 September 1921).
229. OA, DH-İ-UM 3–3/1/03, no. 5 (22 September 1921); CADN, 1SL/1/V, 204, vol. 2—Affaires économiques (25 August 1921).
230. CADN, 1SL/1/V, 164, "Statistique de la population" (21 November 1921).
231. Benjamin Thomas White, "A Grudging Rescue: France, the Armenians of Cilicia, and the History of Humanitarian Evacuations," *Humanity* 10, no. 1 (2019).
232. CADN, 1SL/1/V, 326, vol. 1.
233. Tachjian, *La France en Cilicie*, 173–75.
234. H. P. Poghosean, Հաճընի պատմագիրք պատմութիւն եւ շրջակայ ԳոզանՏաղի հայ գիւղերը (Los Angeles: Bozart Press, 1942); Misak Keleshean, Սիսուան․ պատմական, բանասիրական, տեղեկագրական, ազգագրական եւ Հարակից պարագաներ (Beirut: Hay Chemaran, 1949); Քեսունի պատմագիրք (Buenos Aires: Tp. Ararat, 1960).
235. Hein A. M. Klemann and Sergei Kudryashov, *Occupied Economies: An Economic History of Nazi-Occupied Europe, 1939–1945* (London: Berg Publishers, 2013), 353.
236. Özdemir, *Öyküleriyle Ağıtlar*, 39–42.
237. Akın, *When the War Came Home*, 109.
238. Özdemir, *Öyküleriyle Ağıtlar*, 75–203.
239. Eberhard, *Minstrel Tales from Southeastern Turkey*, 13.
240. Poghosean, Հաճընի բնդհանուր պատմութիւնը, 536.
241. Eberhard, "Nomads and Farmers," 42.
242. Eberhard, *Minstrel Tales from Southeastern Turkey*, 54–56.

243. Watenpaugh, *Bread from Stones*, 91–123.

Chapter 5

1. I have translated *fenni* (meaning "scientific" or "technical") as "modern" because this seems to be the implication of the proposal. In a way not limited to the historical experience of Turkey, science and modernity were very much equated within early republican discourse. On the subject of sciences during the late Ottoman period and emergent understandings of modernity, see M. Alper Yalçınkaya, *Learned Patriots: Debating Science, State, and Society in the Nineteenth-Century Ottoman Empire* (Chicago: University of Chicago Press, 2015).

2. *Cebel-i Bereket Vilayeti'ne ait coğrafi, iktisadi, ictimai, tarihi idari malumatı ihtiva eder bir takaddüme* (Adana: Türksözü Matbaası, 1341 [1925]), 21.

3. Tok, "Adana mıntakasında Sıtma mücadelesi," 1291.

4. Seyfettin Okan, *Türkiye'de Sıtma Savaşı / Malaria Control in Turkey* (Ankara: Sağlık ve Sosyal Yardım Bakanlığı, 1949), 6.

5. See Yasemin Gencer, "We Are Family: The Child and Modern Nationhood in Early Turkish Republican Cartoons (1923–28)," *Comparative Studies of South Asia, Africa and the Middle East* 32, no. 2 (2012): 294–309.

6. See Onur İnal and Ethemcan Turhan, *Transforming Socio-Natures in Turkey: Landscapes, State and Environmental Movements* (London: Routledge, 2020).

7. Seçil Binboğa, "The Soils of Turkey: Nature, Science, and Crisis (1930–1960)," in *Transforming Socio-Natures in Turkey*, ed. Onur İnal and Ethemcan Turhan, 13.

8. See Hale Yilmaz, *Becoming Turkish: Nationalist Reforms and Cultural Negotiations in Early Republican Turkey, 1923–1945* (Syracuse, NY: Syracuse University Press, 2013).

9. Emmanuel Szurek, "To Call a Turk a Turk: Patronymic Nationalism in Turkey in the 1930s," *Revue d'histoire moderne et contemporaine* 60, no. 2 (2013).

10. Oğuz, *Adana Ticaret Rehberi*, 18.

11. *Umumi Nüfüs Tahriri, 28 Teşrinievvel 1927* (Ankara: Türk Ocakları, 1927); *Adana Cumhuriyetten evvel ve sonra* (Ankara: Ulus, 1937); Karpat, *Ottoman Population*.

12. Taha Toros, *Çukurova ve Toroslarda Köy İktisadiyatı* (Adana: Yeni Adana Basimevi, 1939), 10.

13. *Adana Cumhuriyetten evvel ve sonra*, 49.

14. TKA, 210/166, Muhittin to Riyaset, Adana (29 January 1927). An idiosyncratic but thorough map of Muhittin's extensive travels in Çukurova indicates every village and town that he visited. TKA, 210/359.

15. TKA, 210/44, Muhittin to Riyaset, Misis (7 January 1927).

16. TKA, 210/131, Muhittin to Riyaset, Istanbul (26 October 1927); 210/133, Muhittin to Riyaset, Karaisalı (12 October 1927); 210/137, Muhittin to Riyaset, Kozan (10 October 1927); 210/144, Muhittin to Riyaset, Karaisalı (16 November 1927).

17. TKA, 210/382, Muhittin to Riyaset, Adana (11 October 1927). However, in

much of Cebel-i Bereket, the Red Crescent was not well liked, especially in Bahçe, where it had developed a reputation for corruption. TKA, 210/383, Muhittin to Riyaset, Cebel-i Bereket (7 October 1927).

18. TKA, 210/58, Muhittin to Riyaset, Mersin (27 February 1927); 210/187, Muhittin to Riyaset, Mersin (7 January 1927); 210/193, Muhittin to Hilal-i Ahmer Müfettişliği, Mersin (2 January 1927).

19. Asım Karaömerlioğlu referred to peasantism, or *köycülük*, in Turkey as a shared inclination among many countries of the period, offering a detailed comparison and contrast with Bulgaria and Germany. Asım Karaömerlioğlu, *Orada Bir Köy Var Uzakta: erken Cumhuriyet döneminde köycü söylem* (Istanbul: İletisim, 2006), 185–219. For the case of Egypt, see Michael Ezekiel Gasper, *The Power of Representation: Publics, Peasants, and Islam in Egypt* (Stanford: Stanford University Press, 2009); Omnia S. El Shakry, *The Great Social Laboratory: Subjects of Knowledge in Colonial and Postcolonial Egypt* (Stanford: Stanford University Press, 2007).

20. Karaömerlioğlu, *Orada Bir Köy Var Uzakta*, 88–91.

21. "Sıhhî program: Köy ebesi için kurs açıldı," *Yeni Adana*, 21 October 1938. See also "Köylerimiz," *Yeni Adana*, 24 March 1939.

22. Sibel Bozdoğan, *Modernism and Nation Building: Turkish Architectural Culture in the Early Republic* (Seattle: University of Washington Press, 2001), 100–105.

23. Karaömerlioğlu, *Orada Bir Köy Var Uzakta*, 70.

24. Aslı Emine Çomu, "The Exchange of Populations and Its Aftermath in Ayvalık, Mersin and Trabzon," *International Journal of Turkish Studies* 18, nos. 1–2 (2012): 17–38.

25. *Iskân Tarihçesi* (Istanbul: Hamit Matbaası, 1932), 18.

26. Asli Emine Çomu, *The Exchange of Populations and Adana, 1830–1927* (Istanbul: Libra, 2011), 94.

27. *Yeni Adana* cited a case in which a migrant from Serres who had been working formerly Armenian lands given to him as a *mübadil* since 1923, was somehow usurped by an Elassona migrant holding documents of ownership for the same piece of land. "Karışık bir mesele: Yedi senedir verilmiş olan bir tarla nasıl geri alınıyor?" *Yeni Adana*, 4 June 1930.

28. "İskan İşleri," *Yeni Adana*, 18 June 1929.

29. Mehmet Recep, "Dahiliye vekâletine: iskân işleri çok ciddi bir tahkikata lüzum göstermektedir," *Yeni Adana*, 20 June 1929.

30. "Bu nasıl iş?" *Yeni Adana*, 28 August 1929.

31. "Göçmenlerin tapu senetleri," *Yeni Adana*, 9 July 1935. For comparison, see Gingeras, *Sorrowful Shores*, 148–65.

32. Polatel and Üngör, *Confiscation and Colonization*, 115–16.

33. Ayhan Aktar, "Homogenising the Nation, Turkifying the Economy: The Turkish Experience of Population Exchange Reconsidered," in *Crossing the Aegean : An Ap-*

praisal of the 1923 Compulsory Population Exchange between Greece and Turkey, ed. Renee Hirschon (New York: Berghahn Books, 2003), 86.

34. Polatel and Üngör, *Confiscation and Colonization*, 175–80.

35. CA, 300–18–1-1 10/42/16 (7 September 1924).

36. CA, 30–18–1-1 7/23/7 (28 June 1929).

37. Çomu, *The Exchange of Populations and Adana*, 100–101.

38. Çomu, *The Exchange of Populations and Adana*, 104. For more, see Ali Cengizkan, *Mübadele Konut ve Yerleşimleri* (Ankara: Orta Doğu Teknik Üniversitesi, 2004).

39. Polatel and Üngör, *Confiscation and Colonization*, 126.

40. Çomu, *The Exchange of Populations and Adana*, 98.

41. Toros, *Çukurova ve Toroslarda Köy İktisadiyatı*, 5.

42. Sadun Tanju, *Hacı Ömer* (Istanbul: Apa Ofset Basımevi, 1983), 4.

43. NARA, RG 166, Box 438, Turkey—Narrative Reports (1950–54), Economic Conditions (1953–54), 800.05182/4–254, "Notes on Leading Industrialists of the Adana Region" (2 April 1954); *Kayseri Ansiklopedisi*, vol. 1 (Kayseri: Kayseri Büyükşehir Belediyesi, 2009).

44. Çomu, *The Exchange of Populations and Adana*, 108–12, 24. For more on the Kayseri connection during the Ottoman period, see Toksöz, *Nomads, Migrants, and Cotton*, 165. The established commercial elite of Çukurova, according to Üngör and Polatel, benefited from reduced competition due to the elimination of a vast swath of potential Christian competitors. *Confiscation and Colonization*, 131–32.

45. Orhan Kemal, *Bereketli Topraklar Üzerinde* (Istanbul: Everest, 1954, 2008).

46. "Kendini öldürmek istemiş," *Yeni Adana*, 12 June 1929.

47. "Bir amele sefaletten öldü," *Yeni Adana*, 25 June 1931.

48. See "Haftanın Vaziyeti," *Yeni Adana*, 15 June 1931.

49. *İkinci Adana Pamuk Kongresi Zabıtnamesi*.

50. Arıkoğlu, *Hâtıralarım*, 16.

51. Uran, *Adana Ziraat Amelesi*, 20.

52. See Kemal, *Bereketli Topraklar Üzerinde*, 77.

53. Uran, *Adana Ziraat Amelesi*, 21–23.

54. "Adana pamukçuluğu," *Memleket Çukurova'da*, 15 January 1930; "Çukurova Hastahane," *Yeni Adana*, 20 December 1939; Cavit Oral, "Pamuk Ekiminin Başında," *Bugün*, 17 March 1942.

55. "Ceyhanda Amele buhranı mı var?," *Yeni Adana*, 14 September 1929.

56. Uran, *Adana Ziraat Amelesi*, 22.

57. Üngör, *The Making of Modern Turkey*, 122–68.

58. CADN, 8PO/1, Adana, vol. 13.

59. Soner Çağaptay, *Islam, Secularism, and Nationalism in Modern Turkey: Who Is a Turk?* (London: Routledge, 2006), 25. The campaign involved speeches at the local Türk

Ocağıs as well as announcements in local newspapers. See "Vatandaş Türkçe Konuş," *Yeni Adana*, 30 April 1936.

60. Çağaptay, *Islam, Secularism, and Nationalism*, 82–86.

61. "Muhacirler Türkçe öyrenecekler [sic]," *Yeni Adana*, 4 June 1930.

62. Orhan Kemal depicts a humorous scene in *Berektli Topraklar Üzerinde* in which a worker when berated by a factory accountant who corrects his pronunciation, pretends that he is incapable of uttering the phrase "I'm freezing" in proper Turkish. Kemal, *Bereketli Topraklar Üzerinde*, 62.

63. See Uğur Pişmanlık, *Tarsus İşçi Sınıfı Tarihi: 19. yüzyıldan günümüze* (Kadiköy: Yazılama, 2013).

64. Oğuz, *Adana Ticaret Rehberi*; Ravndal, *Turkey*, 97.

65. *Ziraat vekaleti mütehassıs raporları: ziraat kısmı* (Istanbul: Ikdam, 1927), 81; *Memleket Çukurova'da*, 15 February 1930, 3.

66. *1927 senesi ziraat tahriri neticeleri* (Ankara: Istanbul Cumhuriyet Matbaası, 1928), x.

67. Toksöz, *Nomads, Migrants, and Cotton*, 203–4.

68. CADN, 8PO/1, Adana vol. 13, Ronflard to Daeschner, Mersin (18 May 1926) and (15 December 1926).

69. Hilmi Ozansoy, "Pamuklarımızın en büyük müşterisi Almanyadır ve daima da Almanya olacaktır," *Adana Tecim Gazetesi*, 1 November 1936.

70. Stanford J. Shaw and Ezel Kural Shaw, *Reform, Revolution, and Republic: The Rise of Modern Turkey 1808–1975* (Cambridge: Cambridge University Press, 1977), 2:391.

71. Ozansoy made note of how these changes in the boundaries affected the statistics, offering both versions. "Adananın Ökonomi Durumu," *Adana Ticaret Gazetesi*, 21 May 1935.

72. "Adana pamukculuğu"; *Memleket Çukurova'da*, 15 February 1930.

73. "Adananın Ökonomi Durumu."

74. Koudoulian, Հայ էտրը, 12; Teodik, Ամիս մը ի Կիլիկիա, 163. On Jaffa oranges, see Gershon Shafir, *Land, Labor, and the Origins of the Israeli-Palestinian conflict, 1882–1914* (Berkeley: University of California Press, 1996), 29.

75. CA, 30–10–0–0 80/529/18, no. 3 (17 March 1925).

76. "Portakalcılığımız ilerliyor," *Türksözü*, 7 July 1935. Germany became a major recipient of Dörtyol oranges. "Portakal," *Adana Ticaret Gazetesi*, 21 March 1935.

77. Uran, *Adana Ziraat Amelesi*, 25.

78. *1927 senesi ziraat tahriri neticeleri* (Ankara: Istanbul Cumhuriyet Matbaası, 1928).

79. *Memleket Çukurova'da*, 1 May 1930.

80. Kemal, *Pamuk Ziraati*, 24.

81. Lilo Linke, *Allah Dethroned: A Journey through Modern Turkey* (New York: Knopf, 1937), 273–74. On experimentation with sugar in Adana, see also Binboğa, "The Soils of Turkey: Nature, Science, and Crisis (1930–1960)," 11–30.

82. Kemal, *Pamuk Ziraati*, 3–7.

83. *1340–1341 Pamuk mevsiminde Adana Borsasının muamelatını müşir istatistik raporudur* (Adana: Adana Borsası, 1341 [1925]).

84. *İkinci Adana Pamuk Kongresi Zabıtnamesi*, 9.

85. OA, HR-İM 95/62 (23 January 1924).

86. Süleyman Sergici, "Adanada Klevland Pamuğu," *Adana Tecim Gazetesi*, 1 November 1937.

87. "Ovada Ziraat faaliyeti," *Yeni Adana*, 9 July 1937; "Bu yıl Çukurova kâmilen klevland ekecek," *Yeni Adana*, 10 October 1936.

88. Linke, *Allah Dethroned*, 274; "Bu yıl Çukurova kâmilen klevland ekecek."

89. NARA, RG 166, Box 436, Keld Christensen, Iskenderun, "Agriculture on the Cilician Plain" (5 July 1944), 16–19.

90. "Bu yıl çukurova'da Akala'dan başka cins pamuk ekilmiyecek," *Türksözü*, 24 February 1942.

91. NARA, RG 166, Box 436, Keld Christensen, Iskenderun, "Agriculture on the Cilician Plain" (5 July 1944), 16–19.

92. In the latest American report I consulted, the cotton produced in the Çukurova region in 1957 was identified as the "Adana" variety, whereas the cotton of Izmir was labeled as "Acala." NARA, RG 166, Box 804 Turkey (1955–61), Agriculture, "Turkey: Cotton Report," Ankara Embassy to Department of Agriculture (18 September 1957).

93. Fatih Tuğluoğlu, "Türkiye'de Sıtma Mücadelesi (1924–1950)," *Türkiye parazitoloji dergisi* 32, no. 4 (2008): 353.

94. See Kyle T. Evered, "Draining an Anatolian Desert: Overcoming Water, Wetlands, and Malaria in Early Republican Ankara," *Cultural Geographies* 21, no. 3 (2014): 475–96.

95. Kyle T. Evered and Emine Ö. Evered, "Governing Population, Public Health, and Malaria in the Early Turkish Republic," *Journal of Historical Geography* 37, no. 4 (2011): 476–82.

96. RAC, RG 1.1, Series 805, Box 1, Folder 1, Ralph Collins, "Public Health in Turkey" (1926). For biographical detail, see "Dr. Collins," *Türk Hıfzıssıha ve Tecrübî Biyoloji Mecmuası* 2, no. 2 (1940). See also Murat Erdem and Kenneth W. Rose, "American Philanthropy in Turkey: The Rockefeller and Ford Foundations," *Turkish Yearbook* 31 (2000): 131–57.

97. TKA, 210/44–210/477.

98. The budget reached a maximum of 885,000 TL in 1930 but then had a significant decline, perhaps due to the 1929 financial crisis, followed by a gradual rebound. İlhan Tekeli and Selim İlkin, "Türkiye'de Sıtma Mücadelesinin Tarihi," in *70. yılında ulusal ve uluslararası boyutlarıyla Atatürk'ün büyük Nutuk'u ve dönemi*, ed. Gül E. Kundakçı (Ankara: Orta Doğu Teknik Üniversitesi, 1999), 255.

99. Lutfi Aksu, *Malarya (Sıtma)* (Ankara: Ulusal Matbaa, 1943), 28.

100. For example, in 1926 the Turkish government asked the Rockefeller Foundation for $79,000 in assistance that would cover 20 percent of the costs of a new public health institute in Ankara. RAC, RG 1.1, Series 805, Box 1, Folder 1, Gunn to Russel, Paris (14 September 1926). Collins remarked that even though its policies resulted in a tremendous shortage of doctors, the Turkish government did not allow foreigners to practice medicine in Turkey unless they had been licensed before 1915. RAC, RG 1.1, Series 805, Box 1, Folder 1, Ralph Collins, "Public Health in Turkey" (1926), 46.

101. See CA, 30–18–2-2, 116/30/3; 30–18–1-2, 55/45/13; 30–18–1-2, 80/95/9; 30–18–1-2, 84/65/20.

102. Lucien Raynaud, "İtalya'da Sıtma Mücadelesi," *Sıhhiye Mecmuası* 1, no. 3 (1341 [1925]). For more on the emergence of Italian antimalarial campaigns, see Frank M. Snowden, *The Conquest of Malaria: Italy, 1900–1962* (New Haven: Yale University Press, 2006), 53–86.

103. See RAC, RG 1.1, Series 805, Box 1, Folder 1, Ralph Collins, "Public Health in Turkey" (1926).

104. Tok, "Adana mıntakasında Sıtma mücadelesi," 1298.

105. Brumpt and Tok remained in contact and maintained a friendship over subsequent decades, exchanging holiday salutations. IP, BPT-B14, Ekrem Tok, R30/12 Tok to Brumpt, Ankara (25 December 1937); Brumpt to Tok, Paris (7 April 1933). Ekrem Tok even accompanied Brumpt's wife on a trip to the then-disputed Syrian border in 1937. IP, BPT-D13, Tok, Tok to Brumpt, Ankara (1 July 1937). Brumpt's files at the Pasteur Institute Archives in Paris reveal that he maintained continual contact with doctors not only in Adana and Turkey but also in other countries of the Middle East. See IP, BPT-B13; B14; D13; G1.

106. CA, 30–18–1-1, 15/55/10 (9 Eylül 1341 [9 September 1925]).

107. ALON-UNOG, 1919–1927, Class 12B, R874, 28002/37732 "Record of the Proceedings of the First International Malaria Congress held in Rome"; R877, 28002/42825, "Collaboration of Bentmann."

108. Tok, "Adana mıntakasında Sıtma mücadelesi," 1286.

109. Tok, "Adana mıntakasında Sıtma mücadelesi," 1286–89.

110. Tok, "Adana mıntakasında Sıtma mücadelesi," 1291.

111. Linke, *Allah Dethroned*, 249.

112. Throughout the interwar period, the malaria status of more than 10 percent of the population of Turkey was recorded on an annual basis with hopes that every citizen would be tested at least every few years. Tekeli and İlkin, "Türkiye'de Sıtma Mücadelesinin Tarihi," 254.

113. Tok, "Adana mıntakasında Sıtma mücadelesi," 1310.

114. Compiled from *Sıhhiye Mecmuası*, vol. 10, no. 69 through vol. 11, no. 74.

115. Compiled from *Sıhhiye Mecmuası*, vol. 11, no. 76 through vol. 12, no. 83.

116. Tok, "Adana mıntakasında Sıtma mücadelesi," 1306.

117. Linke, *Allah Dethroned*, 242–57.

118. RAC, RG 1.1, Series 805, Box 1, Folder 1, Ralph Collins, "Public Health in Turkey" (1926), 78, 163.

119. RAC, RG 1.1, Series 805, Box 1, Folder 1, Ralph Collins, "Public Health in Turkey" (1926), 165.

120. "Kırmızı ay: Adanada nasıl çalışıyor Sıtma ile mücadele?" *Yeni Adana*, 5 February 1929.

121. See *Sıhhiye Mecmuası*, vol. 11, no. 76 through vol. 12, no. 83.

122. RAC, RG 1.1, Series 805, Box 1, Folder 1, Ralph Collins, "Public Health in Turkey" (1926), 73.

123. RAC, RG 1.1, Series 805, Box 1, Folder 1, Ralph Collins, "Public Health in Turkey" (1926), 46.

124. "Sıtma enstitüsü bu sene 23 Eylül'de açınacaktır," *Yeni Adana*, 30 August 1929; "Sıtma enstitüsü," *Yeni Adana*, 10 September 1929; "Sıtma enstitüsü," *Yeni Adana*, 18 september 1929; "Tıp enstitüsü: evelki gün açılan enstitüde ikinci sıtma tatbikat derslerine başlandı," *Yeni Adana*, 26 September 1929.

125. TBMM, 6. Dönem, vol. 11, p. 873 (27 May 1940).

126. "Seyyar tabip talimatname," *Sıhhiye Mecmuası* 10, no. 70 (October 1934): 316–39.

127. For more, see Zürcher, *The Young Turk Legacy*, 259–70.

128. Linke, *Allah Dethroned*, 249.

129. See Vahid, *Köylü İlm-i Hali* (Istanbul: Matbaa-ı Amire, 1922), 108.

130. For examples, see Kyle T. Evered and Emine Ö Evered, "State, Peasant, Mosquito," *Journal of Political Geography* 31, no. 5 (2012): 311–13.

131. "Sıtmadan kurtulunuz," *Yeni Adana*, 3 July 1929; "Sıtmadan kurtulunuz," *Yeni Adana*, 7 July 1929; "Sıtmadan kurtulunuz," *Yeni Adana*, 24 July 1929; "Sıtma mücade(le)sinin öğütleri," *Yeni Adana*, 1 August 1929.

132. *Sıhhiye nezaret-i celilesinin ısıtmaya tutulmamak için öğütler* (Ankara: Hakimiyet-i Milliye Matbaası, 1927), 1.

133. Pek, *Sıtma Notları*, 65–67.

134. Reşit Galib, *Köy Muallimleriyle Sıhhi Musahebeler* (Istanbul: Devlet Matbaası, 1928), 107–9.

135. *Sıhhiye nezaret-i celilesinin ısıtmaya tutulmamak için öğütler*. See also Aksu, *Malarya (Sıtma)*; Ata Ünalan, *Sıtma: Sıtmalı yerlerde çalışan ve yaşayanlara pratik bilgiler* (Ankara: Titaş Basımevi, 1943).

136. Hamdi Dilevurgun, *Sıtma* (Istanbul: Millî Eğitim Basımevi, 1948), 9.

137. "Flit bayıltmaz, öldürür!" *Yeni Adana*, 3 May 1935.

138. "Sıtmadan korkanlar muntazaman Sıhhat rakısı içsinler," *Yeni Adana*, 25 July 1929.

139. Dilevurgun, *Sıtma*, 18; Rüştü, *Sıtma'ya Karşı Muharebe*, 4. An interesting

op-ed in *Yeni Adana* that described partaking in a drinking session with Ekrem Tok and the other doctors of the Adana region criticized the doctors for being overly tame drinkers. "Doktorlarla içmek belâ imiş: Küçük bir kadeh rakıyı yarım saatte içiyorlar," *Yeni Adana*, 8 March 1929.

140. Linke, *Allah Dethroned*, 250–54.

141. "Ceyhanda sıtma mücadelesi çok işçenlik gösteriyor," *Türksözü*, 17 August 1935; "Adana ve köylerinin sıhhî durumu pek normal görünüyor!," *Türksözü*, 2 September 1936; "Sıtma çoğalıyor," *Türksözü*, 20 July 1935.

142. "Mersin Halkı soruyor: Sıtma her evi sardı. Bataklıklar neden kurutulmadı?," *Türksözü*, 24 September 1935.

143. "Her tarafta sıtma salgını var," *Yeni Adana*, 7 July 1936; "Sıtma salgını devam ediyor," *Yeni Adana*, 23 July 1936.

144. "Sıtma çoğalıyor," *Türksözü*, 20 July 1935; "Her tarafta sıtma salgını var," *Yeni Adana*, 7 July 1936. After all, during his inspection in 1925, Ralph Collins had commented upon the low rates of malaria due to an originally dry season that yielded a remarkable scarcity of anophelines. RAC, 805 Turkey, Box 1 - 1.1 Projects, Folder 1, Ralph Collins, "Public Health in Turkey" (1926), 77.

145. Tevfik, "Adananın sıhhî vaziyeti," *Yeni Adana*, 17 September 1929.

146. Hilmi Ozansoy, *Adana* (Adana: Adana Ticaret ve Sanayi Odası, 1935), appendix 1.

147. "Çeltiklerin vaziyeti çok memnuniyet verici," *Türksözü*, 5 August 1937; "Maraş Çeltikçileri," *Türksözü*, 12 September 1935.

148. "Çeltik ziraatı için bir talimatname hazırlandı," *Yeni Adana*, 2 June 1936.

149. Tekeli and İlkin, "Türkiye'de Sıtma Mücadelesinin Tarihi," 238–40.

150. "Sıtma tahribatı," *Yeni Adana*, 1 August 1929.

151. Toros, *Çukurova ve Toroslarda Köy İktisadiyatı*.

152. Mentioned in "Mersin Halkı soruyor," *Türksözü*, 24 September 1935.

153. "Ekrem Tok Beyin Beyanatı: Dünden itibaren su birikintilerine Mazot dökülmiye başlandı," *Yeni Adana*, 5 June 1929. I have not found any literature on mosquitofish as an invasive species in Turkey, though studies show that their populations are found in Çukurova today in places such as the waters of the Seyhan Dam. S. A. Erguden, "Age, Growth, Sex Ratio and Diet of Eastern Mosquitofish Gambusia holbrooki Girard, 1859 in Seyhan Dam Lake (Adana/Turkey)," *Iranian Journal of Fisheries Sciences* 12, no. 1 (2013).

154. Ekrem Tok, "Sıtma mücadelesinde Kilisifaj balıklar," *Sıhhiye Mecmuası* 5, nos. 26–28 (May 1929).

155. "Ekrem Tok Beyin Beyanatı," *Yeni Adana*, 5 June 1929.

156. Tok, "Adana mıntakasında Sıtma mücadelesi," 1308.

157. "Ekrem Tok Beyin Beyanatı."

158. See Ayşe Gül Altınay, *The Myth of the Military Nation* (New York: Palgrave

Macmillan, 2004), 30–32. Not all national malaria programs evoked an identical rhetoric. Perhaps it was with conscious recognition of this difference that Seyfettin Okan's bilingual work on antimalaria activities in Turkey was published in 1949 as *Türkiye'de Sıtma Savaşı*, or "The War on Malaria in Turkey," in Turkish, but under the title "Malaria Control in Turkey" for its otherwise identical English-language section. Okan, *Türkiye'de Sıtma Savaşı*. Turkey's antimalarial efforts might most closely resemble those undertaken by the fascist government in Italy, which—much as the Turkish public health and public works officials did in Ankara—waged an intense war against the marshes surrounding the capital. Snowden, *The Conquest of Malaria*, 149.

159. Pek, *Sıtma Notları*, 15.

160. See Evered and Evered, "State, Peasant, Mosquito," 320–21.

161. Tok, "Adana mıntakasında Sıtma mücadelesi," 1307.

162. "Ekrem Tok Beyin Beyanatı," *Yeni Adana*, 5 June 1929.

163. CA, 30–10–0-0, 185/277/8 (16 December 1926).

164. See "Çekirge afeti: Tehlikenin önüne geçmek için fedakârlık lazım," *Yeni Adana*, 25 May 1930. See also "Çekirge Kısık boğazında Asker ve ehali tarafından imha ediliyor," *Yeni Adana*, 21 May 1930; "Kozan'da çekirge, halk ve memurların iştirâki ile imha ediliyor," *Yeni Adana*, 25 May 1930; "Çekirge dağ kısmına fazla hücum ediyor," *Yeni Adana*, 25 May 1930; "Tren çekirgeden teehura uğradı," *Yeni Adana*, 25 May 1930; Enver, "Çekirge Fekeye nasıl geldi," *Yeni Adana*, 1 May 1930; Tevfik, "Çekirge," *Yeni Adana*, 27 May 1930; "Kadirlide mücadele," *Yeni Adana*, 27 May 1930; "Osmaniyede bütün köpekler zehirlendi," *Türksözü*, 4 September 1936; "Tarsus haberleri," *Yeni Adana*, 27 March 1937.

165. Aksu, *Malarya (Sıtma)*, 28.

166. *Ziraat Kongresi: Okaliptüs* (Ankara: T. C. Ziraat Vekaleti, 1938); F. Adalı, *Sağlık Ağacı Okaliptüs* (Ankara: Ziraat Vekaleti, 1944).

167. Niyazi Okay, *Okaliptüs Nasıl Yetiştirilir* (Tarsus: Gülek Basımevi, 1947), 9.

168. CA, 30–18–1-2, 80/99/13 (10 December 1937).

169. "Ovamızda okaliptüscülük," *Türksözü*, 27 August 1937.

170. Fikret Saatçioğlu and Besalet Pamay, *Tarsus-Karabucak Mıntıkasında Okaliptüs* (Istanbul: Kurtulmuş Matbaası, 1958), 6.

171. "Karabucak bataklığı son dakikalarını yaşıyor," *Yeni Adana*, 11 August 1939.

172. Okay, *Okaliptüs Nasıl Yetiştirilir*.

173. Mary Gough, *Travel into Yesterday* (Garden City, NY: Doubleday, 1954), 27, 81, 141.

174. Saatçioğlu and Pamay, *Tarsus-Karabucak Mıntıkasında Okaliptüs*, 2.

175. "Adana büyük bir felâkete uğradı," *Türk Sözü*, 6 December 1936.

176. "Sular çekildi, felâketin büyüklüğü heran biraz daha meydana çıkıyor," *Türk Sözü*, 8 December 1936.

177. For examples of the impacts of and responses to significant flooding in

Çukurova during the early republican period from the archives, see CA, 30-10-0-0 6/36/2, Zamir to TBMM (14 April 1924); 30-10-0-0 117/818/22, no. 2–3; 30-18-1-1 8/43/11; 30-10-0-0 117/818/38, no. 2 (15 December 1930); 30-10-0-0 117/821/17, no. 2, Baysal to Dahiliye (3 March 1935). In newspapers, see "Seyhan Yine Taştı: Karşıyaka'nın bir çok yerleri sular altına kaldı," *Yeni Adana*, 5 February 1929; "Amik Ovası sular altında kaldı," *Yeni Adana*, 27 January 1935; "Seyhan setleri yıkdı (sic). Ekili tarlalar su altında kaldı. Zarar çok büyük," *Yeni Adana*, 18 February 1935; "Seyhan, Ceyhan ırmakları dört metreye kadar yükseldiler," *Yeni Adana*, 5 March 1935; "Seyhan ırmağı taştı," *Yeni Adana*, 2 November 1935; "Seyhan Ceyhanla ovada birleşti," *Yeni Adana*, 3 April 1935.

178. Ahmet Rezmi Yüreğir, "Irmakların zararları," *Yeni Adana*, 5 April 1935, and "Fayda yerine zarar," *Yeni Adana*, 5 November 1935.

179. "Uğradığımız son felâketin vukuu ihtimalini on ay önce gazetemiz haber verdiği zaman 'Seyhandan bir tehlike gelmez' diye bizi tekzip edenler şimdi ne diyecek?" *Türksözü*, 13 December 1936.

180. M. Bakşı, "Adananın ikinci kurtuluşu için umumî bir plân lâzımdır," *Türksözü*, 15 December 1936.

181. Nevzad Güven, "Felâketler karşısında Çukurovalı," *Türksözü*, 15 December 1936.

182. Kâmuran Bozkır, "Bayram yapmadım," *Türksözü*, 23 December 1936.

183. "Adanamızın felâketi karşısında Türk matbuatı," *Türksözü*, 11 December 1936.

184. Bozkır, "Bayram yapmadım."

185. Nevzad Güven, "Nehirlerimizin taranması ve etraflarındaki arazinin sulanması için 30 milyonluk bir proje hazırlandı," *Türksözü*, 22 December 1936.

186. Suat Kırış, "Güzel Adanaya," *Yeni Adana*, 9 February 1937.

187. "Çukurovanın sulama işine dün ilk kazma törenle vuruldu," *Yeni Adana*, 6 January 1938.

188. "Seyhan sulama işleri ne safhada?" *Yeni Adana*, 12 January 1939.

189. "Sulama işleri faaliyeti," *Yeni Adana*, 16 January 1939.

190. "Seyhan Sulama," *Yeni Adana*, 2 October 1939.

191. "Seyhan Barajının İnşaatı Tamamlandı," *Türksözü*, 5 June 1942.

192. Hilmi Uran, *Hâtiralarim* (Ankara: Uran, 1959), 388. See Selim Deringil, *Turkish Foreign Policy during the Second World War: An "Active" Neutrality* (Cambridge: Cambridge University Press, 1989).

193. NARA, RG 166, Box 437, Cotton (1939–54), Embassy to State (8 April 1952), p. 16.

194. Those who did heavy labor received 750 g of bread, whereas other adults received 375 g and children 187.5 g. "Ekmek tevzi işlerimiz: Ekmek kartları bugün tevzi ediliyor," *Türksözü*, 17 January 1942. Factory workers in Tarsus published an open letter to the municipality in the newspaper demanding that they be issued cards that listed

them as heavy laborers. "Tarsus'ta İşçilerin dileği," *Türksözü*, 4 March 1942. The ration card process revealed that there were thousands of people in the region who did not yet possess government-issued identity cards. "Ölüler için Ekmek Kartı!," *Bugün*, 3 February 1942.

195. Özdemir, *Öyküleriyle Ağıtlar*, 162.

196. NARA, RG 166, Box 436, Keld Christensen, Iskenderun, "Agriculture on the Cilician Plain" (5 July 1944), p. 22.

197. TNA, FO 195/2485, 507/13/44 (14 October 1944).

198. Okan, *Türkiye'de Sıtma Savaşı*, 4.

199. "Kinin Yokluğu," *Bugün*, 25 March 1942; "Kinin İhtiyacı," *Bugün*, 1 May 1942; Dr. Cezmi Türk, "Tropika," *Bugün*, 18 July 1946; "Kinin," *Türksözü*, 5 May 1942. Well-off politicians complained that malaria was rampant in the places where they vacationed, and that it was impossible to find medicine. CA, 30-10-0-0 177/224/4 (15 September 1943).

200. "Karataşta sıtma mücadelesi," *Türksözü*, 21 July 1942.

201. "Çukurovalı: Buğdayını, arpanı gecikmeden, Ofise teslim et. Sana yaraşan ve sana düşen millet ve yurt ödevi budur," *Bugün*, 23 June 1942; "Ziraat Konferansı," *Bugün*, 15 March 1942.

202. "Muhtaç çiftçiye hükûmetçe çift hayvanı verilecek," *Bugün*, 22 January 1942.

203. NARA, RG 166, Box 436, Keld Christensen, Iskenderun, "Agriculture on the Cilician Plain" (5 July 1944), p. 19.

204. "Ziraat Seferberliği," *Bugün*, 18 February 1942; "Adana okullarında ekim seferberliği," *Bugün*, 5 March 1942; "Zirai Seferberlik Plânı Tatbikatı," *Türksözü*, 25 March 1942; "Zirai Savaş: Bütün Anadoluda Zirai Mücadele devam ediyor," *Türksözü*, 14 May 1942; "Adana Çiftçisi ziraat seferberliğinde ön safta," *Bugün*, 20 March 1942.

205. "Muhtaç çiftçiye ucuz ziraat âlet ve vasıtaları dağıtılacak," *Bugün*, 4 February 1942; "Adana çiftçisi, ekimi 2 misline çıkarmak için Bütün Gayretiyle çalışacaktır," *Bugün*, 11 February 1942; "Ödünç Tohum," *Bugün*, 8 March 1942; "Ziraat aletleri çok ucuz fiyatlarla satılacak," *Bugün*, 27 May 1942.

206. Taha Toros, "Toroslarda Yayla Hayatı," *Yedi Gün*, 5 August 1936.

207. "Yaz tatili Adana mektepleri için pek geç kalıyor," *Yeni Adana*, 27 May 1930.

208. "Havalar kızdı yaylacılar göçüyor," *Yeni Adana*, 23 June 1936; "Adana ateş yağmuru altında: sıcaklar günden güne artıyor," *Yeni Adana*, 22 July 1929.

209. "Yaylalar ve Bağlar," *Türksözü*, 3 July 1937.

210. "Sıcaklar tahammül edilmiyecek bir dereceyi buldu," *Yeni Adana*, 15 August 1929.

211. "Adanada havalar değişti, sıcaklar azalıyor," *Yeni Adana*, 5 September 1929; "Yayla ve bağlardan dönüş başladı," *Yeni Adana*, 24 September 1935; "Yayla ve bağlardan göç başladı," *Yeni Adana*, 26 September 1936.

212. "İbrahim Bey Yaylasında," *Yeni Adana*, 14 August 1929; "Tarsus haberleri,"

Yeni Adana, 10 September 1929; "Yaylâ yolunda," *Toros*, 19 August 1948; M. Sadık, "Yayla Yolunda," *Memleket Çukurova'da*, 15 October 1930; "Sıcaktan kurtuluş," *Toros*, 19 August 1948; "Namrun Yaylasında evim yok diyenlere Müjde," *Gülek*, 4 August 1949.

213. "Bürücek Torosların en eyi yaylası oldu," *Yeni Adana*, 23 June 1936.

214. Yaylacı, "Bürücek yaylasında ilerleme ve hızlanma hamlesi," *Yeni Adana*, 25 July 1939.

215. "Bürücek röportajları, Part 1," *Yeni Adana*, 3 September 1937.

216. "Bürücek Torosların en eyi yaylası oldu."

217. "Bürücek yaylacılarına müjde," *Yeni Adana*, 4 June 1930.

218. "Yaylacılara büyük bir kolaylık," *Türksözü*, 3 July 1936.

219. "Bürücek röportajları, Part 1."

220. "Bürücek röportajları, Part 2," *Yeni Adana*, 4 September 1937.

221. "Bürücek Torosların en eyi yaylası oldu."

222. "Bürücek röportajları, Part 1."; "Bürücek röportajları, Part 2."

223. "Bürücek röportajları, Part 2."

224. "Kiralık yayla yurdu," *Yeni Adana*, 4 June 1935; "Kiralık yayla yurdu," *Yeni Adana*, 21 May 1937; "Satılık yayla yurdu," *Türksözü*, 9 September 1936. *Yeni Adana* reported that the hotels were full on the weekend and empty during the week and that on Monday, most men—including the governor of Adana himself—would return to the city for work, leaving behind only women and children in the village. "Bürücek röportajları, Part 2."

225. "Bürücek yaylacılarına müjde."

226. "Bürücek röportajları, Part 1."

227. BN, Archives Privées du Général F. Taillardat, vol. 1, no. 7, "La Cilicie," p. 177.

228. "Tarsus haberleri," *Yeni Adana*, 10 September 1929

229. Reşat Âkı, "Sıcaktan kurtuluş," *Toros*, 19 August 1948.

230. See "Yayla ihtiyacı karşısında," *Türksözü*, 2 August 1936; "İbrahim Bey Yaylasında"; "Feke'de," *Yeni Adana*, 7 December 1939.

231. TKA, 210/133, Muhittin Nuri to Riyaset-i Hilal-ı Ahmer, Karaisalı (12 October 1927).

232. Sıcramaz, "Karaisalı," *Yeni Adana*, 23 July 1937; Taha Toros, "Karaisalı," *Yeni Adana*, 21 November 1939.

233. "Yayla ihtiyacı karşısında."

234. "Bürücek," *Yeni Adana*, 28 July 1939.

235. Âkı, "Sıcaktan kurtuluş."

236. "Yayla ihtiyacı karşısında."

237. "Bürücek röportajları, Part 1"; "İlbayımız Bürücek yaylasının imarı için büyük alâka gösteriyor," *Yeni Adana*, 4 August 1936.

238. Yaylacı, "Bürücek yaylasında köy heyeti seçimi yapıldı," *Yeni Adana*, 7 August 1939.

239. "Valimizin himmetiyle Torosların pırlantısı," *Yeni Adana*, 9 September 1938.
240. "Bürücek röportajları, Part 2"; Yaylacı, "Bürücek yaylasında ilerleme ve hızlanma hamlesi."
241. "Sıcaktan . . . ," *Yeni Adana*, 3 August 1935.
242. See Seyfettin Arkan, "Yayla Çiçeği," *Yeni Adana*, March–May 1935.
243. Yayla Gülü, "Yayladan ovaya, Parts 1–6," *Türksözü*, 13 July–2 August 1935.
244. Yaşar Zeki, "Anadolu," *Memleket Çukurova'da*, 15 May 1931.
245. Arıkoğlu, *Hâtıralarım*, 34.
246. One could find occasional romanticization of nomadic communities during the Ottoman period, such as the novel *Türkmen Kızı* by Paşabeyzade Ömer Ali, who claimed descent from the Ramazanoğlus of the Adana region. *Türkmen Kızı* (Istanbul: Alim Matbaası, 1307 [1889]).
247. As symbols, the mountains and the *yayla* also carried connotations of authenticity. An illustration of this association can be found in the names of newspapers that emerged in the smaller towns of the Çukurova region. One major newspaper in Mersin was called *Toros* (founded 1948) after the Taurus Mountains; another in Tarsus, *Gülek* (founded 1945), was named after the Gülek Pass through the Taurus Mountains. The main newspaper in Marash, *Engizek* (founded 1947), bore the name of a *yayla* near Marash.
248. Yalgın, *Cenupta Türkmen Oymakları*, 1, 116–26.
249. Müfide Hasan, "Seyahat notları," *Yeni Adana*, 18 August 1929.
250. The caption in Yalgın's account was "An elder woman, one of the most influential figures in the tribe [*oba*] on the *yayla* roads." Yalgın, *Cenupta Türkmen Oymakları*, 1, 299.
251. Alagöz, *Anadoluda Yaylâcılık*, 15–23.
252. Alagöz, *Anadoluda Yaylâcılık*, 16. Genetic research about malaria in the Çukurova region also played an important role in biological conceptions of race and national identity in Turkey. See Elise K. Burton, *Genetic Crossroads: The Middle East and the Science of Human Heredity* (Stanford: Stanford University Press, 2021), 232–33.
253. Kemal Güngör, *Cenubi Anadolu Yürüklerinin etno-antropolojik tetkiki* (Ankara: Ideal Basımevi, 1941).
254. Çağaptay, *Islam, Secularism, and Nationalism*, 86.
255. Ozlem Goner, *Turkish National Identity and Its Outsiders: Memories of State Violence in Dersim* (New York: Routledge, 2017), 31–64.
256. Çağaptay, *Islam, Secularism, and Nationalism*, 109–13.
257. Bates, *Nomads and Farmers*, 21.
258. Alâettin Benal, "Aydınlı Aşiretile bir Konuşma," *Engizek*, 5 June 1947.
259. Yalgın, *Cenupta Türkmen Oymakları*, 1, 221.
260. TKA, 210/86.1, Rasim to Muhittin Nuri, Misis (13 May 1927).

261. Bates, *Nomads and Farmers*, 8–20.
262. CA, 30–18–1-2 22/57/2 (2 August 1931); 30–18–1-2 23/68/12 (4 October 1931).
263. CA, 30–18–1-2 45/37/3 (26 May 1934); 30–18–1-2 45/36/20 (26 May 1934).
264. CA, 30–18–1-2 45/31/1 (26 May 1934); 30–18–1-2 45/31/6 (12 May 1934).
265. Alagöz, *Anadoluda Yaylâcılık*, 38.
266. Alâettin Benal, "Aydınlı Aşiretile bir Konuşma" in *Engizek*, 3 and 5 June 1947.
267. McNeill, *The Mountains of the Mediterranean*, 290.
268. McNeill, *The Mountains of the Mediterranean*, 314, 44.
269. CA, 30–1–0–0 40/241/6, İnönü to Başbakanlık, Adana (23 February 1948).
270. CADN, 36PO/2/66, vol. 2, Folder 1, "Barrage du Seyhan."
271. Yusuf Ayhan, "Seyhan Barajı," *Demokrat (Adana)*, 7 March 1956.
272. Tevfik Can, "Baraj ve Hürriyet," *Demokrat (Adana)*, 8 April 1956. For more on this period and its relationship with late Ottoman and early republican politics, see Nicholas Danforth, *The Remaking of Republican Turkey: Memory and Modernity since the Fall of the Ottoman Empire* (Cambridge: Cambridge University Press, 2021).
273. Kemal, *Çukurova Yana Yana*, 13.
274. M. Serif Korkut, *Isıtma ve Çeltik* (Ankara: Yeni, 1950), 48–49.
275. Kyle Evered and Emine Evered, "A Conquest of Rice: Agricultural Expansion, Impoverishment, and Malaria in Turkey," *Historia Agraria* (2015): 103–36.
276. See "Ceyhan Mektubu," *Yeni Adana*, 10 September 1929.
277. Okan, *Türkiye'de Sıtma Savaşı*, 15.
278. NARA, RG 166, Box 435, Turkey (Agriculture 1950–54), 882.20/1–1852 (18 January 1952).
279. Tekeli and İlkin, "Türkiye'de Sıtma Mücadelesinin Tarihi," 254.
280. *Réceptivité au paludisme et aux autres maladies d'origine parasitaire: Rapport sur la réunion d'un groupe de travail de l'OMS: Izmir 11–15 septembre 1978* (Copenhagen: World Heath Organization, 1979), 10.
281. *Rapport sur la réunion d'un groupe de travail de l'OMS: Izmir 11–15 septembre 1978*, 16.
282. *Köy envanter etüdlerine göre Adana* (Konya: Yıldız Basımevi, 1967).
283. *Economic and Social Aspects of Farm Mechanization in Turkey* (Ankara: Ankara University, 1953), 25.
284. *Economic and Social Aspects of Farm Mechanization in Turkey*, 45.
285. *Çukurova Bölgesi*, 40–44.
286. *Çukurova Bölgesi*, 56.
287. "*Dikkat ettim de Çukurova hala Bereketli Topraklar Üzerinde'nin Çukurovası. Bin yıldır bu böyle.*" Discussion of this quotation can be found in Rahşan Yıldız Eyigün, "Orhan Kemal'in Hayatı, Eserleri ve Orhan Kemal Uyarlamalarının Türk Sinemasındaki Yeri," MA thesis, Mimar Sinan University of Fine Arts, 2006, 137.

288. See Özgür Balkılıç, *Temiz ve soylu türküler söyleyelim: Türkiye'de Milli kimlik inşasında halk müziği* (Istanbul: Tarih Vakfı, 2015).

289. These songs were released on 45 rpm vinyl records under the titles of "Dadaloğlu" by Cem Karaca and "Kalktı Göç Eyledi Avşar Elleri" by Ruhi Su.

290. Atıf Yılmaz, *Kozanoğlu* (1967).

291. Shared by Ötekilerin Postası (6 June 2013).

INDEX

Page numbers in italics indicate figures.

Abdülaziz, Sultan, 62, 225
Abdülhamid II, Sultan, 93, 125, 128–131, 136, 166
Abidin Pasha, 99, 107–108, 112, 270n45
Adana: Armenian properties in, 186; communal relations in, 50, 124; deportation of Armenians from, 144, descriptions of, 2, 32–34, 107, 114; Fair of (1920), 168; floods in, 135, 209–210; Franco-Turkish War in, 168–169; gureba hospitals in, 122–125; labor market in, 102, 188–189; Malaria Institute of, 196–199, 206–207; massacres of 1909, 125, 132–133; mobilization in, 142–143; provincial government of, 25, 63, 97, 115–116, 183; provisioning in, 73, 154, 171–172; Ramazanoğlus in, 45–46; Seyhan hydroelectric dam, 224; summer heat of, 23, 27, 38, 118, 213, 216; travel times in, 108–110; urban growth of, *109*, 184; WWI in 153–154; Ziya Pasha in, 94–95
Adana-Mersin Railway, 107–110
Afghans, 102, 270n52
ağıt. *See* songs

agriculture: Little Ice Age and, 47; commercialization of, 46, 97–101; cotton, 46, 61, 101, 104–105, *106*, 148, 166, *167*, 190–193; mechanization of, 100–101, 156, 192, 227; migrant labor and, 101–104, 188–190; pastoralism and, 51, 53, 86, 221; rice, 46, 91, 99, 120–121, 159, 201, 205, 225; WWI and, 148–150, 156
Aintab, 29, 60, 107, 132, 227
Alawite. *See* Nusayris
Aleppo, 26, 30, 33, 52, 63, 71, 136, 145, 162, 175
Alevi, 46, 127, 143
Amanus Mountains. *See* mountains
Amik, 43, 52–53
Anazarbus, 41–42, 56, 68, 89, 127, 131
Ankara, 62, 72, 163, 174, 194, 219–220
Anopheles superpictus, 159, 290n133
Arabic, 29, 32–34, 43, 182, 190
Arıkoğlu, Damar, 124, 151, 153, 217
Armenian: Catholicos of Sis, 29, 45, 50, 131, 175, 284n27; General Benevolent Union, 172–173; genocide, 143–146, 162–163, 177–178, 186, 282–283; Kingdom of Cilicia,

44; Legion, 170, 173; political organizations, 128, 170; repatriation, 166
Armeno-Turkish, 23–24, 155–156, 241n2
Assyrians, 133, 146
aşirets: conflict with, 63, 112–114, 129; names of, 27–28, 273n108; settlement of, 52, 63–64, 67–69, 75, 77–78, 111, 146, 221–222; studies of, 218–220; transhumance of, 35, 85–87, 219, 223. *See also* pastoralism
Atatürk, Mustafa Kemal, 186, 208
Avşars: conflict between Circassians and, 62–63; descriptions of, 28; folklore of, 1–3, 40, 84, 175–77, 211; settlement of, 84, 111, 223
Ayas, 30, 99
Aydınlıs, 113–114, 222–223, 273n108

Balakian, Grigor, 146
Balkans, 12, 51, 68, 75, 126, 127, 130, 141, 146, 185–187, 218
bandits, 41, 48–50, 89–90, 143, 145, 168, 177, 279n202
banking, 73, 100, 149, 152, 186, 224
banknotes, 154
barley, 86, 101, 111, 152, 191, 271n64, 286n59
Belemedik, 158–164, 174
Bennett, Lieutenant Ferdinand, 68–70, 74–75, 112, 128, 261n60
Bereketli Topraklar Üzerinde, 188, 227
beyliks, Anatolian, 45–46
Bodosakis Athanasiadis, Prodomos, 156–157, 171, 173, 175
buffaloes, 43, 101
Bürücek, 213–217. *See also* yayla
Byzantine Empire, 43–44

Camels, 28, 51, 85, 146, 148, 160, 214
cattle 37, 49, 85, 101, 112, 135, 147, 219
Cemal Pasha, Ahmed, 125, 144, 155, 157, 163, 278n184, 283n21, 284n26, 289n107
Cevdet, Abdullah, 136
Cevdet Pasha, Ahmed: career of, 75: correspondence of Adviye Rabiye and, 80; constitutionalism and, 92–93; *History* of, 56, 76–77; Reform Division and, 63, 77–83, 85
Ceyhan, city of, 61–62, 66–68, 110, 127, 130, 150, 172, 184, 198, 227
Ceyhan River, 26, 32–33, 41, 47, 65, 115–117, 135
Chechens, 62, 66, 89, 126–27, 145,
children, 74, 86, 104–105, 107, 118, 125, 145, 153, 195–196, 203–204
cholera, 71, 73, 119
Churchill, Winston, 211
çiftlik, 89, 98–99, 123, 130–131, 136, 149, 258n17
Cilicia: Armenian Kingdom of, 44; French occupation of, 164–175; Ottoman conquest of, 46; name of, 17, 183
Circassians: banditry and, 89; French military recruitment of, 170; settlement of, 62–63, 68–69, 71, 80, 83–84, 88, 110, 126–27, 131, 278n187, 279n202
citrus, 168, 184, 192
climate: change, 11, 47; descriptions of, 26–27, 31–35, 114, 216, 219, 247n9; malaria and, 20, 35–38, 80–81, 83–84, 88, 119, 122–123, 158, 187
Çokmerzimen. *See* Dörtyol
Committee of Union and Progress, 75, 128, 146, 156
conscription, 58–60, 64, 102, 139, 143, 148–151, 176
constitution, Ottoman, 93, 125
corn, 150, 156
cotton: cultivars of, 104–105, 193; cultivation of, 46–47, 56, 61, 96–98, 101, 167, 184, 187, 189, 211; export of, 97,

INDEX

100, 148–149, 166, 191, 212; malaria and, 118; processing of, 104–107. *See also* Gossypium herbaceum
cows. *See* cattle
Cretans, 14, 127, 185, 187
Crimean War, 59–60
Çukurova: çiftliği (imperial farm), 130–131, 136; description of, 32–33, *42*, 56–57, 65, 79, 184; irrigation in, 117, 224; landowners in, 89, 99, 111, 120, 149, 187; literature and, 8–9, 227; malaria in, 47, 70, 74, 80–82, 84, 119, 172, 195–197, 205; name of, 16–17, 183, 245n46; pastoralism in, 28, 53; settlement in, 62, 64, 66–68, 89, 102, 108, 110, 127, 185–187, 222
Cyprus, 45, 72, 100, 149

Dadaloğlu, 3, 57, 64, 74, 217, 228–29
Davis, E. J., 70, 72, 82, 89, 98, 105, 119
dams, 94–95, 115, 117, 210–211, 224
Demokrat (political party), 224–225
derebey, 48–51, 63–64, 111. *See also* aşirets
Dersim, 63, 78, 221, 224
desertion, 143
Diyarbakır, 120, 129, 132, 227, 269n36
dogs, 201, 208
Dörtyol, 29, 125, 129, 143–144, 146, 168, 174, 184, 192
drought, 72, 92, 104, 211
Dulkadiroğlus, 45–46

ecocriticism, 10
ecology: indigenous, 10–12, 35, 54, 104; political 10, 96, 148, 225
Egypt: cholera in, 71; comparison of Cilicia with, 26, 95–97, 135–137, 165–166; cotton cultivars of, 104–105, export of wood to, 113, First International Malaria Conference and, 196, invasion of Cilicia by, 32, 49, 59, 61, 97, 102–103; Ottoman conquest of, 46

Engizek, 221, 225
eucalyptus, 115, 208–209, 211
Evliya Çelebi, 34–35, 65
exchange of populations. *See* mübadele
exports, 61, 73, 97, 167, 171, 191–192

factories, 103–107, 110, 132, 157, 173, 186, 188, 191
famine, 71–72, 91, 150–151, 155, 171, 174
Fasih, Mehmed, 142
Fırka-i İslâhiye. *See* Reform Division
flour. *See* wheat
floods, 89, 95, 117, 135, 209–210, 223
folklore. *See* songs
forests, 28, 44, 59, 65, 113, 160, 208–209, 215, 217–18, 222–223. *See also* Tahtacıs
France: administration of Cilicia, 164–175, 186; cotton export to, 97, 166, 191; evacuation of Cilicia by, 174; land concessions to, 136; medicine imports from, 122; POWs of, 156; transhumance and, 35, 219; Zeytun rebellion and, 60
French Revolution, 77
frontier: concept of, 12–16, 43, 51; Çukurova as, 65–69

gambling, 102
gambusia (mosquitofish), 206
Germany, 97, 105, 122, 136, 140, 147, 149, 158–164, 191, 201, 211, 293n179, 299n76
al-Ghazzi, Badr al-Din, 32
goats. *See* pastoralism
Gossypium herbaceum, 104–106, 192–193
Gökalp, Ziya, 82, 185
grapes, 38, 48, 86, 151, 168, 187
Great Britain, 32–33, 61, 68, 97, 122, 128, 140–142, 161, 175, 211, 270n52
Greece, 21, 38, 97, 175, 185–186

Greeks, Ottoman. *See* Rum
Gülek, 32
gureba hospitals, 123

Hadjin, 37–38, 40, 44, 50, 60, 107, 109–110, 120–121, 145–146, 151, 170–171, 175, 177, 182–183
hajj, 34, 49, 71
Hakkı Bey, İsmail (Governor of Adana), 102, 144, 149, 151–153, 156, 283n24
halk, 9, 185, 219
Hamidiye cavalry, 128–129, 132–133
Hıdırellez, 40
horses, 33, 38, 41, 62, 79, 83–84, 101, 131, 146, 148, 265n136
hospitals, 122–124, 158–159, 164, 172–174, 199, 203–204. *See also* seyyar doctors

Ibn Khaldun, 57, 75–77, 81–82
Ibrahim Pasha of Egypt, 32, 59, 97, 103, 116
immigration. *See* muhacir
İnce Memed, 8, 112
India, 27, 71, 141–142, 161, 172, 270n52
irrigation, 41, 95–97, 104, 117, 210, 223, 276n147
İnönü, İsmet, 211, 223
Iskenderun, 30–34, 63, 116, 136, 161, 174
İslahiye, 67–70, 80, 87, 99, 112, 123, 129, 151, 168, 197, 205, 223
Istanbul, 46, 60, 64, 75, 80, 134, 143, 154, 157, 170, 172–173, 215, 227, 229
Italy, 31, 42, 91, 97, 191, 195–196, 291n148, 304n158
İzmidi, Feyzullah, 82, 120, 122,

Jazira, 101, 144–145
Jesus, 34

Kadızâde Hacı Hasan Fehmi, 99
Kahramanmaraş. *See* Marash

Kara Fatma (Asiye Hatun), 60, 64
Karabucak, 26, 43, 208–209
Kayseri, 2, 29, 188
Kemal, Orhan, 188, 227
Kemal, Yaşar, 8–9, 57, 83, 90, 112, 227
Kemalists, 168–173, 181, 201
Khaldun, Ibn, 57, 75–77, 81–82
Khirlakyan, Hagop, 99
Kozan. *See* Sis
Kozanoğlu, 50, 64, 89–90, 177–78, 229
Kurds: Armenian genocide and, 145; Cevdet Pasha's views on, 79, 266n144; communities of Cilicia region, 28, 67, 86, 112, 127; Dersim, 220–221; French military recruitment of, 170; Hamidiye cavalry and, 128; impact of settlement on, 70; migrant labor of, 101–103, 190, 281n227; representation in film of, 229; WWI displacement of, 146–147, 294n189

labor: Baghdad railway, 158–159, 163–164; battalions in WWI, 150, 156, 163–164; conditions and wages, 102–104, 188–190, 211, 216, 305n194; factory, 107; household, 104–105; literature and, 227; malaria and, 118–120, 122–124, 160–161, 164, 204–205, 226; migrant, 61, 101, 133–135, 169, 187, 226; POW, 159
land: code of 1858, 59, 75, 98; distribution of, 89, 98–99, 131, 149, 111–112, 185–188, 222. *See also* çiftlik
law, 59, 75, 98, 133, 157, 205, 211, 221–222
League of Nations, 145, 158, 174–175, 196
Lebanon, 60, 89, 95, 99, 150, 155, 175
Lesseps, Paul de, 136, 166, 293n179
Libya, 14, 141
Linke, Lilo, 201, 203–204
Little Ice Age, 47

locusts, 151, 208

machines, agricultural, 101–102, 156, 168, 192, 211, 224, 226–227, 270n45
Mağmumi, Şerafeddin, 109, 124
malaria: agriculture and, 42, 117–121, 205, 225–226; Armenian genocide and, 163–164; control in Turkey, 193–206, 206–208; displacement and, 125, 161–164, 169; in early modern Cilicia, 47; labor and, 118–120, 122–124, 160–161, 164, 204–205, 226; medicine and, 121–124, 157, 164, 172–174, 198–203, 211–212; in medieval Cilicia, 44; modernity and, 20–21; orientalism and, 30–33, 115; settlement and, 52, 68–74, 80–84, 187; transhumance as avoidance of, 33–40, 80, 86–88, 159, 181, 201, 215–216 WWI and, 142, 158–165. *See also* Plasmodium falciparum
Marash: Armenians of, 24, 29, 50, 60, 168; Dulkadiroğlus in, 45–46; Franco-Turkish War in, 168, 182; tribal settlement around, 53, 70, 75, 84, 114, 129, 221; rice cultivation in, 99, 120–121, 205, 225 population of, *109*; WWI in, 148, 150, 154, 178, 283n24
Mavromatis, 100, 103
medicine: education and, 199, 202; German medicine during WWI, 158; humanitarianism and, 172–174, 194–195; international, 195–196; malaria and, 38–40, 82, 121–124, 157, 164, 172–174, 181, 198–203, 211–212; in Ottoman countryside, 73, 122, 124. *See also* hospitals
Memed, My Hawk, 8, 112
Menderes, Adnan, 224–225
Menemenci, 28, 49, 85–86
Mersin: eucalyptus in, 114–115; facto-ries in, 103, 157; soldiers from, 142; finance in, 100; growth of, 61, 83, 100, 108–109, 116, 227; medicine in, 73, 172, 198, 206; WWI in, 143, 149, 152
mevat land, 98–99, 121, 269n29
Midhat Pasha, 59
migration: Armenian, 44, 107, 175; Egyptian invasion of Cilicia and, 61, 270n53; labor, 61, 102, 120, 188–190; medieval, 43–45; Nusayri, 101, 190; Ottoman administration of, 13, 61–62, 146. *See also* muhacir
missionaries, 60, 122, 145–146, 148, 153–154, 179, 277n164
mobilization for war. *See* seferberlik
mosquitos: elimination of, 198, 206–208, 226; folklore and, 2, 57, 225; habitat of, 36–37, 118–120; mountains and, 158–161, 216; representations of, 33, 38, 57, 172, 203, 207. *See also* Anopheles superpictus
mountains, Taurus and Amanus: description of, 25–26, 32; malaria in the, 159, 173–174, 216; as microclimate, 27, 33; pastoralism and, 28, 221; political power and, 44–46, 48–51; rebellions and, 48–51, 60, 77–78, 114, 129, 143, 168, 221; romanticization of, 217–218, 308n247; salubrious quality of, 23–24, 33–35, 37–38, 83–86, 88, 180, 215; settlements of, 1, 27, 29, 44, 47, 108–109, 111, 146, 151, 183; leisure and tourism, 214–215. *See also* yayla
muhacirs, 13, 61–63, 66, 84, 88, 110, 124, 127–128, 130, 146–147. *See also* mübadele
Mustuk, Küçükalioğlu, 49, 60, 64, 255n124
mübadele, 175, 185–187

Namrun, 37, *39*, 44, 46, 110, 169, 174,

215, 219
Nusayris, 29, 40, 101, 107, 127, 169

Oğuz, Remzi, 182
oil. *See* pesticides
oranges. *See* citrus
Orientalism, 30–31, 41, 65, 69
Osmaniye, 67–68, 70, 91, 99, 108, 110, 180, 205–206, 213
oxen, 101, 148, 227

Pasteur Institute, 196, 206, 301n105
Pastoralism: Anatolian beyliks and, 45–46; in early republican Çukurova, 218–223; Hıdırellez and, 40; Little Ice Age and, 47; in Ottoman Cilicia, 28, 49, 85–87, 112–114; Ottoman symbiosis with, 51; Turkish nationalism and, 218, 220; types of, 48–51, 219, 250n55. *See also* aşirets, transhumance
Payas, 34, 49, 60, 73, 86, 197
pesticides: DDT, 226; Paris green, 198, 208; petroleum, 207–208
Pınarbaşı, 1, 62, 84, 223
plague, 31, 35, 45, 251n62
Plasmodium falciparum, 20, 47, 161, 172, 194, 212, 246n50
potatoes, 150
Pozantı, 33, 159–164, 170–173, 213–214, 218
prisoners of war, 142, 156, 161
public health. *See* medicine

quarantine, 71
quinine: administration of, 200, 202; black market, 172; dispensaries, 174, 198–199; importation of, 121–122, 212; law (1917), 157; Ottoman knowledge of, 121; shortages of, 157, 162, 172, 204, 212

Rabiye, Adviye, 80

railways: Armenian genocide and, 144, 163–164; construction of, 107–108, 115–116, 159–160, 208; impact of, 110, 213–214; malaria and, 160–161; WWI and, 141, 158–164
rakı, 161, 203
Ramazanoğlus, 34, 45–46, 131, 170, 308n246
Red Crescent, 142, 157, 169, 173–174, 184, 194, 198–199, 296n17
Red Cross, 174
Reform Division, 63–64, 67–71, 73, 75, 77–81, 87, 91–92, 108–112, 129, 142, 180, 224
rice, 46, 91, 99, 120–121, 159, 201, 205, 225
roads, 49, 60, 65–66, 70, 109–110, 116, 180, 184, 213–214
Rockefeller Foundation, 194–196, 301n100
Roman Empire, 41–42. *See also* Byzantine Empire
Rum (Greek Orthodox), 29, 38, 40, 100, 103–104, 123, 126–127, 157, 175, 186, 191
Russia, 59–62, 66, 128, 142, 161, 191

Sabancı, Hacı Ömer, 188
Saimbeyli. *See* Hadjin
seferberlik, 141–143, 148–149, 153, 155–156, 212
Seljuks, 43–45, 77
sesame, 85–86, 97, 101, 103, 118, 191
settlement: of immigrants and refugees *see* muhacir; of tribes, 52–53, 63–64, 67, 114, 129, 221–222. *See also* aşirets
Seyhan River, 26, 94–95, 102, 114–117, 135, 188, 209–211, 223
seyyar (traveling) doctors, 124, 201
sharecropping, 99, 103
sheep. *See* pastoralism
silt, 43, 47, 113, 223
Sis, 37, 40, 44, 46, 57, 86, 88–89, 114,

117–118, 131, 146, 169, 182, 187. *See also* Armenian Catholicos of Sis
sıtma. *See* malaria
slavery, 41–42, 88, 102, 105
socialism, 92, 128, 184, 225
soil, 26, 51, 65, 70, 82, 89, 113, 120, 136
songs, 2–3, 8–9, 23–24, 57, 74, 84, 90, 120, 156, 170, 175–178, 217–218, 225, 228–229, 247n3
Sudanese, 122, 127
Sursocks, 99, 149, 152
swamps. *See* wetlands
Switzerland, 155, 214
Syria, 29, 32, 59, 60, 63, 101, 144, 151, 164–166, 169, 174–175

Tahtacı, 28, 113, 155, 159, 164–165, 218
Talat Pasha, Mehmed, 145, 163–164, 186, 283
Tanzimat, 12–13, 58–59, 92–93, 94
Tarih-i Cevdet, 76–77
Tarsus: Armenian Red Cross of, 173; businessmen of, 188; city of, 26, 29; credit office of, 100; Egyptian administration in, 97; eucalyptus in, 208–209; factories in, 107, 157; feast of St. George in, 40; gureba hospital in, 123; population of, *109*; public health in, 198; summer in, 37–38; swamps in, 43, 208–209; workers in, 101–103, 190; WWI in, 154, 157
Taurus Mountains. *See* mountains
Teotig, Arshaguhi, 107, 134–135
Terzian, Hagop, 107, 125, 143
timar, 46
Tok, Ekrem, 195–197, 206–207, 226, 301n105
transhumance: definition of, 35–36, 218–220, 250n55; malaria and, 36–38, 80, 85–88, 118, 180–181. *See also* pastoralism
tribes. *See* aşirets

Turcomans (Türkmens), 29, 34–35, 45, 54, 67, 217–221. *See also* aşirets
Turkishness, 184–185, 190, 218
Türksözü, 204–206, 210, 213, 215, 218

Ulaşlıs, 29, 49
United States, 11, 16, 37, 60–61, 91, 104, 119, 129, 146, 150, 175, 177, 188, 193
urbanization, 68, 108–109, 227
Uzunyayla, 1, 28, 62, 80, 84

vakıf. *See* waqf
Varsaks, 29, 50

waqf, 46, 123, 131
wetlands: depictions of, 26, 30–32, 38, 53, 56–57, 65, 70, 225; drainage of, 73, 115–117, 195, *197*, 207–209; formation of, 43, 47, 113, 159; land tenure and, 98–99, 131. *See also* malaria
wheat, 46–47, 72, 86, 97, 101, 103, 152–156, 167, 171, 191, 212,
women: discourses about, 156, 218; households and, 1–2, 46, 80, 124, 216; humanitarianism and, 134–135, 145, 173–74; missionaries, 146, 151; labor and, 102–107, 169, 208–209; malaria and, 74; medicine and, 123, 172–173, 185, 198–199, 201, 203–204; poetry by, 2, 90, 170, 175; war and, 60, 145, 153–155
World Bank, 224
World War I: agriculture and, 148–150, 156; deportation of Armenians during, 143–145, 163–164; desertion during, 142; economic impact of, 152–156, 175–179; locust incursion during, 151; malaria and, 157–165; mobilization during, 139–141; Ottoman refugees during, 146–147; POWs, 142, 161; railways and, 141, 158–161

World War II, 193, 207, 211, 226

yayla: change of air and, 36–38, 84–87, 95, 118, 139, 165, 169, 180; conflict over, 61–62, 129, 132; depictions of, 33–35, *39*, 212–213, 247n3, 308n247; folklore and, 23–24, 57, 120; leisure and, 213–216; pastoralism and, 35, 45–46, 49, 81, 114, 129, 218–223, 250n55; sacred geography and, 40

Yeğenağa, Ali Münif, 170, 283n24

Yeni Adana, 170, 185–186, 188–189, 202–205, 209–210, 214–216, 218

yerli (cotton variety). *See* Gossypium herbaceum

Young Turks. *See* Committee of Union and Progress

Ziraat Bankası, 149, 152

Ziya Pasha, 94–95, 224

Zeytun, 44, 47, 50, 60, 63, 78, 107, 129, 143–144, 175, 182

CPSIA information can be obtained
at www.ICGtesting.com
Printed in the USA
JSHW021911230122
22192JS00003B/8